STANDARD
LOAN

return on or before the last date

WEST SUSSEX INST
HIGHER EDUCATION

AUTHOR

BERNSTEIN

TITLE

RESTRUCTURING

CLASS No.

300.K

D0257387

The Restructuring of Social and Political Theory

This penetrating inquiry grew out of the crisis in the social sciences that erupted in the 1960s, when those sciences were attacked as a disguised form of ideology supporting the status quo. Bernstein explores this controversy and envisions a fundamental restructuring of social and political theory.

He criticizes the social scientists who maintain that their disciplines differ only in degree from the natural sciences. He analyses brilliantly three schools that have challenged these theories: the Anglo-Saxon thinkers (Berlin, Winch, MacIntyre, Taylor, Pitkin); the phenomenologists, especially Alfred Schutz; and the Frankfurt school, including Jürgen Habermas.

Bernstein seeks to integrate from each group what he finds sound, and to reject what is inadequate and false. He argues that the primary problem today is the reconciliation of the classical aim of politics with the modern demand for a scientific knowledge of society. Rejecting either/or positions, he sees the formation of a social theory that will be at once empirical, interpretative, and critical. Cultural pessimism, romantic protest, retreat, or apathy, Bernstein maintains, are not the answer to the alienation of the 1960s, but, rather the re-examination of what human beings are and what they may become.

Bernstein's formidable erudition combined with his recognition of the complexities of the human condition make this volume an invaluable contribution to social and political theory.

Richard J. Bernstein is Chairman of the Department of Philosophy at Haverford College, Pennsylvania.

Books by Richard J. Bernstein

Praxis and Action

John Dewey

EDITED BY RICHARD J. BERNSTEIN
Perspectives on Peirce

John Dewey: On Experience, Nature, and Freedom

RICHARD J. BERNSTEIN

The Restructuring of Social and Political Theory

METHUEN & CO LTD

First published in Great Britain in 1976
by Basil Blackwell, Oxford

First published as a University Paperback in 1979
by Methuen & Co. Ltd
11 New Fetter Lane, London EC4P 4EE
Reprinted 1985

© 1976 Richard J. Bernstein

Printed in Great Britain
by J. W. Arrowsmith Ltd
Bristol BS3 2NT

ISBN 0 416 72240 7

All rights reserved. No part of this book may be
reprinted or reproduced or utilized in any form or
by any electronic, mechanical or other means, now
known or hereafter invented, including photocopying
and recording, or in any information storage
or retrieval system, without permission in writing
from the publishers.

For
Daniel, Jeffrey, Andrea,
and Robin

Contents

Acknowledgments

In preparing this book on the problems and issues of social sciences, I worked closely with colleagues practicing in those disciplines. Haverford College provides a rare opportunity for joint teaching, informal seminars, and interdisciplinary discussions. I have benefited enormously from my exchanges with Thomas D'Andrea (psychology), Samuel Gubins (economics), William Hohenstein (sociology), Wyatt McGaffrey (anthropology), and Sidney Waldman (political science). All have contributed to my thinking on these subjects, but none would agree with all that I say here. I want to single out my debt to Sara Shumer (political theory), with whom I have been arguing for the past eight years. Her incisiveness and her ability to grasp what one is trying to say have always helped to sharpen my own thinking.

I want to express my appreciation to the National Endowment for the Humanities, from whom I received a senior fellowship in 1972–73, when I began work on this book. Haverford College granted me released time from my teaching and provided typing services, for which I am grateful. William McBride and Hanna F. Pitkin read an early version of the manuscript. Their acute criticisms led me to rewrite a great deal. My wife Carol took valuable time from her own demanding academic activities to give me detailed criticisms. Adeline Taraborelli and Mildred Hargreaves typed several versions of the manuscript. Ann O'Donnell prepared the Indexes. Drenka Willen and Clifford Browder, my editors at Harcourt Brace Jovanovich, combined sympathetic understanding with editorial firmness. Finally I want to acknowledge the advice and friendship of William Jovanovich. He has two virtues that every author dreams of finding in a publisher—patience and encouragement.

I started writing this book at the desk used by Michael Ventris in Hampstead, London, and completed it in Jay, New York, overlooking the Adirondack Mountains. The *genii loci* do not always provide a source of inspiration, but in this instance they did.

Richard J. Bernstein

Introduction

During the nineteen sixties when I was working on my book, *Praxis and Action*, I had a profound sense that something new was stirring—something was changing—in the patterns, emphases, and concerns of intellectual life. I dimly perceived that, despite the sharp differences and lack of effective communication among contemporary intellectual orientations, there are fundamental themes to which post-Hegelian movements are constantly and ineluctably drawn. These focused on the centrality of the concepts of praxis and action in the quest to gain a depth understanding of the human condition. I set out to examine the centrality of the themes of praxis and action in four contemporary movements: Marxism, existentialism, pragmatism, and analytic philosophy. But I limited myself primarily to clarifying what each of these diverse approaches contributed to our understanding of human activity. This is why I concluded the study by declaring that it was only a beginning.

When I completed the manuscript, a fresh debate was taking place in which many of the issues that I had been exploring came alive in novel and unexpected ways. One of the consequences of the social and political unrest and protest of the nineteen sixties was a series of attacks on, and radical critiques of, the very foundations of the social disciplines. Just as the end of ideology was being proclaimed in America—when there was a widely shared self-confidence among mainstream social scientists that their disciplines had finally been placed upon a firm empirical foundation where we could expect the steady progressive growth of scientific knowledge of society—troubling issues broke out.

There were those who declared that the very foundations of the social sciences were rotten; that, more often than not, what was supposed to be objective scientific knowledge was in fact a disguised form of ideology that lent support to the status quo; that the most striking characteristic of the social sciences was not their ability to illuminate existing social and political reality, but their inability to provide any critical perspective on what was happening; that the thinking exhibited in these disciplines gave a false legitimacy to the social technical control and manipulation that was infecting all aspects of human life. There was a growing skepticism and suspicion about the liberal faith so entrenched in the social disciplines: the belief that increased systematic empirical understanding of how society and politics work would naturally lead to the intelligent formulation of policies, ameliorate social inequities and injustices, and enable us to solve the problems of society. Even the staunchest defenders of value-free, objective empirical research acknowledged that something was not quite right with their disciplines, although this was frequently ascribed to the youth and immaturity of the social sciences.

More disturbing to professionals than the criticism of outsiders, who could be written off as an uninformed, disenchanted fringe, was the growing criticism of insiders. Presumably the battle in gaining recognition of the social disciplines as genuine sciences had been won. It was reasonable to expect that a new generation of professional students, trained in the most sophisticated quantitative and empirical techniques of research, would carry on the work of furthering the scientific maturity of the social disciplines. Yet it was from these insiders that the greatest dissatisfaction and the most vociferous criticism was heard. Many of the leaders of student protest movements throughout the world were themselves students of the social sciences. Their criticism of society was intimately bound up with their criticism of their own disciplines.

Alternative approaches which had been judged irrelevant, moribund, refuted, or passé suddenly took on a new vitality. Themes worked out in the pure conceptual inquiries of linguistic philosophy were used to challenge the epistemological foundations of the social sciences. New developments in the history and philosophy of science posed a threat to the very conception of scientific knowledge and theory that had been uncritically accepted by social scientists. Phenomenology and hermeneutics, which "tough-minded" empiricists had viewed with suspicion as "tender-minded" woolly foreign intrusions, struck many young thinkers as providing a more genuine and perspicuous insight into social relations than did the weary formulas of those who prided themselves on meticulous, rigorous empirical research. Marxism, which has been pronounced dead or definitely refuted more often than any other contemporary theoretical or practical movement, exhibited a new international vigor.

The initial impression one has in reading through the literature in and about the social disciplines during the past decade or so is that of sheer chaos. Everything appears to be "up for grabs." There is little or no consensus—except by members of the same school or subschool—about what are the well-established results, the proper research procedures, the important problems, or even the most promising theoretical approaches to the study of society and politics. There are claims and counterclaims, a virtual babble of voices demanding our attention.

The polemic and debates so evident in the nineteen sixties were not limited to the narrow academic issue of the status of the social disciplines. The fierceness of these debates reflects a concern with deeper and more general issues. When individuals sense that they are living through a period of crisis, when foundations seem to be cracking and orthodoxies breaking up, then a public space is created in which basic questions about the human condition can be raised anew. My primary objective in this study is to clarify, explore, and pursue these more fundamental issues. I hope to show that in what might otherwise seem a parochial and intramural debate about the social sciences, primary questions have been raised about the nature of human beings, what constitutes knowledge of society and politics, how this knowledge can affect the ways in which we shape our lives, and what is and ought to be the relation of theory and practice.

Many social scientists believe that with the apparently quieter seventies, much of the confusion of the nineteen sixties has happily passed. Those who view society as a complex dynamic equilibrium to be understood by a "structural-functional model," or who think that the new, more advanced "general systems" approach enables us to comprehend how society *really* works, look back upon this period as one of temporary stress and strain where the "steering mechanism" had to be readjusted. They say, let the noisy critics—who are becoming fewer and fewer—shout that this is all "bourgeois ideology." If we are responsible, serious, and honest we will be modest and realistic in our tentative claims, but firm in our conviction that patient empirical work will increase our scientific understanding of society, and can eventually achieve far more to bring about effective social reform than all the polemical tracts of so-called revolutionaries.

I do not deny that this is a prevalent attitude, especially among professionals in the social sciences, nor that weighty reasons support such an attitude. But I hope to show that such an interpretation of what has occurred in the last twenty years is fundamentally distortive. There is another reading of what has happened and what is still very much in the process of happening. When we cut beneath surface rhetoric—when we sort out what is right and wrong, what is exaggerated and what on target in the mounting criticisms of the social disciplines—we can discern the outlines of a complex argument that has been developing: an emerging new sensibility that, while still very fragile, is leading to a restructuring of social and political theory. I am using the expression "argument" in a double sense. In an older usage an argument means a plot or a story. I want to show the outlines of this plot and bring it into the foreground. But I also mean an argument in the more conventional sense of a rational argument. We can detect, in what initially seem to be independent lines of inquiry, steps or stages in a complex argument whose total strength is greater than any of its separate strands. An adequate, comprehensive political and social theory must be at once empirical, interpretative, and critical. What I mean by this, why anything less than this is unsatisfactory, and how empirical research, interpretation, and critical evaluation dialectically involve each other, will become clearer as the underlying plot is revealed.

I did not, however, start this study with a clear thesis that I was setting out to prove. Rather I began with vague intimations and hunches that basic issues about action, society, and theory were being raised only to be smothered in polemic; and that critics and defenders of the social sciences were talking past each other. The first task was to re-examine what had become the target of so much hostility and criticism: the conviction that the social disciplines were to be properly understood as genuine natural sciences of individuals in society, differing in degree and not in kind from the well-established natural sciences. Some of the criticisms offered against the very idea of a social science modeled on the natural sciences are superficial and occasionally silly. Some critics have written as if this belief were based upon a simple or simplistic fallacy; that, for example, all of social science is a naive positivism, and since positivism has been refuted or at least severely modified, we can simply dismiss the claims of a social science that rests upon such faulty foundations. Others have argued that at the core of all social science is the acceptance of a rigid dichotomy between fact and value, and since this rigid distinction is not tenable, the whole of social science collapses. There has been a latent essentialism in some of the critical discussions of the social sciences. It is frequently assumed by critics—and defenders, too—that the idea of social science which applies natural scientific procedures to the study of society and politics involves the acceptance of "one big principle." If this one big principle is exposed and refuted, then the whole edifice collapses, and there is no need to examine the tedious details of the several social sciences.

At a subtler level, ever since the social disciplines have been proposed as genuine *positive* sciences, opponents have advanced a variety of "impossibility," "transcendental," or "conceptual" arguments to prove once and for all that it is not possible to construct such a social science—that the very idea of such a social science is conceptually confused. I do not believe that any of these impossibility arguments have ever been successful, nor, for philosophic reasons, do I think there can be such a definitive a priori argument about the epistemological status of the study of society.[1] For the past hundred years we have repeatedly gone through the tiresome ritual of having transcendental or impossibility arguments put forth about the true nature of the study of society, only to be followed by another round of counterarguments designed to show the inadequacy of these—that there are no insuperable theoretical obstacles to the construction of a positive, empirical natural science of individuals in society. Important considerations for understanding the social disciplines have emerged from these discussions, and I do not suggest that all is well with the view that the social disciplines are immature or youthful natural sciences. But statements that answer the question whether the social studies are *really* scientific, or whether there is some feature of social life that prohibits the application of scientific techniques to the study of social phenomena, tend to obscure rather than clarify critical similarities and differences between the natural sciences and the social disciplines.

What I set out to do first was to recover and articulate the understanding that mainstream social scientists have of their discipline. By "mainstream social scientists" I mean those who conceive of their discipline as one that differs in degree and not in kind from the well-established natural sciences, and who are convinced that the greatest success is to be found in emulating, modifying, and adapting techniques that have proven successful in our scientific understanding of nature. One must *not* think that "mainstream social science" is more monolithic or homogeneous than it really is. As I shall show, there are strong disagreements not only about the essential characteristics of natural science, but also about the basic similarities between the social and the natural sciences. I felt it important, however, to emphasize what practicing social scientists who are methodologically self-conscious tell us, rather than to focus exclusively on what philosophers of the social sciences say. The philosophy of the social sciences has often become a poor stepsister to the philosophy of the natural sciences, and an excuse for dealing with general epistemological issues unrelated to what actually goes on in the social disciplines.

As I will show in Part I, mainstream social scientists are convinced that their discipline is a genuine although young natural science, because of their understanding of the nature and centrality of empirical theory. It is therefore necessary to explore what precisely is meant by empirical theory; how it is to be distinguished from other types of theoretical endeavor such as so-called normative theory; and why it is thought to be so important to the scientific status of the social disciplines. We will see that for all the sharp differences among mainstream social scientists, there is a remarkable unanimity in their understanding of the epistemological and logical features of empirical theory, although there is a lack of any rational consensus about what satisfies or even approximates the criteria of that theory.

Only after a naturalistic interpretation of the social sciences is presented and probed, can we evaluate its strengths and weaknesses, its insights and blindnesses. I decided to concentrate on three contemporary orientations that have directly challenged the claims of a naturalistic understanding of the social disciplines. Each of these has aimed its critique at the foundations of the social sciences, and each has indicated what it takes to be a more illuminating alternative to the study of society and politics.

The first is based upon analytic philosophy, especially "the linguistic turn" taken by Ludwig Wittgenstein and J. L. Austin. Neither of these philosophers was primarily interested in the social disciplines, or even in the relevance of his inquiries to social theory. But many thinkers who have been influenced by them have argued that the new understanding of the complexity of language, especially the language of action, challenges the pretentious claims made by social scientists about the nature, description, and explanation of action. They have argued that there is something desperately wrong and conceptually confused in the relentless attempt to force the description and explanation of human action into the grid of empirical natural science.

Furthermore, one of the most important, controversial, and dynamic areas of recent philosophic investigation among analytic philosophers has been the history and philosophy of science. In the past few decades there has been a virtual revolution in our understanding of the "image of science"—at least when compared with the so-called orthodox understanding of science advocated by positivists and logical empiricists. Most of the work in the history and philosophy of science has dealt with the natural sciences, but it is obvious that it has important consequences for the social sciences. The very case for a naturalistic interpretation of the social sciences depends upon a clear grasp of the primary characteristics of the natural sciences, and especially the role of theory. Insofar as the new postempiricist interpretation of science has altered our understanding of the natural sciences, it affects any informed appraisal of the ways in which the social sciences are like and unlike the natural sciences. Perhaps no work has had a greater influence on recent conceptions of the social sciences than Thomas Kuhn's *The Structure of Scientific Revolutions,* despite the fact that he has scarcely discussed the social sciences. His influence has been a confusing and obfuscating one. Or rather, the fault lies primarily with the way in which his themes have been appropriated by students of politics and society. Kuhn has been used and stretched to bolster the most disparate claims—claims that conflict and contradict each other.

The second major challenge to a naturalistic understanding of the social disciplines comes from phenomenology. Although Edmund Husserl—the founder of contemporary phenomenology—started his investigations by examining the foundations of logic and mathematics, he applied phenomenological methods to the whole domain of human experience. Of the social disciplines, he was most directly interested in psychology; in the reasons for the failures of traditional psychology, and the need to place psychology on a firm phenomenological foundation. As his philosophy developed, the nature of intersubjectivity became thematic and absolutely central to his very understanding of phenomenology.

It was, however, those influenced by Husserl who pursued the implications of phenomenology for describing and understanding social life in its full complexity. Alfred Schutz, who was originally concerned with Weber's notion of interpretative sociology, discovered in Husserl—and in Bergson, too—the intellectual tools required for clarifying the phenomenological foundations of the social disciplines. In France philosophers such as Maurice Merleau-Ponty and Paul Ricoeur, who borrowed freely from Husserl, turned their attention to how phenomenology can aid us to understand social reality. Recently a number of thinkers—most prominently the Italian philosopher Enzo Paci—have attempted a synthesis of Husserl and Marx. What is perhaps most striking about the influence of phenomenology on the social disciplines is that originally it had little effect on empirical work; in the past two decades, however, it has had a vital influence on empirical research, especially in sociology. There is a growing movement of phenomenological sociologists and ethnomethodologists in both America and England; frequently they draw their inspiration from Husserl and Schutz.

The third major challenge to empirical theory, and to the conviction of mainstream social scientists that their disciplines are maturing into full-blown natural sciences, comes from the Frankfurt School of critical theory. The label "The Frankfurt School" gained popularity after the Second World War, and identified a group of thinkers associated with the Institute for Social Research, which was founded in Frankfurt in 1923. Most of the members of the Institute, including the central figures of Horkheimer, Adorno, and Marcuse, were strongly influenced by Hegel and Marx. During the period of their exile from Germany—which corresponded to the most creative period of the Institute—they collectively worked out the foundations of a critical theory of society which they intended as an alternative to bourgeois social science on the one hand, and to doctrinaire Stalinist Marxism on the other. When the Institute was founded, one of its purposes was to engage in empirical research; during its residence in America, it was best known for its study of the authoritarian personality and mass society. But its members always viewed with deep suspicion and disdain Anglo-Saxon traditions of empiricism and American pragmatism.

After the return to Germany in 1950, the most prominent and controversial thinker to emerge from the Institute was Jürgen Habermas. Habermas, unlike the old-timers associated with the Institute, has a more subtle and comprehensive grasp of recent developments in the social sciences, analytic philosophy of science, and the philosophy of language and theoretical linguistics. He has re-examined the foundations of critical theory and sought to develop a comprehensive social theory which is a dialectical synthesis of empiricist, phenomenological, hermeneutic, and Marxist-Hegelian themes. Like Schutz and many post-Wittgensteinian analytic philosophers, Habermas has explicitly criticized the social sciences as conceived of and practiced by mainstream social scientists. He has probed epistemological issues that lie at the heart of our understanding of social reality. And he has begun the difficult task of elaborating an alternative to a naturalistic understanding of the social sciences.

Because each of these orientations is rooted in the philosophic movements that have profoundly shaped modern consciousness, and because each sets out to show what is wrong with the scientism that dominates our age—a scientism that has pernicious theoretical and practical consequences—I decided to examine them in detail. But it was never my intention to write a mere survey, or to take the stance of a presumably neutral referee scoring points for one side or the other. My major objective is to evolve a perspective from which one can integrate what is right and sound in these competing orientations, and reject what is inadequate and false.

The more I worked on and worked through this diverse body of material, the more the pieces fell into place. Gradually it became clearer that we are *not* confronted with a miscellany of critical points and ad hoc arguments coming from unrelated standpoints. My excitement grew as I discovered that, despite tensions and conflicts, there is far more coherence than I had initially anticipated.

When, for example, I explored the several critiques of analytic philosophers of the social sciences, I asked what was the alternative understanding of social knowledge that they were advocating. These critics kept returning to themes which have always been central for the tradition of interpretative sociology and phenomenology. It was natural therefore to explore whether phenomenology offered a clearer account of the understanding and interpretation of social reality. Further, for all the sharp disagreements between "tough-minded" empiricists, their analytic critics, and phenomenologists, there were certain framework assumptions that they shared. They advocated a conception of theory and the role of the theorist that would approximate the ideal of the disinterested observer who explains, understands, interprets, or simply describes what is. But this understanding of theory and the theorist harbored difficulties and unresolved problems that were not brought into the open. These very problems and their ramifications are the *fons et origo* of the critical theory of society.

As I pursued this inquiry, a famous passage from Hegel's *Phenomenology of Mind* kept occurring to me. In the Introduction to the *Phenomenology,* Hegel describes how *Wissenschaft,* or the complete systematic scientific comprehension of what is, and *Das Natürliche Bewusstsein,* or natural consciousness, initially appear to each other. From the perspective of each, the other appears to be topsy-turvy, inverted. Hegel warns us:

For science cannot simply reject a form of knowledge which is not true, and treat this as a common view of things, and then assure us that itself is an entirely different kind of knowledge, and holds the other to be of no account at all; nor can it appeal to the fact that in this other there are presages of a better. By giving that assurance it would declare its force and value to lie in its bare existence: but the untrue knowledge appeals likewise to the fact that it is, and assures us that to it science is nothing. One barren assurance, however, is of just as much value as another.[2]

While I reject Hegel's claim that there is or can be a final complete *Wissenschaft,* one can draw from this passage an extremely important moral which is relevant to this inquiry. In the disputes about the status of the social disciplines, especially those based on different philosophical points of view, it appears as if we are confronted with "one barren assurance" that has "just as much value as another." Opposing claimants write and act as if their point of view is the only correct one and the others of "no account at all." If we are to escape from this type of intellectual skepticism, we must try to see how examining a position—what Hegel calls a form or shape of consciousness—with full integrity, how understanding it in its own terms, and probing it to locate its weaknesses and internal conflicts, can lead us to a more adequate and comprehensive understanding. This is the dialectical movement that Hegel calls the movement from *Gewissheit* (certitude) to *Wahrheit* (truth). There is a truth to be discovered—something right about each of the forms of consciousness that Hegel explores; the task is to bring out this "truth," which necessitates showing what is false and abstract in these several moments, and then passing beyond them to a more adequate comprehension.

So, by analogy, in our study of the competing understandings of political and social theory, it is essential to grasp each from its own internal perspective or self-understanding, and to see how its internal difficulties lead us to comprehend both its falsity or one-sidedness, and its truth. Hegel also teaches us that any serious reflection must begin with what appears to us; it is futile to condemn the common view of things as being of no account. This is why I have begun with an investigation of a naturalistic understanding of the social disciplines and its stress on empirical theory. For this is still—despite the many attacks upon it—the common view of things.

In a study that treats as many thinkers and as much diverse material as this one, questions can always be raised about the principle of selection. I am acutely aware of how much relevant material I have not discussed, and of the many alternative routes that I might have taken. The rationale for my selection of issues and themes will become clearer as I proceed, but I can give a preliminary account here. This book is written primarily for those familiar with and shaped by Anglo-Saxon intellectual traditions. I stress this because the contemporary discussion of the social disciplines, *sciences humaines,* or *Geisteswissenschaften* has taken very different forms in different cultural contexts. If, for example, I were addressing myself to the recent discussions of the *sciences humaines* in France, I would focus on the crosscurrents among phenomenologists, structuralists, poststructuralists, and the new advocates of a comprehensive semiotics. On the other hand, if I were writing for a German and Central European audience, I would have to examine the various forms of Marxism, hermeneutics, *Existenz* philosophy, and phenomenology that have shaped the discussion of the vital issues. In the United States, and to a lesser extent in other Anglo-Saxon countries, there exists a strong naturalistic tradition of the social sciences. Many practitioners have not hestitated to speak of social science as an "American" discipline, and have prided themselves on breaking away from more speculative and philosophic investigations. While I will be exploring the significance of phenomenology and the critical theory of society—both of which have their roots in Continental traditions—I have introduced the discussion of them at those points where they claim to correct the inadequacies of a naturalistic understanding of the social sciences.

Even more important—although it would take another volume or two to establish my claim—is the fact that the same basic problems that emerge in sharp relief in Anglo-Saxon debates about the nature of the social sciences and the role of theory, are also central to Continental investigations of the *sciences humaines* and the *Geisteswissenschaften*. The live options that are taken seriously and the forms of discourse manifestly differ, but there is a concern with the same primary issues.

Here and throughout this study, I have spoken about the "social sciences" and "social studies." I have already warned about the dangers of a misguided essentialism that fails to do justice to the variety and complexity of the inquiries conventionally grouped under these labels. To avoid superficiality, I have concentrated on the fields of sociology and political science. Traditionally it is within these disciplines that primary questions have been raised about the very nature and status of the social sciences, and what it means to have knowledge of society and politics. But throughout I will try to show that what I have to say about these disciplines is relevant to the full range of the social sciences.

One more warning is necessary. I have entitled this inquiry "The Restructuring of Social and Political Theory," but there is a great deal of linguistic confusion—which reflects substantive confusion—about the meaning of "social theory" and "political theory." Sometimes these terms are used primarily to refer to philosophical speculations about the nature of society and politics. More recently, especially as a result of the increasing interest in empirical theory, these terms are used to denote empirical theories about social and political phenomena. Most mainstream social scientists recognize a distinction between sociology and political science, but this distinction is based upon the different types of variables examined, or the typical issues explored, in these different fields. Insofar as both fields aspire to scientific maturity and to well-formulated testable explanatory theories, there are no essential or categorial differences between the "social" and the "political." The distinction between chemistry and physics is analogous. Just as there are many areas of overlap and cross-fertilization in these natural sciences, so too in sociology and political science.

I am, however, sympathetic with those thinkers such as Hannah Arendt and Jürgen Habermas who have examined the history of the concepts of the "social" and the "political," and shown us not only how these concepts were once applied to *categorially distinct* phenomena, but also how the disciplines studying these phenomena had different *aims*.[3] Their inquiries are not limited to the history of the changing meanings of these concepts. They have shown us the significance of the conceptual revolution that took place when moderns came to think of the study of society and politics as basically similar and homogeneous, differing primarily in the types of variables examined. Whatever gains were achieved, something vital was also lost, or rather suppressed. For this modern conceptual revolution has led to a forgetfulness about the classical—especially the Aristotelian—understanding of politics and praxis. The discipline of politics was once conceived of not as a theoretical study of how the political system works, but as a discipline that has as its *telos* a practical end: the leading of a good and just life in the polis. For many social scientists this conception of politics, however noble and inspiring, now seems apocryphal. They think it reflects the confusion between fact and value, the empirical and the normative, which presumably has inhibited the scientific development of the study of society and politics. In Part IV I will explore what is at issue in distinguishing the "social" and the "political," for it is directly relevant to a comprehension of the *critical* function of theory. To be sure, we cannot return to the classical understanding of politics. But I do think, echoing Habermas, that the primary problem today is the reconciliation of the classical aim of politics—to enable human beings to live good and just lives in a political community—with the modern demand of social thought, which is to achieve scientific knowledge of the workings of society.[4]

I want to conclude these introductory remarks by situating this inquiry within my own personal experiences and convictions. These personal experiences have been shared by many thinkers who seek to think clearly about social and political phenomena, and to relate their deepest thoughts to the ways in which they live. Contemporary thinkers in the Anglo-Saxon world cannot underestimate the extent to which their thoughts, attitudes, beliefs, and even feelings have been shaped by empiricist, scientific, and pragmatic traditions—even when one is reacting against these. There are great virtues in these traditions which cannot be lightly dismissed. At their best, they have insisted upon clarity and rigor. They have been committed to the ideal of public and intersubjective tests and criticisms in which any knowledge claim is recognized as fallible and subject to further inquiry. There has been a healthy skepticism toward unbridled speculation and murky obscurantist thought. These intellectual virtues have been closely linked with moral and political ones. It is believed that solid empirical knowledge can help us not only to escape from superstition and prejudice, but also to achieve enlightened action. But many of these beliefs that led to such high hopes and expectations in Enlightenment thinkers have turned sour. There seems to be a natural progression from early Enlightenment ideals to contemporary positivist and empiricist modes of thought. What were once great liberating ideas have turned into suffocating strait jackets. There is a hidden nihilism in the dialectic of this development which Anglo-Saxon thinkers have not often honestly confronted. The history of intellectual life during the past two hundred years has imposed ever more severe restrictions on what counts as genuine knowledge and on limits of rational argument. Wittgenstein in his *Tractatus* carried this dialectic to its inevitable conclusion: that, strictly speaking, we cannot even meaningfully talk about values, for values lie outside the world of facts and meaningful propositions about these facts.

The movement of thought reflected in this dialectic has had the most profound theoretical and practical consequences—especially in the study of society and politics. On the one hand we are told that we cannot turn our back on the relentless progression of science, that our task as theorists is to interpret the world—that is, to give theoretical explanations of the facts that meet the rigorous standards of scientific knowledge. Enlightenment ideals are still verbally endorsed, for we are constantly told that as we accumulate empirical knowledge, we can better engage in enlightened action and social reform. But on the other hand, the very possibility of rational discourse about what is enlightened and what is better has been called into question. Such discourse, we are told, not only lies outside the domain of science, but outside *any* form of rational argument. Presumably, in the final analysis, all value positions are subjective, arbitrary, and equally unjustifiable. There are no rational decision procedures that are *sufficient* for judging among competing value orientations.

The problems and tensions that have resulted are not merely intellectual. They affect the ways in which we think of ourselves in the world and conduct our lives. During the nineteen sixties this central experience of self-alienation and crisis was shared by many. Something was desperately wrong with prevailing forms of social and political reality, and with the established ways of thinking about them. The disparity between what one had been taught to accept as the most sophisticated forms of human knowledge, and what one felt in one's "gut," became critical. During this period there were many excesses and a good deal of thrashing around. But one serious consequence cannot be ignored. Many came to feel the need of a more penetrating understanding of what had gone wrong, of how the straitjacket of established thought had come to dominate human life. Shallow protest and polemic are not enough. What is needed is a critique that aims to get at the roots; a rethinking of what it means to live a rational life; and a relating of theory to practice. It is the story of this turning and probing that I want to tell in this inquiry—a story whose conclusion has not yet been decided.

Part I

Empirical Theory

It is one of the assumptions of intellectual life in our country that there should be amongst us men whom we think of as political philosophers. Philosophers themselves and sensitive to philosophic change, they are to concern themselves with political and social relationships at the widest possible level of generality. . . . For three hundred years of our history there have been such men writing in English, from the early seventeenth to the twentieth centuries, from Hobbes to Bosanquet. To-day, it would seem, we have them no longer. The tradition has been broken and our assumption is misplaced, unless it is looked on as a belief in the possibility that the tradition is about to be resumed. For the moment, anyway, political philosophy is dead.

Peter Laslett, 1956[1]

All mature scientific knowledge is theoretical. Obviously this does not mean that facts are immaterial. . . . Facts must be ordered in some way so that we can see their connections. The higher the level of generality in ordering such facts, the broader will be the range of explanation and understanding. . . .

Clearly, if political science could arrive at such a general theory, the understanding of political life that it would give would be both profound and extensive. There is no need consequently to point out that such a theory would be desirable because of its utility. The only thing that is not apparent, however, is that the formulation of such a theory is a possible and necessary step along the road to reliable and perceptive knowledge about politics.

No such theory is visible on the horizons of political research in the United States today.

David Easton, 1953[2]

Among the many motives which impelled the so-called 'behavioural revolution' in political science, two major and potent anxieties have played an important part. Both have persuaded political scientists to turn away from the traditional political science curriculum, and both have persuaded the practitioners of the new political science that their new science was to be one natural science among others. . . . The first anxiety was the fear of what David Easton's *The Political System* labelled as 'hyperfactualism'. Political scientists had all too often become mere compilers of facts about political

3

systems, especially facts about the minutiae of constitutions. No one denied the importance of facts; indeed, it was freely admitted that a developed political science would demand far more factual evidence than we presently possess. But it was recognized that the developed and prestigious physical sciences were very far from being compilations of facts; and it was seen that, by itself, sticking to the facts was quite inadequate to generate anything that aspired to the name of political *science*. The cure for 'hyperfactualism' was to be the creation of an organized body of theory, for theory alone enables us to classify and assess the significance of the factual data acquired by experiment and observation. But such theory would also assuage the second anxiety —the fear that political scientists might be taken for political ideologists. For such theory was to be quite different from 'traditional' political theory; it was to be empirical and descriptive, not moral and prescriptive theory. The goal was the creation of a properly validated body of scientific theory, not the production of ideology.

Alan Ryan, 1972[3]

The Positivist Influence

THESE passages reflect the dominant mood that prevailed during the nineteen fifties about the state of political philosophy and political science. They also provide a perspective for exploring the nature and significance of empirical theory in the social sciences. Although they are about political philosophy and political science, one could cite similar passages reflecting the same intellectual attitudes throughout the range of the social sciences. The rhythms of development have been different, but during the twentieth century each of the social sciences has passed through a decline of speculative and philosophical reflection, and a rise of optimism about results to be expected once a firm scientific and empirical foundation was achieved.

Laslett's declaration, "For the moment, anyway, political philosophy is dead," was provocative, but appeared to be the brutal truth. One could not single out a contemporary philosopher whose political and social thought exhibited the comprehensiveness of Hobbes, Locke, Bentham, or the Mills. No contemporary displayed the power, scope, and depth of Montesquieu, Rousseau, Hegel, or Marx. Laslett was right: the great tradition had been broken, even though he suggested weakly that it might be resumed.

But it was not for any superficial reasons or lack of creative genius that this happened. The break in the tradition seemed to be the ineluctable consequence of the most deeply rooted and prevalent intellectual attitudes in Anglo-Saxon cultural life. Few Anglo-Saxon thinkers have been positivists in the strict sense of either Comte or the Vienna Circle, but the positivist temper has had a profound influence upon them. Basically, the positivist temper recognizes only two models for legitimate knowledge: the empirical or natural sciences, and the formal disciplines such as logic and mathematics. Anything which cannot be reduced to these, or cannot satisfy the severe standards set by these disciplines, is to be viewed with suspicion. There is the task of analysis, the job of clarifying the distinctive characteristics of these models, but analysis itself is a second-order discipline, a parasite that exists on the first order, the empirical and formal sciences.

Few social scientists are willing to suggest that the study of political and social philosophy is of no value whatsoever. Such an historical study might enlarge one's vision, suggest empirical hypotheses to be tested, and occasionally reveal acute observations that can be salvaged. But the trouble with these grand philosophical systems is their tendency to confuse fact and value, descriptive and prescriptive judgments. Whatever worth such a study might have, these traditional systems do not lend themselves to systematic, rigorous formulation by which they can be empirically tested.

Mainstream social scientists came to view the history of their own disciplines through the spectacles of positivism. Some opted for the "break" theory, which emphasized that what was now happening in the twentieth century was comparable to what had happened in the sixteenth and seventeenth, when the natural and physical sciences broke away from the older tradition of natural philosophy. The potential revolutionary consequences of this new scientific era in the human sciences would be no less consequential than what had already occurred in the physical sciences. Others favored the "continuity" theory, which saw the new scientific approach as the fulfillment of the latent promise of the tradition that began with Plato and Aristotle. Either version views the history of intellectual life as passing through the dark ages of theological, metaphysical, and philosophical speculation, only to emerge in the triumph of the positive sciences.

The understanding that social scientists have of their own disciplines was reinforced by what was happening in philosophy. Once the triad of the early logical positivists had taken hold—analytic, synthetic, or meaningless—there was no legitimate place for social and political philosophy. Such a grand edifice had to be dismantled—sorted out into its proper empirical (synthetic) components and its definitional (analytic) components. Attitudes about the normative aspects of such disciplines ranged from the more extreme and militant stance that all such discourse is meaningless or at best emotive, to the less extreme view that philosophical analysis can at least clarify the uses of normative terms and discourse. Ethics was to be replaced by metaethics. The job of the philosopher is to elucidate ethical discourse, not to make normative pronouncements. Presumably the same would hold in the normative discourse appropriate to social and political life. I say "presumably" because, while a great deal of intellectual energy went into the study of metaethics, there was scarcely any serious interest in social and political issues among philosophers influenced by logical positivism and logical empiricism. They shared the prevalent contemporary belief that once the really hard issues in epistemology and ethics were cleared up, we could apply these results to other problems.

Even with the "ordinary language" revolution that occurred within analytic philosophy, the situation at first did not change. In the first flush of the ordinary language movement there were severe attacks on the excessive scientism of orthodox positivism, and a growing sensitivity to the complexity, variety, and nonreducibility of different forms of language, as well as a new understanding of philosophical analysis. One could now say that moral discourse—or more generally, normative discourse—was not defective because it failed to satisfy the canons of scientific discourse. Moral discourse exhibits its own structure, grammar, and rules. The task of the philosopher is to elucidate and probe this discourse and to clarify the subtle nuances of moral terms. But ordinary language philosophers shared, with their more positivistically inclined opponents, the conviction that the proper philosophical task is elucidation of moral discourse, not making disguised normative claims or specious justifications. Here too, philosophy was thought of as a second-order—although extremely important—discipline.

In short, the tradition of political and social philosophy had been broken because the most sophisticated and rigorous developments in Anglo-Saxon philosophy had presumably shown that there was not, and could not be, any such rational discipline yielding genuine knowledge. Mainstream social scientists certainly did not lament the passing or breaking of this tradition. On the contrary, the lack of scientific development of their own fields was frequently attributed to the inhibiting influence of this tradition, and to conceptual confusions that it harbored about the categorial distinction between empirical and normative theory.

Kant, in his *Critique of Pure Reason,* had perceptively characterized how mathematics and the natural sciences underwent conceptual revolutions which transformed them into genuine sciences. Once this revolution had occurred, they then exhibited the characteristics of progressively maturing disciplines involving the growth of human knowledge. Mainstream social scientists believe that during the twentieth century an analogous revolution has been taking place in the scientific study of individuals in all their complex human relationships. This collective sense of what has been happening, and this optimism about the future development of the social or behavioral sciences, was expressed by Clark Hull when he wrote in 1943:

. . . there is reason to hope that the next hundred years will see an unprecedented development in this field. One reason for optimism in this respect lies in the increasing tendency, at least among Americans, to regard the "social" or behavioral sciences as genuine natural sciences rather than *Geisteswissenschaft*. Closely allied to this tendency is the growing practice of excluding the logical, folk, and anthropomorphic considerations from the list of presumptive primary behavioral explanatory factors. Wholly congruent with these tendencies is the expanding recognition of the desirability in the behavioral sciences of explicit and exact formulation, with empirical verification at every point. If these three tendencies continue to increase, as seems likely, there is good reason to hope that the behavioral sciences will presently display a development comparable to that manifested by the physical sciences in the age of Copernicus, Kepler, Galileo, and Newton.[4]

As social scientists became increasingly confident about the scientific status of their own discipline, they felt a need to clarify its logical and epistemological features, especially the respects in which it could be significantly compared with the well-established natural sciences. Ryan refers to the fear of "hyperfactualism," but other influences also urged an elucidation of the scientific status of the social disciplines, and especially the nature and significance of empirical theory. Practicing social scientists became concerned about the internal confusion in their own fields. And as philosophers of science became clearer about the primary characteristics of the natural sciences and the precise role that theory plays in them, they exerted a powerful influence on methodologically sophisticated social scientists.

The Mainstream Position: Robert Merton

O NE of the best brief contemporary statements concerning the scientific status of the social disciplines appears in Robert Merton's *Social Theory and Social Structure*.[5] Because Merton is a social theorist who has contributed substantially to sociological research, and who exhibits a detailed knowledge of the range of the social sciences, and an historical awareness of their development, his statement about theory provides an excellent starting point for an investigation of empirical theory. Merton has always been an intellectual moderate, and during the nineteen fifties his conception of "theories of the middle range" served as a credo which many diverse social scientists could happily endorse.

Merton takes on the challenge of accounting for the immature development of the social sciences as compared with the natural sciences. He claims that to compare the present state of the social sciences, especially sociology, with contemporary physics is not only misleading, but tends to be a "misplaced masochism." An understanding of the history of science may be both humbling and liberating, especially for those optimists who think that social theory can achieve grand results in one fell swoop. For this naive optimism ignores the way in which centuries of research prepared the terrain for the great breakthroughs in physical science. It is an error to assume that *"all cultural products existing at the same moment of history must have the same degree of intellectual maturity"* (p. 6). "Perhaps sociology is not yet ready for its Einstein because it has not yet found its Kepler. Even the nonpareil Newton had, in his day, acknowledged the indispensable contribution of cumulative research, saying: 'If I have seen farther, it is by standing on the shoulders of giants' " (p. 7).[6]

The moral to be drawn is that if we are to compare sociology with the physical sciences, it is more illuminating to compare the present state of sociology with the fledgling state of the physical sciences. "Between twentieth-century physics and twentieth-century sociology stand billions of man-hours of sustained, disciplined, and cumulative research" (pp. 6–7).

Although Merton emphasizes the disparity in development of the social and the physical sciences, he does not doubt the possibility of bringing the social sciences to the same type of scientific maturity. Like Hull, he is certain there can be a Kepler, Newton, or Einstein of the social sciences. His advocacy of theories of the middle range is intended as a sensible strategy for the present in order to approach this goal. Merton is acutely aware that much of social science research has fluctuated between the violent extremes of "abstracted empiricism" and "grand theory"—extremes which were brilliantly caricatured and devastatingly criticized by C. Wright Mills.[7]

But before one can adequately characterize theories of the middle range, we must become clearer about the theoretical orientation in the social sciences. Merton's sketch of activities that are frequently confused with theory proper is not only extremely helpful in serving as a warning, but also in locating the specific functions of theory.

Theory is *not* to be understood as consisting of *"general orientations toward data, suggesting types of variables which need somehow to be taken into account, rather than clear, verifiable statements of relationships between specified variables"*—even though this is "a large part of what is now called sociological theory" (p. 9). According to Merton, this is unsatisfactory because it is entirely too amorphous. Theory does not consist of "points of view" or "approaches." Theory which yields definite theorems must at least consist of "clear verifiable statements of the relationships between specified variables."

Theory is not to be confused with methodology. Of course social scientists must be methodologically sophisticated. They must know how to use statistical and other quantitative techniques, and how to design experiments; they must understand the nature of inferences and the requirements of a theoretical system. "But such knowledge does not contain or imply the particular *content* of sociological theory" (p. 84). One of the curiosities of the social sciences—unlike the natural sciences—is that methodology has become a subfield with its own professional specialists. The excessive preoccupation with methodology can and frequently has become a diversion from the task of constructing substantive theoretical systems. Merton shares the view of many practicing scientists that methodological discussions are frequently most fruitfully pursued when they arise in relation to specific substantive problems of research.[8]

Nor is theory to be confused with the "analysis of sociological concepts" such as status, role, *Gemeinschaft,* social interaction, social distance, *anomie,* etc. Once again, sociological theorizing cannot proceed without the analysis of central concepts which may enter a theoretical system. But a miscellaneous analysis of such concepts, which has preoccupied so many social theorists, does not generate or add up to a theoretical system. Such a system consists of logically interrelated propositions which have empirical consequences.

We come closer to one of the central confusions about theory when we mistake *"post factum* sociological interpretations" (p. 90) for theory proper. Frequently such interpretations are offered in order to explain observations. A social theorist is confronted by a variety of data, and he sees that this material "makes sense" or "fits" with a given interpretation. But the logical fallacy underlying *post factum* interpretations is that there are a variety of crude hypotheses which are in some measure confirmed or verified by the "facts," but which are designed to account for conflicting and contradictory states of affairs. *Post factum* interpretations and explanations are frequently so flexible, vague, or open that they can "account" for almost any data. Merton is alert to a point that has been emphasized by Peirce and reiterated in our own time by Karl Popper: scientific theories must be refutable and falsifiable, and not merely verified or confirmed.

Some social scientists have thought that the proper function of theory is making well-founded empirical generalizations. Empirical generalizations are a necessary condition for establishing theoretical systems, but they are not sufficient. Here we can see most clearly what Ryan means by the anxiety of "hyperfactualism" or what C. Wright Mills called "abstracted empiricism." A primitive myth which has deeply affected social science research is the belief that the real business of science is the collection of data and the advancing of empirical generalizations based on it. In the twentieth century our techniques for collecting data have become considerably more sophisticated. We now have data banks and institutes whose primary business is refining techniques for gathering data. It is also frequently believed that when and if we collect enough data and discover correlations that hold among these data, then we will be in a position to arrive at those higher empirical generalizations that constitute genuine science. Even those who are dimly aware that there is more to science than collecting data and formulating empirical generalizations based upon data, are nevertheless convinced that this is the proper way of preparing the terrain for more advanced theories. This is a "primitive myth" because—even though it is widely held, and Bacon and Mill are cited frequently as having endorsed and advocated it—it is completely fallacious. It would be difficult to name any philosopher who ever held such a simplistic conception of the nature of science—certainly not Bacon and Mill. Further, despite the wide and sometimes sharp disagreement among contemporary philosophers about the nature and role of theory in the sciences, there is a rational consensus that it does not simply consist of empirical generalizations based on the collection or observation of facts.

This point will be extremely important when we consider some of the challenges to the conception of the social sciences as genuine natural sciences. Many social scientists wedded to naive empiricism are convinced that these challenges are specious or "off base." They are incredulous when their opponents assert that it is impossible or mistaken to collect data, search for correlations, and advance testable empirical generalizations suggested by the data. They are convinced that this not only *can* be but *is* being done in the best empirical research. Insofar as they consider such activity the quintessence of scientific inquiry, they simply cannot understand what their opponents find so objectionable; how, they ask, can one even question the possibility or importance of a social science that employs methodologically sound techniques of research? But we will see later that the primary issue is not the possibility of collecting and interpreting data, but rather the significance of this enterprise and what inferences we can draw from it.

Merton tells us that sociological literature abounds in empirical generalizations—"isolated propositions summarizing observed uniformities of relationships between two or more variables" (p. 92). But "a miscellany of such propositions only provides the raw material for sociology as a discipline. The theoretic task, and the orientation of empirical research toward theory, first begins when the bearing of such uniformities on a set of interrelated propositions is tentatively established" (p. 92).

Having distinguished a variety of activities that are confused with theory, Merton is now ready to explain what systematic theory is, not only for sociology but for the social sciences in general. The first point he emphasizes is that generalizations appropriate to systematic theory differ significantly from miscellaneous empirical generalizations based on the observation of specific variables. "The second type of sociological generalization, the so-called 'scientific law,' differs from the foregoing inasmuch as it is a statement of invariance *derivable* from a theory" (p. 92). Like most social scientists, Merton is willing to concede that to date there is a lack of good examples of such laws, although he believes that approximations of this second type of sociological generalization "are not entirely wanting" (p. 92). "The paucity of such laws in the sociological field perhaps reflects the prevailing bifurcation of theory and empirical research. Despite the many volumes dealing with the history of sociological theory and despite the plethora of empirical investigations, sociologists (including the writer) may discuss the logical criteria of sociological laws without citing a single example which fully satisfies these criteria" (p. 92). This admission appears almost like a refrain among the defenders of the scientific status of the social disciplines, especially those who are convinced that the role of theory and scientific explanation is essentially the same in the natural and social sciences. Merton, however, gives an example of what he means. It is worth while to consider his example in detail, because many of the points that Merton wants to stress about systematic theory, scientific explanation, and the role of scientific laws can be clearly seen with reference to it. The example is a "reformulation" of Durkheim's explanation of the differential in suicide rates among Catholics and Protestants.[9]

"It has long been established as a statistical uniformity that in a variety of populations, Catholics have a lower suicide rate than Protestants" (p. 92). To the extent that such a claim is carefully formulated, with other factors remaining constant, we have only an empirical generalization—one which does not purport to state an invariance. The problem was to give a theoretical explanation of this regularity. Restating Durkheim's theoretic assumptions in a formal fashion, Merton offers the following account of Durkheim's analysis:

1. Social cohesion provides psychic support to group members subjected to acute stresses and anxieties.
2. Suicide rates are functions of *unrelieved* anxieties and stresses to which persons are subjected.
3. Catholics have greater social cohesion than Protestants.
4. Therefore, lower suicide rates should be anticipated among Catholics than among Protestants. (p. 93)

In the context of his discussion, Merton is not concerned to justify that this is a proper reconstruction of Durkheim. Nor does he argue for the truth of the relevant premises, or analyze such crucial and slippery concepts as "psychic support" or "*unrelieved* anxieties and stresses." His sole purpose is to comment on some of the formal features of this paradigm of theoretic analysis.

First, he observes, the scope of the original empirical finding is considerably extended by such an analysis, because the generalization is conceptualized in abstractions of a higher order: "Catholicism—social cohesion——relieved anxieties—suicide rate" (p. 93). The advantage of this move to greater abstraction is that we no longer see the uniformity as an isolated one, but as a relation "between groups with certain conceptualized attributes (social cohesion) and the behavior" (p. 93).

Second, this type of analysis at once explains and establishes "the theoretic pertinence of uniformity by deriving it from a set of interrelated propositions" (p. 93). Consequently it provides for an accumulation of theory and research findings. "The differentials-in-suicide-rate uniformities add confirmation to the set of propositions from which they—and other uniformities—have been derived. This is a major function of *systematic theory*" (p. 93).

Third, the above reformulation allows us to draw diverse consequences, and enables us both to test the adequacy of the theoretic analysis and to explain other seemingly unrelated regularities. Thus, for example, the initial premise about social cohesion enables us to investigate other phenomena besides suicide as factors influencing the breakdown of "social cohesion"—phenomena such as obsessive behavior or morbid preoccupations.

Fourth, the theory introduces a ground for prediction. If, for example, independent measures should reveal a decrease in the social cohesion of Catholics, the theorist (if other variables are constant) would be able to predict a tendency toward increased suicide rates in this group.

Fifth, the above functions of theory suggest another important characteristic of theories which Merton tells us is "not altogether true of the Durkheim formulation" (p. 94). If a theory is to be productive, it must be sufficiently *precise* and *determinate*. "Precision is an integral element of the criterion of *testability*" (p. 94). Merton sensibly warns that at this stage of sociology, the degree of precision and determinateness that a theory has is a matter of good judgment. The pressure toward excessive precision in the social sciences can lead to unproductive activity. But on the other hand a theorist must strive to achieve at least a degree of precision, so that theories can be empirically tested and refuted.

Merton's reformulation of Durkheim's theoretic analysis, and the several points that he emphasizes, are meant only as illustrations. It would be ungenerous, at this stage of my inquiry, to accuse him of failing to confront the many problems that arise in gaining a determinate and precise understanding of theory proper. But I do think that Merton touches upon the most central themes that have preoccupied both social scientists and philosophers of the social sciences when they elucidate the nature of systematic theory and scientific explanation. The model of theoretical scientific explanation that Merton adumbrates is what has been called the "hypothetical-deductive" model. It is "deductive" because the explanation—in this case, of the empirical regularity about suicide rates—is by nontrivial derivation. Given the first three premises, the conclusion drawn is logically derivable. And if any of the three premises were challenged, one could presumably give reasons for their tentative acceptance. It is hypothetical, because no claim is being made that any of the premises in this schema is infallible. Further conceptual or empirical inquiry may challenge, modify, or even abandon them.

Merton also recognizes that in systematic theory there is explicitly or implicitly a need to employ laws—or, more cautiously, lawlike statements. Such laws must be carefully distinguished from mere empirical generalizations. It is by virtue of these presumed laws—what philosophers have labeled "nomological statements"—that we are warranted in drawing those counterfactual statements so essential for scientific explanation and prediction. This is illustrated when Merton tells us that Durkheim's theoretic assumptions would enable us to predict that, *if* there should be a decrease in the social cohesion among Catholics, *then* (*ceteris paribus*) we would expect in this group a tendency toward increased suicide rates.

Finally, Merton is alert to the close connection between scientific explanation, precision, testability, and prediction. A well-formulated scientific theory is one that explains by showing how empirical phenomena and regularities can be derived from theoretical assumptions and appropriate initial conditions. But it must be stated with sufficient precision so that it is testable. Otherwise we would be unable to distinguish it from a *post factum* explanation, since these pseudo-scientific explanations can also satisfy the criterion of derivability.

The above sketch of sociological theory proper—a sketch intended to capture the essential features of systematic theory in any of the social sciences—helps to situate Merton's specific strategic recommendation of the need for theories of the middle range. On the one hand, Merton opposes those empiricists who think that we can get along without theory. Throughout his writings he argues that such an attitude is narrow-minded, unproductive, and ultimately unscientific. At best such a naïve empiricism leads to the directionless collection of data and the chaotic accumulation of miscellaneous empirical generalizations. This is not what science is about, and it certainly is not the key to the success of the natural sciences. Empirical research without theory is blind, just as theory without empirical research is empty. We must also be modest and realistic in our aspirations. It is only by slowly building and testing theories of the middle range—"theories intermediate to the minor working hypotheses evolved in abundance during the day-by-day routines of research, and the all-inclusive speculations comprising a master conceptual scheme from which it is hoped to derive a very large number of empirically observed uniformities of social behavior" (p. 5)—that we can add to the cumulative tradition of scientific inquiry. As our more modest theories are tested and their consequences examined, we can expect—as progress in the physical sciences teaches us—that we will discover more comprehensive theoretical schemes within which theories of the middle range can be integrated.

Although Merton is one of the few contemporary social scientists interested in both the history and the sociology of the social sciences, he distinguishes the history of theory from the "systematics of theory." Frequently—as reflected in the university curricula of the social sciences —what is labeled "theory" consists of little more than a survey of the history of the grand systems of the past. There is an "attractive but fatal confusion of utilizable sociological theory with the history of sociological theory" (p. 4).

Although the history and the systematics of sociological theory should both be of concern in training sociologists, there is no reason for merging and confusing the two. Systematic sociological theory . . . represents the highly selective accumulation of those small parts of earlier theory which have thus far survived the tests of empirical research. But the history of theory includes also the far greater mass of conceptions which fell to bits when confronted with empirical tests. It includes also the false starts, the archaic doctrines and the fruitless errors of the past. Though acquaintance with all this may be a useful adjunct to the sociologist's training, it is no substitute for training in the actual use of theory in research. We can with profit study much of what the forefathers of sociology wrote as exercises in the conduct of intellectual inquiry, but this is quite another matter. (pp. 4–5)

What Merton is saying here seems so plausible and sensible that we may miss its radical implications. It certainly reflects a prevailing orthodoxy of mainstream social scientists. The plausibility of Merton's claim about the attractive but fatal confusion between the history of theory and the systematics of theory assumes acceptance of the analogy between the natural and the social sciences. In his view there are many reasons why one would read the original texts of Newton and study his period. Our interest might be the historical one of discovering what Newton said and did, as contrasted with textbook versions of his accomplishments; or we might probe Newton's work as a model for understanding how scientific inquiry proceeds. But the study of the historical Newton is neither essential nor important to the physicist concerned with research in his discipline and with a theoretical understanding of the physical world.

Furthermore, the above passage indicates the standards by which the contemporary systematic theorist judges these "noble" attempts of the past. His primary concern is and should be "those small parts of earlier theory which have thus far survived the tests of empirical research" (p. 4). At best, acquaintance with the history of one's discipline is a useful adjunct to the sociologist's education, but no substitute for training in the actual use of theory in research. This basic attitude of Merton, which is so widely shared, also regards earlier theorists as having dimly perceived what we only now see so much more clearly. Present theory—to the extent that it is rigorously formulated and empirically tested—is the measure of the success or failure of past theory.

Merton's view has significant consequences for the education and training of social scientists. At this stage I want to call attention to one of its side effects. Given the pluralist structure of the modern university in America, where there has typically been a tolerance for different approaches, almost every respectable social science department has a place for at least one "theorist." But this usually means a person who has a curious antiquarian or historical interest, and whose primary function is to teach the past classics in the field. While the study of these classics may be edifying, and useful in broadening the training of social scientists, it is not thought comparable to the serious business of advancing systematic theory. Thus a manifest tolerance for the study of "theory" —grand theoretical schemes of the past—is combined with a not-so-latent bias against it.

Merton's reflections on the nature of systematic theory, and his attempt to distinguish this from other sorts of activities commonly labeled theoretic, are intended to set the stage for his own attempt to advance substantive empirical theory. He tells us "functional analysis is at once the most promising and possibly the least codified of contemporary approaches to problems of sociological interpretation" (p. 21). Merton conceives of his own theoretical work as directed to the reformulation and codification of functional analysis, so that it meets or approximates the criteria laid down for theory proper. But before turning to a brief examination of Merton's version of functionalism, I want to show how pervasive and deeply entrenched the idea of systematic empirical theory is among mainstream social scientists.

While Merton's statement virtually served as a position statement endorsed by many sociologists during the nineteen forties and fifties, one of the objects of his criticism was the grand theorizing of Talcott Parsons, who dominated American sociology at the time. Merton's attempt to distinguish theory proper from general sociological orientations, the analysis of sociological concepts, and *post factum* interpretations, can be read as an implicit critique of Parsons' thought. Merton's advocacy of theories of the middle range was a direct challenge to Parsons' endeavor to construct a comprehensive systematic theory. It was to be expected that Parsons would take on this challenge and answer the explicit and implied criticisms of Merton. In his presidential address to the American Sociological Society subsequent to the formulation of Merton's position, Parsons directed himself to this challenge. Merton in turn replied to Parsons in the 1968 enlarged edition of *Social Theory and Social Structure*.

The most important aspect of this exchange is not the points of difference but the points of agreement. It becomes clear that on the substantive points of what is systematic theory in sociology and the social sciences, there is no essential disagreement. Their disagreement—to the extent that there is one—concerns the *strategic* matter of how sociologists interested in advancing theory should proceed. Parsons, no less than Merton, expects that an adequate general theory will explain phenomena and regularities by showing how they can be derived from theoretic assumptions; will be sufficiently precise and determinate so as to lend itself to empirical tests and refutations; will reveal sociological laws that warrant proper counterfactual conditionals, together with relevant auxiliary hypotheses; and, at least in principle, will enable us to make predictions about social systems and social change.

To show how much agreement there is between Merton and Parsons, it is worth while citing Merton's long footnote on this debate.

I attach importance to the observations made by Talcott Parsons in his presidential address to the American Sociological Society subsequent to my formulation of this position. For example: "At the *end* of this road of increasing frequency and specificity of the islands of theoretical knowledge lies the ideal state, scientifically speaking, where *most* actual operational hypotheses of empirical research are directly derived from a general system of theory. On any broad front, . . . only in physics has this state been attained in *any* science. *We* cannot expect to be anywhere nearly in sight of it. But it does not follow that, distant as we are from that goal, steps in that *direction* are futile. Quite the contrary, *any* real step in that direction is an advance. Only at this *end* point do the islands merge into a continental land mass.

"At the very least, then, general theory can provide a broadly orienting framework [*n.b.*] . . . It can also serve to codify, interrelate and make available a vast amount of existing empirical knowledge. It also serves to call attention to gaps in our knowledge, and to provide canons of criticism of theories and empirical generalizations. Finally, even if they cannot be systematically derived [*n.b.*], it is indispensable to the systematic clarification of problems and the fruitful formulation of hypotheses." (Italics supplied.)

Parsons, "The Prospects of Sociological Theory," *American Sociological Review,* February 1950, 15, 3–16 at 7. It is significant that a general theoris , such as Parsons, acknowledges (1) that in fact general sociological theory seldom provides for specific hypotheses to be derived from it; (2) that, in comparison with a field such as physics, such derivations for most hypotheses are a remote objective; (3) that general theory provides only a general orientation and (4) that it serves as a basis for codifying empirical generalization. and specific theories. Once this is acknowledged, the sociologists who are committed to developing general theory do not differ significantly in principle from those who see the best promise of sociology today in developing theories of the middle range and consolidating them periodically.[10]

Many social scientists would agree that Merton's *Social Theory and Social Structure* is one of the contemporary classics in sociology. A major reason for its success and influence is Merton's clear, moderate statement of the state of sociology as a young but growing science, and his optimism about its future development as a scientific enterprise slowly building and consolidating its theoretical foundations.

The Restatement by Neil Smelser

I N 1968 Neil Smelser published a collection of essays, *Essays in Sociological Explanation,* with the subtitle, "Theoretical Statement on Sociology as a Social Science and Its Application to Processes of Social Change." Just as Merton's original study epitomizes the understanding that mainstream social scientists had of their own discipline for the nineteen fifties, so Smelser's essays performed a similar function for the nineteen sixties. During the twenty-year period between Merton's original essays and Smelser's, there had been an extraordinary growth in the number and diversity of studies not only in sociology, but in all the social sciences. A significant dent had been made in the "billions of man-hours of sustained, disciplined, and cumulative research" that Merton claimed stood between twentieth-century physics and twentieth-century sociology. But it would be naive to think that this period had seen only the steady progress of sociology as a scientific discipline. It was during this same period that a wide variety of new approaches—ranging from the work of Erving Goffman to Harold Garfinkel and the new school of ethno-methodologists—began to influence sociology. These new approaches did not easily fit the picture of theories of the middle range projected by Merton. This was a period too when insiders and outsiders were calling into question the achievements and foundations of the social sciences.

Smelser, as a professor of sociology at the University of California, Berkeley, was at the very center of this intellectual storm. Closely associated with Talcott Parsons (they jointly published *Economy and Society*), Smelser had already published two substantial and influential sociological works, *Social Change in the Industrial Revolution* (1959) and *Theory of Collective Behavior* (1963). The titles indicate two of Smelser's central concerns: social change and theory.

Smelser has always been sensitive to two frequent charges brought against a Parsonian framework: that the theory was so grand and abstract that it did not explain or guide concrete empirical research, and that Parsons' theoretical structure was unable to account for or to illuminate the all-important processes of social change. Smelser's own contributions to sociology, and his wide and intimate knowledge of the range of the social sciences—including economics, psychology, and even history—make him an ideal spokesman for restating the case for a naturalistic interpretation of the social sciences: an interpretation that sees the social sciences as "immature" natural sciences containing the potential for sophisticated and mature development.

Smelser is aware of the criticisms of sociology as a scientific discipline, and of recent developments in the philosophy of science. He expresses his optimism about the future development of the social sciences more cautiously than Hull or Merton. But what is most striking is his fundamental agreement with Merton on the nature, function, and prospects for empirical theory in the social sciences. He is willing to concede that sociology, as of 1967, is "too comprehensive, diffuse, soft in the center, and fuzzy about the edges" (p. 49).[11] "The contemporary scene yields a bewildering patchwork of fields that is anything but scientifically optimal" (p. 53). Nevertheless, he believes that the structure of the several social sciences as *scientific* disciplines can be clarified, and steps taken toward achieving greater maturity. Smelser examines the types of dependent and independent variables that characterize the different social sciences, and the research methods to be employed in both specifying these variables and discovering correlations and relationships among them. But like Merton, he insists that listing dependent and independent variables "does not tell the whole story. It is necessary . . . to specify the ways in which a discipline imposes a *logical ordering* on its variables" (p. 5). He explicitly distinguishes three types of logical ordering: *hypotheses,* or "statements of the conditions under which dependent variables may be expected to vary in certain ways" (p. 5); *models,* where a number of hypotheses are combined and organized into a system; and *theories,* where models are embedded in definitions, assumptions, and postulates. "Such definitions, assumptions, and postulates constitute the *theoretical framework* of a scientific discipline. Within this framework, specific hypotheses 'make sense.' To put it more strongly, the hypotheses and models should be *derived,* as rigorously as possible, from the theoretical framework" (p. 6).

Smelser's characterization is general enough to reveal the basic structure of any scientific discipline, including both physical and social sciences. He shares with Merton the conviction that in the social sciences it is not sufficient to collect data, propose hypotheses about the correlation of variables, or limit ourselves to ad hoc empirical generalizations. There must also be logical ordering, culminating in the discovery and construction of theoretical frameworks that *explain* the data and "make sense" of our hypotheses. Although Smelser does not explicitly discuss the role of laws in sociological explanation, he concedes:

I would be the last to dispute the central importance of laws in sociological explanation, and the last to deny that these laws must be both derived theoretically and grounded empirically. On the other hand, in dealing with a field like social change, I have discovered a real scarcity of laws and a deficit of theoretically derived propositions, to say nothing of firmly established empirical regularities. The discrepancy between knowing what should be done and possessing the resources to do it was considerable.[12]

Smelser also meets—and defeats—a common objection against the very idea of a social science modeled on the natural sciences. It has been argued that social science rests upon a naive epistemology. Social scientists assume that there is a realm of objective facts. The facts which are reported in observation statements are taken to be the foundation and touchstone for all higher theories. Critics then argue that a more sophisticated understanding of epistemology has conclusively shown the inadequacy of such a naïve view. We have learned that what we call facts or observations are themselves "theory-laden" and shaped by our conceptual schemes. There are no uninterpreted or brute facts that are simply "out there," unaffected by our theoretical and conceptual schemes.

Although I think that the recent appreciation of the ways in which facts and observations are "theory-laden" has important consequences for understanding the social disciplines, I do *not* think that it in any way shows or even suggests the impossibility of the scientific status of the social disciplines. Ironically, most of the controversies over the precise meaning and significance of the claim that all observation is "theory-laden" have focused on the physical sciences. While sorting out the problems involved does not have important consequences for our understanding of science, no one has claimed that the lack of a sharp distinction between facts and theories, or between observations and theories, in the physical sciences is sufficient to call into question the very idea of physical science.

Smelser addresses himself to this problem.

In one form or another, this distinction [between theory and fact] is almost universally accepted by social and behavioral scientists. According to the distinction, the world may be divided into empirical facts (behavioral data) that are given in the "real world" and theory (concepts, constructs, models) that is in the "world of ideas"; and the core task of scientific inquiry consists in systematically generating explanations by bringing theory and fact into some appropriate relation with one another. (p. 58)

But as Smelser points out, although there is something right about this distinction, it is far too simplistic. Citing Lawrence J. Henderson's characterization of a fact as "an empirically verifiable statement about phenomena in terms of a conceptual scheme" (p. 58), Smelser emphasizes the importance of the phrase "in a conceptual scheme." There is no such thing as a sociological fact apart from a conceptual scheme to which it is referred. "When we refer to facts or behavioral data, then we actually refer to a universe of statements, the rules for the organization of which are commonly rooted in the unexamined structures of common language and common sense. There cannot be a fact without a conceptual framework" (p. 58). But while we must abandon the naive picture of a world of facts which make up the "real world," this does not mean that we must give up the importance of the *intended* distinction between facts and theory. Rather this distinction is to be reformulated as "*a relation between two conceptual frameworks*" (p. 58).

It consists in comparing the linguistic and conceptual conventions by which we organize phenomena we call the empirical world with the linguistic and conceptual conventions by which we organize phenomena we call ideas. If a certain relation between the two frameworks is attained, we judge an assertion to be "valid" or "verified"; if another relation is attained, we judge the assertion to be "rejected" or "in need of modification." (pp. 58–59)

Many complex issues arise once we speak about the relation between different conceptual frameworks—issues at the center of controversies in the philosophy of science, but not pursued by Smelser. At this stage of my inquiry, I simply want to note that while many social scientists have a naive conception of what constitutes facts and data (as do many physical scientists), a naturalistic interpretation of the social sciences is *not* refuted by showing that there is no hard and fast distinction between fact and theory.

Functionalism and Its Critic, George Homans

LIKE Merton, Smelser intends his remarks about the scientific status of sociology, the nature of sociological explanation, and especially the importance of theory in the social sciences, as prolegomena to his own approximations toward constructing substantive theories, theories which can scientifically explain social change. When we turn to an examination of these, we will not only discover theoretical hedgings, but an enormous disparity between the requirements that he lays down for theory and what he actually proposes. But it may be objected that by focusing on Merton, Smelser, and Parsons, my discussion of the nature of theory in mainstream social science has been skewed. After all, these three distinguished sociologists have all been associated with the movement called "functionalism" or "structural-functionalism"—an orientation that Merton claims is "the most promising and possibly the least codified of contemporary orientations to problems of sociological interpretation." But although functionalism has been a dominant influence on both social anthropology and sociology, it has been severely criticized. The literature criticizing functionalism on substantive, methodological, epistemological, and ideological grounds has reached voluminous proportions. So it may be thought that framework assumptions shared by functionalists concerning the scientific status of the social disciplines, and the emphasis that they place on empirical theory, are wedded to their misguided functionalist orientation.

This is not true at all. While there is plenty of disagreement on all sorts of issues between functionalists and some of their mainstream critics, there is no significant disagreement about the nature of an adequate theory in the social sciences. The disagreements are about whether or not we can discover empirical theories through a functionalist orientation.

One of the sharpest critics of functionalism has been George Homans. His paper "Bringing Men Back In"—his presidential address to the American Sociological Association in 1964—caused quite a stir in the sedate world of professional sociologists. Homans, who at least in opposition to functionalists has occasionally been an *enfant terrible,* polemically attacks the entire school from Durkheim to Smelser. He says that "where functionalism failed was not in its empirical interests but, curiously, in what it most prided itself on, its general theory" (p. 811).[13] The source of this failure was that "with all their talk about theory, the functionalists never—and I speak advisedly—succeeded in making clear what a theory was" (p. 811). The time has come "to stop talking to our students about sociological theory until we have taught them what a theory is" (p. 811). Twitting his opponents, Homans gives them an elementary lesson in the philosophy of science, instructing them about "what a theory is." He presents what has become virtually the canonical understanding of empirical theory advocated by logical empiricists and proponents of the hypothetical-deductive model of scientific explanation.

What is most ironical about Homans' polemical attack is that, when it comes to tell us "what a theory is," it reads like a gloss on Merton's 1949 characterization of "systematic theory," and Smelser's 1968 statement of the type of "logical ordering" which is theoretical.

To constitute a theory, the propositions must take the form of a deductive system. One of them, usually called the lowest-order proposition, is the proposition to be explained, for example, the proposition that the more thoroughly a society is industrialized, the more fully its kinship organization tends towards the nuclear family. The other propositions are either general propositions or statements of particular given conditions. The general propositions are so called because they enter into other, perhaps many other, deductive systems besides the one in question. Indeed, what we often call a theory is a cluster of deductive systems, sharing the same general propositions but having different *explicanda*. The crucial requirement is that each system shall be deductive. That is, the lowest-order proposition follows as a logical conclusion from the general propositions under the specified given conditions. . . . When the lowest-order proposition does follow logically, it is said to be explained. The explanation of a phenomenon is the theory of the phenomenon. A theory is nothing—it is not a theory—unless it is an explanation. (pp. 811–12)

Although the prose is harsher and tougher than Merton's or Smelser's, the content about "what theory is" is essentially the same.[14] Think too of the way in which Merton discriminated theory proper from other activities frequently labeled theoretical, when Homans goes on to explain:

One may define properties and categories, and one still has no theory. One may state that there *are* relations between properties, and one still has no theory. One may state that a change in one property will produce a definite change in another property, and one still has no theory. Not until one has properties, and propositions stating relations between them, and the propositions form a deductive system—not until one has all three does one have a theory. Most of our arguments about theory would fall to the ground, if we first asked whether we had a theory to argue about. (p. 812)

I do not want to underestimate Homans' sharp disagreements with functionalists. But these disagreements are *not* about "what theory is"— or ideally what it should be. The essence of Homans' attack is that "as a theoretical effort, functionalism never came near meeting these conditions" (p. 812).

Furthermore, Homans thinks that "even if the functionalists had seriously tried" to meet the standards of theory, "they would still have failed" (p. 812). Homans' skepticism is based on this conviction that functionalists have been misguided in the types of general propositions or lawlike statements that they employ in their purported scientific explanations. For, according to Homans, adequate explanations of social phenomena can be given only "by propositions of learning theory in psychology" and not by "any distinctively sociological propositions" (p. 812). In short, according to Homans, functionalism in sociology has been based on a mistake, for functionalists assume that there are sociological laws or general propositions that explain social phenomena. But there are no such things, there are only psychological laws.

Lack of Explanatory Theory in the Social Sciences

THUS far my major objective has been to show that, despite many sharp disagreements among mainstream social scientists, there is a basic unanimity about the nature of empirical theory in the social sciences; about the importance of such theory in attaining or approximating scientific explanations; and about the importance of developing testable explanatory theories, if the social sciences are to mature as the natural sciences have done. Hull, Merton, Parsons, Smelser, and Homans agree not only that this is a real possibility, but also that this is the direction in which the social disciplines *ought* to progress. While I have focused primarily on the work of sociologists, the same basic story could be told throughout the social sciences. Once we achieve empirical theories, so the argument goes, there will no longer be any serious question about the scientific status of the social disciplines, and it will be clearly seen that the form and success of explanations differ in degree only from the natural sciences; the social sciences are in the process of becoming genuine natural sciences. As I proceed in this inquiry, I will show that this conception of empirical theory has powerful theoretical and practical consequences for the role of the social theorist in society; for the relation between theory and action, fact and value; and for empirical and normative theory.

But it is at this point that many of the really difficult problems come into the foreground. What emerges from our discussion thus far is at best a sketch of "what theory is" in the social sciences. The social scientists discussed have explored the methodological and epistemological status of theory only insofar as it has been necessary to clarify what they are doing in their substantive work, and to gain some perspective on the contemporary social sciences. Frequently, practicing social scientists leave off their discussions at the very place where philosophers of social science begin. Merton and Smelser, for example, emphasize the importance of distinguishing ad hoc empirical generalizations from the types of generalizations needed for theoretical explanations. Can we then give a precise analysis of this difference? Can we specify the conditions which are necessary and sufficient to single out those general propositions or nomological statements essential to theoretical frameworks?

Further, all the thinkers discussed have emphasized that an essential characteristic of scientific explanation involves deduction and derivability. Can we then clearly distinguish trivial derivations from those which are explanatory? We also want to know whether all scientific explanation must be explanation by derivation. Are there other forms of legitimate scientific explanation? How, for example, are we to analyze those explanations that involve probability and statistical principles? Once it is granted that there is no sharp difference between fact or observation and theory, how then can we distinguish those conceptual schemes by which we report facts and observations from those conceptual schemes that state theories intended to explain phenomena? What precisely is the relation between scientific explanation and prediction?

Contemporary philosophy of social sciences—as well as the philosophy of the natural sciences—has revolved about these questions.[15] There is no doubt that much of this work—as can be seen so clearly with Homans—has exerted a profound influence on mainstream social scientists' notions of what they are "up to," and of what the canons are for theory and scientific explanation in their fields. But there is also something troubling about these discussions and the amount of intellectual energy and sophistication involved. While they do have extremely important consequences for our understanding of science, and more generally for epistemology, they often have little relevance to the practical and substantive problems that social scientists face in their research.

Whatever analogies one wants to draw and stress between the social sciences and the physical disciplines, there is one significant difference that virtually no one disputes. The philosophy of the natural sciences has recently become a very exciting and controversial field in which few issues have been finally settled or resolved. But there is certainly no disagreement among either practicing scientists or philosophers that an adequate understanding of the physical sciences must account for and do justice to the work of such giants as Copernicus, Kepler, Newton, Einstein, Bohr, Dirac, and many others. One can argue about the characteristics and analyses of their theoretical contributions, but their work serves as the exemplars of scientific investigation and theoretical advance. But there is simply no comparable corpus in sociology and political science where one can point to exemplars of powerful explanatory empirical theories. It seems that in the social sciences the stress on "what theory is" is inversely proportional to the ability to come up with "theory proper."

Of course this is not denied by even the most militant defenders of scientific status of the social disciplines. Typically they appeal to the youth of the discipline, arguing that the terrain is now being prepared for the Copernicus or Newton of the social sciences, and that there are now at least approximations to the rigorous standards of genuine explanatory theory. Yet when we take a hard look at these so-called approximations, they fall far short of those very standards of theory advocated by social scientists themselves. Unlike those critics who claim that they can demonstrate the impossibility of a science of human beings, I do not think this can be proven in one fell swoop by a priori conceptual arguments. In Part II I will consider the arguments of analytic philosophers such as Peter Winch and A. R. Louch, who claim to show that the very idea of social science modeled on the natural sciences involves insurmountable conceptual confusions and logical fallacies.

Many philosophers—and especially Karl Popper—have stressed it is not a failure of scientific inquiry that hypotheses and theories are constantly refuted, being superseded by better falsifiable theories. According to Popper, this is precisely the feature of scientific inquiry that demarcates it from other forms of intellectual inquiry. But this pattern—the pattern of conjecture and refutation—is *not* found in the social disciplines. There are general orientations that have their rise and fall, supplanted by what are taken to be more fruitful and promising ones. But although this pattern bears a superficial resemblance to the physical sciences, there is certainly no rational consensus among social scientists that these proposed theories are genuine empirical theories refuted by further empirical inquiry and experiment. The succession of general orientations in the social sciences bears a greater resemblance to the succession of what Thomas Kuhn calls "schools."

To establish conclusively these claims about the paucity of well-formulated empirical theories in the social sciences is beyond the scope of this inquiry. However, there is an extensive and growing body of literature that reveals the empirical, methodological, logical, and ideological inadequacies of empirical theories, including "functionalist theories," "equilibrium theories," "systems theories," and "social exchange theories." While there are vehement disputes about how fruitful these theories really are, and in what sense, if any, they approximate the ideal of empirical theory, no responsible social scientist has asserted that we

have yet achieved anything comparable to what was achieved in sixteenth-
and seventeenth-century physical science.

To illustrate the types of difficulties encountered, and why I think
that even to speak of approximations is to obscure and mystify issues,
I want to consider briefly the theories advanced by Merton and Smelser.
One can certainly *not* draw the inference that the failures of their theoretical attempts show the impossibility of ever attaining an adequate
theory in the social sciences. But one can see from their work the types
of stumbling blocks encountered over and over again in the many attempts to advance empirical theory.

To see what is wrong with functionalism, we need not turn to its numerous hostile critics, but to those who have defended it and championed a
naturalistic interpretation of the social sciences. Merton himself is an
acute critic of some of the prevailing forms of functionalism. His starting
point in *Social Theory and Social Structure* was to clear away the dross
that overlay loose talk about functionalism and functional analysis. His
chapter on "Manifest and Latent Functions" sought at once to codify
and advance our understanding of functional analysis. In the process
Merton brilliantly exposes what was wrong in earlier attempts to articulate a functional theory. In this respect his analysis serves as a critique
of those formulations of functionalism that do little more than sketch a
general orientation, and fall short of theory proper.

But does Merton do any better than some of his predecessors in codifying functional analysis so that we can see how it meets the criteria of
theory proper? Some have thought that he does, and have attempted to
further the analysis of what is required for an adequate functional analysis. For example, in an important paper inspired by Merton's work, the
eminent philosopher of science Ernest Nagel set forth "A Formalization
of Functionalism." Nagel's "primary objective" is "to exhibit the several
items in Merton's codification as intimately related features in a coherent
pattern of analysis, and thereby to make more evident than he has done
the indispensable requirements which an adequate functional account in
sociology must seek to satisfy."[16] But while this is Nagel's *intention,* his
analysis is actually a devastating critique of Merton. Nagel carefully
shows in his closely reasoned analysis the many problems and distinctions
Merton glosses over. Nagel actually shows the disparity between Merton's codification, and the "indispensable requirements which an adequate functional account in sociology must seek to satisfy" *before* one
can consider it a well-formulated empirical theory. Merton's codification
is an approximation in the sense that early Greek theories of the atomic

structure of the universe are approximations of contemporary atomic theory in physics.

It is difficult to dissent from the conclusions of two philosophers of the social sciences with very different perspectives, who have reviewed the arguments pro and con about functional analysis and functional theory: Richard S. Rudner and Alan Ryan.

Rudner, who strongly defends a naturalistic interpretation of the social sciences, says the following about functionalism:

Not a single one of the myriad claims in anthropological literature [and Rudner would also include sociological literature] can be accepted without serious qualification—not because it is, in principle, impossible to achieve functional explanation (indeed, part of the import of the preceding sections of this chapter has been to indicate how, *in principle*, such explanations could be given), but rather because it is too difficult, much more difficult than the claimants appear to have realized. All too frequently these claims may be counted as at most containing some more or less accurate *descriptions,* rather than explanations, of specific phenomena, ·couched in or accompanied by a rhetoric that may be mistaken for explanations by the unwary. . . . The results produced to date must be seen to· amount only (so far as explanation is concerned) to the articulation of some prescientific hunches or pious hopes that a functional explanation for the item in question *can* ultimately be given.[17]

Alan Ryan not only agrees with the logical and methodological inadequacies noted by Rudner, but adds some further criticisms of his own. Merton, like other mainstream social scientists, advances an empirical theory in order to further the scientific status of sociology, and also to escape the charge that theory in the social sciences is a disguised form of ideology. (Merton explicitly attempts to show that functionalism is neutral in regard to ideological biases.) But Ryan points out that

in Merton's work, the term 'function' serves no purpose at all, save to make a nod to those who believe in the autonomy of sociology, and to decorate the word 'consequences,' indicating that Merton was impressed with the unlooked-for goodness of the consequences of much social life in America. And it is this equation of 'function' with 'good consequences' which dominates the sociological literature of recent years, as a glance at such a journal as *The American Sociological Review* illustrates: articles on such topics as 'Some Social Functions of Ignorance' turn out to be articles on 'Some Unthought-of Good Effects that Ignorance Produces for Almost Everyone'. The reader who doubts this is recommended to verify it for himself.[18]

The case of Neil Smelser is even more instructive for locating the difficulties that sociologists encounter when they actually get down to advancing substantive explanatory theories. As I have indicated, Smelser has been acutely aware that the type of "structural-functionalist theory" that he has adopted from Parsons and sought to refine is accused of being vacuous, of failing to explain empirical phenomena or to illuminate the central issues of social change. In his *Essays in Sociological Explanation* there are several papers that re-examine some of his earlier work, and in 1969 he published a revealing retrospective analysis of his intellectual career: "Some Personal Thoughts on the Pursuit of Sociological Problems."

In his first major book, *Social Change in the Industrial Revolution,* Smelser used the model of "structural-differentiation" as the "logical ordering" device to present his historical study of the structural change in the British cotton industry, and in the family structure of the working classes of that industry, between 1770 and 1840. As Smelser informs us, he was greatly influenced by Parsons in writing this work, especially by the "potential empirical applications"[19] of the model of structural differentiation. The model is intended to specify a general pattern applicable to a variety of types of social change. According to Smelser's own report, "I wanted to assess the potential of the theory of action for analyzing social dynamics in a concrete historical setting." His historical study of the British cotton industry means to show that its development exhibits the stages of structural differentiation.

Subsequently, however, Smelser became increasingly dissatisfied with the theoretical underpinning of his work. He realized that he had made a number of "simplifying assumptions" which needed to be re-examined. He conceded that, contrary to his original expectations, "my account of structural change during the British industrial revolution was not, strictly speaking, derivable from the categories of the framework of [Parsons'] theory of action."[20] And finally, Smelser was aware of a certain amount of theoretical hedging:

On the one hand, I had presented the model as a temporal sequence of steps: but on the other hand I had acknowledged the possibilities of "skipping steps," "regressions to earlier steps," "truncated sequences," etc.—all of which could be used as theoretical escape hatches if some particular historical sequence did not happen to match the one that was called for by the model of differentiation. I felt a vague uneasiness that the representation of the model of differentiation as a sequence of temporal steps or stages was theoretically unsatisfactory, but as yet I didn't know how it might be represented in any better way.[21]

In short, Smelser dimly perceived that the model of structural differentiation lacked what was supposed to be its primary virtue—explanatory power. At best it constitutes a disguised empirical generalization which formally represents a general pattern of social change. But unless we can indicate some of the causal or nomological connections among the several stages of this temporal sequence—unless we are able to explain why some historical sequences diverge from the model and some do not—we may have a generalized description, but certainly not an *explanation* of the historical sequence. This is not to say that the use of such a model has no value. It may have—although many have disputed this—great value in revealing hidden similarities among apparently diverse phenomena, but it certainly is not sufficient to advance or approximate empirical explanatory theory.

In his second major work, *Theory of Collective Behavior,* Smelser thought he could rectify some of the theoretical difficulties that he was increasingly coming to appreciate. In this work he uses a "value-added" model. The basic idea of this model is very simple: instead of assuming that the variables specified stand in relation of a simple temporal sequence (as Smelser had done with the model of structural differentiation), one now assumes that there is a "logic of the combinatorial cumulation of variables."[22] A set of variables, each of which is indeterminate by itself, nevertheless results in a determinate result when it occurs in a specific combination:

The value-added model was an effort to gain an increase in explanatory determinacy by *combining* a number of variables—each indeterminate by itself—into a number of different patterns, each one of which would be associated with a distinctive type of collective behavior. And finally, the value-added model was conceptualized as a purely analytic rather than a temporal sequence; this was an attempt to avoid some of the problems that arose in connection with the notion of temporal stages in the model of structural differentiation.[23]

But is this really an advance? Does such a model succeed in increasing "explanatory determinacy"? From a conceptual point of view, we are really no closer to theoretical explanation. For the same problem that plagued Smelser in his study of the British cotton industry crops up here in a more sophisticated but not less devastating form. Once again the explanatory power of the value-added model depends on specifying what are the nomological or causal relations among the many variables that are discriminated. Unless we can specify these relations, it is difficult to see in what sense, if any, the value-added model scientifically explains the relevant phenomena. Smelser, like so many other mainstream social scientists, has stressed that an adequate theory ought to enable us to derive empirical generalizations from our theoretical assumptions. He acknowledges that one should be able to derive counterfactual statements about what *would* happen if certain independently specifiable variables were altered. But his value-added model does not satisfy this requirement. Smelser himself poses the really tough question when he writes: " 'If a variable in the model is not activated by the variable immediately "preceding" it in the value-added series, what are the conditions that activate it?' This question was not satisfactorily answered in *Theory of Collective Behavior,* and I have not been able to answer it to my satisfaction since the book's appearance."[24]

The case for success or failure in the social sciences does not rest on Merton's or Smelser's approximations. There are some, like Homans, who would claim that their attempts were doomed to failure, not because there is anything intrinsically wrong with the search for theoretical explanations in the social sciences, but because those wedded to functionalism have been looking in the wrong place.[25]

It should at least make us pause when such prominent social scientists as Merton and Smelser, who are knowledgeable about a wide variety of approaches in the social sciences, are unable to come up with anything that genuinely resembles or even approximates explanatory scientific theory. The situation is aggravated when we realize that none of the alternatives proposed to date in sociology or political science have come any closer to offering such theory.

It is precisely this paradox, or at least this tremendous disparity between the concept of empirical theory endorsed by mainstream social scientists, and the failure to achieve it, that has led an increasing number of thinkers to question the very foundations of social science conceived of as a natural science. What is even more disturbing—from the perspective of what mainstream empirical theorists tell us they are doing—is the realization of how much of what has been advanced as theory in the social sciences turns out to be disguised ideology. No matter how ambitious or modest the claims of mainstream social scientists to advance empirical theory, they have insisted that the hypotheses and claims they put forth are value-neutral, objective claims subject only to the criteria of public testing, confirmation, and refutation. Yet as we shall see in Part II, these proposed theories secrete values and reflect controversial ideological claims about what is right, good, and just.

There are a variety of justifications or rationalizations of what Rudner has called this "melancholy consideration"—the gap between our methodological understanding of what theory and scientific explanation is, and the "scarcity of bodies of well-confirmed, well-articulated theory throughout all of the sciences of human behavior."[26] Most of these justifications revolve about the claim that the social sciences are young or immature disciplines—even though some have acknowledged that they are really older than the natural sciences. But when one hears these rationalizations made over and over again—as they have been, during the past hundred years—with so little to show in the way of theoretical achievements, one has a right to be incredulous. Is the primary source for this failure perhaps *not* a lack of imagination or genius, but rather a radical misunderstanding of the type of explanation and theory appropriate to the social disciplines? This has been a primary point of criticism for the three orientations I will examine in the three subsequent parts of this study. But since my intention in this first part is both to comprehend and to present the strongest possible case for a naturalistic understanding of the social sciences, I want to examine the responses made to this challenge that there are insuperable obstacles in the way of developing empirical explanatory theories.

The Defender of Social Scientific Inquiry: Ernest Nagel

M OST mainstream social scientists—especially in America—have not addressed themselves to those critics who challenge the very foundations of what they are doing. Hull, Merton, Smelser, Homans, Parsons, and—among political scientists—Easton, Truman, Almond, Eulau, and many others view contemporary disputes about the scientific status of the social and political disciplines as analogous to antiquarian disputes about the physical sciences when they were breaking away from philosophy, or the tedious polemics about science and religion in the nineteenth century. The prevailing point of view has been that the battle over the scientific status of the social sciences has been won, and that the central task now is to get on with the serious business of empirical research and theory construction.

There are those who have sought in a responsible way to meet the charge that there are insuperable obstacles and conceptual confusions at the heart of social scientific inquiry. One of the most prominent is Ernest Nagel. It is not uncommon for social scientists to appeal to Nagel as a definitive and authoritative answer to those critics who claim that the foundations of contemporary social science are shaky.

Nagel's work, *The Structure of Science,* is a contemporary classic. It is one of the most judicious, comprehensive, and systematically developed statements of the nature of scientific explanation and theory. Furthermore, Nagel, unlike many philosophers of science, does have an intimate knowledge of the social sciences. Nagel directly challenges those arguments which purport to demonstrate that there are insuperable obstacles in the way of social scientific inquiry. He seeks to show that none of these arguments establish such a conclusion. Although there are special problems to be confronted in social inquiry, there are no sharp differences or radical breaks between a properly conceived social science and the natural sciences.

While I do not intend to deal with all of Nagel's points, I want to touch on some of the highlights of his analysis for two reasons: first, it will help to further our appreciation of the case for a naturalistic understanding of the social sciences; secondly, it will forestall some of the more superficial criticisms of a scientific study of individuals in society.

But first, I think it extremely important to call attention to Nagel's strategy of argumentation. Although Nagel does not think that there is any single or simple characteristic that distinguishes science from non-science, he does argue that an adequate account of science involves a clarification of the role of laws, explanations, theories, and the complex ways in which theoretical explanations are tested, confirmed, and refuted. In *The Structure of Science* he is primarily concerned with the clarification and explication of interrelations of these structural elements. He does not think it profitable to discuss whether social inquiry is "real science." "The important task, surely, is to achieve some clarity in fundamental methodological issues and the structure of explanations in the social sciences, rather than to award or withhold honorific titles" (p. 449).[27] Nagel does not deny that there are serious practical obstacles, frequently more formidable than many social scientists realize, but such practical difficulties must be carefully distinguished from conceptual impossibilities.

Nagel begins his analysis by admitting—as so many mainstream social scientists do—that "in no area of social inquiry has a body of general laws been established, comparable with outstanding theories in the natural sciences in scope of explanatory power or in the capacity to yield precise and reliable predictions" (p. 477).

Many social scientists are of the opinion, moreover, that the time is not yet ripe even for theories designed to explain systematically only quite limited ranges of social phenomena. Indeed, when such theoretical constructions with a restricted scope have been attempted, as in economics or on a smaller scale in the study of social mobility, their empirical worth is widely regarded as a still unsettled question. To a considerable extent, the problems investigated in many current centers of empirical research are admittedly concerned with problems of moderate and often unimpressive dimensions. (p. 498)

But even granting all this, the present unimpressive state of the social sciences does not preclude the potentiality for scientific development.

The first major confusion that Nagel seeks to clarify concerns the difference between "controlled experimentation" and "controlled investigation." It is frequently objected that because controlled experimentation is the *sine qua non* for achieving scientific knowledge, and in particular for establishing general laws, therefore, since such experimentation is impossible with large-scale social phenomena, we cannot discover and test general laws pertaining to such phenomena. But Nagel points out that there are well-developed physical sciences such as astronomy and astrophysics which are not, strictly speaking, "experimental sciences." It is true that in every branch of scientific inquiry there must be procedures that have "the essential logical functions of experiment in inquiry" (p. 452). There must, for example, be an opportunity for contrasting occasions and for discriminating those hypotheses which can be confirmed or rejected. Furthermore, the putative artificiality of experiments in the social disciplines is frequently exaggerated and misunderstood. In the natural sciences there are also artificial experiments which, because they exclude many normal factors, help us understand "real" physical processes. "It is a misguided criticism of laboratory experiments in social science that, since a laboratory situation is 'unreal,' its study can throw no light on social behavior in 'real' life" (p. 456). In short, criticism of social science along these lines misfires. Critics misunderstand the role and function of experiments in scientific inquiry, and obscure the central issue of whether there are procedures for carrying on controlled investigation.

A second difficulty often cited in establishing general laws in the social sciences is that social phenomena are "historically conditioned" or "culturally determined" (p. 458). Nagel admits it is possible that "nontrivial but reliably established laws about social phenomena will always have only a narrowly restricted generality" (p. 460). But while the discovery of transcultural laws is an open empirical question, Nagel rejects the arguments advanced to show that they are in principle impossible. Neither the inability to forecast an indefinite future because of the complexity of human phenomena, nor the fact that many aspects of social phenomena are beyond human control, are good reasons to declare such laws impossible. With physical phenomena we can encounter the same difficulties.

Furthermore, those who claim that transcultural laws are impossible because all social phenomena are historically conditioned, frequently emphasize the manifest complexity and diversity of these phenomena. Certainly if, in our theoretical explanations, we used concepts which denoted characteristics that appeared in just one special group of societies, we would be unable to discover general transcultural laws. But, as with physical phenomena, there is nothing in the study of societies that precludes the discovery of more basic underlying structures or correlations which are not immediately apparent. Presumably, if there are such underlying common structures—as many social scientists have claimed—their discovery would enable us to explain theoretically the common features of what appears to be culturally relative. None of the arguments advanced by critics rule this out as a logical but unrealized possibility. One is certainly not warranted to confuse present ignorance with permanent impossibility.

A fashionable argument employed to demonstrate the impossibility of social science is based on the consideration that the *knowledge* of social phenomena, unlike that of physical phenomena, is a social variable. For example, in interviewing techniques which form a major part of social science research, one has to note that typically the respondents *know* they are being interviewed, which may affect their answers. There have been many criticisms of interviewing techniques and conclusions based upon such interviews, because the investigator fails to take this into account. Here, too, Nagel does not deny the seriousness of the difficulty, nor does he offer a general formula for outflanking it. But the very posing of the problem points to the solution. In the social as in the physical sciences, difficulties arise because changes are produced in the subject matter by the very techniques used to investigate it. Further, Nagel certainly concedes that in the social sciences such changes can in part be attributed to the knowledge or beliefs of individuals. But this difference bears on the techniques that must be used to discriminate and discount the bias involved, not on the logic of the situation. On the contrary, this problem presents a practical challenge, not a theoretical obstacle, to social science research. It requires the development of techniques to eliminate or minimize any distortion resulting from the participant's awareness.

There are two other popular arguments concerning knowledge as a social variable that Nagel wants to deflate. These have to do with what is called "suicidal predictions" and "self-fulfilling prophecies." "Suicidal predictions" are those that are solidly grounded at the time they are made, but falsified because of actions undertaken as a consequence of their announcement. This occurs when economic experts make predictions about the future state of the economy, and businessmen—in response to these publicly announced predictions—act in such a way that the predictions become falsified. But what does all this prove? Only "that beliefs about human affairs can lead to crucial changes in habits of human behavior that are the very subjects of those beliefs" (p. 469). It does not prove that we cannot make predictions, or even that we cannot take into account the ways in which predictions may be affected by subjects aware of these predictions. Arguments against social science that are based on "self-fulfilling prophecies"—predictions false at the time made, but which turn out to be correct because of actions resulting from belief in them—can be defeated in the same manner.

The next two types of objections that Nagel considers have been prominent in recent criticisms of the social sciences. In the subsequent parts of this inquiry, we will explore in fuller detail how they have been made and explicated. But it is instructive to see how Nagel anticipates and formulates them, and how he seeks to answer them.

There are those who claim that "objectively warranted explanations of social phenomena are difficult if not impossible to achieve, because those phenomena have an essentially 'subjective' or 'value-impregnated' aspect" (p. 473). Here it is objected that no account of social phenomena can be adequate unless it considers motives, dispositions, intended goals, and values. But these aspects of human phenomena are not open to sensory inspection; they are essentially subjective. Consequently a type of inquiry that limits itself to publicly observable subject matter, or what is "purely behavioral"—as the natural sciences do—cannot be adequate to describe or explain human phenomena.

Nagel focuses on three primary questions that are raised by this and similar arguments about the subject matter of the social sciences:

(1) Are the distinctions required for exploring that subject matter exclusively "subjective"? (2) Is a "behavioristic" account of social phenomena inadequate? and (3) Do imputations of "subjective" states to human agents fall outside the scope of the logical canons employed into "objective" properties? (p. 475)

Nagel's answer to these questions—once the issues are clarified—is an emphatic *No!* In the first place, even when the behavior studied by social scientists is indisputably directed toward some conscious goal, the social sciences need not restrict themselves to the study of psychological states. For we want to know how natural factors such as scarcity or availability of resources, or the objective study of the laws of modern soil chemistry, affect social behavior. It would be self-defeating and overly restrictive to narrow social inquiry so that it excludes the influence of such nonsubjective factors.

Secondly, Nagel thinks that the charge of behaviorism has become an intellectual red herring, and that frequently what is labeled "behaviorism" by its critics is a caricature. There have been those who advocate a philosophical version of behaviorism as a form of reductive materialism, claiming that all behavior will eventually be reduced and explicitly defined in terms of purely physical movements. And there are scientific behaviorists who advocate a "science of man" that limits itself to concepts definable in terms of molar human behavior. But Nagel emphasizes that this latter is only one type of program in science and that its objectives "have certainly not been attained, and perhaps never will be" (p. 480). But such substantive and philosophical versions of behaviorism ought to be carefully distinguished from behaviorism as a "methodological orientation" which insists that "the controlled study of overt behavior is nevertheless the only sound procedure for achieving reliable knowledge concerning individual and social action" (p. 480). From the perspective of such a liberal methodological behaviorism, one can interpret introspective reports not as statements about private psychic states, but as observable responses to be included among the objective data studied. Further, one can even admit that private psychic states exist, but still insist that the only procedure for achieving reliable scientific knowledge is by the study of overt behavior. When behaviorism is interpreted as such a methodological doctrine and disentangled from its caricatures, there is no longer any reason to think that a behavioristic account of social phenomena is inadequate.

In answering the third of the questions listed above, Nagel considers what *he* takes to be the objection by those who say that the aim of the social sciences is to understand social phenomena, and that this involves categories of meaningful action by which we grasp the "subjective" states of human agents. I emphasize that this is Nagel's understanding of the objection because, when I consider the work of Schutz in Part III, we will see that Schutz charges Nagel and others with misunderstanding the nature of *Verstehen*. Nagel is not denying that there are subjective, psychological states attributable to human agents, or that frequently we must understand them if we are to grasp what the agents are doing. But his major point is that "the logical canons in assessing the objective evidence for the imputation of psychological states do not appear to differ essentially (though they may often be applied less rigorously) from the canons employed for analogous purposes by responsible students in other areas of inquiry" (p. 984).

In answering the question about the procedures needed to understand subjective phenomena, Nagel reiterates a distinction and a doctrine accepted by almost all mainstream social scientists, and by those philosophers who have defended a naturalistic interpretation of the social sciences: the sharp distinction between the context of *discovery* and the context of the *validation* of claims to knowledge.

In sum, the fact that the social scientist, unlike the student of inanimate nature, is able to project himself by sympathetic imagination into the phenomena he is attempting to understand, is pertinent to questions concerning the origins of his explanatory hypotheses but not to questions concerning their validity. His ability to enter into relations of empathy with the human actors in some social process may indeed be heuristically important in his efforts to *invent* suitable hypotheses which will explain the process. Nevertheless, his empathic identification with those individuals does not, by itself, constitute *knowledge*. The fact that he achieves such identification does not annul the need for objective evidence, assessed in accordance with logical principles that are common to all controlled inquiries, to support his imputation of subjective states to those human agents. (pp. 484–85)

The final set of arguments against the very possibility of objective social science research that Nagel considers has to do with the so-called fact-value problem. This has figured most prominently in recent criticisms and attacks on the social sciences. But to speak of the "fact-value" problem is a misnomer, for analysis shows that this is a label used for a variety of distinct and loosely related issues. Common to many of those who focus on this problem in their attacks is the claim that "the 'value neutrality' that seems to be so pervasive in the natural sciences is . . . often held to be impossible in social inquiry" (p. 485).

Nagel isolates several subissues. There are questions concerning the selection of problems. Many critics have called attention to the hidden and not-so-hidden social influences on the selection of problems that social scientists investigate. These influences can range from the types of research encouraged because funding is available—either from government sources or from private foundations with special interests—to the types of data readily available, as for example from census surveys. Nagel does not claim that social science research—or any scientific research—takes place in a social vacuum. I have no doubt that he would welcome the new field of the sociology of science, which attempts to study and isolate the variables that affect the problems investigated by scientists. But however important or interesting it is to discover what influences the selection of problems investigated—in both the physical and the social sciences—social influence on the selection of problems "represents no obstacle to the successful pursuit of objectively controlled inquiry in any branch of study" (pp. 486–87). One can ask why a scientist studies what he does, but this is logically distinct from assessing the validity of his hypotheses and objective claims.

Furthermore, it is sometimes objected that social scientists are affected implicitly or explicitly by "considerations of right and wrong." Much of social science research during the past hundred years has been motivated by strong moral and reforming zeal—as well as by the opposite: fear or suspicion of radical social change. "It is surely beyond serious dispute that social scientists do in fact often import their own values into their analyses of social phenomena" (p. 488). But what does this prove? According to Nagel, it only shows the fallibility of human beings and the ease with which they can be mistaken in their claims to objective knowledge. After all, "it has taken centuries to develop habits and techniques of investigation which help safeguard inquiries in the natural sciences against the intrusion of irrelevant personal factors" (p. 488). The fact that personal biases color the conclusions of social scientists should not be a cause for surprise. The important logical and methodological issue is whether we can, in principle, through self-corrective inquiry, sort out these biases even when we are initially unaware of them. According to Nagel, the very posing of the problem points to its resolution—at least as an obstacle to objective inquiry. For "the problem is intelligible only on the assumption that there is a relatively clear distinction between factual and value judgments, and that however difficult it may sometimes be to decide whether a given statement has a purely factual content, it is in principle possible to do so" (p. 488).

A more "sophisticated" argument that the social sciences cannot be value-free maintains that the distinction between fact and value which is assumed above is itself an untenable distinction. An ethically neutral social science is not just difficult but impossible to achieve, because, in the description and explanation of human action, fact and value are so fused that they cannot be distinguished.

In order to meet this objection, Nagel introduces a distinction between two types of value judgment which he claims are frequently confused. The first type of value judgment is one that "expresses *approval* or *disapproval* either of some moral (or social) ideal, or of some action (or institution) because of a commitment to such an ideal" (p. 492). The other type of value judgment is one that "expresses an *estimate* of the degree to which some commonly recognized (and more or less clearly defined) type of action, object, or institution is embodied in a given instance" (p. 492).

To illustrate these quite different types, Nagel uses the example of anemia from biology. We do judge certain animals to be anemic. And in making such a judgment, an investigator is aware of the relevant factors to be taken into account. Although the meaning of the term "anemia" can be made quite clear, it is not defined with complete precision. When an investigator judges that a particular specimen is anemic, he can be said to be making a value judgment because he must judge whether the available evidence warrants the conclusion—whether this particular specimen deviates sufficiently from the normal number of red blood corpuscles to be called anemic. But this type of value judgment—which is prevalent in biology and the medical sciences, and can raise many difficult technical issues—is essentially a "characterizing value judgment." If one went on to judge that anemia is bad or an undesirable condition, one would then be making an "appraising value judgment"—one that expresses approval or disapproval. The essential point is to realize the logical independence of these two different types of "value judgment."

With these distinctions Nagel claims that he can clear up the confusion of those who think value judgments so deeply embedded in social inquiry, and so deeply fused with descriptive claims, that it is impossible to develop a value-neutral social science. In the description and explanation of social phenomena we frequently do and must use characterizing value judgments. We speak of various actions as "mercenary, cruel or deceitful" (p. 499), or what may seem more neutral, we classify actions as "dysfunctional." Furthermore, it would be absurd to deny that in characterizing actions, institutions, and agents, we are frequently stating or implying our disapproval or approval.

Nevertheless—and this is the main burden of the present discussion—there are no good reasons for thinking that it is inherently impossible to *distinguish* between the characterizing and the appraising judgments implicit in many statements, whether the statements are asserted by students of human affairs or by natural scientists. To be sure, it is not always easy to make the distinction formally explicit in the social sciences—in part because much of the language employed in them is very vague, in part because appraising judgments that may be implicit in a statement tend to be overlooked by us when they are judgments to which we are actually committed though without being aware of our commitments. Nor is it always useful or convenient to perform this task. For many statements implicitly containing both characterizing and appraising evaluations are sometimes sufficiently clear without being reformulated in the manner required by the task; and the reformulations would frequently be too unwieldly for effective communication between members of a large and unequally prepared group of students. But these are essentially practical rather than theoretical problems. The difficulties they raise provide no compelling reasons for the claim that an ethically neutral social science is inherently impossible. (pp. 494–95)

What are we to make of the battery of arguments that Nagel brings to bear on the varied claims that a social science sharing the same logical canons and aims as the natural sciences is inherently impossible? His arguments represent a qualified success. But it is important to specify in what sense his position is "qualified" and in what sense "successful." It is qualified because while Nagel defeats the objections as he formulates them, he does not always appreciate the full force of these objections. Let me be perfectly clear. It is not that I think there are other objections that Nagel fails to consider, or variations of those which he does examine, which demonstrably prove the impossibility of social science. When the issue is put in this way, Nagel wins. But if we get away from the obsession of setting up and shooting down impossibility arguments— as I believe we should—then the objections raised by more sophisticated critics may be viewed in a very different perspective. Rather than questioning the logical or conceptual possibility of social science, they can be seen as questioning present and prevailing emphases, concerns, and problems. Intellectual orientations—including Nagel's—lend weight to a sense of what are the important issues, the fruitful lines of research to pursue, the proper way of putting the issues. The most important and interesting challenges to any dominant orientation are those which force us to question the implicit and explicit emphases, that make us self-conscious not only of what is included in the foreground, but excluded or relegated to the background as unimportant, illegitimate, or impractical.

Furthermore, we must not be misled by the fundamental dichotomy that sets the entire context for Nagel's discussion—the distinction between theoretical and practical obstacles. For what Nagel means by "theoretical" in this context is logical impossibility—arguments that purport to demonstrate the logical or conceptual impossibility of social science. All other obstacles are lumped together as practical.

Nagel is quite clear about this, although many who cite him as an authority are far less clear. His success consists in showing that none of the arguments that he reformulates and examines can deny the possibility of the scientific development of the social disciplines. Ironically, however, as he considers many of the objections, he actually shows that in most cases they do have a point. For while they fail as impossibility arguments, they do reveal the complex obstacles encountered—practical difficulties far more formidable than many mainstream social scientists realize.

But we must be careful not to draw the wrong conclusions from Nagel's analysis. There is a slippery path here along which many mainstream social scientists have all too easily moved. No good reasons have been advanced to demonstrate the impossibility of social science, therefore it is possible. From this it seems a small step to claim that since it is possible, it is likely or probable that a genuine social science will be achieved—if we work hard enough and are sufficiently ingenious in formulating and testing hypotheses, models, and explanatory theories. Then it appears almost irresistible to believe that one *ought* to adopt a properly scientific attitude to advance the maturity of the social disciplines. One need not cite Hume, who warned about the dangers of moving without friction from talk about what is, or what is possible, to what ought to be done. This is a danger that mainstream social scientists themselves keep warning us about, though not always conscious of their own tendencies to succumb to it.

The most fitting conclusion to Nagel's deflationary strategy in attacking critics of the scientific status of the social disciplines is given by Nagel himself: "Problems are not resolved merely by showing that they are not necessarily insoluble; and the present state of social inquiry clearly indicates that some of the difficulties we have been considering are indeed serious" (p. 503).

The Naturalistic Interpretation: A General View

Thus far in exploring empirical theory in the social sciences, and the case for interpreting the social disciplines as natural sciences, I have kept close to the thoughts and words of prominent spokesmen. I have done this deliberately for two reasons. First, as indicated earlier, I want to avoid the charge that I am presenting a caricature. I do not think that the very idea of social science can be dismissed by labeling it "positivism," "behaviorism," or "naive empiricism." Secondly, only by presenting the case in its most judicious and responsible way can one distinguish criticisms that are superficial from those that cut deep. But now we can see a generalized picture emerging: one that can do justice to the shared assumptions and framework principles, as well as the areas of internal disagreement. It is a picture that has significant consequences for a whole range of issues, including the history of social and political theory, the essential aims of social inquiry, the type of education appropriate to social scientists, the role of the theorist, the relation of theory and action, as well as that of fact and value.

At the core of this naturalistic interpretation is the conviction that the aim of the social sciences is the same as that of the natural sciences. Collecting and refining data, discovering correlations, and formulating testable empirical generalizations, hypotheses, and models, all have important roles to play, but they are not sufficient to establish the social disciplines as mature sciences. There must also be the growth of testable and well-confirmed theories which explain phenomena by showing how they can be derived in nontrivial ways from our theoretical assumptions. At the heart of scientific explanation there must be discovery of and appeal to laws or nomological statements.

There are those who think our present ignorance so vast that it is best to stick to the task of refining techniques for collecting data and making low-level empirical generalizations about independent and dependent variables. There are those who think that such an endeavor is blind and directionless unless guided by the search for general theories. There are those who recommend a more modest endeavor of advancing theories of the middle range. There are disputes concerning what types of lawlike statements will figure in the explanation of social phenomena—whether there are, for example, any genuine sociological laws, or whether the only suitable laws for theoretical explanations are psychological laws pertaining to individuals. And of course there are disputes about which theoretical orientations hold out the most promise and most closely approximate the logical and methodological criteria of theory proper. But all these disagreements and disputes are inside the general framework that we have isolated; indeed they "make sense" within this framework.

This framework fosters a distinctive attitude toward the history of the social sciences and especially social and political theory. This attitude draws a basic distinction between the history of theory and systematic theory. Whether we think of the social disciplines as ancient or relatively new, and whether we admire or disdain the great theorists of the past, our primary interest in past theories—insofar as our concern is systematic theory—will be to look to them for clues, insights, and suggestions that can help us to develop empirical theory. From a scientific point of view, the measure of past theories is and ought to be the present state of systematic theory.

Such an attitude has tremendous consequences for the education of social scientists. And it would be difficult to underestimate the transformation of curricula and attitudes that has taken place during the past fifty years, especially in American universities. Whatever value the study of the history of a discipline and the past classics in the field may have, this is not considered the main intellectual content for the training of social scientists. As in the case of progressive physical sciences, students must be taught the most advanced quantitative and empirical techniques of research; they must be introduced to the problems at the frontiers of empirical research; they must master the best theories presently available, and be encouraged to develop the creative imagination to discover new and better theories.

The theorist and the empirical researcher, it is felt, ought to cultivate a disinterested attitude when investigating social and political phenomena. As a private citizen, or expert who assumes public responsibilities, he may bring his tentative knowledge to bear on the vital issues of his time. But qua theorist he must strive to be objective and neutral. Since we know how easy it is to let one's biases distort the description and explanation of social phenomena, the theorist must always be willing to submit his hypothetical claims to public discussion and testing, and ought to abandon any claims which have been refuted according to the canons of scientific research. His job qua theorist is to interpret the world, not to change it; he interprets it by offering and testing theoretical explanations. He knows, or at least believes, that if one is seriously interested in "changing the world," this can best be accomplished through scientific knowledge—especially knowledge of the probable consequences of different courses of action.

Therefore, he endorses a categorical distinction between theory and practice or action. Whatever senses of "action" are appropriate to understanding scientific inquiry—for example, controlled experimentation—they must be sharply distinguished from the forms of activity in which we consciously apply our theoretical knowledge to the solution of practical problems of society.

Finally, a sophisticated defender of mainstream social science can admit that there are many ways in which values and norms are relevant to social science research. We can study values and norms scientifically. We can try to locate the variables that reinforce certain values or foster the breakdown of norms. We can admit, and even study, the ways in which values affect the selection of problems in social research. We can be sensitive to the role of values in assessing evidence. We can even acknowledge that social science research cannot proceed very far without making use of "characterizing" value judgments, and that we must be extremely cautious in making these. We can recognize how social scientists have fused and confused characterizing value judgments with judgments that implicitly or explicitly express approval and disapproval. But none of these admissions lessens or compromises the one basic sense in which there is a categorial distinction between fact and value. The task of the social scientist is to describe and explain social phenomena as accurately as he can. In this broad sense his task is to describe and explain the facts. His task is *not* to make prescriptive claims about what ought to be—not to advocate a normative position.

This last point brings into the foreground a distinction which we have thus far only obliquely explored—the distinction between empirical and normative theory. I have followed the practice of mainstream social scientists in speaking of empirical theory or explanatory theory as rough equivalents, but the rhetorical significance of the expression "empirical theory" distinguishes it sharply from "normative theory." There is far less unanimity among mainstream social scientists about the nature of normative theory than about empirical or explanatory theory proper. But there is essential agreement that whatever it is or however it is characterized, normative theory must not be confused with empirical theory. To complete our picture of mainstream social science, we need to confront the prominent issues involved in distinguishing empirical from normative theory.

The Problems of Normative Theory

Iɴ exploring the positivist influence on mainstream social science, we have detected an ambivalent attitude toward normative theory. On the one hand, there is an insistence on a categorial distinction between empirical and normative theory, but on the other hand there is a widespread skepticism about the very possibility of normative theory. Consider the following claim made by David Easton in 1953:

This assumption, generally adopted today in the social sciences, holds that values can ultimately be reduced to emotional responses conditioned by the individual's total life-experiences. In this interpretation, although in practice no one proposition need express either a pure fact or a pure value, facts and values are logically heterogeneous. The factual aspect of a proposition refers to a part of reality; hence it can be tested by reference to the facts. In this way we check its truth. The moral aspect of a proposition, however, expresses only the emotional response of an individual to a state of real or presumed facts. It indicates whether and the extent to which an individual desires a particular state of affairs to exist. Although we can say that the aspect of a proposition referring to a fact can be true or false, it is meaningless to characterize the value aspect of a proposition in this way.[28]

If we draw out the implications of this passage, we can see why normative theory is undermined: there is not and cannot be any such rational discipline. The factual aspect of a proposition refers to a part of reality. As such, it can be true or false. But the value aspect of a proposition does *not* refer to any facts. Strictly speaking, there are no moral facts—except in the Pickwickian sense of facts *about* values. We may be interested in what individuals desire, or in what variables influence these desires, but such questions are factual empirical questions, not normative questions. In asserting "moral propositions" we are either making disguised factual claims—which can be assimilated by science—or expressing only our emotional responses to a state of real or presumed facts. But if we accepted all these claims and their implications, then it follows that there is no rational discipline that we can call normative theory.

I suggested earlier that despite Easton's claim that this assumption is generally adopted in the social sciences, most mainstream social scientists have not been willing—or consistent enough—to go this far and rule out the very possibility of normative theory.

The thinker who struggled most seriously with the issues involved was Max Weber. His basic position still forms the background for discussion of the status of normative theory, as well as what social science can and cannot achieve. One must be careful in exploring Weber's influence, for the Weber who is cited as an authority in laying the groundwork for a conception of social science as *Wertfrei* is a domesticated Weber. Few social scientists have appreciated the Nietzschean themes in his reflections and the complex ways in which Weber directly and indirectly returned to the issues over and over again. As he became clearer about the limits of social science, he became more and more concerned with its moral and social consequences, and specifically its consequences in regard to individual choice.[29]

The basic contours of Weber's thought were shaped by Kantian and neo-Kantian themes—in particular, the Kantian distinction between the "is" and the "ought"—the dichotomy between scientific discourse about phenomena, and moral discourse grounded in pure practical reason. Kant emphasized this absolute distinction in order to justify the autonomy, objectivity, and universality of moral judgment. He certainly was not dubious about the possibility of rationally justifying the categorical imperative. But one of the strains in nineteenth-century thought was an increasing skepticism about the autonomy and objectivity of moral judgment and its presumed rational foundation. No critic is the equal of Nietzsche in his searching and profound criticisms of the moral or normative half of the Kantian dichotomy. Weber, as philosopher and social scientist, accepted the logical absoluteness of the Kantian dichotomy and felt the full power of Nietzsche's critique of moral judgment. Weber insisted on the "absolute heterogeneity" of facts and values, and recognized that science, including the social sciences, can only deal with the factual side of the dichotomy. He put the issue dramatically and incisively when he considered the question, What is the meaning of science?

Tolstoi has given the simplest answer with the words: "Science is meaningless because it gives no answer to our question, the only question important for us, 'What shall we do and how shall we live?' " That science does not give an answer to this is indisputable. The only question that remains is the sense in which science gives "no" answer, and whether or not science might yet be of some use to the one who puts the question correctly.[30]

Weber, however, was not a positivist, and he certainly did not advocate an emotivist theory of normative discourse. Once we get clear on fundamentals, he believed, it is possible to see how science is relevant to normative discourse, and even how there can be rational discussion of basic value positions. Such discussion is essentially limited to three functions:

(1) "The elaboration and explication of the ultimate, internally 'consistent' value axioms, from which the divergent attitudes are derived."[31] This type of analysis does not directly use empirical techniques nor does it produce knowledge of new facts. But it is important insofar as it can make us aware of different types of value axioms and whether a specific set value statement is consistent.

(2) "The deduction of 'implications' (for those accepting certain value judgments) which follow from certain irreducible value axioms, when the practical evaluation of factual situations is based on these axioms alone." To do this well requires careful analysis and articulation of value axioms, and an understanding of their logical implications. It also requires "empirical observations for the completest possible causistic analyses of all such empirical situations as are in principle subject to practical evaluation."[32]

(3) "The determination of the factual consequences which the realization of a certain practical evaluation must have (1) in consequence
of being bound to certain indispensable means, (2) in consequence
of the inevitability of certain, not directly desired repercussions."[33]

This last is the most important area in which empirical social research
can have a bearing on our values. We may discover that we have not
thought out the empirical consequences of our choices and actions, or
that we are ignorant of what is likely to be their repercussions, or that
when we become aware of some of the probable unintended .conse-
quences of proposed courses of action, these discoveries may lead to a
revision of our practical evaluations. A more detailed understanding of
the probable consequences of different courses of action may lead to
abandonment or modification of existing value axioms, or adoption of
new ones. We may, for example, cease to favor recycling of energy
sources, if we discover that the amount of energy required for recycling
is greater than that which would be produced by this means.

It should be obvious that none of these three functions of the rational
discussion of value axioms and value judgments lessens the gap between
fact and value, or lessens the burden of choice placed upon us. Indeed,
Weber's intention is to sharpen our perceptions of the consequences of
human choice. The social scientist as teacher can say to us: "If you take
such and such a stand, then according to scientific experience, you have
to use such and such a *means* in order to carry.out your conviction practically. Now, these means are perhaps such that you believe you must
reject them. Then you simply must choose between the end and the
inevitable means. Does the end 'justify' the means? Or does it not? The
teacher can confront you with the necessity of this choice. He cannot do
more, so long as he wishes to remain a teacher and not to become a
demagogue."[34] If we are absolutely consistent with the position that
Weber advocates, then even the three functions of the discussion of
values are based on a prior acceptance of certain values which themselves cannot be rationally justified. Only if we accept the value of being
consistent, of being responsibly aware of what follows from the value
axioms we hold, and of basing our decisions and choices on an informed
empirical understanding of their probable consequences, will such analyses rationally influence our choices. But according to Weber, it is absolutely hopeless to think that we can justify such basic values; we can
only choose to accept them.

With his characteristic acuteness, Weber saw where his arguments
were leading him, but he did not flinch from their conclusion. He feared
the social consequences of the increasing "rationalization" of social life,

with its inevitable disenchantment with the world. Few mainstream scientists, including those who think of themselves as following Weber, have pressed their inquiries as far as he did. Most have been content to stop at an unstable halfway point. They have assumed that "enlightened" men share the same basic values, and that the important task is to gain a fuller empirical understanding of the consequences of possible courses of action, and the empirical means to foster those values which enlightened men endorse. But by this change of emphasis they blur and gloss over the abyss that Nietzsche had uncovered and Weber looked into— that there can be no ultimate rational foundations for our basic values.

Many of the prevailing contemporary attitudes about normative theory, and about the relation between empirical science and normative theory, are a series of footnotes to Weber. Weber also provides a rationale for those who advocate that the social sciences can have practical consequences when they are thought of as policy sciences—or that the policy sciences are an important subdivision of the social sciences. We can empirically study the probable consequences of different proposed courses of action. The policy sciences can "fill out" hypothetical imperatives. They take the logical form of showing us that if we do choose, desire, or value *x,* then *y* will certainly or probably result. We cannot expect to become very sophisticated about probable empirical consequences, especially in complex situations of modern industrial societies, unless we press our scientific inquiries as far as we can. It is naive, for example, to favor full employment, unless we are aware that under certain empirical circumstances, such full employment can lead to runaway inflation which may in turn lead to severe unemployment. Any rational person would certainly modify his opinion about the value of full employment, once he is more fully informed about its probable empirical consequences.

The hypothetical character of the information gained from the social sciences which lends itself to technical application has been the basis for those who advocate "social engineering." Although the expression "social engineering" is abhorrent to many because of the specter it raises of conscious manipulation by technocrats, the central idea of how the knowledge gained in social science research can be applied to practical problems is widely shared. A classic statement and defense of the social engineering approach was made by Karl Popper in *The Poverty of Historicism.* Popper contrasts "piecemeal social engineering" with what he claims is the misguided notion of utopian or holistic social engineering. The piecemeal social engineer "is to design social institutions, and to reconstruct and run those already in existence" (p. 64).[35] Unlike the utopian or holistic thinker, the piecemeal social engineer knows how little he knows and that we learn from our mistakes. "Accordingly he will make his way, step by step, carefully comparing the results expected with the results achieved, and always on the look-out for the unavoidable unwanted consequences of any reform; and he will avoid undertaking reforms of a complexity and scope which make it impossible for him to disentangle causes and effects, and to know what he is really doing" (p. 67).

For Popper neither technology, engineering, nor science itself is sufficient to determine and warrant the ends to be achieved or approximated by our cautious steps of social reform. He concedes that "public or political social engineering may have the most diverse tendencies, totalitarian as well as liberal" (p. 66). The task of carrying out the final solution to the Jewish problem by the Nazis was an "engineering" one involving many technical questions about the most effective means of rounding up Jews, transporting them to concentration camps, and killing them. From a logical point of view, the technical knowledge required to perform these tasks efficiently (while conducting a war at the same time) is of the same type needed to design and control institutions to foster high employment in a peacetime economy. Piecemeal social engineering is neutral with regard to the ends to be achieved. Popper does think there can be rational critical discussion of ends, but there are grave difficulties in his defense of this central claim.

In 1969, at a time when the idea of social engineering was being vehemently attacked from a variety of points of view, Philip M. Hauser restated and defended this ideal.[36] Hauser seems to think that the social engineering approach is an entirely new one, and the only approach adequate to the solution of contemporary social problems. He describes the role of the social scientist qua scientist, whose primary task is to generate knowledge through his data collection, processing, and analysis. This knowledge can then serve as the basis for the formation of social policy by the social engineer, who is interested in "social accounting"—"an information-control system to serve the needs of administrators of an organization or a program" (p. 15). This new approach is "beyond the naiveté of traditional forms of liberalism and conservatism" (p. 14). It is the only approach that can seriously cope with our contemporary social problems. Almost in passing, Hauser tells us:

Social accounting will become possible only after consensus is achieved on social goals. The development of social goals is neither a scientific function nor a social engineering function. It is a function that must be performed by society as a whole, acting through its political and other leaders. In a democratic society it presumably reflects the desires of the majority of the people. (p. 15)

But Hauser emphasizes the role that the social scientist and the social engineer can play in such goal formation. They are the experts who "must work closely with political and other leaders to help develop a broad spectrum of choices, which will reflect, insofar as possible, the requirements and consequences of specific goals" (p. 15). Hauser glosses over the really difficult and sticky issues at the heart of social engineering. The very possibility of social engineering depends on a specification of the social goals to be attained. It is not very illuminating, to say the least, to tell us that "this must be performed by a society as a whole." How? By whom? What reason do we have to suppose that there are any goals that are shared by a society as a "whole"? How are we—whether as citizens, administrators, or social engineers—to decide what goals *ought* to be realized? Hauser obscures the central normative issues that must be honestly confronted if the social engineering approach is to have any plausibility at all, and not used to enforce social domination and repression.

Conclusion: A Growing Sense of Crisis

WITH this review of the various attitudes toward normative theory, I have completed the generalized picture that mainstream social scientists have of their own discipline. Far more is involved than an understanding of the nature and centrality of empirical explanatory theory. The central role assigned to such theory reflects a *total* intellectual orientation. This orientation holds up to us an ideal of what constitutes theoretical knowledge of social and political phenomena, and how we are to progress in order to approximate this ideal. It is an orientation that colors our understanding of the history of these disciplines, and what directions they may reasonably expect to take in the future. It reflects a distinctive understanding of the categorial difference between theory and action, when action is viewed as the technical application of what we learn from theory. It has normative consequences for both the training of social scientists and the disinterested attitude that ought to be adopted by the theorist. I call this the "mainstream" position because, despite numerous internal disagreements, it has been and still is shared by the dominant group of professional social scientists.

One more element can be added as a capstone to this presentation.

Historically, one cannot underestimate the role that the Enlightenment has played in both shaping and giving impetus to the development of the social sciences. The ideal has long been cherished that the advancement of science, and of scientific knowledge of social and political phenomena, must bring progress toward ideals and social goals accepted by reasonable human beings. We have learned how much more difficult it is to achieve and utilize such knowledge than was anticipated by some of our Enlightenment forefathers, but this goal—this regulative ideal—is still advocated by social scientists.

Indeed, many may wonder if there is any reasonable alternative. Yet for all the attractiveness, power, and reasonableness that this orientation represents, there are severe problems and conflicts within it. I have already noted the tremendous disparity between the insistence on what theory is and the failure to actually produce it. One could write the history of much of social science during the past hundred years in terms of declarations that it has just become, or is just about to become, a genuine scientific enterprise. Many of the standard apologies for the primitive state of sociology and political science, when measured against the criteria advocated by mainstream social scientists, seem thin and unconvincing.

Furthermore, despite official modesty about the state of the social sciences, there is frequently a dangerous arrogance. This is typified by Hauser, who acknowledges that, "strictly speaking," social engineering depends on a specification of the social goals to be achieved, but immediately goes on to claim that "the social scientist and the social engineer are in a strategic position to participate in goal formation" (p. 15) by working closely with political and other leaders to develop a broad spectrum of choices. Hauser's own normative judgments become perfectly apparent when he has the temerity to declare:

It is my judgment that had this nation possessed a Council of Social Advisors since 1947, along with the Council of Economic Advisors, and had the recommendations of such a Council been heeded by the Administration and the Congress, the "urban crisis" which sorely affects us would not have reached its present acute state. (p. 15)

As we shall see in Part II, the way in which Hauser so easily passes off "appraising value judgments" while supposedly engaging in an objective and neutral analysis of social science and social engineering, represents only the tip of the iceberg. Despite all the talk of objectivity and value neutrality, social science literature and so-called empirical theory are shot through with explicit and implicit value judgments, and controversial normative and ideological claims.

But there are further and even more deeply disturbing aspects in the orientation presented. Knowledge, and in particular detailed empirical knowledge of how society and politics really work, is supposed to provide the basis for enlightened action and social reform. Yet when we concentrate on the dialectic of the epistemological foundations of mainstream social science, we detect the powerful tendencies to undermine this very Enlightenment ideal. When unmasked, there is not only an enormous skepticism about the possibility of normative theory as a rational discipline, but also the constant suggestion that in the final analysis "values" are only individual emotional responses, subjective and irrational. We are told over and over again that the formation of policies, the application of scientific knowledge, and the enterprise of social engineering depend on a specification of goals. But we are given no or little guidance as to how such ends ought to be established. If we do not squarely confront these issues, it becomes only too obvious that techniques of control and manipulation can just as well be used for the most evil or undesirable ends.

Furthermore, with all the insistence on the social scientist as disinterested observer, something has been lost or suppressed from the tradition of *theoria* out of which social science theory emerged. One of the classical functions of theory was supposed to be its practical efficacy—its ability to help us distinguish appearance from reality, the false from the true, and to provide an orientation for practical activity. To anticipate a point that has been incisively made by Habermas, what once was supposed to be a primary function of the *bios theoretikos* is now ruled out by "methodological prohibitions."[37]

Mainstream social scientists would deny that they have abandoned this function of theory. They claim that only now, for the first time in history, are we able to distinguish the more manifest and superficial aspects of society and politics from the way in which they "really" are; only now are we achieving solid empirical knowledge rather than opinion and speculation. But even if such a dubious claim were granted, the practical consequences of this accumulation of empirical knowledge are not at all clear. The gap between such knowledge and its utilization for creating a good and just society is increasing. We have not closed the gap between theory and practice, but created an intellectual and practical vacuum. Rather than the utilization of knowledge by social and political reformers, we find the use of it by whomever has the power to do so. And for all the concern with the scientific status of the social and political disciplines, the very idea of the theorist as a critic of society and politics is avoided or ruled out by "methodological prohibitions."

This situation, with its potentially ominous consequences, has led to a growing sense of crisis, to protest, and a desperate need to re-examine the very foundations of the mainstream understanding of social and political inquiry. In the subsequent parts of this study, I will explore the most serious attempts to re-examine and restructure social and political inquiry.

Part II

Language,
Analysis,
and Theory

The history of thought and culture is, as Hegel showed with great brilliance, a changing pattern of great liberating ideas which inevitably turn into suffocating straightjackets, and so stimulate their own destruction by new emancipating, and at the same time, enslaving conceptions. The first step to understanding of men is the bringing to consciousness of the model or models that dominate and penetrate their thought and action. Like all attempts to make men aware of the categories in which they think, it is a difficult and sometimes painful activity, likely to produce deeply disquieting results. The second task is to analyse the model itself, and this commits the analyst to accepting or modifying or rejecting it, and in the last case, to providing a more adequate one in its stead.

Isaiah Berlin, 1962[1]

The Reassessment of Theory in the Social Sciences

THE above passage is from Isaiah Berlin's eloquent and passionate essay, "Does Political Theory Still Exist?", which appeared in the Second Series of *Philosophy, Politics and Society*. It was written as a direct response to the situation described by Peter Laslett when he declared, "For the moment, anyway, political philosophy is dead." This forthright statement by Laslett in the First Series of *Philosophy, Politics and Society* "became the text most cited from the volume as a whole."[2] But by 1962 the editors of the Second Series wrote: "It would be very satisfactory if we were able here to proclaim the resurrection, unreservedly and with enthusiasm. We cannot quite; but the mood is very different and very much more favorable than it was six years ago."[3]

Berlin was an ideal person to write an apologia for political theory. He was Chichele Professor of Political and Social Theory at Oxford when he wrote the essay. Oxford was the center of the linguistic movement, and Berlin was intimate with many of the leaders of this movement. Unlike some of his Oxford colleagues, Berlin, through his extensive and subtle

57

appreciation of the history of culture, and his commitment to the centrality of political and social issues in human thought and action, brought a much needed perspective to the ahistorical—and sometimes antihistorical—bias of contemporary analytic philosophers.

I plan to use Berlin's essay as a guide for interpreting what has happened, and still is happening, among Anglo-Saxon thinkers who are influenced by the linguistic movement in philosophy, and concerned to apply insights gained from it to social and political theory. Although I will be discussing topics not explicitly treated by Berlin, they all can be related to themes in his essay and lines of inquiry that he opens up. Berlin's essay indicates the changing intellectual mood in the reassessment of political theory and its relation to the social sciences. He was aware of what was stirring at the time and about to come into the foreground of discussion. Once we sort out some of the exaggerated and misguided claims, and cut beneath the surface polemic, we will discover a remarkable coherence and power in the thinking about social and political theory. Since the story has several complicated subplots, I will give a brief preview of what I will examine and what I hope to show.

After presenting some of the major themes in Berlin's essay, I will turn to an examination of the language and concept of action, which has become a focal concern for contemporary analytic philosophers. In another work, I have investigated why this has become dominant, as well as the conflicting theses about the concept of action and such related concepts as motive, intention, reason, and cause.[4] Here I will pursue those themes which directly bear on social and political action, and the ways in which we describe, explain, and interpret such action.

I will then examine the new "image of science" that has been emerging in recent postempiricist history and philosophy of science. Most of this recent discussion has centered upon the natural or physical sciences, but these discussions have important consequences for the social sciences. The understanding that mainstream social scientists have of their own discipline is based upon the logical empiricists' conception of the natural sciences. But this view of science has been severely criticized. Consequently, many fundamental questions have recently been raised about what empirical theory really is in both the physical and social sciences. Furthermore, when I examine the use and abuse of the work of Thomas Kuhn by social scientists—especially the varied uses of the slippery concept of a paradigm—we will see how Kuhn's work has been made to bolster conflicting and even contradictory theses.

Finally I will examine some of the ways in which linguistic analysts have called into question many of the dichotomies that have shaped mainstream social science—dichotomies such as fact and value, description and evaluation, and empirical versus normative theory. Analytically trained philosophers, joined by others, have shown how so-called empirical theory in the social sciences harbors ideological biases.

But while analytic investigations have taken a critical stance toward mainstream social science and its epistemological foundations, the cumulative result of these investigations has not been merely negative. On the contrary, they indicate a new awareness of the importance of interpretation in any adequate social and political theory—interpretation which cannot be reduced or eliminated in favor of the collection of data and the study of existing regularities. Some linguistic or conceptual analysts have claimed to show, once and for all, that the very idea of a social science conceived of as a natural science is based upon conceptual confusions, and that it is logically impossible. Although I do not think they have succeeded in establishing this strong and dramatic thesis, they have shown some of the profound conceptual difficulties in achieving or even approximating such an ideal—difficulties ignored by mainstream social scientists. More important, they have shown that the obsession with transforming social studies into natural sciences obscures, distorts, and suppresses the legitimacy of issues vital for theorizing about political and social life. When we follow the shift of emphasis that has been taking place, we will find a natural transition to phenomenology, which has been much concerned with the nature of intersubjectivity and the meaning of interpretation.

Isaiah Berlin's Critique of Empirical Theory

BERLIN begins his essay by describing the two methods for answering questions that have become the very standard for rational discourse and the legitimacy of knowledge claims: the empirical and the formal. He underscores what is so prominent for positivist thinkers, and those mainstream social scientists who would view their discipline as an empirical science. In line with Berlin's claim that Hegel showed how "great liberating ideas . . . inevitably turn into suffocating straight-jackets," it is important to emphasize that the conviction that all "real" questions could be answered by formal or empirical methods was historically liberating. We can trace this positivist doctrine back to its origins in the Enlightenment. Science, especially empirical experimental science, was seen as a touchstone for distinguishing superstition, bias, and mere opinion from hard fact and empirically warranted knowledge. One could point with pride to the tremendous growth of human knowledge once the sure paths of the formal and empirical sciences had been secured. Modern positivists went one step further: they interpreted the history of thought as one where disciplines floundered until reformulated into the canons of scientific discourse. In its boldest phase, positivism claimed that anything which cannot be so reformulated was to be judged meaningless, or to be seen as raising pseudo-problems incapable of rational solution. In this more doctrinaire stage, what had once been a "great liberating idea" indeed became a "suffocating straightjacket." What had long been central to discourse about political and social life— the fate and critical evaluation of that life—was now to be dumped in the dustbin of cognitively meaningless discourse.

Berlin directly challenges this dogma. Without denying the success of the empirical and formal disciplines, he argues that there is a third major category of legitimate and vital questions that cannot be clarified by formal or empirical techniques. He calls these philosophical and concentrates on those that are important to political philosophy and theory.

When we ask why a man should obey, we are asking for the explanation of what is normative in such notions as authority, sovereignty, liberty, and the justification of their validity in political arguments. These are words in the name of which orders are issued, men are coerced, wars are fought, new societies are created and old ones destroyed—expressions which play as great a part as any in our lives to-day. What makes such questions *prima facie* philosophical is that no wide agreement exists on the meaning of some of the concepts involved. There are sharp differences on what constitutes reasons for actions in these fields; on how the relevant propositions are to be established or even rendered plausible; on who or what constitutes recognized authority for deciding these questions; and there is consequently no consensus on the frontier between public criticism and subversion, or freedom and oppression and the like. (p. 7)[5]

Now it may be thought—and most likely would be, by mainstream social scientists—that Berlin is not at all calling into question the conception of social science as a natural science seeking to discover empirical theories. The very use of the term "normative," they would say, gives the clue to what he is advocating. By "political theory" Berlin means "normative political theory." Whether one is sympathetic or unsympathetic to this proposal, normative theory is distinct from, and not to be confused with, empirical theory. But this representation of what Berlin is saying distorts his meaning and ignores some of the more controversial implications of his analysis.

Berlin stresses that "men's beliefs in the sphere of conduct are part of their conception of themselves and others as human beings; and this conception in its turn, whether conscious or not, is intrinsic to their picture of the world" (p. 13). Human beings are *self-interpreting* beings, and this fact is of central importance for understanding social and political life. The beliefs that human beings have about themselves and others are not simply subjective states in their minds; they are—to use a Kantian expression—*constitutive* of the actions, practices, and institutions that make up social and political life. Human beings, Berlin tells us, are dominated by one or more models of what the world is like, and "this model or paradigm determines the content as well as the form of beliefs and behaviour" (p. 14). Consequently, "any change in the central model is a change in the ways in which the data of experience are perceived and interpreted. The degree to which such categories are shot through with evaluation will doubtless depend on their direct connexion with human desires and interests" (p. 17). We are interested not only in the variety of beliefs and dominant models, but in their origins, and in the causes for their dominance, reinforcement, and collapse—causal issues that do indeed form an important part of social studies. But if we are to understand human beings, we must also explore the adequacy of these models, the ways in which they do and do not correspond to the actual behavior of men, and their validity.

To suppose, then, that there have been or could be ages without political philosophy, is like supposing that as there are ages of faith, so there are or could be ages of total disbelief. But this is an absurd notion; there is no human activity without some kind of general outlook: scepticism, cynicism, refusal to dabble in abstract issues or to question values, hard-boiled opportunism, contempt for theorizing, all the varieties of nihilism, are, of course, themselves metaphysical and ethical positions, committal attitudes. . . . The idea of a completely *Wertfrei* theory (or model) of human action (as contrasted, say, with animal behaviour) rests on a naïve misconception of what objectivity or neutrality in the social studies must be. (p. 17)

Once again it may be objected that no responsible mainstream political or social scientist thinks that we can ignore the beliefs, attitudes, and interpretations of human agents in an adequate social science. Rather he insists that if we are to investigate these essentially subjective and private phenomena in methodologically sound ways, we must relate them to objective behavior, including the verbal behavior exhibited in response to questionnaires and surveys. But as Berlin suggests, the primary issue is a categorial one. Mainstream social scientists tend to think that all relevant phenomena can be divided neatly into subjective and objective, private and public. The methodological problem in studying what is subjective and private is to show how it can be correlated with what is objective and public. But if Berlin is right these dichotomies, which are so entrenched in mainstream social science and have a long philosophical lineage, actually misrepresent human action. Human action does not consist of two externally related separable parts—an element of mental belief and an element of physical movement. Human action—at least the forms of action relevant to social and political life—is such that what we take to be an action, and even its proper description, is internally related to the interpretations that are intrinsically constitutive of it. The description and identification of human action are "shot through with evaluation."

If we ignore or play down the extent to which human action is constituted by the interpretations of human agents, then even our empirical studies of regularities will be misleading. The discovery of regularities in social and political life may *not* be an indication of even a starting point for discovery of invariant features of human life; these regularities may only reflect the entrenchment and uncritical acceptance of dominant models of political reality. As Berlin acutely points out, it is in a society that is unanimously agreed upon its goals that a social science would work best that aims at prediction and the reduction of all questions to empirical ones.

In a society dominated by a single goal there could in principle only be arguments about the best means to attain this end—and arguments about means are technical, that is, scientific and empirical in character: they can be settled by experience and observation or whatever other methods are used to discover causes and correlations; they can, at least in principle, be reduced to positive sciences. In such a society no serious questions about political ends or values could arise, only empirical ones about the most effective paths to the goal. (p. 8)

The replacement of political theory by a natural science of human beings would *not* be the triumph of value neutrality and objectivity. It would be thoroughly value-laden: primary questions about what men are would no longer be seriously asked; instead, there would be the uncritical acceptance of ideological biases. Political theory is primarily concerned with

such questions as what is specifically human and what is not, and why; whether specific categories, say those of purpose or of belonging to a group, or law are indispensable to understanding what men are; and so, inevitably, with the source, scope and validity of certain human goals. If this is its task, it cannot, from the very nature of its interests, avoid evaluation; it is thoroughly committed not only to the analysis of, but to conclusions about the validity of, ideas of the good and the bad, the permitted and the forbidden, the harmonious and the discordant problems which any discussion of liberty or justice or authority or political morality is sooner or later bound to encounter. (p. 17)

Berlin's essay is more suggestive than definitive. He has raised many issues without pursuing them in detail or providing adequate support for his main theses. But we will soon see how many of the themes touched upon by Berlin have been explored by other investigators. Berlin is not simply urging a revival of normative political theory to complement empirical theory. The alternative understanding of political theory that he sketches challenges the most basic and cherished dogmas of mainstream social science. At the heart of his criticism is an attack on the notions of what is "empirical" and what constitutes the "hard facts" about political agents. What men are—not what they ought to be—is determined by the interpretative models that penetrate the thought and action of human agents. Consequently, if we are to understand what human beings *are,* then we must understand the models that dominate their thought and action. Any conception of the empirical that ignores or underestimates the power and pervasiveness of these models, is emasculated. The conception of the empirical that restricts itself to publicly observable behavior, and relegates such models and interpretations to what is "merely" subjective, misrepresents human action.

Conceptual Analysis and the Language of Action: Peter Winch

A few years before the appearance of Berlin's essay, Peter Winch published a short but much discussed monograph, *The Idea of a Social Science.* The significance of this work lies more in the historical and polemical role that it played than in the clarity of its central theses or the adequacy of the conclusions reached. Winch was one of the first to explore the implications of linguistic analysis—especially the investigations of Ludwig Wittgenstein—for critically assessing the social sciences and explicating the "concept of the social." Further, Winch also links up the work in linguistic philosophy with the notion of *Verstehen* and the concept of "meaningful behavior" which had been central to the Weberian tradition of interpretative sociology. The monograph was written at a time when the dogmas of mainstream social scientists seemed so well entrenched that it was difficult to discern any rational alternative. Winch is protesting against the restrictions and distortions of a positivist conception of knowledge, and the ways in which this has infected mainstream social science.

Not content to point out difficulties, Winch wants to show that the idea of a social science based upon the natural sciences is a mistake, that it rests upon deep conceptual confusions which the new study of language helps expose. According to Winch, "the notion of a human society involves a scheme of concepts which is *logically incompatible* with the kinds of explanation offered in the natural sciences"; "The understanding of society is *logically different* from the understanding of nature"; and "The central concepts which belong to our understanding of social life are *incompatible* with concepts central to scientific prediction."[6] These are strong claims. If Winch is right, then the difficulties in the way of developing a mature social science modeled on the natural sciences are not just practical obstacles, but "logical" and "conceptual" impossibilities. Although Winch is much vaguer about the alternative he proposes, he suggests that the study of society should emulate the "a priori methods" of philosophy rather than the empirical ones of natural science.

Most of the criticism of Winch's work has focused on these extravagant claims: his attempts to provide a priori "impossibility" or "transcendental" arguments against the type of empirical theory advocated by mainstream social scientists. I agree with those critics who have found Winch's arguments seriously deficient.[7] Ironically, Winch's position rests upon a set of dichotomies that are just as dubious as those he attacks. For example, without ever justifying his position, Winch uncritically claims that there is a sharp distinction between "conceptual questions" and "empirical questions," or between philosophy, which employs a priori methods of analysis, and science, which uses empirical and experimental procedures. In certain contexts it is illuminating to distinguish a conceptual from an empirical issue, but unless one can establish that there is a categorial distinction between the conceptual and the empirical—which Winch fails to do—his claims about "incompatibility" collapse. Further, his picture of empirical science borders on caricature. Winch fails to do justice to the important role of conceptual analysis in empirical science itself, or to help us distinguish the conceptual analysis appropriate to science from the conceptual analysis presumably characteristic of philosophy.

But while Winch's claims about "logical incompatibility" do not withstand critical scrutiny, he succeeds in calling attention to a number of complex issues that must be confronted in any adequate theorizing about society—issues which are played down or suppressed by mainstream social scientists. Winch emphasizes the Wittgensteinian notion of a "form of life," and Wittgenstein's remarks about rule-following behavior. Human behavior—what many linguistic philosophers have called "action," to distinguish it from "behavior" understood as physical movement—is rule-governed.

Fundamental to Winch's position is his interpretation of the Wittgensteinian claim, "What has to be accepted, the given, is—so one could say—forms of life" (p. 40). While Winch claims that the various branches of philosophy, such as the philosophy of science, art, and history, have "the task of elucidating the peculiar natures of those forms of life called 'science,' 'art,' etc., epistemology will try to elucidate what is involved in the notion of a form of life as such" (p. 41).[8] To clarify the notion of a form of life is to "understand the nature of social phenomena." Forms of life involve rule-following and rule-governed behavior. The very notion of following a rule presupposes intersubjective conventions and agreements. Rule-following behavior is therefore essentially social behavior.

Conversely, Winch claims that *all* social behavior itself involves the acceptance and following of rules. "It is only in a situation in which it makes sense to suppose that somebody else could in principle discover the rule which I am following that I can intelligibly be said to follow a rule at all" (p. 30). This does not mean that an individual can always formulate the rule which governs his actions, or even that if he does formulate the rule, it is the one that he is actually following. But the "notion of following a rule is logically inseparable from the notion of making a mistake. If it is possible to say of someone that he is following a rule, that means that one can ask whether he is doing what he does correctly or not" (p. 32). Winch also claims that the concepts of a "form of life" and "rule-governed" behavior clarify Weber's notion of "meaningful behavior." "All behavior which is meaningful (therefore all specifically human behavior) is *ipso facto* rule-governed" (p. 52). With reference to "forms of life," we can also clarify two other concepts that must be introduced to understand what is involved in rule-governed behavior—reason and motive.

Consider an example that Winch gives as a paradigm of someone performing an action for a reason. "Suppose it is said of a certain person, *N*, that he voted Labour at the last General Election because he thought that a Labour government would be most likely to preserve industrial peace. What kind of explanation is this? The clearest case is that in which *N*, prior to voting, has discussed the pros or cons of voting Labour and has explicitly come to the conclusion 'I will vote Labour because that is the best way to preserve industrial peace' " (pp. 45–46). Winch does not claim that this example is a paradigm for *all* types of meaningful or rule-governed behavior, but it does exhibit a feature of all such behavior. In order for the above explanation to count as an explanation of *N*'s action, *N* must "have some idea of what it is to 'preserve industrial peace' and of the connection between this and the kind of government which he expects to be in power if Labour is elected" (p. 46).

Generalizing this point, Winch tells us that "the acceptability of such an explanation is contingent on *N*'s grasp of the concepts contained in it" (p. 46). It should also be obvious that an activity such as voting would not make any sense unless we are speaking about a society in which there are certain specific political institutions. Reference to these institutions is essential for understanding the very activity of voting, what counts as a vote in the particular society, and what procedures must be followed in order to vote. Voting behavior is not the type of activity that can be translated or reduced to a set of physical movements. Certain physical movements, such as pulling a lever or marking a ballot, may count as a vote under appropriate circumstances. But these "appropriate circumstances" involve relevant rules.

We can begin to see what is required for describing, explaining, and understanding distinctively human actions. We must grasp the nature of those institutions that enable us to identify the very action in question, and this means grasping the forms of life and the rule-governed behavior involved. It is only by reference to the rules implicit in these forms of life that we can explain an individual's reasons and motives. This is just as true for "motives" as for "reasons." To be sure, the concepts of motive and reason are not identical: "To say, for example, that *N* murdered his wife from jealousy is certainly not to say that he acted reasonably" (p. 82). Nevertheless, "learning what a motive is belongs to learning the standards governing life in the society in which one lives; and that again belongs to the process of learning to live as a social being" (p. 82). If such concepts as "reason" and "motive"—and one can add "intention," "purpose," "goal," and "desire"—are wedded as intimately as Winch suggests to the standards governing life in a society, it would indeed be a conceptual confusion to think it possible to identify such concepts with physical or psychological states or events. A language limited to what is purely physical or psychological leaves out what is essential for making such concepts intelligible—"the standards governing life in the society."

There is a further important consequence of Winch's emphasis on forms of life as the key for understanding social phenomena. In the example above, Winch stresses that the acceptability of the explanation of *N*'s action is contingent upon *his* grasp of the concepts involved. Winch also maintains that "the social relations between men and the ideas which men's actions embody are really the same thing considered from different points of view" (p. 121). "Social relations between men exist only in and through their ideas" (p. 123). "Language," "ideas," and "concepts" cannot be neatly separated from social relations; they are *constitutive* of these relations. Consequently—and here Winch's analysis complements Berlin's—fundamental changes in the concepts, ideas, and language used by men *necessarily* entail fundamental changes in their social relations.

From this brief sketch of Winch's views, we can grasp his general orientation. The philosopher's task is to elucidate the concept of a form of life that involves rule-following behavior, and to show how this is essential for understanding the "concept of the social." The student of society must elucidate the variety of forms of life which characterize our own and other societies. He seeks to comprehend "the point or meaning of what is being done or said."[9] When we elucidate these varied forms of life, it is a mistake—and one Winch thinks is all too common—to assume that our own deeply embedded forms of life are the standard for judging alien forms of life. The very notion of a standard is itself dependent on a given form of life. Winch never tells us precisely how to go about understanding what is distinctive about different forms of life, nor does he claim to provide a methodology. His emphasis on different forms of life and different standards becomes most intriguing and controversial when he suggests that, in understanding an alien society, we must even be prepared to grasp "forms of rationality" different from our own. Presumably, actions which seem irrational by our standards may be intelligible and rational when we relate them to alien forms of rationality.[10]

Much of what Winch says may be interpreted as sound and sensible, albeit vague. Why then does Winch claim that the "notion of a human society involves a scheme of concepts which is logically incompatible with the kinds of explanation offered in the natural sciences"? Winch's main argument for this strong claim follows:

Now if the position of the sociological investigator (in a broad sense) can be regarded as comparable, in its main logical outlines, with that of the natural scientist, the following must be the case. The concepts and the criteria according to which the sociologist judges that, in two situations, the same thing has happened, or the same action performed, must be understood *in relation to the rules governing sociological investigation.* But here we run into a difficulty; for whereas in the case of the natural scientist we have to deal with only one set of rules, namely those governing the scientist's investigation itself, here *what the sociologist is studying,* as well as his study of it, is a human activity and is therefore carried on according to rules. And it is these rules, rather than those which govern the sociologist's investigation, which specify what is to count as 'doing the same kind of thing' in relation to that kind of activity. (pp. 86–87)

He elaborates his point further:

Two things may be called the 'same' or 'different' only with reference to a set of criteria which lay down what is to be regarded as a relevant difference. When the 'things' in question are purely physical the criteria appealed to will of course be those of the observer. But when one is dealing with intellectual (or, indeed, any kind of social) 'things,' that is not so. For their *being* intellectual or social, as opposed to physical, in character depends entirely on their belonging in a certain way to a system of ideas or modes of living. It is only by reference to the criteria governing that system of ideas or mode of life that they have any existence as intellectual or social events. It follows that if the sociological investigator wants to regard them *as* social events (as, *ex hypothesi,* he must) he has to take seriously the criteria which are applied for distinguishing 'different' kinds of actions and identifying the 'same' actions within the way of life he is studying. It is not open to him to arbitrarily impose his own standards from without. In so far as he does, the events he is studying lose altogether their character as *social* events. (p. 108)

This does not mean that we must stop at the kind of unreflective understanding that the participants have of their actions, "but any more reflective understanding must necessarily presuppose, if it is to count as genuine understanding at all, the participant's unreflective understanding" (p. 89).

But what does this argument really establish? Suppose we return to Winch's example of the paradigm of acting for a reason. If we did not understand the concept of voting, we could not investigate why *N* voted as he did. To understand such a concept, we must understand a particular society's institutions and rules for voting. Of course the effective rules may (and do) vary in different societies; we cannot arbitrarily impose other standards from without. One can also agree with Winch that if we limited ourselves to the observation of exclusively physical motions, or to the concepts required for the description of such motions, we would be unable to understand voting as a distinctive type of human activity.

But such an understanding of voting is not the end of the matter, and it is difficult to see in what sense it is incompatible with empirical research or scientific investigation. On the contrary, it is precisely what is required in order to ask intelligent empirical and scientific questions about voting behavior. One of the things that we may want to know is whether the reasons given by participants are indeed the reasons that explain their action. But it is difficult to see how we could answer such a question unless we investigated systematically a variety of empirical factors that may influence such behavior. Or we may want to see if patterns of voting behavior can be correlated with other variables such as socio-economic status, race, religion, etc., on the bases of which we might even make predictions, and formulate hypotheses and modest theories, concerning this or any other form of meaningful behavior. As Alasdair MacIntyre has pointed out, "What Winch characterizes as the whole task of the social sciences is in fact their true starting point. Unless we begin by a characterization of a society in its own terms, we shall be unable to identify the matter that requires explanation. Attention to intentions, motives, and reasons must precede attention to causes. . . ."[11] MacIntyre is also correct when he says:

We can in a given society discover a variety of systematic regularities. There are the systems of rules which agents professedly follow; there are the systems of rules which they actually follow; there are causal regularities exhibited in the correlation of statuses and forms of behavior, and of one form of behavior and another, which are not rule-governed at all; there are regularities which are in themselves neither causal nor rule-governed, although dependent for their existence perhaps on regularities of both types, such as the cyclical patterns of development exhibited in some societies; and there are the interrelationships which exist between all these. Winch concentrates on some of these at the expense of others.[12]

Furthermore, Winch insists that forms of life are not static and unchangeable: they develop, change, and sometimes disappear. Nothing in what he has said would rule out the legitimacy of empirical questions about what factors influence the forms of life that constitute social life. Any serious inquiry would attempt to sort out which factors are causally effective and which are not.

Winch might object that this criticism is based on a conceptual confusion, for it presupposes that causal categories are applicable to the study of social phenomena, whereas the main burden of his argument is to show that causal terms and causal explanation belong to a different conceptual scheme or "language strata."[13] If one believed that the concept of cause is only applicable to physical motions or to the correlation of discrete mental events, then there would be some grounds for such a view. But here one must protest that the careful conceptual analysis that Winch and others demand when we consider the concept of action seems to be entirely lacking when he speaks about causality and causal explanation.[14] If one takes Winch's own claim that science itself is a form of life—or rather that science consists of varied forms of life—then what is demanded is a careful discrimination of these forms of life, and an understanding of the family resemblances and differences between the study of social and natural phenomena, including the ways in which we legitimately speak of and inquire into the causes of social phenomena. What seems so ironical and paradoxical is Winch's assumption that, even within the natural sciences, "causal talk" *must* mean one sort of thing. It is as if all the warnings of Wittgenstein are repressed or forgotten when one speaks about the concept of causality—a concept no less complex and varied than that of action.

Something seems to have gone wrong with Winch's argument. Although we can agree with much of what he has to say concerning what is distinctive about one type or aspect of social phenomena, his elucidation of social phenomena fails as an argument for incompatibility. A similar point is made by Hanna Pitkin.

The language of action . . . is characteristically shaped by being used in the course of action by the actors; but those are not its only uses, or the only influences on its grammar. Sometimes we do (what is called) describe an action objectively; sometimes we do (what is called) predict an action; sometimes we do (what is called) give a causal explanation of action. So the problem for social science is not that prediction and causation do not apply to actions, or that objectivity is impossible, but that these concepts apply to actions in distinctive ways, ways which give rise to conceptual difficulties when we try to generalize about them.[15]

If, then, we read Winch—as he intended us to read him—as trying to demonstrate the incompatibility of the concepts used in studying social phenomena with those used in science and empirical research, we must judge his argument a failure. But to leave the matter here would be to miss what is most valuable in his investigations. Instead of viewing what he says in the context of proposing—and failing to justify—an impossibility argument, we can, following Pitkin's suggestion, interpret his claims as attempts to clarify the ways in which concepts employed in the study of natural phenomena undergo a subtle shift of emphasis and meaning when applied to social phenomena. Further, we can see that Winch is highlighting important conceptual problems that must be confronted in the systematic study of social phenomena. Let me indicate three areas where Winch locates important conceptual problems but offers little guidance in their solution.

Winch is right when he emphasizes the importance of understanding and interpreting social practices and institutions. When dealing with an activity like voting we may not find significant obstacles in the way of such an understanding, but when we turn to religion, witchcraft, or magic there are difficult conceptual problems in both principle and fact in deciding even what counts as a proper interpretation of the phenomena involved. Commenting on Weber's notion of *Verstehen* as a process of arriving at sociological interpretations, Winch takes strong exception to the claim that we check the validity of a suggested interpretation by appealing to "statistical laws based on observation of what happens." "Against this view, I want to insist that if a proffered interpretation is wrong, statistics, though they may suggest that that is so, are not the decisive and ultimate court of appeal for the validity of sociological interpretations in the way Weber suggests. What is then needed is a better interpretation, not something different in kind" (p. 113).

Winch, however, never tells us how to decide which among competing interpretations is the best. He might reply that this can only be determined in particular cases when we examine the alternative interpretations, and that there are a variety of ways in which to decide. But this only pushes the problem back one stage further. On Winch's own epistemological grounds, the interpretation of social phenomena is itself a rule-governed activity and must necessarily involve criteria of correctness and incorrectness. Yet Winch never presents these criteria. It is precisely the suspicion that there are no such criteria in the assessment of competing sociological interpretations that makes so many mainstream social scientists skeptical of concepts like "interpretation" and "understanding" in the study of society.

Secondly, Winch is right when he emphasizes that, in the systematic study of *some* social phenomena, we must pay careful attention to the rules governing the activity of the participants, and to *their* criteria for what counts as "doing the same kind of thing." While Winch insists that a "more reflective understanding must necessarily presuppose, if it is to count as genuine understanding at all, the participant's unreflective understanding" (p. 89), he never pins down the *logical* relation between the concepts and categories employed by the sociological investigator and those of the participants studied. Of course this will vary from situation to situation, and Winch himself tells us that a psychoanalyst "may explain a patient's neurotic behavior in terms of factors unknown to the patient and of concepts which would be unintelligible to him" (p. 89). Presumably this situation would also arise wherever we believe the participants have a "false consciousness" or ideological misconception of forms of life in which they participate. But if it is admitted that participants may be mistaken in their "unreflective understanding," and that their activity may be explained in terms of factors unknown and even unintelligible to them, then it is not at all clear what limits are placed upon the sociological investigator. At times all Winch seems to claim is that before we can offer, from an external point of view, any interpretation of social phenomena, we must first be sure that we understand the situation as conceived by those involved. If this is to amount to more than the trivial claim that in any study—in the natural and social sciences alike—we must account for what we are trying to explain, then what is required is some specification of the effective limits on our more reflective modes of understanding.

Thirdly, Winch tells us that "the social relations between men and the ideas which men's actions embody are really the same thing considered from different points of view" (p. 121), and that "our language and our social relations are just two different sides of the same coin" (p. 123). Consequently, "if social relations between men exist only in and through their ideas, then, since the relations between ideas are internal relations, social relations must be a species of internal relation too" (p. 123).

Once again one is inclined to say that there is something right and important about what Winch *wants* to say, but something wrong and misleading about his actual claims. We cannot even begin to understand some social relations unless we understand the beliefs and concepts of the participants involved. To understand the variety of even such non-discursive social relations as love, friendship, hostility, hatred, etc., we must understand how the participants interpret and conceive of each other. Against the view that we can ignore or disregard the "intentional descriptions" of the participants, Winch is making a telling point.

However, the claim that social relations are a species of internal relations easily slides into the claim that to understand social relations, it is sufficient to understand the ways in which they are internally related. Winch ignores or at least minimizes the variety of ways in which social relations are influenced by nonlinguistic *external* factors—factors which may be unknown to or hidden from the participants involved. We have seen already that in psychoanalysis Winch admits that the therapist may legitimately explain the behavior of an individual—and his social relations—by reference to factors unknown to the patient. But Winch fails to appreciate how the logic of this situation can be generalized. Frequently in our very attempt to understand a type of social relation, just this sort of empirical information is required. Whatever criticisms one may make of Freud and Marx, they have taught us that hidden factors can have a powerful influence on what men think, and on their social relations. As in so many of his arguments, Winch seems to be operating with a spe-cious dichotomy: we must think of social relations on the model of either language or the interaction of physical forces. This very dichotomy is the basis for ruling out as conceptually confused what are legitimate and important empirical questions: what nonlinguistic factors influence our social relations.

Winch's strategy of argument is wrongheaded, for it is a mirror image of what he opposes. The real object of Winch's attack is a form of sci-entism which refuses to recognize that there is anything distinctive about our social life and the concepts required for describing and explaining it. He is ferreting out the a priori bias which declares that talk of "under-standing," "interpretation," "forms of life," and "rule-governed behavior" has no place in a tough-minded scientific approach to the study of social phenomena.[16] But the consequence of Winch's arguments—despite occa-sional protests that this is *not* what he intends—is to isolate social life and the concepts pertaining to it from the rest of nature and empirical in-quiry. If we were to accept many of Winch's claims, it would be a con-ceptual confusion to investigate the external causal influences on our social life. This itself turns out to be nothing but an unjustified a priori bias. More seriously, the very type of understanding and interpretation of social phenomena that Winch demands frequently requires that we search for the causal determinants of the specific forms of life that are "given."

We see the same sort of curious mirror image in the "descriptivism" that pervades so much of what Winch says. He tells us:

Science, unlike philosophy, is wrapped up in its own way of making things intelligible to the exclusion of all others. Or rather it applies its criteria un-selfconsciously; for to be self-conscious about such matters is to be philo-sophical. This non-philosophical unselfconsciousness is for the most part right and proper in the investigation of nature (except at such critical times as that gone through by Einstein prior to the formulation of the Special Theory of Relativity); but it is disastrous in the investigation of a human society, whose very nature is to consist in different and competing ways of life, each offering a different account of the intelligibility of things. To take an un-committed view of such competing conceptions is peculiarly the task of phi-losophy; it is not its business to award prizes to science, religion, or anything else. It is not its business to advocate any *Weltanschauung*. . . . In Wittgen-stein's words, 'Philosophy leaves everything as it was.' (pp. 102–103)

Although Winch stresses that taking such an uncommitted view is peculiarly the task of philosophy, clearly he advocates it as well for the "acceptable forms of social scientific theory." The social investigator must not impose his own standards of rationality or intelligibility, but rather must uncover the standards of the forms of life he investigates. Such claims seem eminently reasonable: they are a plea for openness to the variety of forms of life, and a warning against biases that color and distort what we investigate. But such claims are also double-edged. Winch lacks an awareness that the "self-consciousness" that he takes as characteristic of philosophy, involves a critical distance and perspective. A primary objective of the tradition of *theoria*—not only in philosophy but in social and political theory, too—has been to distinguish the true from the false, the apparent from the real and essential. It is not the business of philosophy to "award prizes," but it is indeed the business of philosophy and genuine theory to provide the basis for critical evaluation of the forms of life. Winch tells us that "the concept of *learning from* which is involved in the study of other cultures is closely linked with the concept of *wisdom*. We are confronted not just with different techniques, but with new possibilities of good and evil, in relation to which men may come to terms with life."[17] But such a "wisdom" is empty unless it also provides some critical basis for evaluating these "new possibilities of good and evil." Certainly we can recognize that there are forms of life which are dehumanizing and alienating, and we want to understand precisely in what ways they are so; to insist that philosophy and social theory remain neutral and uncommitted undermines any rational basis for such a critique of society.

Human Action as a Moral Concept: A. R. Louch

W INCH was among the first philosophers to show the relevance of linguistic investigations for an understanding of "the concept of social," and for criticizing the understanding of social knowledge as natural scientific knowledge. A far more radical and skeptical thesis has been advanced by A. R. Louch. Like Winch, Louch believes that analytic philosophy—especially the linguistic investigations of Wittgenstein, Ryle, and Austin—can illuminate human action and social phenomena. But one of the main targets of Louch's attack is Winch, whom he accuses of the grossest conceptual confusions.[18] Whereas Winch claims that "the requirements of philosophy place limits on acceptable forms of social scientific theory,"[19] Louch declares that "my main intent has been to show that the very idea of a science of man or society is untenable" (p. viii).[20] Louch's highly polemical stance in his *Explanation and Human Action* (1969) is shaped by his conviction that the very quest for a scientific un-

derstanding of human society has dangerous and pernicious moral consequences. It reinforces a "scientific or engineering attitude" that is
primarily concerned with effective techniques of manipulation.

Totalitarianism is too weak a word and too inefficient an instrument to describe the perfect scientific society. For in the totalitarian regimes known to
us, one is still conscious of coercion and thus of alternatives, however disastrous to the individual such alternatives may be. In the engineers' society,
perhaps unwittingly promoted by psychologists and sociologists bent on being
scientists, we should have to give up the concept of an open or civil society
which, however inefficiently, serves as a prop for a social order based on
respect for men as persons or autonomous agents.

A programme having such ultimate consequences cries out for refutation.
(p. 239)

Louch uses a variety of strategies in his attack on the very idea of a
science of man and society. He shows that much of what passes for social scientific knowledge is platitudinous and empty, or expresses common sense judgments disguised in technical jargon. He seeks to establish
that the obsession with the quest for generality and covering laws has led
many social scientists astray. "We have, in fact, a rather rich knowledge
of human nature which can only be assimilated to the generality pattern
of explanation by invoking artificial and ungainly hypotheses about which
we are much less secure than we are about the particular cases the generalizations are invoked to guarantee" (pp. 3–4). Louch wants to cut
deeper and expose what he takes to be the epistemological biases in the
mainstream conception of what a proper explanation of social phenomena involves. Against the view that there is something inadequate, deficient, or incomplete about ad hoc explanations, he argues that it is just
this type of explanation that accounts for human performances. He even
attacks a common interpretation of the doctrine of causal explanation.
"The view that causal explanation depends upon repeated observations
of temporal succession derives its support chiefly from an atomistic view
as to what we may be said to observe, a view which I hope to show cannot be intelligibly stated" (p. 4). Louch wants not only to debunk the
pretentious claims of social science and undermine the epistemological
foundations on which it rests, but also to clarify the ways in which we
actually describe and explain human actions. What, then, is so distinctive
about the description and explanation of human actions as to justify the
claim that a "science of man or society is untenable"?

Louch states his view succinctly:

Observation, according to a prevailing orthodoxy, is one thing, appraisal
quite another. Consequently, the activity of appraisal or evaluation gives us no
new information about the world. I shall maintain against this view that ob-

servation, description, and explanation of human action is only possible by means of moral categories. The concept of action itself, I hope to show, is in a broad sense a moral concept. (p. vii)

Since moral categories are not scientific concepts and cannot be reduced or replaced by scientific concepts, a *science* of human action is impossible. But what does it mean that the observation, description, and explanation of action is possible only in terms of *moral* categories? The sense in which Louch uses "moral" is characterized as the procedural view of morality.

In the procedural view, a man whose actions are guided by his assessments, and his understanding of his own and others' actions by the grounds he finds for those actions in the situation of the actor, is looking at behaviour morally. So long as he describes his own and others' conduct as doing something well or poorly, effectively or clumsily, appropriately or mistakenly, he is a moral agent and observer. It may be that the grounds he discovers as the end products of his diagnosis shock or offend various moral sensibilities; but this is relatively unimportant. The point is, he thinks in terms of grounds. He acts or describes actions, not by seeking temporal antecedents or functional dependencies, but by deciding that the situation entitles a man to act in the way he did or is likely to do. (p. 51)

Louch is fully aware that he is challenging one of the main doctrines of much contemporary philosophy and social science.

It is the tendency among behavioural scientists to think of value as a subtle and dangerous obstacle to the business of objective description of human action. So these scientists feel that if they set their values to one side, articulate them, and isolate them in a preface all will be well. But values do not enter descriptions of human affairs as disruptive influences; rather, they allow us to describe human behaviour in terms of action. *Inasmuch as the units of examination of human behaviour are actions, they cannot be observed, identified, or isolated except through categories of assessment and appraisal.* There are not two stages, an identification of properties and qualities in nature and then an assessment of them, stages which then could become the business of different experts. There is only one stage, the delineation and description of occurrences in value terms. (p. 56, italics added)

Louch presents his thesis in the strongest possible form when he says, "The man or situation is not seen and then appraised, or appraised and then seen in distortion; it is seen morally. Value and fact merge" (p. 54).

Exactly how are we to interpret Louch's assertions? There is a minimal interpretation by which they are both plausible and important, and a stronger one—essential to Louch's argument—by which they are implausible and mistaken. Against those who think that there is a univocal sense of "observation" and "description" which consists solely in the reporting of sense data or physical objects, and who think that any other sense of "observation" or "description" is illegitimate, Louch's claims have force. There are contexts and paradigms in which we do describe our own and others' "conduct as doing something well or poorly, effectively or clumsily, appropriately or mistakenly." To claim that this is not "really" describing tells us more about one's epistemological biases concerning description than it does about the grammar of description. It is a classic instance of the type of bias that Wittgenstein so brilliantly exposes in his *Philosophical Investigations*—the bias where, blinded by a "picture" of what *must* be the case we fail to "look and see" the various ways in which we actually use concepts. But to admit this is to make a much more modest claim than Louch makes. He argues that "inasmuch as the units of examination of human behaviour are actions, they cannot be observed, identified, or isolated except through categories of assessment and appraisal." Yet this is certainly a mistake. We can and do describe actions as voting, or signing a contract, or committing suicide. Of course we cannot describe such actions unless we understand the concepts we are using. We may—although we need not—go on to *describe* these activities "as doing something well or poorly, effectively or clumsily," etc. In some doubtful cases we will be called upon to evaluate the basis for claiming that an action was performed. But this would seem to be just as true in the description of any physical phenomena.

Furthermore, if we appeal to the paradigmatic ways in which we speak —as Louch does—then much of what he says is just as applicable to the description of nonhuman as to human actions. We may describe the movement of a horse as graceful, or the way a chimpanzee solves a problem as intelligent, or the behavior of lions as cowardly. One might even argue that his discussion is applicable to some of our descriptions of inanimate objects. The fact that we sometimes talk in such ways reveals nothing distinctive about human action.

In a curious way Louch himself seems to be the victim of his own generality thesis, when he moves from the observation that we sometimes use "moral" categories in describing actions, to the general and mistaken claim that we cannot observe, identify, or describe human actions without the employment of moral categories. Actually, the point that he is making is important for pinpointing a set of difficult issues that must be confronted, rather than for demonstrating that the scientific study of individuals and society is untenable. Operating under the dogma of a value-free social science, many mainstream social scientists are unaware how much of their research involves categories of assessment and appraisal. This is true not only when they speak of "democracy," or of "deviant" or "dysfunctional" or "normal" or "pathological" behavior, but in less obvious ways when they use concepts like "role," "status," "equilibrium," and "system."[21]

Even Nagel's distinction between the two types of "value judgment" is not very helpful here, for he glosses over many of the difficulties in demarcating the boundaries between these, and fails to appreciate the discriminations necessary when we proceed from relatively uncontroversial concepts like "anemia" to such treacherous ones as "intelligence," and "mental health," where the very criteria for the application of these concepts are at issue. There is a standard reply that Nagel and mainstream social scientists can make, when the pervasiveness of "moral" categories in the description of human action is pointed out. If the terms "democracy," "intelligence," and "mental health," are found objectionable because of their moral overtones, they say, more neutral terms can be substituted without logically affecting the truth or falsity, correctness or incorrectness of the descriptions. One may, for example, object to calling the contemporary political community in the United States a "democracy" because of the evaluative connotations of this term; call it what you wish, the task remains of providing an adequate description of how this political system works. But there is something ingenuous about this reply; it minimizes the extent to which "descriptive-evaluative" concepts pervade and shape not only our ordinary discourse about human actions, but social science literature as well—especially "empirical theory."

In short, I do not think that Louch's remarks concerning human action as a moral concept establish an "impossibility" thesis about a science of man or society. But they do indicate what would be required to rewrite social science literature antiseptically in a language of "pure description." It is not even clear what the concept of "pure description" means, or what a language intended for describing human action but devoid of all evaluative aspects would be like. Yet one point is clear: in the attempt to carry out such a project systematically, we would find ourselves with an artificial and emasculated vocabulary bearing little or no relation to the ways in which we—and social scientists—speak about human action.

Thus far I have focused on Louch's attempt to show that the observation, description, and identification of human actions involve categories of assessment and appraisal—what he calls moral categories. But we need to consider what he has to say about the explanation of human action to understand fully why he thinks a science of man untenable. He wants to show that the type of explanation appropriate for human actions is "moral explanation," not scientific explanation, and further that moral explanations are ad hoc and context-bound. His polemic is directed against what he takes to be the unwarranted bias of a "scientific mentality" convinced that there is something illegitimate and unsatisfactory about such ad hoc explanations.

The nature of explanation depends upon the kinds of things investigated and on the exemplary cases we bring, often unconsciously, to our inquiries. Explanation, in Wittgenstein's phrase, is a family of cases, joined together only by a common aim, to make something plain or clear. This suggests that a coherent account of explanation could not be given without attending to the audience to whom the explanation is offered or the source of puzzlement that requires an explanation to be given. There are many audiences, many puzzles, and a variety of paradigmatically clear cases that give rise, by contrast, to puzzles about other cases. The means of explaining are thus quite heterogeneous. (p. 233)

Louch states this as a conclusion, but throughout his discussion of such concepts as liking, desire, need, emotion, motive, intention, purpose, etc., he has attempted to *show* how heterogeneous are the puzzles that confront us in understanding human performances and the variety of ways in which we make something clear. Because Louch thinks that a science of man or society presupposes belief in a "univocal theory of explanation where all explanation consists in bringing a case under a law" (p. 233), he doubts the possibility of such a science.

There has indeed been an overwhelming belief among mainstream social scientists that there is or ought to be a univocal sense of explanation, and that a proper scientific explanation will take the form of deduction from fundamental laws. In our investigation of Merton, Smelser, and Nagel we have seen different forms of this bias. Furthermore, this bias has blinded many to the variety of ways in which we offer explanations of human performances in ordinary life. There has also been a conviction that "genuine" scientific explanation is more basic and perspicuous than the variety of ad hoc explanations that we ordinarily give of our actions. Thus social scientists have tended to explain *away* the heterogeneous types of explanations rather than to give a proper account of them. If this were all that Louch was claiming, one would welcome his analyses as a healthy corrective.

But Louch makes much stronger claims that are dubious. He tells us that "relativism thus means that actions can only be judged in context, and that there happens to be no universal context. Explanation of human action is context-bound. . . . What is important is the variety, the detail, not the general features which afford grounds for the statement of

laws" (p. 207). And Louch draws some very substantial and controversial moral conclusions from his insistence on the heterogeneity and
variety of human conduct and the explanations of this conduct.

And so the only moral recommendations, as the only recommendations for
the empirical study of man, come to the same thing—a move here, a move
there, zig and zag, after the manner of Aristotle's recommendations with regard to the Mean, everything tentative and subject to change. It is both from
overweening generalizations in ethics and the pretentions of general theory in
behavioural science that we stand most to fear the sorts of impositions on our
lives that make for totalitarian regimes. Things, so to say, are always bad, or
at least not nearly so good as we could imagine them being; but wholesale
changes, whether backed by Plato's ethics, Marx's historicism, or Skinner's
laws of conditioning will most likely make matters worse. For men and situations represent a variety and a changing variety, which makes the application
of general laws trivial or false and universal moral principles a positive evil.
(p. 208)

This passage brings out a dichotomy that is fundamental for Louch's
argument and polemic—a dichotomy which is suspect. He writes as if we
are confronted with an either/or. *Either* we concern ourselves exclusively
with the variety, complexity, and detail of specific contexts of human performances, and with ad hoc descriptions and explanations of these, *or* we
will be ensnared in the futile search for generality that results in empty,
platitudinous, dubious claims and in universalistic doctrines that are
positively evil.

What seems to be squeezed out as illegitimate is the genuine need to
gain some perspective on the multifarious contexts in which we find ourselves, in order to understand and explain them. In his concern—almost
an obsession—to attack the "generality thesis" in all its forms, Louch
has run together several strands of his argument that need to be carefully
distinguished. There is the claim that in ordinary life we frequently describe and explain human performances using moral categories, and further that the explanations we offer are ad hoc. The bias which assumes
that such explanations are wrong or incomplete is unwarranted and needs
to be exposed. There is also the important claim that many descriptions
and explanations offered in the social sciences involve categories of assessment and evaluation, and that many social scientists have lacked a
critical self-consciousness that they are offering moral descriptions and
explanations. This results in passing off highly dubious and controversial
appraisals as if they were simply based on a description of value-neutral
facts. Also there is Louch's persistent attack on the conception that a
genuine explanation of human action *must* take the canonical form of
subsumption of instances under general theories and laws.

But once we separate out the various elements in Louch's polemical attack, then we must distinguish the various *senses* of the search for generality. His arguments do not justify a blanket condemnation of all forms of generality in the explanation of human actions. At times Louch himself seems to be aware of this, although he represses this point when he emphasizes the variety and detail of human contexts, and the types of explanations appropriate to them. In discussing economic theory, he writes:

With exception of the purely statistical studies of the business cycle, the volume and velocity of credit, money, and products, economics as a theory is a moral theory. Nor does this discredit it. We require a clear statement of the aims of the economy in order to make pertinent inquiries into the physical possibilities of the economic situation, enabling us to decide how altering one circumstance will affect others. Difficulties arise only when a concept like need, after having saturated the study of the economy with moral considerations, is then trotted forth as an innocent and discoverable fact, which then makes us prone to take special interests as if they reflected inevitable laws of nature. (p. 76)

And he adds:

Take, for example, the view one hears so much of nowadays that man is by nature a profit-seeking animal. This view is stated as a law of human nature, which can then be employed to explain all the variety of human actions. It is derived from Adam Smith but, if its role there is examined with care, its essentially polemical nature will emerge. The search for profit is essential to Smith's exhortation to let the economy govern itself. The assumption is that men, left to themselves, will, in fact, act so as to maximize profit, and thus contribute to the general good (wealth) of the community as a whole. . . . In the first place, it is clear that it does not hold for all societies or all times and places. It belongs rather among the conventions subscribed to by particular men in particular cultures. And in a sense, Adam Smith had much to do with articulating the moral view that makes the pursuit of profit a *sine qua non* of human activity. The point is, we know what men will do for profit, and we can expect a person involved in a bargaining position to buy as cheaply as he can and sell as dearly as he can, because those are the conventions under which he operates in the market-place. We have not divined some hitherto hidden truth about human nature to which we must bow, but have noted the conventions common to certain institutions and practices, which we can and do work to alter. (pp. 76–77)

If we analyze the above passages carefully, we see that Louch is *not* criticizing the search for generality, but a misconception of the type of generality appropriate to social inquiry. The type of economic theory that he is speaking about rises above the particularistic contexts and seeks to discern general patterns and regularities exhibited in such contexts.

And Louch himself notes that to point out that an economic theory is a moral theory is not to discredit it. Rather it clarifies what is involved, so that we see as illegitimate the move from the claim that there are "conventions common to certain institutions and practices," to the mistaken conclusion that this reveals "hidden truths about human nature" or reflects "inevitable laws of nature."

Contrary then to Louch's intentions, his insights concerning how some accounts of human actions implicitly or explicitly involve categories of assessment and appraisal, help to illuminate a proper function of social theory. For we want not only to understand the structure and dynamics involved in the "conventions common to certain institutions and practices," but also to assess critically the status and consequences of these institutions and practices. Statistics, empirical observation, and the formulating of modest hypotheses, models, and theories, can and do have a role in this endeavor. They enable us to discern the structure and dynamic interrelationships within such institutions and practices. I fail to see that Louch has provided us with any reason for thinking that such an endeavor is untenable or unimportant. It can be value-neutral in that it seeks to give a correct description of these institutions and practices and tries to avoid distortion. But if we think that what we are describing and explaining consists of value-neutral "brute facts"[22]—if we fail to realize that embedded in the very institutions and practices analyzed are value commitments—then we are on the brink of misunderstanding this activity. And there is ample evidence that, over and over again, these are just the sort of illicit moves that mainstream social scientists have a tendency to make.

Louch—like so many others who insist upon the ways in which description and explanation are context-dependent—never squarely faces the issue of what *is* the appropriate context that we are speaking about, how it is to be construed, and how extensive it really is. It may be that there is no "universal context," but this does not exclude general contexts from which we can gain a more perspicuous understanding of the types of description and explanation that we use in understanding human actions.

Louch is very sensitive to, and critical of, the moral consequences of the scientistic attitude that he finds so objectionable. But while so alert to the dangers of scientism, Louch seems to lack a critical self-consciousness about the moral consequences of the very point of view that he advocates, and how compatible it is with the totalitarian tendencies that he deplores. When he tells us that "the only moral recommendations, as the only recommendations for the empirical study of man, come to the same thing—a move here, a move there, zig and zag . . . everything tentative and subject to change," this makes eminently good sense if one *pre-supposes* that it takes place in the type of open society that Louch so cherishes. But in a closed society, or in one where there are powerful forces leading to closure—which, in the twentieth century, is no mere abstract possibility—then Louch's recommendations amount to moral defeatism. It is little solace to those victimized by such a society to be told, "Things, so to say, are always bad, or at least not nearly so good as we could imagine them as being." For all his skepticism about a priorism in philosophy, the consequence of Louch's own position is to rule out a priori the possibility of an informed general critique of social institutions and practices—to tell us that such a general assessment is morally inde-fensible and epistemologically unwarranted. One may turn Louch's own words against him: "a programme having such ultimate consequences cries out for refutation."

A balanced assessment of the contributions and limitations of the work of Winch and Louch must take account of the dialectical context in which their arguments were developed. One cannot underestimate the naturalistic influence in shaping both the direction and self-understand-ing of the social sciences. Mainstream social scientists have held that the social sciences had finally been placed on a firm scientific foundation, that we could now expect the progressive cumulative development of knowledge characteristic of the natural sciences. Against this outlook, both Winch and Louch have advanced strong countertheses, the former claiming that the concepts required for describing and understanding social life are incompatible with those of the natural sciences, and the latter questioning the very idea of a science of man or society. I have argued that neither really justifies these countertheses, though their in-vestigations have made us more sensitive to aspects of social and political phenomena and of human action ignored by mainstream social scientists. In different ways, they have shown how much of human action is con-stituted by the manner in which men intentionally describe and under-stand their own and others' actions. The search for "brute data" has been criticized as an illusory and conceptually confused ideal, and the failure to appreciate how assessment and appraisal are involved in accounts of human action has been shown to produce empty generalizations.

Insofar as both Winch and Louch draw upon linguistic investigations to show what is involved in accounts of human action, they can be read as "filling out" some of the claims made by Isaiah Berlin. This new linguistic orientation helps us to understand what it means to say that "men's beliefs in the sphere of conduct are part of their conception of themselves and others as human beings; and this conception in its turn, whether conscious or not, is intrinsic to their picture of the world." Further, like Berlin, they have explored the ramifications of this in criticizing the blindness of those who seek to force accounts of human action into the forms of scientific discourse and theory.

Even so, something that Berlin saw clearly is obscured in Winch and Louch. Berlin emphasizes that the task of the theorist is not only to understand and analyze the models and paradigms that shape the conduct of human beings, but to evaluate these models critically. There is a deep irony in the intellectual stance of Winch and Louch—one that reveals a tension plaguing much (though not all) of the conceptual investigations of human action. On the one hand, it is clear that the investigations of Winch and Louch are informed by a moral point of view. Their protest against rampant scientism and positivism is not limited to epistemological considerations. Or rather, they are arguing for the intrinsic connection between epistemology and a moral point of view. But on the other hand, both are victimized by a latent descriptivism which undermines rational criticism of existing social and political phenomena. They come down hard on the demand for the theorist to provide adequate and perspicuous accounts of the many ways in which men actually describe and explain human performances. But they do not indicate in what ways we can gain a rational critical perspective on the quality of social and political life. This seems to be left to the individual to do in his ad hoc ways. In this respect, despite occasional protests to the contrary, they undermine one of the primary functions of theory in political and social studies —its critical, negative function.

Max Weber, who struggled heroically with the nature and limits of social science, concluded that science is "meaningless" in that it could not answer "the only important question for us": "What shall we do and how shall we live?" But even Weber held out the possibility that philosophy might help answer this question. He only dimly perceived that what he had to say about science would soon be said about philosophy itself, and declared the new wisdom of the age.

Thomas Kuhn's Ambiguous Concept of a Paradigm

THE criticisms leveled against the social sciences by Winch and Louch have been based on their linguistic investigations of human action. Despite occasional forays into the philosophy of science, in the main they have accepted the picture of science advocated by logical empiricists and endorsed by many social scientists. The rhetorical force of what they have to say depends on this acceptance. In effect they have argued that, given this notion of what science and scientific explanation are, we can show how different the description and explanation of human action are. But recently another attack on mainstream social science has emerged which is concerned with the very concept of science and theory that is implicit or explicit in the naturalistic interpretation of the social sciences.

This new discussion has relied very heavily on the work of Thomas Kuhn. His short book which he describes as an essay—*The Structure of Scientific Revolutions* (1962)—has been one of the most provocative to appear in the past fifteen years, at least if one judges by the amount of critical attention it has received. Although Kuhn has been almost exclusively concerned with the natural sciences, limiting his remarks about the social sciences to occasional observations, social scientists have "discovered" Kuhn and claimed that his work offers fresh illumination for understanding social sciences and theory. We will soon see how tangled the issues become. For Kuhn has been used, and more frequently abused, to support the most divergent and contradictory claims. With appropriate self-irony, Kuhn himself has recently written of *The Structure of Scientific Revolutions:* "Part of the reason for its success is, I regretfully conclude, that it can be too nearly all things to all people."[23] After presenting a general account of Kuhn's position and locating certain of its central ambiguities, I want to consider some of the ways in which he has been appropriated. Once we work through these controversies, we will discern emphases and insights that support and complement those which have emerged in the linguistic analyses of the concept of action.

As Alan Ryan has noted, "Kuhn's case resists summary, if only because it is hard to produce a summary which does not beg the analysis of the numerous ambiguities in his own statement of that case."[24] On the most abstract level, it runs as follows.

If we examine the history of any of the well-established natural sciences, we discover a period in which investigation is dominated by competing schools and subschools which fail to exhibit a single generally accepted view about the phenomena in question, or about the proper procedures of investigation and research. Although schools can and have made important contributions to scientific investigation, there is a marked and qualitative difference that arises in a history of a science when a paradigm emerges. When Kuhn first introduces the concept of paradigm, he tells us that paradigms are "universally recognized scientific achievements that for a time provide model problems and solutions to a community of practitioners" (p. viii).[25] The significance of paradigms is that they give rise to what Kuhn calls normal science: "research firmly based upon one or more past scientific achievements that some particular scientific community acknowledges for a time as supplying the foundation for its further practice" (p. 10). The achievements that can serve as paradigms may include "law, theory, application, and instrumentation together" (p. 10). Paradigms serve a regulative function in directing future research. Most of what scientists do is to engage in normal science, and this, as characterized by Kuhn, is essentially a type of puzzle-solving. In the initial stages of the acceptance of a paradigm, there is still largely the promise of success in solving specific problems. Normal science actualizes that promise by extending the knowledge of those facts revealed by the paradigm, by increasing the extent of the match between those facts and the paradigm's predictions, and by further articulation of the paradigm.

There are a variety of ways in which the scientific community imposes a paradigm: scientific education, a textbook tradition, expulsion from the profession of those who reject the paradigm. Kuhn emphasizes how little normal science and research aim to produce major novelties. Their primary aim is to articulate and fill out what is suggested by the accepted paradigm. Normal science as a puzzle-solving activity is a cumulative enterprise, and is eminently successful in extending scientific knowledge. Indeed, the picture of what *all* science is like is frequently based on the mistaken extrapolation that all science is like normal science. But in the course of normal science, novelties of fact and theory arise. "Discovery commences with the awareness of anomaly, i.e., with the recognition that nature has somehow violated the paradigm-induced expectations that govern normal science" (pp. 52–53). The initial reaction to the awareness of anomalies is to attempt in various ways to assimilate them to the existing paradigm, or to ignore or suppress them. Scientific discovery is essentially a process which can be extended over a long period of time. The awareness of anomalies opens a period in which conceptual categories are adjusted until the initially anomalous has become the anticipated. While scientific discoveries contribute to paradigm change, there are also more dramatic and radical shifts that result in the invention of new theories.

Anomalies can resist integration into an accepted paradigm, causing a pronounced failure in the normal problem-solving activity guided by the paradigm. A variety of factors can contribute to this breakdown, which brings a crisis where the tools that a paradigm supplies can no longer solve the problems it defines. Kuhn does not maintain that persistent and recognized anomalies *always* lead to crisis, because the fit between a paradigm and nature is never perfect: there are always unresolved problems. But when an anomaly "comes to seem more than just another puzzle of normal science, the transition to crisis and to extraordinary science has begun" (p. 82). More and more attention is devoted to attempting to explain the anomaly. It is at this stage that extraordinary science and research develop to meet the crisis. And at such moments scientists themselves turn to philosophical analysis and speculative hypotheses. A "proliferation of competing articulations, the willingness to try anything, the expression of explicit discontent, the recourse to philosophy and to debate over fundamentals, all of these are symptoms of a transition from normal to extraordinary research" (p. 91).

At such times, revolutions in science occur—revolutions that involve the proposal of new paradigms, new ways of characterizing problems. "As in political revolutions, so in paradigm choice—there is no standard higher than the assent of the relevant community" (p. 94). Paradigm choice "can never be unequivocally settled by logic and experiment alone" (p. 94). The relation between a paradigm and its successor is *not* that the former is a special case of a more general theory that replaces it. On the contrary, "the normal-scientific tradition that emerges from a scientific revolution is not only incompatible but often incommensurable with that which has gone before" (p. 103). The new paradigm often necessitates a redefinition of the corresponding science as the source of new problems, new methods, and new standards of solution. Kuhn argues that paradigms are constitutive not only of science but of nature. Consequently, in a scientific revolution, what we take to be nature must itself, in a sense, change. Furthermore, "The decision to reject one paradigm is always simultaneously the decision to accept another." (p. 77).

But if the differences among competing paradigms are as radical as Kuhn suggests, and if there is no set of standards for proving the superiority of one paradigm over another, how are we to account for such changing paradigms and for the switch of paradigm allegiance? Kuhn compares this switch to a conversion. To understand how such a conversion is induced or resisted, we must turn not to the logic of proof and experimental evidence, but to the "techniques of persuasion." Kuhn insists that the case for the new paradigm can never be decisively "proven"; a variety of arguments—the promise of the new paradigm to solve problems created by the crisis, aesthetic considerations, etc.—are all used as techniques of persuasion. "Rather than a single group conversion, what occurs is an increasing shift in the distribution of professional allegiances" (p. 158), resulting eventually in the triumph of a new paradigm with new problems, standards, and procedures.

It is not difficult to see why Kuhn's work has caused so much controversy. Kuhn criticizes those who think that all science is like normal science, with its steady, cumulative development of research. Social scientists of an empiricist or behaviorist persuasion have at times stressed the need to begin with facts and to build up correlations and hypotheses in a cumulative fashion. But Kuhn sees such a view of science as both naïve and mistaken. He is just as critical of those—especially philosophers of science—who think that scientists are or ought to be always advancing radical hypotheses—a view that underestimates the overwhelming role that normal science plays in preparing the way for genuine revolutions.

Further, Kuhn cuts across lines which many have thought fixed and sacred, to use a variety of psychological, sociological, historical, and logical arguments in order to support his claims. He sees the scientific community less as one with an impartial interest in the quest for truth than as a political community where authority is imposed, and novelty and deviance suppressed. As in the case of political communities, there can be a breakdown in authority leading to a period of crisis. In the crisis new paradigms are proposed, and defenders of the old order and champions of the new order frequently argue at cross purposes. But in the case of a successful scientific revolution, a new paradigm emerges to set new directions for normal science. And while Kuhn at times draws back from the claim that the world itself is different after a scientific revolution, he does say that after a revolution "scientists are responding to a different world" (p. 135), for what we take to be the world is shaped by the paradigms that we employ in understanding it.

There is scarcely an aspect of Kuhn's work that has not been severely criticized—frequently from conflicting points of view. Critics have argued that the central notion of a paradigm is ambiguous and confused; that Kuhn has misinterpreted the history of science; that he has inaccurately described what he calls normal science; that the distinction between normal and revolutionary science is not nearly as sharp as he suggests; that his analysis of the paradigm shift makes science into an irrational, subjectivistic, and relativistic discipline, and fails to explain how sciences in fact do progress; that he not only confuses the history of science with the logic of science, but also surreptitiously passes off normative claims about what science ought to be, based on descriptions that do not warrant such norms.[26] I will not attempt the laborious task of evaluating these diverse and conflicting criticisms; but to show the relevance of Kuhn's theses to the social sciences, I will indicate some important problematic areas and the ways Kuhn has attempted to meet his critics' objections.

The first problem concerns the central and elusive concept of paradigm. Much of what Kuhn says depends on the notion of a paradigm: the paradigm's emergence presumably distinguishes science from the pre-paradigmatic school phenomena; it is with reference to a paradigm that normal science is characterized; it is the breakdown of a paradigm that leads to crisis and the triumph of a new paradigm. But a close reading of *The Structure of Scientific Revolutions* indicates just how slippery this concept is, and one commentator has listed at least twenty-two senses in which the term is used in the book.[27] Kuhn has acknowledged his ambiguity and confusion, admitting that "the term 'paradigm' points to the central philosophical aspect of my book but that its treatment there is badly confused."[28]

In the 1969 postscript to *The Structure of Scientific Revolutions,* Kuhn has attempted to clarify this troubling concept—or rather to indicate the ways in which his thinking about paradigms has altered. He now argues for the necessity of "disentangling that concept from the notion of a scientific community" (p. 174), and claims that there are nontrivial empirical techniques for studying the characteristics of scientific communities. He also acknowledges that in the original book "the term paradigm is used in two different senses. On the one hand, it stands for the entire constellation of beliefs, values, techniques, and so on shared by members of a given community. On the other, it denotes one sort of element in that constellation, the concrete puzzle-solutions which, employed as models or examples, can replace explicit rules as a basis for the solution of the remaining puzzles of normal science" (p. 175). He suggests that the transition to maturity in a given scientific discipline is not associated with the *acquisition* of a paradigm.[29] "What changes with the transition to maturity is not the presence of a paradigm but rather its nature. Only after the change is normal puzzle-solving research possible" (p. 179).

But if we can describe a community of scientists by some of the empirical techniques that Kuhn indicates,[30] we may ask what its members share that accounts for the relative fullness of their professional communication and the relative unanimity of their professional judgments. And Kuhn suggests that, instead of referring to a paradigm or a set of paradigms, it is more helpful to use the term "disciplinary matrix": " 'disciplinary' because it refers to the common possession of the practitioners of a particular discipline; 'matrix' because it is composed of ordered elements of various sorts, each requiring further specification" (p. 182). This revision seeks to clarify the elements originally lumped together in the blanket term "paradigm," such as symbolic generalizations, beliefs in particular models, values, exemplars. It is exemplars, or shared examples, that Kuhn claims are "the central element of what I now take to be the most novel and least understood aspect of this book" (p. 187). These exemplars serve normal scientists as models for puzzle solutions.

While these various revisions are helpful in opening up the complexity and components of what were originally called "paradigms," I don't think that Kuhn has made much progress in clarifying a more fundamental ambiguity. What is frequently forgotten or neglected is that a primary aim of his book is to help us understand what is *distinctive* about science, and not only what science shares with other forms of intellectual or artistic endeavor. The notion of a paradigm was introduced precisely to make this distinction. This is why Kuhn's initial characterization of a paradigm—a "universally recognized *scientific* achievement that for a time provides model problems and solutions to a community of practitioners" (italics added)—seems circular (supposedly it is the appeal to paradigms that enables us to distinguish an achievement as scientific), yet at the same time is so vital for his entire project. What he has to say about paradigms, their acceptance, the ways in which they are imposed, their breakdown, and the emergence of new paradigms, is just as true for the history of schools. There are many disciplines such as philosophy—which Kuhn distinguishes from science—where what Kuhn says about science is perfectly applicable.[31] Kuhn himself gently chides those enthusiastic readers of his book who fail to realize that his intention was to bring into focus what is distinctive about science.

Kuhn does not think that there is any single criterion by which we can distinguish science from other disciplines. But even when he attempts to sort out the structure of community life, the disciplinary matrix, and the exemplars, it is troubling to note that there are analogues for all these components in nonscientific disciplines. We can put the issue sharply by asking what it is about paradigms that helps to set off science from other disciplines; or—if we use "paradigm" in its more general sense—what it is about *scientific* paradigms that distinguishes them from other sorts of paradigms. As I will show, the failure of social scientists to discriminate the various senses of "paradigm," and to ask hard questions concerning what, if anything, is distinctive about paradigms in science, has led to much confusion and many conflicting claims.

The second problematic area concerns the type of debate that takes place when a new paradigm is proposed and eventually replaces an older one. Kuhn claims to be shocked by the misunderstanding of so many of his critics, who think that he is advocating some sort of mob rule, or that what is involved is an irrational, subjective decision. Kuhn cannot escape responsibility for such inferences because of his talk of conversion, his insistence that what is involved is *not* proof, and statements such as these: "As in political revolutions, so in paradigm choice—there is no standard higher than the assent of the relevant community" (p. 94); "Like the choice between competing political institutions, that between competing paradigms proves to be a choice between incompatible modes of community life" (p. 94). But Kuhn denies that new paradigms triumph ultimately through some "mystical aesthetic" (p. 158), and insists that arguments are vital in advocating them. "Because scientists are reasonable men, one or another argument will ultimately persuade many of them. But there is no single argument that can or should persuade them all. Rather than a single group experience, what occurs is an increasing shift in the distribution of professional allegiances" (p. 158).

Since Kuhn has been so persistently attacked on this point, he has sought to clarify what he means in his various responses to his critics. His 1969 postscript tells us that in denying that debates over theory choice (or paradigm choice) are matters of proof, he intended to make a simple point.[32] By proof he means logical or mathematical proof. "In the latter, premises and rules of inference are stipulated from the start. If there is disagreement about conclusions, the parties to the ensuing debate can retrace their steps one by one, checking each prior stipulation. At the end of the process one or the other must concede that he has made a mistake, violated a previously accepted rule" (p. 199). But in a scientific revolution, debate does not concern conclusions drawn from agreed-upon premises, but rather the premises themselves. If this is what Kuhn means by proof when he denies that theory choice is a matter of proof, then the point is not only simple but simplistic. One wonders whom he is opposing, for who indeed claims that debates over theory choice involve assessing the validity of deductive arguments?

Debates about theory choice or paradigm choice involve persuasion, but Kuhn sees a significant difference between rational and nonrational persuasion.

Nothing about the relatively familiar thesis [that theory choice is not a matter of proof as characterized above] implies either that there are no good reasons for being persuaded or that those reasons are not ultimately decisive for the group. Nor does it even imply that the reasons for choice are different from those usually listed by philosophers of science: accuracy, simplicity, fruitfulness, and the like. What it should suggest, however, is that such reasons function as values and that they can thus be differently applied, individually and collectively by men who concur in honoring them. If two men disagree, for example, about the relative fruitfulness of their theories or if they agree about that but disagree about the relative importance of fruitfulness and, say, scope in reaching a choice, neither can be convicted of a mistake. Nor is either being unscientific. There is no neutral algorithm for theory-choice, no systematic decision procedure which, properly applied, must lead each individual in the group to the same decision. (pp. 199–200)[33]

If we want to understand the type of rationality involved in disputes about theory choice, then we must understand "the manner in which a particular set of shared values interacts with the particular experiences shared by a community of specialists to ensure that most members of the group will ultimately find one set of arguments rather than another decisive" (p. 200). These considerations also help to qualify and clarify Kuhn's claim that the choice between competing paradigms is a choice between incompatible modes of community life. Kuhn now insists—and claims he always meant—that such incompatibility does not lead to complete mutual incomprehension. There is a breakdown of communication, but such a breakdown is a "partial" one: in such disputes there is a search for common ground on which the advocates of different paradigms can argue with each other.

But Kuhn still insists that the heart of the matter in a paradigm switch is conversion.

The conversion experience that I have likened to a gestalt switch remains, therefore, at the heart of the revolutionary process. Good reasons for choice provide motives for conversion and a climate in which it is more likely to occur. Translation may, in addition, provide points of entry for the neural reprogramming that, however inscrutable at this time, must underlie conversion. But neither good reasons nor translation constitute conversion, and it is that process we must explicate in order to understand an essential sort of scientific change. (p. 204)[34]

Although these modifications help clarify what Kuhn intends—or, as some critics have suggested, indicate how he has changed his mind—he is opening a vast tangle of issues rather than providing a solution. Even if we accept Kuhn's claims that "reasons constitute values to be used in making choices rather than rules of choice,"[35] we still must ask what are and what ought to be the "shared values" that are the basis for making theory choices. In what ways are the "shared values" of the scientific community or communities similar to and different from the "shared values" of other types of community? Talk of "good reasons" rather than "proof" provides little advance in clarification, unless one can specify the standards for distinguishing better and worse reasons. Unless one can make headway in both specifying and answering these questions,

Kuhn's analysis of scientific revolutions is in danger of foundering. Echoing the question that Socrates asks of Euthythro concerning piety, one wants to know whether the "shared values" of the scientific community serve as standards of rationality because these are the *accepted* values, or whether such values are accepted because they *are* the standards of rationality or because they *ought* to be. At times Kuhn seems to be aware of the Pandora's box of problems he is opening. The most sympathetic way of representing his views is to say that, while he does think that the process of a theory choice or paradigm switch is rational, our standard theories of what constitutes rationality are not adequate to illuminate this complex process.

In a curious way, Kuhn is trapped more deeply than he realizes in the very positivism that he battles. When he comes to the conclusion that neither "strict proof" (logical deduction) nor simple verification or falsification is sufficient to account for the choice of theories or paradigms, he seems to be left only with "persuasion"—just as positivists were, when they attempted to characterize moral disputes. But while Kuhn has always *intended* to distinguish rational from irrational persuasion, he has not succeeded in clarifying this vital distinction. I think even he would agree that what is required is a more comprehensive and subtle understanding of rationality, to let us grasp the complex argumentative processes involved in adjudicating among competing paradigms. But he has not pursued the problems in any depth. I do not want to suggest that there are any simple or easy solutions to the issues raised. Many independent lines of inquiry resulting from the work of Popper, Quine, Davidson, Sellars, Feyerabend, Lakatos, Toulmin, and others have focused on clarifying what is involved in theory change and conceptual change, and in what ways this is a rational process. It is also clear that the issues involved extend far beyond an understanding of science, for they affect almost every aspect of contemporary philosophy.[36]

The Use and Abuse of Thomas Kuhn: Truman, Almond, Wolin

WITH this awareness of some of the deep and unresolved issues in Kuhn's "image of science," I can turn to the ways in which his ideas have been taken up by social scientists. I want to show that an insensitivity to the problems that Kuhn's analysis harbors, and an uncritical application of his views, have led to confusion and contradiction. But it should be noted that Kuhn himself has very little to say about the social sciences, partly because he believes that much of what goes under their name exhibits characteristics of the pre-paradigmatic stages of natural sciences. To say even this is misleading, for it suggests that eventually the social sciences will indeed undergo the same type of transformation as the natural sciences. Kuhn tells us:

> To a very great extent the term 'science' is reserved for fields that do progress in obvious ways. Nowhere does this show more clearly than in the recurrent debates about whether one or another of the social sciences is really a science. These debates have parallels in the pre-paradigmatic periods of fields that are today unhesitatingly labeled sciences. (p. 160)

Or again he writes:

> There are many fields—I shall call them proto-sciences—in which practice does generate testable conclusions but which nevertheless resemble philosophy and the arts rather than established sciences in their developmental patterns. I think, for example, of fields like chemistry and electricity before the mid-eighteenth century, of the study of heredity and phylogeny before the mid-nineteenth, or of many of the social sciences today. . . . No more than in philosophy and the arts, do they result in clearcut progress.
>
> I conclude, in short, that the proto-sciences, like the arts and philosophy, lack some element which, in the mature sciences, permits the more obvious forms of progress. . . . I claim no therapy to assist the transformation of a proto-science to a science, nor do I suppose that anything of the sort is to be had. If . . . some social scientists take from me the view that they can improve the status of their field by first legislating agreement on fundamentals and then turning to puzzle solving, they are badly misconstruing my point.[37]

I have already indicated that in their enthusiasm for what they take to be Kuhn's insights, social scientists have applied his central concepts in conflicting and contradictory ways: they have, in fact, used them both to justify and to criticize mainstream social science. Let us first consider the way Kuhn has been used by political scientists David Truman and Gabriel Almond.[38] Soon after the publication of *The Structure of Scientific Revolutions,* each in turn cited Kuhn in his presidential address to the American Political Science Association. Since they present an overview and assessment of the state of political science, both these addresses are good indicators of the self-understanding of mainstream political scientists during the mid-nineteen sixties.

In his 1965 address Truman tells us that Kuhn's notion of a paradigm is particularly suggestive in thinking about the development of contemporary political science, although he declares that "in the formative years of political science in the United States, in the decades around the turn of the century, the field did not have a paradigm, nor has it acquired one since" (p. 866).[39] From the context it appears that the sense of "paradigm" that Truman has in mind is an exemplar or model that guides the development of normal science, setting the standards for precision that "permits an investigator to know when something is wrong, i.e., contrary to what should be expected, and to see the need for a paradigm change" (p. 866).

If we accepted Truman's judgment quite literally, we would expect an inquiry into the basic differences between political science and Kuhn's understanding of science. For despite his qualifications, Kuhn never waivers in his conviction that what distinguishes genuine science from other disciplines is the acceptance of a paradigm by a scientific community, and the role that paradigm plays in guiding normal research. But this is not the line of inquiry that Truman explores. Instead he writes:

I think it is accurate to argue, nevertheless, that something loosely analogous to a paradigm characterized American political science for at least the half-century running from sometime in the 1880's into the 1930's. In order not to distort Kuhn's provocative conception, this should be thought of as simply an implicit though fairly general agreement on what to do and how to proceed in the field. Because the matters in agreement were vague and the terms applicable to them loose and imprecise, they permitted a product diverse in quality and intent. (p. 866)

But this "something" which is "loosely analogous to a paradigm" is so distant from what Kuhn means by a paradigm—even in the twenty-two senses in which he uses the term—that one may wonder whether such talk of paradigms obscures more than it illuminates. The existence of a "fairly general agreement on what to do and how to proceed" characterizes most fields of human endeavor—as Kuhn himself notes; it is just as characteristic of "schools" as of "science." What concerns Kuhn is the *type* of consensus that characterizes scientific communities. Truman's failure to tackle this problem directly blurs the vital issue of whether the consensus that has been or can be achieved in political science is similar to that achieved in various stages of the natural sciences.

What I think most significant about Truman's application of Kuhn's insights is not the analogies that he draws, but the differences that arise from his own analysis. This becomes clear when he explores the developments that led to a breakdown of the prevailing consensus in American political science. For example, he singles out two developments since the Second World War that have contributed to the dissolution of that consensus. "One was the drastically altered character of world politics after

Potsdam" (p. 868). The other has been the "breakup of the colonial system, the emergence of new nations or national entities, and the awakening of older ones, which revealed the inadequacy of a disciplinary posture that was essentially parochial, that took the nature of the political system for granted, and that lacked an adequate and explicit view of political change" (p. 868).

If one seeks loose analogies with Kuhn's understanding of the development of science, we might say that what caused the breakdown in the consensus was the increasing awareness of anomalies. But if we analyze the type of anomaly that Truman indicates, we can see how strikingly different it is from the various anomalies that Kuhn considers. The developments that Truman singles out are not scientific discoveries or a recognition that "nature has somehow violated the paradigm-induced expectation that governs normal science," but a change in the world of politics itself, a change of the political reality. But this suggests a very different relationship between the type of professional consensus that Truman likens to a paradigm, and the political reality it is intended to describe and explain. Such a view comes remarkably close to suggesting that a professional consensus may be only an ideological reflection of a prevailing social or political order, rather than a perspective providing critical insight into the nature and status of this order. And when Truman characterizes and judges the professional consensus that existed in American political science—when he tells us that it represented a disciplinary posture that was "essentially parochial"—he himself is bringing out the ideological and nonscientific character of this paradigm.

Do we have reason to think that political science can overcome this parochialism—that it can make the breakthrough that Kuhn considers essential when science ceases to be a matter of competing schools and achieves the status of normal science? Truman is optimistic, but what is most revealing is his frankness about alternative possibilities. Truman's understanding of the situation in political science—as of 1965, but the situation is much the same in 1976—is that there is "a confusion of competing and divergent, if not incompatible, views of the appropriate questions to be asked and the proper methods to be used" (p. 869). And he tells us that, as a result, political science may be "so uninsulated from its environment that it will have to wait for a broad intellectual and social movement to give it implicit coherence" (p. 869).

But if this is a real possibility, Truman fails to appreciate the extent to which he is denying or at least questioning whether political science can overcome its ideological biases. The issue is not merely the verbal one of whether we want to award the honorific label of "science" to the study of political reality. Rather it involves the relationship between the types of consensus that have been and can be achieved among political scientists, and the "reality" with which they are concerned. Truman does not clarify this issue, but obscures it.

In 1966 Gabriel Almond succeeded Truman as president of the American Political Science Association and enthusiastically applied Kuhnian themes to the history and present state of political science. He organized his address around three assertions:

First, there was a coherent theoretical formulation in the American political theory of the eighteenth and nineteenth centuries.

Second, the development of professional political science in the United States from the turn of the century until well into the 1950's was carried on largely in terms of this paradigm, to use Kuhn's term. The most significant and characteristic theoretical speculation and research during these decades produced anomalous findings which cumulatively shook its validity.

Third, in the last decade or two the elements of a new, more surely scientific paradigm seem to be manifesting themselves rapidly. The core concept of this new approach is that of the political system. (p. 369)[40]

The very way in which Almond formulates his claims should alert us that something is wrong with his application of Kuhn's ideas. Again, the serpent is the slippery concept "paradigm." Clearly, Almond thinks that only now—in the last decade or so—is political science finally becoming a genuine science. If this were true, then what preceded this state of affairs should be a pre-paradigmatic period. Ironically, Almond here endorses the very conception of scientific development that Kuhn attacks. Commenting on historians of science, Kuhn tells us:

The more carefully they study, say Aristotelian dynamics, phlogistic chemistry, or caloric thermodynamics, the more certain they feel that those once current views of nature were, as a whole neither less scientific nor more the product of human idiosyncrasy than those current today. If these out-of-date beliefs are to be called myths, then myths can be produced by the same sorts of methods and held for the same sorts of reasons that now lead to scientific knowledge. If, on the other hand, they are called science, then science has included bodies of belief quite incompatible with the ones we hold today. Given these alternatives, the historian must choose the latter. (p. 2)

What one critic has called Almond's "self-serving misunderstanding of Thomas Kuhn's *The Structure of Scientific Revolutions*"[41] becomes even clearer when Almond argues that "we are becoming a science by inference from changes in the magnitude, structure, age distribution, and intellectual environment of the political science profession" (p. 869).

What follows is a variety of statistics intended to show how rapidly the profession of political science has grown in the United States in an age of "scientific revolution." But it is difficult to see what any of this really establishes, because Almond is speaking about the growth of *profession-alism* and not the growth of *science*.

Much of what he has to say about the growth of professionalism in political science is equally applicable to almost all the academic professions, including philosophy and art history. One may be tempted to think that professionalism is a necessary condition for the existence of science—although an understanding of the history of science would lead us to question this claim—but it certainly is not a sufficient condition for science, nor does it provide any basis for inferring that "we are becoming a science."

Because Almond believes that at the present time political science is "predominantly an American discipline," he gives a brief sketch of the historical background of "political theory in America on the eve of the development of political science as a specialized discipline" (p. 870)—a quick guided tour from the time of the Greeks until the nineteen fifties in America. Almond concludes, "Thus far we have described a sequence much like that presented by Thomas Kuhn in his theory of scientific revolutions" (p. 875).[42] Even Almond seems to be aware that something is not right, for he adds, "If it does not quite fit his model, then we must remember that the social sciences may have a dialectic somewhat different from the physical and biological sciences" (p. 875). But it is difficult to see what—except for terminology—is preserved from Kuhn.[43] Again, what is most significant is the way in which Almond accounts for changes in the development of political theory. They are not the response to an awareness of anomalies revealed through the practice of normal science, but rather a response to changes in politics itself.

There is an even more fundamental issue that Truman and Almond never confront. Like many mainstream social scientists, they are confident that the social sciences will, or even are just about to, reach a stage of scientific maturity. But they fail to realize how misleading the language of "paradigms" and "pre-paradigmatic stages" can be. What is at issue is not only whether political science is or is not in a "pre-paradigmatic" or "paradigmatic" phase, but whether this very way of speaking is appropriate and illuminating. Once we adopt the language of paradigms, we are implicitly assuming that the success or maturity of a discipline is measured by the extent to which it achieves the paradigmatic phase characteristic of the natural sciences. But it is precisely this issue— whether or not this is the standard by which political science, especially in its theoretical aspirations, should be evaluated and judged—that needs to be honestly faced and not begged. If one thinks that political science is in a pre-paradigmatic stage, this suggests that surely a scientific para-digmatic stage must arise if we are patient and work toward it. But there is absolutely no warrant for such an inference on Kuhn's grounds or any others. It is curious how in the hands of Truman and Almond the new talk of paradigms is reminiscent of the old talk of positivism—which Kuhn set out to attack explicitly. Despite the use of Kuhn's terminology, both Truman and Almond share—albeit in a sophisticated form—the old nineteenth-century positivistic belief that intellectual disciplines such as political science pass through a dark ages and only "mature" when the methods of positive science triumph.

Sheldon Wolin makes a very different use of Kuhn in elucidating po-litical theory. Whereas Truman and Almond have appropriated Kuhn to vindicate the behavioral revolution in political science and to show how political science is finally becoming a science,[44] Wolin's primary intention is to criticize the self-understanding of that behavioral revolution and its distorted conception of political theory. Earlier I referred to social scien-tists who have discovered in Kuhn the weapons for a critique of main-stream social science; Wolin is one of them.

Wolin claims that many political scientists have accepted some version of the incremental view of scientific progress. He cites Hans Eulau:

A science of politics which deserves its name must build from the bottom up by asking simple questions that can, in principle, be answered: it cannot be built from the top down by asking questions that, one has reason to suspect, cannot be answered at all, at least not by the methods of science. An em-pirical science is built by slow, modest, and piecemeal cumulation of relevant theories and data. (p. 127)[45]

For the most part, political scientists' "conceptions of science, its meth-ods and its history, have no other basis than some view which they be-lieve to be authoritative. Wanting nothing more than to be allowed to get on with the work of empirical investigation, they are not anxious to engage in disputes concerning the theoretical foundations which support and justify their work" (p. 131). Kuhn's work is challenging, Wolin feels, because it no longer allows us to be content with the overly simplified view of science and its development accepted by so many political scien-tists.

But Kuhn's investigation also provides a new perspective for under-standing the history of political theory itself. Wolin's purpose is "not to argue that political theory is a species of scientific theory, but rather that political theories can best be understood as paradigms and that scientific study of politics is a special form of paradigm-inspired research" (p. 139). It is clear that Wolin is using the concept of paradigm in an extremely broad sense.

When applied to the history of political theory, Kuhn's notion of a paradigm, 'universally recognized scientific developments that for a time provide model problems and solutions to a community of practitioners', invites us to consider Plato, Aristotle, Machiavelli, Hobbes, Locke, and Marx, as the counterparts in political theory to Galileo, Harvey, Newton, Laplace, Faraday, and Einstein. Each of these writers in the first group inspired a new way of looking at the political world; in each case their theories proposed a new definition of what was significant for understanding that world; each specified distinctive methods for inquiry; and each of their theories contained an explicit or implicit statement of what should count as an answer to certain basic questions. (p. 140)

If we use the concept of paradigm in such a generous way, one wonders what has happened to the central Kuhnian problematic of differentiating the development of natural science from that of other disciplines. By a paradigm Wolin means a general orientation, a "new way of looking at things," rather than a specific scientific exemplar or model that is "universally recognized."[46] If we pursue this analogy between Kuhn's understanding of the development of natural science and the history of political theory, what becomes evident is not so much similarities as important differences.

We are told that the theories of the great political philosophers are to be understood as master paradigms. But is there anything comparable to "normal science" in the history of political theory? Wolin suggests that in each case "lesser writers" exploited these master paradigms "in a manner comparable to that of 'normal science' " (p. 141). Wolin views these "paradigm-workers" not as tiresome and repetitious epigone" (p. 142), but rather as underlaborers attempting to apply the master paradigm to "unexpected puzzles." He further claims that there are similarities between the highly efficient enforcement of paradigms in the natural sciences and the enforcement of paradigms in political theory. Yet what he actually shows are fundamental differences in the intent of this enforcement: "By means of his theory the scientist hopes to transform the outlook of the members of the scientific community and to gain the support and power of that community for the application of his theory to the investigation of nature. The aim of many political theorists has been to change society itself: not simply to alter the way men look at the world, but to alter the world" (p. 144). According to Wolin, this impulse is characteristic of Plato, Machiavelli, Hobbes, Rousseau, Bentham, Saint Simon, and Marx.

Wolin also finds other possibilities open to the political theorist to achieve paradigm enforcement. "Today the modern American university offers an even more enticing prospect, for to the natural influence at its disposal there has been added the power of foundations. In concert they provide a powerful mechanism for enforcing paradigms and subsidizing research. Until recently, one vital ingredient has been lacking in political science departments—the paradigm itself" (p. 146)—but the situation has changed dramatically. "The growth of social science and the successful behavioral revolution have supplied the missing element, and there appears to be a convergence between a paradigm, a mechanism of enforcement and ample resources for carrying on paradigm-directed research" (p. 146).

Ironically, Wolin's reading of recent developments in political science converges with that of Almond and Truman. He essentially agrees with them that the behavioral movement "satisfies most of Kuhn's specifications of a successful paradigm." "It has come to dominate the curricula of many political science departments throughout the country; a new generation of students is being taught the new methods of survey analysis, data processing, and scaling; behavioural textbooks are increasing in evidence; and there are even signs that the past is being reinterpreted in order to demonstrate that the revolution is merely the culmination of 'trends' in political science over the past few decades" (p. 147).

But at this point the tension between Wolin's intentions and what he is actually saying becomes acute. If we are faithful to Kuhn's analysis of the development of science and accept the judgment that the behavioral movement "satisfies most of Kuhn's specifications for a successful paradigm," then this development should be welcomed, not deplored. The acceptance of paradigms is essential for normal science: only by working through paradigms can puzzles be solved; only by making paradigms more precise can anomalies be discovered. And normal science is absolutely necessary for scientific development of a discipline.

Furthermore, while Kuhn stresses the importance of the study of the history of science in order to gain a proper "image of science," such a study is not important for a practicing normal scientist, and may even distract him from his work of puzzle-solving. What Wolin fails to realize is that pressing the analogy between the development of political theory and Kuhn's understanding of natural science has the consequence, not of justifying serious study of the history of political theory, but of undermining it. There is no necessity for the practicing normal scientist qua scientist—or even for the extraordinary scientist—to study the history of his discipline. The normal scientist's historical sense need not extend any further than the paradigm within which he operates.[47] And even the extraordinary scientist is primarily concerned with the development of a new paradigm that can account for existing anomalies. In times of scientific crisis, when there is a "willingness to try anything," a fresh look at the history of the discipline *may* help the revolutionary scientist, but it is neither a necessary nor a sufficient condition for coming up with a new paradigm.

Furthermore, when Wolin characterizes the types of crisis to which the great political theorists have responded, he also stresses the differences between these and those which generate extraordinary natural science.

> Many of the great theories of the past arose in response to a crisis in the world, not in the community of theorists. It was not a methodological breakdown that prompted Plato to commit himself to the *bios theoretikos* and to produce the first great paradigm in Western political thought; it was instead the breakdown of the Athenian *polis*. Again, it was not a simple desire to replace theological with Aristotelian methods that led to *Defensor Pacis,* but a continuing crisis in the relations of church and state. There is no need to multiply instances; the paradigms of Machiavelli, Bodin, Harrington, Hobbes, Locke, Toqueville, and Marx were produced by a profound belief that the world had become deranged. (pp. 147–48)

But while Wolin notes this crucial difference, he does not explore its consequences.

I am suggesting that there is a hidden logic in Wolin's line of argument which, when taken literally, undermines what he intends to demonstrate. If behaviorism represents a new universally recognized scientific paradigm, then the moral to be drawn is the one that Almond and Truman draw: the task now is to get on with empirical puzzle-solving and specification of the new paradigm—the only way in which a science can develop the precision required for the discovery of anomalies. Something, then, seems to have gone wrong. To leave the matter here would be a parody of what Wolin *intends* to say, yet I think it important to see the consequences of pressing the analogy between political theory and Kuhn's understanding of the development of natural science.[48]

It is at this point in his analysis—almost at the close of his essay—that Wolin "amends" Kuhn's concept of a paradigm. But when we appreciate the full ramifications of this emendation, we will see that it radically transforms our understanding of "paradigms" in the sciences of society and politics, and brings out striking differences from anything in the natural sciences. We will see too how many lines of argument explored in Part II come together here.

Political Society as a Moral Paradigm

WOLIN proposes that we not only think of the grand theories of classical political theorists as paradigms, but that "we conceive of *political society* itself as a paradigm of an operative kind" (italics added).

From this viewpoint society would be envisaged as a coherent whole in the sense of its customary political practices, institutions, laws, structure of authority and citizenship, and operative beliefs being organised and interrelated. A poltically organised society contains definite institutional arrangements, certain widely shared understandings regarding the location and use of political power, certain expectations about how authority ought to treat the members of society and about the claims that organised society can righfully make upon its members. . . . This *ensemble* of practices and beliefs may be said to form a paradigm in the sense that the society tries to carry on its political life in accordance with them. Further, in its agencies of enforcement and in its systems of rules, a political society possesses the basic instrumentalities present in Kuhn's scientific community and employs them in analogous ways. Society, too, enforces certain types of conduct and discourages others; it, too, defines what sorts of experiments—in the form of individual or group actions —will be encouraged, tolerated, or suppressed; by its complex organisation of politics through legislatures, political parties, and the media of opinion, society also determines what shall count in determining future decisions. (p. 149)

If we continue to use the language of "paradigms"—and the term's use in so many loose, ambiguous, and conflicting ways suggests that we might well avoid it—then it is important to stress how different this conception of "paradigm" is from anything that Kuhn discusses.[49] In speaking of political society itself as a paradigm, Wolin is not speaking of the theoretical activity of the political theorist, but of the political reality that he studies. And in singling out the importance of practices and institutions, expectations and beliefs, he is noting some of the distinguishing features of this political reality. Wolin's point is similar to the one that Winch makes when he says, "Whereas in the case of the natural scientist we have to deal with only one set of rules, namely those governing the scientist's investigation itself, here what the sociologist is studying, as well as his study of it, is a human activity and is therefore carried on according to rules."[50] It is also similar to the point that Louch makes when he attempts to explain in what sense disciplines like economics can be construed as moral disciplines. Louch even uses the language of "paradigms."

> We expect a man to behave in certain ways in economic situations, not because it is inevitable that he do so, but because, if he didn't, we would think of him as a poor business man or a lunatic. Profit-seeking is not a causal law, but a paradigm of activity in specialized situations. Persons entering into such situations are expected to match the paradigm if they can, because that is the thing to do. But it does not disrupt the place of the paradigm to discover, even most of the time, that economic behaviour does not quite match up to it. As a causal law, profit-seeking would entitle us to infer the future behaviour of economic agents; if discrepancies turn up, so much the worse for the law. But as a rule of practice, we are entitled rather to moral expectations; when discrepancies turn up, so much the worse for the merchant.[51]

Alan Ryan has also noted how different the role of paradigms is in the human sciences. He helps to bring out a further consequence implicit in Wolin and explicit in Louch; that such political and social paradigms are *moral* paradigms. They are moral paradigms in the sense that they contain beliefs and expectations about what is correct, appropriate, or "rational" behavior. "It is important not to be confused over this; they do not commit us to any particular moral or political evaluation. But, again, in the manner [of] the natural science paradigm, they do define the range of *possible* moral arguments, and define what *sort* of puzzle a particular moral puzzle is."[52]

In this sense, then, the very reality with which we are concerned in the human sciences is itself value-constituted, not an indifferent value-neutral brute reality. And it is precisely this insight that clarifies the basis of Wolin's criticism of behavioral studies. For it is not the case, as so many behavioral scientists profess, that they are seeking to match or test empirical claims against a political reality which is *itself* "objective" and "value-neutral." Rather, says Wolin, "the most striking characteristic among the numerous studies on voting, community power, political participation, and decision-making is their acceptance of the prevailing political paradigm as the frame of reference and as the source of research problems" (p. 151). While the dominant paradigm of political society does not dictate the methods of inquiry by which it is to be investigated, "it does set limits around what is to be considered useful inquiry" (p. 152).[53]

Wolin characterizes the difference between behavioral "theory" and traditional theory as resembling that between normal and extraordinary science—although here, too, the analogy is remote from anything that Kuhn intends. Wolin stresses that behavioral studies are wedded to the dominant political paradigm that now exists, while "traditional theory is preoccupied with possible rather than actual worlds and, as a consequence, it jeopardizes rather than repairs the regnant paradigm" (p. 152). At the heart of Wolin's indictment of behavioral theory or the behavioral paradigm is the ease with which it embraces and reflects a deranged world. A "theory corresponding to a sick world would itself be a form of sickness" (p. 148).[54]

Let us stand back and ask what the infatuation with Kuhn's work by social scientists and theorists has taught us. Does Kuhn's "image of science" help to gain a more perspicuous understanding of social and political studies? The initial answer must be no, nor does Kuhn himself ever claim that it does. There are two main reasons why the use of Kuhn by social scientists is unhelpful. First, Kuhn's theses are most ambiguous and unsatisfactory precisely where one most needs illumination. Kuhn does not help to distinguish scientific paradigms from ideological paradigms—a fundamental point ignored by those who are so eager to see Kuhn's relevance to social and political studies. Secondly, when social scientists get down to showing the relevance of Kuhn, what actually emerges are the significant nonanalogies between the natural sciences and social and political studies. This is just as true for Truman and Almond as it is for Wolin. All three indicate that the anomalies that effect a change in these studies result from changes in the world of politics, and not from factual or theoretical discoveries that nature violates what we have come to expect in normal research. Therefore what is so vital and essential to the development of natural science—a tradition of normal science—may be disastrous in political and social studies. The success of a paradigm in explaining and predicting human behavior may result from men's acceptance of rigid normative constraints about what is rational and acceptable behavior.[55]

Kuhn's work, together with other postempiricist theories about the nature of science, does help to overthrow the simplistic picture of science that has been accepted by many empirically minded social scientists. These investigations have taught us how vital and central the role of theory is for any scientific discipline. And they have also shown that even the logical empiricists' concept of scientific theory as consisting of hypothetical-deductive systems is far too narrow and misleading to account for the varied functions of theory in science. In this respect the attempt to press the analogy between the social sciences and Kuhn's image of the natural sciences has the paradoxical but extremely important consequence of making us more alert to important differences.

Nothing I have said is intended as an attack on the legitimate scientific status of political and social studies. On the contrary, we are now in a position to see how competing claims about these disciplines can be reconciled. One common theme in Berlin, Louch, Winch, Ryan, and Wolin is that social and political reality constitutes a complex inter- locking set of institutions, practices, rules, and forms of life. This is what Wolin means when he suggests that political society itself can be con- ceived of as a "paradigm of an operative kind." It is what Ryan empha- sizes when he tells us that such paradigms are "moral paradigms" in- volving the acceptance of norms of behavior and action by political agents. But these forms of life and practices *do* exhibit regularities and systematic interrelationships. In studying these regularities, we can use a variety of empirical and quantitative techniques successfully employed in the natural sciences. The basic conviction by empirical social scientists that this is *now* being done reinforces their belief that "we are becoming a science."

But by now we should see how the primary issue has to be concep- tually relocated. The issue is not whether it is possible to employ em- pirical and quantitative techniques, but rather how to interpret the results. There has been an overwhelming tendency in mainstream social science toward reification, toward mistaking historically conditioned social and political patterns for an unchangeable brute reality which is simply "out there" to be confronted. In the eagerness to build a new natural science of human beings, there has been a tendency to generalize from regularities of a regnant moral paradigm, and to claim we are discovering universal laws that govern human beings. The most serious defect in this endeavor is not simply unwarranted generalizations, but the hidden ideological bases. There has been a lack of critical self-consciousness among main- stream social scientists that the admonition to be "realistic," to study the way things are, is not so much a scientific imperative as a dubious moral imperative that has pernicious consequences in limiting human imagina- tion and political and social possibilities. Scientism in social and political studies has become a powerful albeit disguised ideology.[56]

Ideology and Objectivity

AT the beginning of Part I, I cited a passage from Alan Ryan in which he emphasizes "two major and potent anxieties" that have played an important part in the so-called behavioral revolution in politi- cal science: the fear of "hyperfactualism," and the fear that political scientists might be taken for political ideologists. The cure for both was to be the creation of an organized body of empirical explanatory theory. Ryan's point can be generalized, for it is applicable to the entire range of the social sciences. But now we can frankly ask whether the cure has been successful. Is there any hard evidence that the creation of empirical explanatory theories has overcome these potent anxieties? The answer—for two primary reasons—is a definitive no. First, despite virtual unanimity among mainstream social scientists about the epistemological and methodological requirements of empirical explanatory theory, no "organized body" of such theory exists. Despite all the talk about such theory, if we are as tough-minded in assessing the results of their investigations as empirical social scientists keep telling us to be, we find no theories that satisfy the stringent standards which *they* advocate as essential.

Secondly—a point that emerges with greater clarity in this part—there are serious questions about whether the so-called empirical theories of social scientists escape ideological bias. Since the expression "ideology" has been used so loosely, it is important to pin down the claim that "empirical theories" are ideological. First, one must stress that the explicit intention of those who advance such theories is to give an objective and value-neutral account of the "facts," not to pass off their value judgments as factual descriptions. Furthermore, by virtue of the belief that they are simply doing good empirical science, social scientists give a false legitimacy to claims that are not merely empirical and scientific. The critique of empirical theory as ideology seeks to reveal these hidden and dubious value biases.

In using the concepts of ideology and ideological mystification, I have relied upon the context to convey my meaning. I can now pin down what I mean by ideology and the critique of ideology. My understanding of these concepts is based upon Marx and Hegel. But since there are varying and conflicting interpretations of what Marx and Hegel meant, let me specify what I take to be the basic characteristics of the concept and critique of ideology.

First, by "ideology" I do *not* mean what is frequently meant in the common or vulgar sense of this term. An ideology is not any set of moral, social, or political beliefs and attitudes that informs and shapes an individual's (or a class's) interpretation of the world and his behavior. I reject this excessively liberal conception of ideology because of its hidden relativism and nihilism. It suggests—and many think this is entailed by the concept of ideology—that all "belief-systems" ultimately have the same epistemological status, that all are equally unjustifiable. According to this view, when we criticize a given ideology, we are presupposing another ideological stance that we do not question. This permissive use of the concept of ideology obscures the fact that ideologies are based upon beliefs and interpretations which purport to be true or valid. These beliefs and interpretations are consequently subject to rational criticism.

Second, an ideology is not an epiphenomenal "reflex" that arises mechanically in response to the dynamics of a material substructure. I reject this view of ideology because (1) it ignores the complex ways in which the form and content of an ideology are shaped by a variety of historical factors (and are never merely a mechanical response to an underlying material substratum); (2) it ignores the efficacy of ideology in shaping the ways in which men interpret the world and understand their own actions and those of others; (3) it has the consequence of placing ideology beyond criticism. If ideology is understood as a reflex only to a material substratum, then it makes no sense to speak of the falsity of an ideology. It is sometimes thought that this "reflex" theory of ideology is Marx's view. But it is difficult to think of a more horrendous distortion of Marx's understanding of ideology. According to Marx, an ideology must be deciphered, must be critically understood. This means that we must understand how it both *reflects* and *distorts* the historical material conditions of social life, and grasp what factors influence and sustain the acceptance of an ideology.

Further, the *power* of ideologies is related to the way in which they are used to justify and legitimize actions. Those who accept an ideology do not think of it as arbitrary or unwarranted. On the contrary, they claim their ideological interpretation is valid. They think of it as "self-evident," "what any rational man will hold," "realistic," "based on what human nature is," or—more recently—"what science tells us." In each case an ideology is being used to determine what counts as "realistic" action, and to define the limits of "rational" choice.

The critique of ideology has several interrelated functions: (1) It must describe and accurately characterize the ideology, and be wary of caricature. (2) It seeks a depth interpretation of the ideology which will at once reveal how the ideology reflects and distorts an underlying social and political reality. (3) It seeks to discover the material and psychological factors that reinforce and sustain it. (4) It seeks to isolate the fundamental beliefs and interpretations that are the basis of the ideology, and to criticize them in order to expose their falsity. (5) It seeks to dissolve the legitimizing power of ideologies by overcoming resistance in the ideologies' defenders.

The concept of ideology or "false consciousness" is reciprocally related to the concept of a nonideological understanding or a "true consciousness." I do not think that there are any fixed criteria by which we can, once and for all, distinguish "false consciousness" from "true consciousness." The *achievement* of "true consciousness" is a regulative ideal of the critique of ideology, and the relation between "false consciousness" and "true consciousness" is asymmetrical. This does not mean that we must remain intellectually agnostic, that we are never in a position to evaluate and judge the ways in which an ideology is systematically distortive and reflects reified powers of domination. On the contrary, since every ideology is based on beliefs and interpretations that make the claim to validity, we can examine these claims to validity and show their falsity. We can show the falsity of an ideology without claiming that we have achieved a final, absolute, "true" understanding of social and political reality.[57]

The investigations of Berlin, Louch, Winch, Wolin, and Ryan contribute to exposing ideological biases. But the issue has been attacked more directly. The critical literature showing the variety of ways in which so-called objective and value-neutral research is ideological is extensive, but one of the most succinct and acute analyses is Charles Taylor's "Neutrality in Political Science." It is not just an accident that value biases have been confused with factual descriptions; Taylor's critique shows that the "connection between the factual base and the valuation is built-in, as it were, to the conceptual structure" of these theories.[58] To be sure, mainstream social scientists admit that social scientists are fallible and frequently do confuse factual descriptions with value judgments, but they believe that—in a manner argued by Nagel—these appraising value judgments will be purged as the social sciences achieve greater maturity. But when we actually examine the prominent candidates for empirical theory in political science and sociology, we find we cannot adopt the theoretical framework and neatly isolate the value judgments implied by it. For the "adoption of a framework of explanation carries with it the adoption of the 'value slope' implicit in it."[59]

Taylor illustrates this value bias in the work of Lipset, Almond, and Laswell.

We can say that a given explanatory framework secretes a notion of good, and a set of valuations, which cannot be done away with—though they can be over-ridden—unless we do away with the framework. Of course, because the values can be over-ridden, we can only say that the framework tends to support them, not that it establishes their validity. But this is enough to show that the neutrality of the findings of political science is not what it was thought to be. For establishing a given framework restricts the range of value positions which can be defensively adopted. For in light of the framework certain goods can be accepted as such without further argument, whereas other rival ones cannot be adopted without adducing over-riding considerations. The framework can be said to distribute the onus or argument in a certain way. It is thus not neutral.

The only way to avoid this while doing political science would be to stick to the narrow-gauge discoveries which, just because they are, taken alone, compatible with a great number of political frameworks, can bathe in an atmosphere of value neutrality. That Catholics in Detroit tend to vote Democrat can consort with almost anyone's conceptual scheme, and thus with almost anyone's set of political values. But to the extent that political science cannot dispense with the theory, with the search for a framework, to that extent it cannot stop developing normative theory.[60]

Taylor's conclusion about the role of theory in political science is also supported by Alasdair MacIntyre in his article, "Is a Science of Comparative Politics Possible?" After showing the empty pretentiousness as well as the distortions of the empirical theory of comparative politics, MacIntyre compares this work with the argument about justice in the *Republic*. He concludes that "Lipset and Bierstedt are thereby taking sides in an ancient philosophical argument: is it important for the ruler to be just, or is it only important for him to be thought to be just? What Lipset and Bierstedt do in defining legitmacy is not unlike what Thrasymachus did in defining justice and what Glaucon and Adeimantus did in developing Thrasymachus' case. We may now recall that Thrasymachus too claimed to be merely reporting how the world went, to be a neutral and value-free observer."[61]

Quentin Skinner, who reviews the controversy over the empirical theory of democracy and takes some of its critics to task, nevertheless concludes that even Robert Dahl's sophisticated theory of democracy is ideological. The very "application of the term *democracy* to the type of political system Dahl describes constitutes an act of political conservatism: it serves to commend the recently prevailing values and practices of a political system like that of the United States, and it constitutes a form of argument against those who have sought to question the democratic character of those values and practices."[62] What is characteristic of the way in which Taylor, MacIntyre, and Skinner attack the ideological biases of mainstream social science—especially so-called empirical explanatory theories in political science—is that each attempts to show how these biases are built into the very language and concepts employed. Here too we see a confirmation of one of the central points in Berlin's essay "Does Political Theory Still Exist?" Berlin suggested there that it is precisely because our linguistic practices and concepts are so deeply embedded in the ways we think and act that we are frequently blind to their powerful influence. A central task of the theorist is to make these prevailing concepts and models explicit; he must achieve the type of self-consciousness which not only clarifies these concepts and linguistic practices, but subjects them to critical evaluation.

It is sometimes thought by mainstream social scientists that arguments challenging the value-neutrality of their orientation are an attack on the very ideal of objectivity essential to responsible intellectual inquiry. But this is not what is at issue. One can be right or wrong about divorce rates, birth rates, the number of persons who vote in an election, etc., although seemingly straightforward empirical claims—even about such "hard" facts as crime and suicide—may prove dubious because they involve conceptual decisions about what counts as an instance of the phenomenon studied. It is essential to make a sharp distinction between "objectivity" and "objectivism." If by "objectivity" we mean that in any domain of human inquiry—whether physical phenomena, or an existing political system, or even the interpretation of a text—there are intersubjective standards of rationality or norms of inquiry by which we attempt to distinguish personal bias, superstition, or false beliefs from objective claims, then adherence to such an ideal of objectivity governs any systematic inquiry.

This does not mean, however, that there is a simple or direct way of stating the norms of the appropriate inquiry, or that there cannot be significant disagreement about these norms and their application, or even whether what counts as objective in one domain of inquiry can do so in another. The attempt to specify a single univocal set of criteria as a basis for distinguishing what is genuinely objective from what is not, has been one of the most obsessive and futile preoccupations of modern thinkers since Descartes. But we are not therefore obliged—as it is often claimed —to retreat to skepticism, self-defeating relativism, or irrational subjectivism. The lesson to be learned, rather, is how difficult and complex it is to articulate the standards of objectivity relevant to different domains of inquiry, and the ways in which these standards are themselves open to criticism. Furthermore—and this is perhaps the most important point— the very standards of objectivity and rationality themselves depend on the existence of communities of inquirers who are able, willing, and committed to engage in argumentation.

But "objectivism" is a substantive orientation that believes that in the final analysis there is a realm of basic, uninterpreted, hard facts that serves as the foundation for all empirical knowledge. The appeal to these "facts" presumably legitimizes empirical claims about the world. "Objectivism"—a doctrine which in its primitive or sophisticated forms is shared by many mainstream social scientists—turns out to coincide with the "myth of the given" which has been so devastatingly criticized by contemporary philosophers.[63] "Objectivism" in the study of social and political life is not an innocent mistaken epistemological doctrine. It has dangerous consequences insofar as it tends to distort and reify "facts" which are historically conditioned—"facts" which reveal only one among the many different possibilities that human action may take.[64]

Conclusion: The Convergence of Critiques of Mainstream Social Science

THROUGHOUT this part I have been attempting to demonstrate the power and coherence in seemingly varied critiques of mainstream social science by Anglo-Saxon thinkers. Initially, it seemed a consequence of logical positivism and the ordinary language revolution in analytic philosophy, that these movements undermined the very possibility of substantive political and social theory. At best, observers thought that philosophic analysis might help to clear up conceptual confusions. But gradually it was perceived that analytic philosophy, especially the type of investigations carried on by Wittgenstein and J. L. Austin, had an enormous potential for elucidating the concept of human action, and the ways in which we describe and explain such action. Indeed, a dialectical extreme was adopted. It was argued that the "linguistic turn" in philosophy could be used to show the conceptual or logical impossibility of a social science modeled on the natural sciences. The preoccupation—one is inclined to say the obsession—with advancing and knocking down "impossibility" arguments has obscured the real contribution of linguistic analyses. What has been emerging more recently, as illustrated by the work of Charles Taylor, MacIntyre, Pitkin, Ryan, and many others, is a more moderate but more penetrating orientation. None of them set out to "prove" the impossibility or worthlessness of empirical studies in the social sciences. But all of them have helped us to see how limiting and constraining are the framework assumptions of mainstream social science. Their work, and the new intellectual orientation that it represents, are not merely negative.

These thinkers have contributed to the creation of a new universe of discourse where we are much more profoundly aware of the complex ways in which linguistic practices, concepts, and institutions shape political and social reality. The new universe of discourse and sensibility that is emerging requires that we become increasingly aware that human beings are *self-interpreting* creatures, and that these interpretations are constitutive of what we are as human beings. At the heart of their critique is an attack on the categorial foundations of mainstream social science and the picture of human agents it projects.

Charles Taylor, whose work illustrates this new sensibility, articulates this when he writes: "It is not just that people in our society all or mostly have a given set of ideas in their heads and subscribe to a given set of goals. The meanings and norms implicit in these practices are not just in the minds of the actors but are out there in the practices themselves, practices which cannot be conceived as a set of individual actions, but are essentially modes of social relation, of mutual action."[65] Like many of the other thinkers examined, Taylor challenges the categorial distinction that runs so deep in mainstream social science: that phenomena must be either classified as objective—"out there," and consequently in the category of the observable—or lumped together as beliefs, attitudes, and opinions which are "merely" subjective and private. On the contrary;

The situation we have here is one in which the vocabulary of a given social dimension is grounded in the shape of social practice in this dimension; that is, the vocabulary wouldn't make sense, couldn't be applied sensibly, where this range of practices didn't prevail. And yet this range of practices couldn't exist without the prevalence of this or some related vocabulary. There is no simple one-way dependence here. We can speak of mutual dependence if we like, but really what this points up is the artificiality of the distinction between social reality and the language of description of that social reality. The language is constitutive of the reality, is essential to its being the kind of reality it is.[66]

We have now come full circle. Taylor phrases in the new linguistic mode the central point of Berlin's essay with which we started. Many lines of development converge here. From the philosophy of language we have learned to appreciate how language is embedded in practices and shaped by intersubjective constitutive rules and distinctions. From the theory of action we have learned that a proper analysis of human action involves references to those social practices and forms of life in which actions can be described and explained. From the analysis of social and political reality, we have come to see how this reality itself consists of practices and institutions that depend on the acceptance of norms about what is reasonable and acceptable behavior. From the postempiricist philosophy and history of science, we have learned how misleading and simplistic the empiricist theories of science are, and how central are interpretation and understanding even in the hard natural sciences.

Once the limiting perspective of mainstream social science has been challenged and the biases at its foundation exposed, new questions and problems emerge. These cluster about the interpretation and understanding of political and social reality. How are we to engage in this activity? What is the relevance of empirical studies of regularities and correlations to the interpretative process? Looming in the background is the central question of how one can rationally adjudicate among competing and conflicting interpretations. We have reached the threshold of these questions. There are illuminating hints and suggestions about how they may be further specified and answered. But we do not find in the work of Anglo-Saxon thinkers a systematic attempt to probe them and to carry us further in the restructuring of social and political theory. It is not surprising, however, that among thinkers trained in Anglo-Saxon intellectual traditions, there has been a growing interest in hermeneutics and phenomenology. As we shall see in Part III, the analysis of intersubjectivity, and the understanding of theory as an interpretative process, have been at the very center of phenomenological investigations of social and political reality.

Part III

The Phenomenological Alternative

I T is increasingly evident that in order to gain a critical understanding of the social and political disciplines, we must face not only epistemological but metaphysical issues. Before examining the phenomenological critique of the naturalistic interpretation of the social and political disciplines, I want to reflect on some of the global philosophic problems that confront us. Specifically, I want to sketch two competing pictures of man-in-the-world which have been, and continue to be, fundamental to our view of individuals. After exploring the clash of these images, I will consider two very different attempts to reconcile or join them—attempts to achieve a genuine synthesis or synoptic vision which does justice to the truth implicit in this dialectical opposition. These are the syntheses proposed and explored independently by two philosophers: Wilfrid Sellars, an American, and Edmund Husserl, a German. This will then serve as a basis for a more detailed examination of Alfred Schutz's phenomenological investigation into the foundations of social reality.

Admittedly, there is something artificial in contrasting the views of Sellars and Husserl. They are not contemporaries, and consequently have not directly encountered or argued with each other. But Sellars has been one of the most ambitious analytic philosophers. He has sought to integrate the various strains of analytic thought—and the history of philosophy, too—in order to develop a synoptic vision of man-in-the-world. He has systematically articulated a subtle and sophisticated version of scientific realism—a type of naturalism that attempts to meet the objections of its critics. While few mainstream social scientists have been concerned with basic philosophic issues, Sellars' synoptic vision constitutes a powerful and persuasive statement of the naturalism that lies at the heart of so much contemporary thinking about the sciences.

On the other hand, if Husserl wrote before logical empiricism and analytic philosophy had reshaped contemporary thought, he nevertheless had a penetrating insight into the foundations and direction of modern naturalism. He sought to focus on these foundations and subject them to radical criticism. Therefore a confrontation between him and Sellars can help clarify two of the major visions of man-in-the-world that have shaped contemporary thought, and that are reflected in opposing conceptions of the proper study of human beings.

The Scientific versus the Manifest Image of Man

Implicit in the modern scientific tradition has been an ideal based on the conception of human beings as complex physical systems differing in degree, but not in kind, from the rest of nature. If, then, we are really to understand what human beings are, our primary task is to explain how this complex system works. Though not necessarily wedded to outdated and simplistic concepts of materialistic mechanism, this view holds that whatever concepts and categories ultimately describe and explain the physical world will also describe and explain what human beings are. There are no gaps or breaks in nature; science and science alone tells us what really exists.

Defenders of this concept frequently admit that we may be at a far more primitive stage of scientific development than has been realized; that the obstacles in the way of comprehensive scientific knowledge may be greater than we imagine. But our primary task as serious inquirers is to make whatever contribution we can toward such an ideal comprehensive scientific theory. This is an ideal accepted and advocated not only by many natural and social scientists, but by philosophers, too, including some who have reasserted it with renewed sophistication in our own time.[1]

Any adequate history of modern philosophy and science would also have to examine the ways in which this conception has been opposed and criticized. When such a scientific materialism or reductionism is pressed to its limits, it has called forth its dialectical antithesis. Opponents claim that it involves the grossest distortion of the human condition, and of what is most basic for the understanding of it. In our time this dialectic has involved a revolution against the reductionism and physicalism so characteristic of early logical positivism and logical atomism.[2] In different ways the later Wittgenstein, Austin, Ryle, Strawson, and many others have attempted to show how the understanding of man as a complex physical system is topsy-turvy—an inversion that results from being caught in the grips of scientism. P. F. Strawson gives an emphatic statement of the alternative to this scientific image:

There is a massive central core of human thinking which has no history—or none recorded in the histories of thought; there are categories and concepts which, in their most fundamental character, change not at all. . . . They are commonplaces of the least refined thinking; and are yet the indispensable core of the conceptual equipment of the most sophisticated human beings. It is with these, their interconnections, and the structure that they form, that a descriptive metaphysics will be primarily concerned.[3]

From Strawson's point of view it makes no sense to speak of this "central core" as being replaced or displaced by a "more adequate" scientific account of man, for science—like any "conceptual equipment of man"—presupposes this core.

It is also important to appreciate the various ways in which these competing perspectives on human beings—and their understanding of the tasks of philosophy—have attempted to account for each other. Using the terminology of Wilfrid Sellars, who characterizes these two "ideal types" as the scientific image of man-in-the-world and the manifest image of man-in-the-world,[4] we can ask how the scientific image accounts for the manifest image. It is sometimes argued that the manifest image is only a realm of "appearance" and "opinion"; that if we want to understand man, only science can provide the answers. Or it may be argued that what is required is a *grounding* of the manifest image by explaining it through more fundamental scientific principles. But whatever option is taken, the basic conviction remains that science alone is the measure of reality, and the standard for assessing legitimate knowledge of what human beings are.

From the perspective of the manifest image—or more precisely, of those who endorse it—there are also several options open to explain the scientific image of man, the most common being an instrumental interpretation. But whatever account they give of science, those who endorse the manifest image remain firm in their conviction that it makes no sense, or is "conceptually impossible," to think that a scientific understanding of man can threaten the manifest image. Why? Because ultimately science as a conceptual activity presupposes those categories and concepts that are the indispensable core of *any* conceptual thought.

Sellars indicates that the manifest image is important because "it defines one of the poles to which philosophical reflection has been drawn."[5] Not only have the great speculative systems of ancient and medieval philosophy been built around the manifest image, but in our own time the careful analysis and description of that image have been central for both Anglo-Saxon conceptual analysts and many continental phenomenologists. Thus, although the language and primary concerns of a philosopher like Merleau-Ponty are very different from those of Strawson, Merleau-Ponty has given forceful expression to what he takes to be the derivative status of science.

The whole universe of science is built upon the world as directly experienced, and if we want to subject science itself to rigorous scrutiny and arrive at a precise assessment of its meaning and scope, we must begin by reawakening the basic experience of the world of which science is the second-order expression. Science has not and never will have, by its very nature, the same significance *qua* form of being as the world which we perceive, for the simple reason that it is a rationale or explanation of that world. . . . Scientific points of view, according to which my existence is a moment of the world's, are always both naïve and at the same time dishonest, because they take for granted, without explicitly mentioning it, the other point of view, namely that of consciousness, through which from the outset a world forms itself round me and begins to exist for me.[6]

Now it may be thought that there is some straightforward way of reconciling the competing claims of these two images. After all, science can help us to understand what human beings are, and while this might be supplemented by a careful articulation and description of the manifest image, are not these just two different perspectives on, or aspects of, the *same* human reality? But such a happy synthesis, which suggests we need both images and do not have to choose between them, fails to take seriously the claim of each "to constitute *the* true and, in principle, *complete* account of man-in-the-world."[7] Each asserts that it can account for the other. Each makes the claim of completeness, and purports to represent the fundamental ontological stance from which the other must be seen as derivative.

Thus those who endorse the scientific image maintain that science will provide not a partial but a complete account which can in principle, if not yet in fact, explain even the "indispensable core" of human concepts, by showing how they are based on more fundamental scientific principles. And those who endorse the manifest image declare not just that a scientific account of man is incomplete, but that, if we "subject science itself to rigorous scrutiny," we will see in it a second-order discipline based on a more fundamental understanding of man-in-the-world.

These competing images of man-in-the-world, and the competing intellectual orientations behind them, have substantial consequences for the sciences of human life. If we are convinced that man is nothing but a complex physical system, or that it is best to operate with this assumption, then we will look to science as the only proper means for explaining how this system works. We will look upon the successes of scientific development as gradually revealing these truths to us, and on its failures as only temporary. But if we are convinced that "scientific points of view . . . are always both naïve and at the same time dishonest," then we must use some other approach to understand what human beings are. We will read the history of failures in the sciences of human life—sciences shaped in the image of the natural sciences—as indicating deep conceptual or categorial confusions. Such an "ideal" scientific theory is necessarily doomed to failure.

Can the clash between these two images be reconciled? Can the claim of each be understood in a way that does justice to both, and avoids the distortions that result when we view one through the spectacles of the other? Is there a perspective from which we can gain a synoptic vision of both? Sellars and Husserl answer these questions in the affirmative, though the answers they give are quite different—at crucial points, indeed, incompatible.

The Synoptic Vision of Wilfrid Sellars

I want first to specify more precisely what Sellars means by the manifest and scientific images of man-in-the-world, in order to indicate how he conceives of their clash and their ultimate resolution. Sellars realizes that in speaking of two images he is speaking of "ideal types" or constructs (p. 5), therefore of "fictions" (p. 7), although they are heuristic or methodological fictions used to clarify two contrasting poles in philosophy. In calling them "images" he tells us that he does "not mean to deny to either or both of them the status of 'reality.' I am, to use Husserl's term, 'bracketing' them, transforming them from ways of experiencing the world into objects of philosophical reflection and evaluation" (p. 5).

The manifest image can be characterized in two complementary ways. It is "the framework in terms of which man came to be aware of himself as man-in-the-world. It is the framework in terms of which, to use an existentialist turn of phrase, man first encountered himself—which is, of course, when he came to be a man" (p. 6). But he makes a stronger claim: man is *essentially* a being who thinks of himself in the framework of the manifest image; consequently, if "this image, insofar as it pertains to man, is a 'false' image, this falsity threatens man himself, inasmuch as he is, in an important sense, the being which has this image of himself" (p. 18). It is a mistake to think that such an image is one that arose only in the prehistory of man or that it is even a "pre-scientific, uncritical, naive conception of man-in-the-world" (p. 6). What Sellars means by the manifest image can best be understood as a "refinement or sophistication of what might be called the 'original' image" (p. 6) of man-in-the-world. The manifest image involves both *empirical* and *categorial* refinement.

By empirical refinement, Sellars means the refinement obtained through the use of techniques for discerning and establishing correlations. Consequently the manifest image is itself, in an appropriate sense, a "scientific image." "It is not only disciplined and critical; it also makes use of those aspects of scientific method which might be lumped together under the heading of 'correlational induction' " (p. 7).

By categorial refinement, Sellars means a type of alteration in the categories used to classify the basic objects of the manifest image. The primary objects of the manifest image are persons. According to Sellars, there has been a refinement in the historical development of the manifest image from a primitive stage in which the category of persons had a much greater range than today; what we today classify as *things* were once thought of as *persons*. Thus, for example, *"originally* to be a tree was a *way of being a person,* as, to use a close analogy, to be a woman is a way of being a person, or to be a triangle is a way of being a plane figure. . . . When primitive man ceased to think of what we call trees as persons, the change was more radical than a change of belief; it was a change in category" (p. 10).

But the major difference between the manifest image—even when we take account of these two types of refinement—and the scientific image proper, is that the latter "involves the postulation of imperceptible entities, and principles pertaining to them, to explain the behaviour of perceptible things" (p. 7). Roughly speaking, then, the manifest image is restricted to what can be observed and described in the everyday world (where description and observation are broadly conceived to include persons and their behavior), while the scientific image involves the postulation of nonobservable entities to account for our observations of "perceptible things."

Sellars takes up the standard objection to displacing the manifest with the scientific image. He concedes that in a sense the scientific image is dependent on the manifest image. But while *methodologically* we begin with the manifest image before constructing the scientific image, it does not follow that "the manifest image is prior in a *substantive* sense; that the categories of a theoretical science are logically dependent on categories pertaining to its methodological foundation in the manifest world of sophisticated common sense in such a way that there would be an absurdity in the notion of a world which illustrated its theoretical principles *without also illustrating categories and principles of the manifest world"* (p. 20).

We must isolate what is at issue here. Defenders of the primacy of the manifest image have frequently appealed—as Strawson and Merleau-Ponty do—to some version of the claim that the scientific image is dependent on the manifest image, so as to establish the sense in which the manifest image is basic. But if Sellars is right, then all they have shown is a *methodological,* and not a substantive or ontological, dependence. But does it make any sense to think that the scientific image of man-in-the-world as a "complex physical system" could ever, even in principle, displace the manifest image? If this were really possible, then, though we could distinguish true and false claims made *within* the manifest image, we might also speak of the entire framework of the manifest image as a "false" one, in that its basic categories do not indicate the way things really are.

In pursuing this possibility, Sellars locates three main obstacles that the image presents to any displacement by the scientific image. The first concerns the status of thoughts or concepts; the second, "conscious sensations"; and the third, the "categories pertaining to man as a *person* who finds himself confronted by standards (ethical, logical, etc.) which often conflict with his desires and impulses, and to which he may or may not conform . . ." (p. 38).

In his treatment of these three obstacles, the full dialectical subtlety and complexity of the synthesis that Sellars proposes are most clearly evidenced. While many scientific reductionists fail to see that the manifest image presents any obstacles to the primacy of the scientific image, Sellars argues that these reductionists distort the manifest image. In this respect he seems to agree with those who argue that the manifest image is basic and not reducible. But Sellars claims that, while they are right in arguing against any simple or direct reduction, these defenders of the manifest image themselves draw mistaken ontological conclusions from their arguments.

Take, for example, the issue of thoughts or concepts. Sellars agrees that it is not possible to explain away or explicitly define thoughts in terms of physical behavior. He acknowledges that there is an "intentionality" of thoughts which must be given its due. But he develops a two-stage argument to show, first, that the intentionality of thoughts can be analyzed in terms of the semantic properties of overt speech acts; and second, that since "thoughts are items which are conceived in terms of the roles they play, then there is no barrier *in principle* to the identification of conceptual thinking with neurophysiological process" (p. 34).[8]

In the case of sensations, Sellars argues that we need a different strategy if we are to make intelligible the claim that sensations can be conceived of as aspects of neurophysiological process. "Whereas both thoughts and sensations are conceived by analogy with publicly observable items, in the former case the analogy concerns the *role* and hence leaves open the possibility that thoughts are radically different *in their intrinsic character* from the verbal behaviour by analogy with which they are conceived. But in the case of sensations, the analogy concerns the quality itself" (p. 35). The distinctive feature of sensations is that they possess a quality or "ultimate homogeneity" (p. 35) that does not seem to be identifiable with, or reducible to, neurophysiological processes. But here, too, Sellars does not think this distinctive feature of sensations an insuperable obstacle to the primacy of the scientific image of man. Roughly speaking—and his argument here is extremely complex—Sellars thinks that there is no a priori reason why we cannot conceive of a more robust sense of physical process, in which the scientific correlates of what we *now* call "sensations" are taken to be "a dimension of natural" or physical process.[9]

It would seem, then, that Sellars is arguing for the substantive primacy of the scientific image, insofar as he thinks that thoughts and sensations do not present any insuperable obstacles to it. But what about the categories pertaining to man as a person? After all, by Sellars' own insistence this is the heart of the manifest image. It is the nonreducibility of these categories to those of the scientific image that has been the basis of the perennial philosophy's endorsement of the manifest image as the measure of what is ultimately real. Here we do seem to have an insuperable obstacle.

To understand the denouement of this battle of the images, we must clarify what it is regarding persons that Sellars takes to be essential and nonreducible. He tells us that "the conceptual framework of persons is the framework in which we think of one another as sharing the community intentions which provide the ambience of principles and standards (above all, those which make meaningful discourse and rationality itself possible) within which we live our own individual lives. A person can almost be defined as a being that has intentions" (p. 40). And "it follows that to recognize a featherless biped . . . as a person requires that one think thoughts of the form, 'We (one) shall do (or abstain from doing) actions of a kind A in circumstances of kind C' " (p. 39)[10]

It seems now that we are left with a new dualism which countenances, on the one hand, all that the scientific image recognizes as real, and on the other, the "conceptual framework of persons." But this is not where Sellars ends up! He thinks there is a way out of such a dualism once we recognize that, in thinking thoughts of the kind required for "person-talk," we are not classifying or explaining, but rather rehearsing intentions.

Thus the conceptual framework of persons is not something that needs to be *reconciled with* the scientific image, but rather something to be *joined* to it. Thus, to complete the scientific image we need to enrich it *not* with more ways of saying what is the case, but with the language of community and individual intentions, so that by construing the actions we intend to do and the circumstances in which we intend to do them in scientific terms, we *directly* relate the world as conceived by scientific theory to our purposes, and make it *our* world and no longer an alien appendage to the world in which we do our living. We can, of course, as matters now stand, realize this direct incorporation of the scientific image into our way of life in imagination. But to do so is, if only in imagination, to transcend the dualism of the manifest and scientific images of man-of-the-world. (p. 40)

Sellars' denouement of the clash of the images has been so rapid that we can easily miss the point. If we think of these images as clashing concerning their claim to ultimate reality and the categories required for a description and explanation of this reality, then, according to Sellars' synthesis, the scientific image has substantive or ontological primacy. "In the dimension of describing and explaining the world, science is the measure of all things, of what is that it is, and of what is not that it is not."[11] But at the same time that Sellars insists on the epistemological and ontological priority of the scientific image, and claims that in principle—if not yet in fact—it can give a rational account of the manifest image, he also recognizes there is something "more" to human beings than even an ideally complete scientific account represents. But this "more" does not drive us to an epistemological or ontological dualism. It is the "more" that is conveyed in "person-talk." Such talk is not to be conceived of as another way of describing and explaining man. If we take the standpoint of man acting in the world—in the robust sense in which actions involve intentions—then we can "directly relate the world as conceived by scientific theory to our purposes." According to Sellars, the "manifest image is not overwhelmed in the synthesis" (p. 9). This is why he uses the analogy of stereoscopic vision to convey how we must "see" *both* images of the world.

To use the Kantian terminology, Sellars is telling us that if we take a speculative stance and ask what man is, then the theoretical scientific image has primacy; but if we are concerned with man as a being who acts intentionally in the world—who shares community intentions and can guide his actions with reference to principles and standards—then we can understand the sense in which the core of the manifest image is primary.

For from this perspective, Sellars is asserting the primacy of practical reason. And these two claims to primacy are now understood to be *compatible* in the synoptic, stereoscopic vision of man-in-the-world that Sellars has adumbrated for us.

These philosophic reflections may appear to have taken us quite far from the social and political disciplines, but the substantive consequences for an understanding of those disciplines should be clear already. According to Sellars, there is a sense in which the manifest image "itself is a scientific image," i.e., insofar as it involves a critical and disciplined use of the methods of correlational induction. The sciences of human life— the behavioral sciences—may then be understood as sciences of the manifest image which study the systematic correlations of molar behavior.[12] This supports and provides a rationale for the self-understanding that behavioral social scientists have of their discipline. Further, when we turn to the scientific image proper—the image of man that involves "the postulation of imperceptible entities, and principles pertaining to them, to explain the behaviour of perceptible things" we must realize that there are no a priori limitations to the development of such a science. Insofar, then, as we are concerned with the description and explanation of what is, not only is it possible that we can develop sciences of human beings analogous to the sciences of nature, but we already have good reason to believe in a convergence of the theoretical sciences. The "scientific image of man turns out to be that of a complex physical system" (p. 25).

What is so attractive and forceful about Sellars' synthesis is that it avoids the errors and pitfalls of less sophisticated forms of scientific materialism, reductionism, and positivism. It appears to meet the strongest challenges of those who have defended the autonomy and nonreducibility of the manifest image, yet provides a philosophic framework for both understanding and justifying the basic conviction of naturalistically oriented social scientists who are convinced that "we are becoming a science."

The Transcendental Phenomenology of Edmund Husserl

THE care, subtlety, and comprehensiveness with which Sellars has delineated this synoptic vision of man-in-the-world helps to sharpen the contrast with a rival synthesis which has also had a powerful influence:

the synthesis of Edmund Husserl. As we pursue the details of Husserl's overview, we will see that it also has substantive consequences for the sciences of human life—consequences which are radically different from those of Sellars' overview.

Sellars' characterization of the scientific and the manifest image provides an excellent starting point for understanding Husserl. That characterization bears a strong resemblance to Husserl's own characterization of objective or positive science and the world it projects, as contrasted with the *Lebenswelt* (though we will find some crucial differences, too). But there is a fundamental ambiguity in Sellars that must be cleared up if we are to understand Husserl. In characterizing the manifest image, Sellars claims that "it defines one of the poles to which philosophical reflection has been drawn. It is not only the great speculative systems of ancient and modern philosophy which are built around the manifest image, but also many systems and quasi-systems in recent and contemporary thought, some of which seem at first to have little if anything in common with the great classical systems. That I include the major schools of Continental thought might be expected" (pp. 7–8). And Sellars goes on to assert that the "perennial philosophy of man-in-the-world" not only aims at giving an adequate account of the structure of the manifest image, but also *endorses* this image as real. It is not entirely clear whether Sellars thinks that Husserl's phenomenology is an example of this perennial philosophy, although the context suggests that he does. But if this is what Sellars means, then he fundamentally misconstrues Husserl's primary intention. Husserl is absolutely clear that what is required for a phenomenological understanding of the world of objective science and the *Lebenswelt* is the bracketing of *both* these worlds—the suspension of judgment about their "reality." We must examine the structures of meanings in these worlds, and suspend any judgment concerning ontological primacy.

But what does Husserl mean by "objective science" and the *Lebenswelt?* Husserl stresses that objective science involves an essential mathematization and idealization of the world. He is also aware that this image of the world has a history, but he singles out Galileo to clarify what such a conception of the world involves. What took root in the origins of modern science is the ideal of a science which is "rational and all-inclusive, or rather the idea that the infinite totality of what is in general is intrinsically a rational all-encompassing unity that can be mastered, without anything left over, by a corresponding universal science" (p. 22).[13] Just as Sellars emphasizes that what is distinctive about the scientific image proper is "the postulation of imperceptible entities, and principles pertaining to them, to explain the behaviour of perceptible things," so too Husserl emphasizes the idealization required in Galileo's mathematization of nature.

Galileo, the discoverer—or, in order to do justice to his precursors, the consumating discoverer—of physics, or physical nature, is at once a discovering and a concealing genius [*entdeckender und verdeckender Genius*]. He discovers mathematical nature, the methodical idea, he blazes the trail for the infinite number of physical discoveries and discoverers . . . he discovers what has since been called simply the law of causality, the "a priori form" of the "true" (idealized and mathematized) world, the "law of exact lawfulness" according to which every occurrence in "nature"—idealized nature—must come under exact laws. All this is discovery-concealment, and to the present day we accept it as straightforward truth. In principle nothing is changed by the supposedly philosophically revolutionary critique of the "classical law of causality" made by recent atomic physics. For in spite of all that is new, what is essential in principle, it seems to me, remains: namely, nature, which is in itself mathematical; it is given in formulae, and it can be interpreted only in terms of the formulae. (pp. 52–53)

As Husserl continues his analysis, he projects what might be called the *telos* of this scientific image.

Thus one lives in the happy certainty of a path leading forth from the near to the distant, from the more or less known into the unknown, as an infallible method of broadening knowledge, through which truly all of the totality of what is will be known as it is "in-itself"—in an infinite progression. To this always belongs another progression: that of approximating what is given sensibly and intuitively in the surrounding life-world to the mathematically ideal, i.e., the perfecting of the always merely approximate "subsumptions" of empirical data under the ideal concepts pertaining to them. This involves the development of methodology, the refinement of measurements, the growing efficiency of instruments, etc. (pp. 65–66)

But just as Sellars emphasizes the clash between the scientific and the manifest image, so does Husserl. For the very conception of an ideal universal objective science which involves the mathematization of nature appears to depend on something more fundamental; as Sellars has stressed, it presupposes the manifest image of man-in-the-world, or what Husserl calls the *Lebenswelt*. Again one seems to find depth similarities between Husserl's *Lebenswelt* and Sellars' manifest image.

Husserl claims that, even as early as Galileo, what began to take place is "the surreptitious substitution of the mathematically substructed world of idealities for the only real world, the one that is actually given through perception, that is ever experienced and experienceable—our everyday life-world" (p. 48). And for Husserl, too, this everyday life-world is prescientific not only in that it existed prior to the development of modern science, but also in that it is presupposed in all our scientific endeavor. This is the world in which man first encounters himself as man. When we forget or conceal that natural science itself is rooted in and presupposes this world, we are threatened with distortions, with "portentous misunderstandings" (p. 53). Like Sellars, Husserl shows us that the enigmas which resulted from the several attempts to account for the "subjectivity" of human experience, and the various forms of dualism that arise in modern philosophy, can be traced back to a conviction that the world of mathematical, objectized nature is the measure of all that is genuinely real. Objective scientific endeavor—and the theoretical and technical interest it embodies—"presupposes as its point of departure, both historically and for each new student, the intuitive surrounding world of life, pregiven as existing for all in common" (p. 121). No matter how far the development of objective science is carried, this surrounding world of everyday life is always presupposed and pregiven.

Like Sellars, Husserl draws the contrast between the scientific and the manifest image as sharply as possible, in order to accentuate the clash.

If we have made our contrast with all necessary care, then we have two different things: life-world and objective-scientific world, though of course [they are] related to each other. The knowledge of the objective-scientific world is "grounded" in the self-evidence of the life-world. The latter is pregiven to the scientific worker, or the working community, as ground; yet, as they build upon this, what is built is something different. If we cease being immersed in our scientific thinking, we become aware that we scientists are, after all, human beings and as such among the components of the life-world which always exists for us, ever pregiven; and thus all of science is pulled, along with us, into the—merely "subjective-relative"—life-world. And what becomes of the objective world itself? What happens to the hypothesis of being-in-itself, related first to the "things" of the life-world, and also human beings within the "space-time" of the life-world—all these concepts being understood, not from the point of view of the objective sciences but as they are in prescientific life? (pp. 130–31)

From Sellars' perspective, it looks as if Husserl is confusing methodological with substantive or ontological dependence. Sellars would agree that the surrounding world of everyday life is always presupposed by the activity of science, but would insist that this dependency does not establish the ontological primacy of the manifest image or the *Lebenswelt*. But Husserl is *not* asserting the ontological primacy of the *Lebenswelt*. We must also bracket the *Lebenswelt* if we are to understand its structures of meaning. We must perform a type of *epoché* in which we transform what seems to be so obvious and unproblematic into an enigma, and make it the subject of an independent investigation. "The paradoxical interrelationships of the 'objectively true world' and the 'life-world' make enigmatic the manner of being of both" (p. 131). What is required, then, is a new beginning, a new type, and indeed a new conception of science (when contrasted with objective science), by which we understand the general structures of meaning of the *Lebenswelt* and how these meanings are constituted.[14] Husserl tells us that the "complete personal transformation" required for taking a total phenomenological attitude is "comparable in the beginning to a religious conversion which . . . bears within itself the significance of the greatest existential transformation which is assigned as a task to mankind as such" (p. 137).

It is clear even from Husserl's preliminary characterizations of the *Lebenswelt,* and what he takes to be its general structures, that he would criticize Sellars' own account of the manifest image—especially in regard to what Sellars calls empirical and categorial refinement—as being infected by categories rooted in objective science. He would accuse Sellars of not being "philosophically radical" enough in bracketing the manifest image and providing an analysis of its structure.

But how are we to perform such an investigation? What is the ground for such a "new" science? Here we touch upon the most fundamental theme in Husserl, one which he took to be a *radical* turn—though he also claims it has been the *telos* of philosophical reflection itself: the transcendental *epoché* that makes possible a transcendental reduction. When we bracket the ontological claims of the *Lebenswelt* and perform the *epoché,* "we are not left with a meaningless, habitual abstention, rather, it is through this abstention that the gaze of the philosopher in truth first becomes fully free: above all, free of the strongest and most universal, and at the same time most hidden, internal bond, namely, of the pregivenness of the world" (p. 151). When we have freed ourselves by means of this transcendental *epoché,* is it possible to recognize the *Lebenswelt* and mankind itself as "a self-objectification of transcendental subjectivity" (p. 153).

The transcendental *epoché*—the philosophical act of pure reflection—which involves a personal and intellectual transformation of the philosopher, is not to be understood as a "turning away" from "natural human life-interests."

. . . the world is the totality of what is taken for granted as verifiable; it is "there" through an aiming [*Abzielung*] and is the ground for ever new aimings at what is—what "actually" is. In the epoché, however, we go back to the *subjectivity* which ultimately aims, which already has results, already has the world through previous aims and their fulfillment; and [we go back] to the ways in which this subjectivity . . . "has brought about," and continues to shape the world through its concealed internal "method." The interest of the phenomenologist is not aimed at the ready-made world or at external, purposeful activity in it, which itelf is something "constituted." . . . Rather, he takes being-an-end as such, this living toward goals in world-life and terminating in them, as the subject of his own investigation in respect to the subjective aspects pervading them; and thus the naïve ontic meaning of the world in general is transformed for him into the meaning "system of poles for a transcendental subjectivity," which "has" a world and real entities within it, just as it has these poles, by constituting them. (pp. 176–77)

From Husserl's perspective, Sellars' "failure"—and the failure of all forms of naturalism, materialism, positivism, objectivism, and scientific realism—is the failure to take this transcendental turn.[15] Husserl sees this failure as part of the general "crisis of European sciences."

This is not the place to explore the many questions and difficulties posed by Husserl's conception of transcendental phenomenology and philosophy, which has appeared so dubious to naturalistically inclined Anglo-Saxon philosophers, and even to some phenomenological "followers" of Husserl.[16] But we can now understand the clash between the two syntheses or synoptic visions, and the consequences for the sciences of human life. Sellars' stereoscopic vision of man-in-the-world involves a *joining* in which the scientific image has ontological primacy, but where we enrich this scientific image "with the language of community and individual intentions." But from Husserl's perspective, Sellars' vision of man-in-the-world conceals the underlying transcendental subjectivity and its a priori structures, which serve as the ultimate ground for both the world of objective science and the *Lebenswelt*. If we are to understand the structures of both the world of objective science and the *Lebenswelt,* and the ways in which these two worlds are interrelated—if, in short, we are to gain a perspective from which we can reconcile the competing claims of these two worlds when each is taken as a self-contained and self-sufficient totality—then we must do this from the basis of a transcendental phenomenology grounded in transcendental subjectivity. We must make both these "transcendentally understandable" (p. 189).

For the transcendental philosopher, however, the totality of real objectivity— not only the scientific objectivity of all actual and possible sciences but also the prescientific objectivity of the life-world, with its "situational truths" and the relativity of its existing objects—has become a problem, the enigma of enigmas. The enigma is precisely the taken-for-grantedness in virtue of which the "world" constantly and prescientifically exists for us, "world" being a title for an infinity of what is taken for granted, what is indispensable for all objective sciences. As I, philosophizing, reflect in pure consistency upon myself as the constantly functioning ego throughout the alteration of experiences and opinions arising out of them, as the ego having consciousness of the world and dealing with the world consciously through these experiences, as I inquire consistently on all sides into the *what* and the *how* of the manners of givenness, and the modes of validity, and the manner of ego-centeredness, I become aware that this conscious life is through and through an intentionally accomplishing life through which the life-world, with all its changing representational contents [*Vorstellungsgehalten*], in part attains anew and in part has already attained its meaning and validity. (p. 204)

Now at last we can appreciate the consequences of Husserl's transcendental phenomenology for an understanding of the sciences of human life, and see how sharply it contrasts with Sellars' understanding. According to Sellars—although he primarily addresses himself to behavioristic psychology—there are two compatible ways of understanding the sciences of human life. First, we may think of such sciences as primarily dealing with the specification and discovery of regularities or correlations of variables *within* the manifest image. Such a behaviorism will be rich enough to include both verbal and nonverbal behavior. This is the sense in which the manifest image itself can be conceived of as a scientific image; there are, in fact, sciences based on correlational induction of molar behavior. But Sellars also outlines a second possibility—that of theoretical postulational sciences which will account for the correlations that we discover in the manifest image. This is the way in which Sellars conceives of an adequately developed neurophysiology.

I shall, therefore, provisionally assume that although behaviouristics and neurophysiology remain distinctive sciences, the correlational content of behaviouristics points to the structure of postulated processes and principles which telescope together with those of neurophysiological theory, with all the consequences which this entails. On this assumption, if we trace out these consequences, the scientific image of man turns out to be that of a complex physical system. (p. 25)

According to Sellars, once we clarify the differences and relationships between the types of scientific activity appropriate to the manifest image and to the scientific image proper, then we grasp the essential unity of science. This unity not only reconciles the two types of scientific endeavor appropriate to the two images, but also indicates the essential unity between the natural and the social sciences. Extrapolating what Sellars says about behaviouristics, we can extend his principle to the distinctively *social* sciences such as economics, political science, and sociology, and claim that these disciplines also involve the techniques of correlational induction appropriate to the manifest image.

But it is precisely here that we find the deepest and the most consequential clash between Sellars and Husserl. Husserl too takes psychology itself as a "decisive field" (p. 203). And his judgment about the science of psychology—both behavioristic and nonbehavioristic—is that it has been a failure. "Psychology had to fail because it could fulfill its task, the investigation of concrete, full subjectivity, only through a radical completely unprejudiced reflection, which would then necessarily open up the transcendental-subjective dimension" (p. 211). And while Husserl also focuses on psychology, it is clear that he is pressing an indictment against all forms of naturalism and objectivism in the sciences of human life. In the attempt to apply the methods of the natural sciences to an understanding of human subjectivity and intersubjectivity, these disciplines have not only failed, but distorted the phenomena studied. This failure is not one that can be overcome by more sophisticated development of the methods and techniques of the natural sciences. "Our task is critically to make transparent, down to its ultimate roots, the naturalistic—or, more exactly, the physicalistic—prejudice of the whole of modern psychology." (p. 223). "It has already become clear to us that an 'exact' psychology, as an analogue to physics . . . is an absurdity. Accordingly, there can no longer be a descriptive psychology which is the analogue of a descriptive natural science. In no way, not even in the scheme of description vs. explanation, can a science of souls be modeled on natural science or seek methodical counsel from it. It can only model itself on its own subject matter, as soon as it has achieved clarity on this subject matter's own essence" (p. 223). If it is objected that a "genuine" psychology is not a "science of souls," but a science of observable behavior, this does not weaken Husserl's charge, for psychology conceived in this manner will never be able to illuminate the structures of human subjectivity and intersubjectivity.

We must also discriminate two stages in Husserl's analysis of psychology. The first stage is to delineate what *ought* to be the structure of a proper phenomenological psychology, or a properly conceived descriptive psychology which is modeled "on its own subject matter," i.e., the fundamental intentional acts of human consciousness. Such a phenomenological psychology is a psychology based on the natural attitude—the acceptance of the *Lebenswelt*. But such phenomenological psychology is not to be confused with the more fundamental transcendental phenomenology, which requires a further *epoché* and would reveal the ultimate transcendental ground of the *Lebenswelt* itself. There is no doubt that, for Husserl, such a transcendental phenomenology is the *telos* of all philosophical reflection. It is clear that Husserl wrote *The Crisis of European Sciences and Transcendental Phenomenology* in a dramatic context, believing that only the development of a transcendental philosophy and phenomenology could meet the crisis which has shaken the very foundations of the special sciences, modern philosophy, and "modern European humanity itself." I emphasize this distinction between the two stages—or more properly, the two levels—of his analysis of psychology, because there are many deep and confusing issues which Husserl left unanswered concerning the nature, possibility, and procedures of such a transcendental phenomenology. Many phenomenologists (including Schutz) who have serious reservations about such a transcendental phenomenology, have nevertheless taken Husserl's lead in developing a phenomenological understanding of the *Lebenswelt*.

In concluding this philosophic interlude, let me sum up Husserl's indictment of Sellars, and all versions of scientific realism, materialism, physicalism, and objectivism. He considers Sellars' synthesis defective because Sellars fails to take the transcendental turn. Husserl might well argue that if Sellars had thought through what is involved in the very project of transforming the manifest and scientific images "from ways of experiencing the world into objects of philosophical reflection and evaluation"—if Sellars had radically reflected on the very presuppositions of such an inquiry—he might (and should) have realized that the "ground" of this philosophical reflection is transcendental subjectivity itself. Further, Husserl would charge Sellars with distorting the structure of the everyday world by his excessive reliance on "objectivistic" categories. Consequently, Sellars fails to grasp the distinctive subject matter and character of an adequate psychology. More generally, Sellars distorts what is required for the range of disciplines primarily concerned with human subjectivity and intersubjectivity. We need a new foundation for the entire range of the sciences of human life, and a new understanding of the character of such sciences. A phenomenological understanding of the life-world is one that aims at elucidating the essential structures of this life-world, structures which are themselves constituted by intentional consciousness.[17] It is not a discipline concerned with "correlational induction." Husserl is suggesting a new "impossibility" argument—the impossibility of reducing the sciences of man to, or even modeling them on, the natural sciences.

My forceful statement of Husserl's views, and my description of his radical opposition to all forms of naturalism and objectivism, should not be mistaken as an endorsement of his stance. Husserl, no more than any of the other philosophers I have examined, justifies his "impossibility" argument. My purpose has been to draw as sharp a contrast as possible between two sophisticated but profoundly different conceptions of the sciences of human life, in order to set the stage for an examination of the phenomenological analysis of social reality.

Phenomenological Foundations of the Social Sciences: Alfred Schutz

IN pursuing the inquiry into the phenomenological basis of the social sciences, I plan to focus on the work of the German-born phenomenologist Alfred Schutz for three reasons. First, although Husserl suggested many of the leading themes for a phenomenological approach, he did not systematically develop these insights with regard to the range of the social sciences. Husserl's primary emphasis is on phenomenological psychology, and even here we find the beginnings only—in the writings published during his lifetime—of the shape of such a discipline.[18] But from Schutz's earliest work, an interest in the phenomenological foundations of the social sciences was at the very center of his investigations. Although other philosophers influenced by Husserl—including Maurice Merleau-Ponty and Paul Ricoeur—were led to an examination of the human sciences, we do not find in their work the sustained systematic inquiry into the foundations of the social sciences characteristic of Schutz.

Secondly, the "Americanization" of Schutz offers a distinct advantage in relating his views to mainstream social science and the naturalistic self-understanding of these disciplines. By "Americanization" I am not simply referring to the fact that Schutz was among the European refugees who came to America in the late 1930s and continued his work in a new intellectual environment.[19] Schutz established new roots in American intellectual traditions. He was one of first to discover and integrate themes in American philosophy (especially in the work of James, Mead, and Dewey) that complemented and supported the insights of phenomenology.[20] Furthermore, Schutz developed his own understanding of the phenomenological basis of the social sciences at a time when Nagel, Hempel, and others were elaborating a naturalistic interpretation of the social sciences. Schutz directly commented on their work, contrasting a phenomenological orientation with the varieties of naturalism.[21]

Thirdly, Schutz has had a profound influence both on philosophers concerned with the social sciences such as Maurice Natanson, Peter Berger, Thomas Luckmann, and Richard Zaner (all of whom were students or colleagues), and on a number of leading practicing social scientists, including Harold Garfinkel and Aaron Cicourel.[22] The development of a phenomenological sociology and ethnomethodology in both America and England is directly indebted to Schutz's pioneering work.[23] Husserl and Schutz believed that once we achieved clarity about a proper phenomenological foundation of the social sciences, the way would be open for empirical research to further develop these disciplines. If we are to judge by how phenomenological themes have influenced the type and direction of empirical research in the social sciences—especially sociology—the expectation of Husserl and Schutz has been partially fulfilled. Phenomenology not only offers an interpretation of the social sciences, but has a direct influence on current empirical research.

The Analysis of *Verstehen*

Schutz did not begin his philosophic inquiry with the explicit attempt to apply Husserl's insights to the social sciences.[24] As he tells us in the preface to his first book, *The Phenomenology of the Social World,* he started with reflections on Weber's theoretical writings, in particular with Weber's attempt to delineate an interpretative sociology.

> The present study is based on an intensive concern of many years' duration with the theoretical writings of Max Weber. During this time I became convinced that while Weber's approach was correct and that he had determined the proper starting point of the philosophy of the social sciences, nevertheless his analyses did not go deeply enough to lay the foundations on which alone many important problems of the human sciences could be solved. Above all, Weber's central concept of subjective meaning calls for thoroughgoing analysis. As Weber left this concept, it was little more than a heading for a number of important problems which he did not examine in detail, even though they were hardly foreign to him. (*PSW,* p. xxxi)[25]

Schutz claimed to have found in Husserl's (and Bergson's) work on internal time-consciousness the intellectual resources to solve the problems raised by Weber. The aspect of Weber's contribution that Schutz emphasized was quite different from that of many mainstream social scientists.

Among many naturalistically oriented social scientists and philosophers of social science, Weber's insistence that social science research ought to be *Wertfrei* was taken over as an almost unquestioned dogma. They placed primary emphasis on Weber's "basic thesis . . . that generalized theoretical categories are essential to the proof of causal relationships in the human and cultural field as they are in the natural sciences."[26] The importance that Weber assigned to *Verstehen,* and to the subjective point of view of the social actor, has been interpreted as a vestige of his romanticism and his desire to accommodate the tradition of *Geistewissenschaften.* Whatever heuristic value empathic imagination and interpretation may have for arriving at and formulating hypotheses, these hypotheses are subject to the canons of testing by objective evidence —as is any claim to empirical knowledge. Nagel epitomizes this attitude toward *Verstehen* when he says, "This crucial point is that the logical canons employed by responsible social scientists in assessing the objective evidence for the imputation of psychological states do not appear to differ essentially . . . from the canons employed for analogous purposes by responsible students in other areas of inquiry."[27]

Schutz shares the views of Ernest Nagel and Carl G. Hempel on a number of fundamental issues. He agrees that "all empirical knowledge involves discovery through processes of controlled inference, and that it must be statable in propositional form and capable of being verified by anyone who is prepared to make the effort to do so through observation" (I, 51). He agrees that " 'theory' means in all the empirical sciences the explicit formulation of determinate relations between a set of variables in terms of which a fairly extensive class of empirically ascertainable regularities can be explained" (I, 52). Furthermore, Schutz agrees that the fact that regularities in the social sciences have a restricted universality, and that they permit prediction only to a limited extent, does not constitute a basic difference between the natural and the social sciences. Schutz himself rejects the claim that the "methods of the social sciences are *toto coelo* different from those of the natural sciences" (I, 48), and insists that "a set of rules for scientific procedure is equally valid for all empirical sciences whether they deal with objects of nature or with human affairs" (I, 49). And he never questions Weber's general thesis that social science ought to be a *Wertfrei* discipline.

But although he shares this common ground with naturalistically oriented social scientists, Schutz argues that they fundamentally misunderstand Weber's "postulate of subjective interpretation" and the primary goal of the social sciences. Their primary goal is to obtain organized knowledge of social reality.

By the term "social reality" I wish to be understood the sum total of objects and occurrences within the social cultural world as experienced by the common-sense thinking of men living their daily lives among their fellow-men, connected with them in manifold relations of interaction. It is the world of cultural objects and social institutions into which we are all born, within which we have to find our bearings, and with which we have to come to terms. From the outset, we the actors on the social scene, experience the world we live in as a world both of nature and of culture, not as a private but an intersubjective one, that is, as a world common to all of us, either actually given or potentially accessible to everyone; and this involves inter-communication and language. (I, 53)

Naturalism is defective insofar as it simply takes this social reality for granted, as the presupposed but unclarified foundation of the social sciences. Naturalists do not account for the way in which this social reality is constituted and maintained, in what ways it is intersubjective, or how actors in their common-sense thinking interpret their own actions and the actions of others. A proper foundation of the social sciences requires that we describe, grasp, and elucidate the basic structures of this every-day world or life-world. Once we properly locate the subject matter and aim of the social sciences, we have a perspective for clearing up many of the mistakes and confusions concerning *Verstehen*. Schutz argues that the "whole discussion suffers from the failure to distinguish clearly be-tween *Verstehen* (1) as an experiential form of common-sense knowl-edge of human affairs, (2) as an epistemological problem, and (3) as a method peculiar to the social sciences" (I, 57).

Verstehen as an experiential form of common-sense knowledge of hu-man affairs has nothing to do with introspection; it is neither a form of "private" knowledge about oneself nor an inference regarding the "purely" private or subjective psychological states of others. Like Hus-serl and many other phenomenologists, and post-Wittgensteinian analytic philosophers as well, Schutz is challenging the basic ontological and epistemological dichotomy that infects the various forms of naturalism and empiricism. This bias has its ancestry in Cartesian dualism, which as-sumes that human life can be neatly divided into what is physical—and therefore observable like any nonhuman physical process—and what is mental, or supposedly private, subjective, and inaccessible to observa-tion. Whether we come down on the side of those physicalists and be-haviorists who confine the social sciences to a study of what is "strictly speaking" observable, or on the side of a more old-fashioned psychology that limits itself to what is mental, we are operating within and accepting this basic dichotomy. But a human actor is constantly interpreting his own acts and those of others. To understand human action we must not take the position of an outside observer who "sees" only the physical manifestations of these acts; rather we must develop categories for un-derstanding what the actor—from his own point of view—"means" in his actions. *Verstehen,* according to Schutz, is first of all the name of a complex process by which all of us in our everyday life interpret the meaning of our own actions and those of others with whom we interact.

The epistemological problem of *Verstehen* asks how such common-sense understanding or interpretation is possible. It is the "scandal of philosophy" (I, 57) that until recently there has been no satisfactory solution of this question. We must make what is familiar into an enigma if we are to gain understanding. It is a manifest fact in the everyday world that we constantly engage in common-sense interpretation and thinking. Schutz believes that Husserl has provided us with the intellectual tools for confronting the many issues raised once we critically investigate intentionality, meaning, internal time consciousness, and intersubjectivity —all of which are presupposed in our common-sense interpretations.

The third problem concerning *Verstehen* arises when it is conceived as a "method peculiar to the social sciences." If our goal is an understanding of social reality as experienced by men in everyday life, and if everyday life is characterized by the intersubjective context in which common-sense interpretation takes place, then a scientific understanding of this life-world requires that we develop and elaborate categories and constructs adequate to explaining its structures.

In a manner reminiscent of Winch, Schutz tells us:

The world of nature, as explored by the natural scientist, does not "mean" anything to molecules, atoms, and electrons. But the observational field of the social scientist—social reality—has a specific meaning and relevance structure for the human beings living, acting, and thinking within it. By a series of common-sense constructs they have pre-selected and pre-interpreted this world which they experience as the reality of their daily lives. It is these thought objects of theirs which determine their behavior by motivating it. The thought objects constructed by the social scientist, in order to grasp this social reality have to be founded upon the thought objects constructed by the common-sense thinking of men, living their daily life within their social world. Thus, the constructs of the social sciences are, so to speak, constructs of the second degree, that is constructs of the constructs made by actors on the social scene, whose behavior the social scientist has to observe and explain in accordance with the procedural rules of his science. (I, 59)

This analysis of the three aspects of *Verstehen* indicates how Schutz understands the "postulate of subjective interpretation." It is the postulate or the demand that the scientific constructs of the social sciences include a first-level reference to the meaning that an action has for an actor. "The postulate of subjective interpretation has to be understood in the sense that all scientific explanations of the social world *can,* and for certain purposes *must,* refer to the subjective meaning of the actions of human beings from which social reality originates" (I, 62). Schutz's remarks about the constructs involved in common-sense experience, and the constructs on the second level developed by the social scientists, indicate what he takes to be the significance of Weber's notion of ideal types. Just as we need to make a careful distinction between *Verstehen* as a first-level process by which we all interpret the world, and *Verstehen* as a second-level process by which the social scientist seeks to understand the first-level process, so too we can say that the purpose of the second-level ideal types that the social scientist constructs is to explain the first-level ideal types that we use in everyday interpretation.

There are three dimensions of the activity of the social scientist that must therefore be carefully distinguished. Like every other man, he is a participant in the everyday life-world and engages in the interpretation of this *Lebenswelt.* As a social scientist, like any other scientist he participates in distinctive forms of social interaction with his scientific colleagues; indeed, one can investigate the structure and dynamics of the social interaction of scientific communities. But qua *social* scientist he is concerned with an objective representation and explanation of the structures and dynamics of the everyday life-world. His stance then is a theoretical one—rather than the practical one characteristic of action in the everyday world.[28] The hypotheses, interpretations, explanations, and theories that he proposes about the *Lebenswelt* are objective in that they are subject to the intersubjective norms of the scientific community. But these *objective* claims concern actors in the everyday life-world. Schutz —no less than the naturalists whom he opposes—is committed to the objectivity of scientific knowledge, and to the requirement that any knowledge claim be submitted to intersubjective scientific inquiry.

But "how is it possible to form objective concepts and an objectively verifiable theory of subjective meaning structures" (I, 62)? We will examine this in detail, but can already anticipate Schutz's answer:

How does the social scientist proceed? He observes certain facts and events within social reality which refer to human action and he constructs typical behavior or course-of-action patterns from what is observed. Thereupon he coordinates to these typical course-of-action patterns models of an ideal actor or actors, whom he imagines as being gifted with consciousness. . . . He thus ascribes to this fictitious consciousness a set of typical notions, purposes, goals, which are assumed to be invariant in the specious consciousness of the imaginary actor-model. This homunculus or puppet is supposed to be interrelated in interaction patterns to other homunculi or puppets constructed in a similar way. . . . Yet—and this is the main point—these constructs are by no means arbitrary. They are subject to the postulate of logical consistency and to the postulate of adequacy. The latter means that each term in such a scientific model of human action must be constructed in such a way that a human act performed within the real world by an individual actor as indicated by the typical construct would be understandable to the actor himself as well as to his fellow-men in terms of common-sense interpretation of everyday life. Compliance with the postulate of logical consistency warrants the objective validity of the thought objects constructed by the social scientist; compliance with the postulate of adequacy warrants their compatibility with the constructs of everyday life. (I, 63–64)

The expressions "everyday world," "common sense world," "world of daily life," and "life-world" (*Lebenswelt*) are all variant expressions for the intersubjective world that every man in his wide-awake consciousness experiences and participates in during his daily life. It is the world that Husserl originally called the world of the "natural attitude," and which is dominated by our practical interests and the problems at hand. Schutz conceived of his investigations as a phenomenology of the natural attitude or the everyday life-world rather than a "transcendental phenomenology."[29] The primary feature of this everyday world is its intersubjectivity and its social character. The analysis of intersubjectivity as manifested in the *Lebenswelt* is the dominant concern of almost all Schutz's work. For the everyday world in which we find ourselves is from the outset intersubjective. "It is intersubjective because we live in it as men among other men, bound to them through common influence and work, understanding others and being understood by them. It is a world of culture because, from the outset, the world of everyday life is a universe of significance to us, that is, a texture of meaning which we have to interpret in order to find our bearings within it and come to terms with it" (I, 10). The problem of the "existence" of others does not arise within our everyday life-world. Therefore a phenomenology of this life-world is not concerned with proving that others exist, but rather with how we come to interpret others and their actions; with the complex ways in which we understand those with whom we interact; and with the ways in which we interpret our own actions and those of others within a social context.[30]

Basic Concepts

Three closely interrelated types of inquiry are required for a phenomenology of the social world. The first is an explication and clarification of the basic concepts involved, especially the concepts of "subjective meaning," "action," and "intersubjectivity"; the second is the development of distinctions and categories required to understand properly the dynamics and structure of the *Lebenswelt;* and the third is the application of this categorial scheme for the investigation of specific social phenomena.[31] Schutz was primarily concerned with foundational studies, although he did engage in all three types of inquiry. As one might expect, his first book—which can be translated literally as "The Meaning-Construction of the Social World," or more precisely, "The Meaningful-Construction of the Social World"—explores the groundwork for such a phenomenology. It is here that one will find the most detailed and subtle attempt to clarify the central concepts for a phenomenology of the social world, especially the theory of meaning and action.

The problem of *meaning,* as Schutz conceives of it, is essentially a "time problem," not in the sense of physical time but rather "internal time consciousness." It is within an individual's *durée* that the meaning of his experience is constituted for him as he lives through that experience. This formulation of the problem of meaning, which owes a great deal to Husserl and Bergson, indicates how Schutz structures his inquiry. He first examines how meaning is constituted in the individual experience of a solitary ego, then methodologically introduces a variety of more complex distinctions leading up to a "general theory of the structure of the social world."[32]

Building on Husserl's basic understanding of the ego or consciousness as consisting of a series of intentional acts—which Schutz attempts to integrate with Bergson's concept of *durée*—Schutz distinguishes the completed act by which an ego constitutes various meaning structures, products, or objectifications, and the processes involved in this constitution: the ways in which a dynamic stream of consciousness functions. The distinction between process and product is fundamental:

On the one hand, I can look upon the world presenting itself to me as one that is completed, constituted, and to be taken for granted. When I do this, I leave out of my awareness the intentional operations of my consciousness within which their meanings have already been constituted. . . . The meaning-structure thus abstracted from its genesis is something I can regard as having objective meaning, as being meaningful in itself, just as the proposition $2 \times 2 = 4$ is meaningful regardless of where, when, or by whom it is asserted. *On the other hand,* I can turn my glance toward the intentional operations of my consciousness which originally conferred the meanings. Then I no longer have before me a complete and constituted world but one which only now is being constituted and which is ever being constituted anew in the stream of my enduring ego: not a world of being, but a world that is at every moment one of becoming and passing away—or better, an emerging world. As such, it is meaningful for me in virtue of those meaning-endowing intentional acts of which I become aware by a reflexive glance. (*PSW,* pp. 35–36)

Meaning is "*a certain way of directing one's gaze at an item of one's own experience*" (*PSW*, p. 42). Normally, "I live *within* the meaning-endowing acts themselves and am aware only of what is objectively constituted in them, i.e., objective meaning. It is only after I . . . turn away from the world of objects (*Gegenstände*) and direct my gaze at my inner stream of consciousness, it is only after I 'bracket' the natural world and attend only to my conscious experiences within the phenomenological reduction, it is only after I have done these things that I become aware of this process of constitution" (*PSW*, pp. 36–37).[33]

There are many problems that these preliminary considerations introduce concerning the precise nature and types of constitution; the procedures employed in everyday life and by social scientists in grasping objective and subjective meanings; and the ways in which I can come to know my own subjective meanings and the subjective meanings of others. Schutz is aware of these problems and explores some of them in depth. But we have laid the groundwork for seeing how the distinction between subjective and objective meaning bears on the concepts of *behavior* and *action*.

If we simply live within the flow of duration characteristic of our stream of consciousness, "we encounter only undifferentiated experiences that melt into one another in a flowing continuum" (*PSW*, p. 51). Not until I turn my attention to a segment of this flow by an act of reflection, do I single out discrete experiences, and only in a retrospective glance do discrete experiences exist for me. "Only the already experienced is meaningful, not that which is being experienced. For meaning is merely an operation of intentionality, which, however, only becomes visible to the reflective glance" (*PSW*, p. 52). Consequently we must distinguish "experience" from "behavior."

A pain, for instance, is not generally called behavior. Nor would I be said to be behaving if someone else lifted my arm and then let it drop. But the *attitudes* I assume in either of these cases *are* called behavior. I may fight the pain, suppress it, or abandon myself to it. I may submit or resist when someone manipulates my arm. So what we have here are two different types of lived experience that are fundamentally related. Experiences of the first type are merely undergone or suffered. They are characterized by passivity. Experiences of the second type consist of attitudes taken to experiences of the first type. (*PSW*, p. 54)

Behavior, then, as Schutz used this term, is the "meaning-endowing experience of consciousness." Consequently, "experience" is a more generic term than "behavior," for behavior consists only of "meaning-endowing experiences."[34]

Once Schutz has clarified what he means by "behavior," he is able to characterize the more specific concept of *action,* which is one type of behavior. "Every action is a spontaneous activity oriented to the future" (*PSW,* p. 57). Every action involves a *project;* the span and unity of an action is determined by the project. Once again we must carefully distinguish between action (*Handeln*) as process and act (*Handlung*) as product. If we define an act as the product of the completed action, we can say that it is the completed act that is projected in my anticipation of the future. "What is projected is the act, which is the goal of the action and which is brought into being by the action" (*PSW,* p. 60).

Suppose I imagine myself getting up out of my chair and going over to the window. What I really picture to myself is not a series of muscle contractions and relaxations, not a series of specific steps—one, two, three—from chair to window. No, the picture that I have in mind is a picture of the completed act of having gone over to the window. (*PSW,* p. 60)

Of course one can break up this process and imagine the various steps involved—walking across the room, moving away a chair, etc.—but Schutz's point is that it is always the "completed act" that one imagines, no matter how much one breaks up the process.

Schutz is delimiting a range of concepts which stand in a hierarchial relationship. "Experience" in its most generic sense refers to the undifferentiated flow of the inner stream of duration. "Behavior" refers to the "meaning-endowing experiences of consciousness" and involves those intentional *attitudes* that I take to the experiences that I live through. "Action" refers to those forms of behavior involving the execution of a projected act. And "the *meaning of any action is its corresponding projected act.*"[35]

We can appreciate these distinctions when we realize how they serve as a commentary on Weber's famous definition of action: "In 'action' is included all human behavior when and insofar as the acting individual attaches a subjective meaning to it" (*PSW,* p. 15). The phrase "attaches a subjective meaning to it" suggests that meaning gets attached to behavior in some mechanical or external fashion—as if "subjective meaning" were externally related and simply antecedent to behavior. Thinking of "subjective meaning" in this way has given rise to much misunderstanding and criticism of both Weber's definition of action and the conception of interpretative sociology that depends on it. Schutz uses these distinctions to make, as forcefully as he can, the substantive point that human behavior, and a fortiori human action, are *not* something merely physical and observable in the same way as any other physical process.

Action is intrinsically meaningful; it is endowed with meaning by human intentionality, i.e., by consciousness. If the meaning of an action is its "corresponding projected act," then it makes no sense to speak of an action without reference to its meaning. And in focusing on action, we can and must speak of its subjective meaning, the meaning it has by virtue of the meaning-endowing intentional acts of a human consciousness, as well as its objective meaning—the meaning-structure that the action exhibits and that can be abstracted from it.

Thus far, following Schutz, I have not yet brought in the concept of the "social." I have spoken of "experience," "behavior," and "action" from the perspective of a single solitary ego. But the centrality of *intersubjectivity* should already be clear. We can see this in two ways. "The ordinary man in every moment of his lived experience lights upon past experiences in the storehouse of his consciousness. He knows about the world and he knows what to expect. With every moment of conscious life a new item is filed away in this vast storehouse" (*PSW*, p. 81). We are continuously ordering, classifying, and interpreting our ongoing experiences according to various interpretative schemes. But in our everyday life these interpretative schemes are themselves essentially social and intersubjective. Intersubjectivity lies at the very heart of human subjectivity. The analysis of behavior and action leads to a realization that we are continuously endowing our lived experiences with meaning. In order to do this, we must choose interpretative schemes.[36] But these schemes themselves, which come to be and pass away, are not intrinsically private; they are essentially social or intersubjective interpretative schemes.

Furthermore, in our everyday lives our actions do not take place in a vacuum. What we have said so far about experience, behavior, action, and interpretative schemes is abstracted from a richer and thicker social context. We not only interpret our own actions but also those of others with whom we interact, and there is a reciprocal relation between the ways I interpret my own actions and the actions of others. The projects that I choose, and which define my actions, are themselves affected by the projects and actions of others, as well as by my understanding of the subjective meanings of the actions of others. So if we are to understand the interpretative schemes by which an individual endows his lived experiences with meaning, we must understand not only how such schemes are intrinsically intersubjective, but also how they are affected by and oriented to the varied forms of social interaction.

On the basis of his analysis of the central concepts of meaning, experience, behavior, action, and intersubjectivity, Schutz seeks to develop a conceptual scheme that will elucidate the everyday life-world. This is what I have called the second phase of the project of developing a phenomenology of the social world. Schutz's first book has explicated the most basic concepts required for such a phenomenology. And while he returned to, refined, and further clarified these basic concepts throughout his career, the papers that he wrote during the American stage of his intellectual development were primarily devoted to showing how these concepts could be integrated and applied in understanding the social reality of the everyday life-world.

The World of Everyday Life

For the wide-awake individual as he acts in the intersubjective world of daily life, Schutz observes, "all interpretation of this world is based on a stock of previous experiences of it, our own and those handed down to us by parents or teachers; these experiences in the form of 'knowledge at hand' function as a scheme of reference" (I, 7). Every wide-awake, grown-up individual approaches his world with a *stock of knowledge at hand*. Schutz uses this concept broadly to include not only knowledge but also the beliefs, expectations, rules, and biases by which we interpret the world. This stock of knowledge at hand is formed by both our personal experiences and the socially preformed knowledge that we inherit; in the course of our experience, it is constantly being tested, refined, and modified. At any moment in an individual's life, he finds himself in a *biographically determined situation*. He is not merely a physical being in an objective spatial-temporal world. As a living being who endows his experiences with meaning, he has a *position* in a world that is meaningful to him. Even the type of phenomenological time and space within which he lives is constituted by the meaning he gives to this world. To say that an individual's situation is "biographically determined is to say that it has a history; it is the sedimentation of all man's previous experiences, organized in the habitual possessions of his stock of knowledge at hand, and as such his unique possession given to him and to him alone" (I, 9). In the everyday world an individual's primary interest is not theoretical but *practical*. "A pragmatic motive governs our natural attitude toward the world of daily life. World, in this sense, is something that we have to modify by our actions or that modifies our actions" (I, 209).

Schutz shares and develops the point of view characteristic of many contemporary philosophers, who argue that traditional epistemological analyses of knowledge—and indeed analyses of the whole range of cognitive attitudes, including belief and perception—have resulted in mistakes and distortions because they are dominated by a spectator or contemplative view of knowledge. Whatever role we may assign to contemplation and to disinterested theoretical orientation, this is *not* the primary stance of man in his everyday life. His knowledge is oriented toward interaction with the world, and is conditioned by the ways in which he acts and is acted upon.[37]

But although the individual's stock of knowledge at hand is continually undergoing change, the total configuration of this knowledge is *structured*. The wide-awake individual does not encounter the world as a *tabula rasa,* nor does he start from scratch in experiencing and interpreting the world. An individual approaches the world with common-sense constructs. "The outer world is not experienced as an arrangement of individual unique objects, dispersed in space and time, but as 'mountains,' 'trees,' 'animals,' 'fellow-men.' I may have never seen an Irish setter but if I see one, I know that it is an animal and in particular a dog, showing all the familiar features and typical behavior of a dog and not, say, of a cat" (I, 7–8). My actual experience will confirm or modify my anticipation of the typical conformity with other objects; typification is never completely closed or fixed.

While the configuration of *typifications* characteristic of anyone is distinctive, there is a dynamic system of *relevances* by which it is structured —relevances determined by our interests. As used by Schutz, the concept of typification includes the most universal and stable types, as well as those which are quite specific and changing. If we were to freeze an individual's stock of knowledge at any given time, we would discover how his set of typifications is organized by a system of relevances. And as his situation changes, this system of relevances also changes. Given any object, innumerable aspects of it *may* be relevant to me, but for the purposes at hand I *take* certain features to be relevant and others to be irrelevant.

Asserting of this object S that it has the characteristic property p, in the form "S is p," is an elliptical statement. For S, taken without any question as it appears to me, is not merely p but also q and r and many other things. The full statement should read "S is, among many other things, such as q and r, also p." If I assert with respect to an element of the world as taken for granted: "S is p," I do so because under the prevailing circumstances I am interested in the p-being of S, disregarding as not relevant its being also q and r. (I, 9)

Yet even this statement may be misleading, because I do not self-consciously formulate the ways in which I typify the world. Although Schutz does not refer explicitly to the concept of "tacit knowledge," he is claiming that most of our typifications are tacit in the sense that we normally lack explicit awareness about the typifications by which we structure our experience. We can begin to see what problems and tasks open up for us if, as theoretical observers, we want to understand men in their everyday life. We must not only elucidate the different forms of typifications and the ways in which they are related to systems of relevance, but also understand the various ways in which such typifications arise, are sustained, and are modified.[38]

The stock of common-sense knowledge is socially preformed, and it is also socially distributed. This is an aspect of common-sense knowledge that Schutz did not explore in depth, but which has enormous potential significance.[39] The actual stock of knowledge at hand in the everyday world differs not only among individuals, depending on personal experience, but also among various groups and classes, depending on the common-sense knowledge that they share. An individual is an expert in a small field and a layman in many others. But no matter how distinctive or unique one's stock of knowledge is in its content, style, clarity, and distinctness, one also shares with others elements of this common-sense knowledge, and there is an overlap in our system of relevances.

In its intersubjective character the life-world can be stratified into several social dimensions, each with its own distinctive spatial-temporal structures. There is first of all the social world of face-to-face relations and interactions. Schutz calls this the "pure" We-relation, which can be actualized with different degrees of concreteness and specificity. My experiences are not identical with those of my fellow man with whom I interact in a face-to-face situation, but we "participate" in each other's conscious life. There is a community of time and space, i.e., a "synchronization of two interior streams of consciousness" (II, 26), as well as a direct bodily presence by which we interpret each other's words, gestures, facial expressions, and movements. The process by which I apprehend the conscious life of another is necessarily a process in my own conscious life. As we interact, "we grow older together" and I have immediate contact with my fellow man—although, of course, even this immediate contact is mediated by the past experience and the stock of knowledge of each of us.

As I look at you in the community of space and time I have direct evidence that you are oriented to me, that is, that you experience what I say and do, not only in an objective context of meaning but also as manifestations of my conscious life. I know that the same goes for you, and that you refer your experience of me back to what you grasp of my experiences of you. In the community of space and time our experiences of each other are not only coordinated but also reciprocally determined by continuous cross-reference. I experience myself through you, and you experience yourself through me. The reciprocal mirroring of Selves in the partners' experience is a constitutive feature of the We-relation in face-to-face situations. (II, 30)

Although Schutz stresses the primacy of the face-to-face or "We" relation, he does not think this sufficient to develop a general theory of social reality. On the contrary, his main purpose is to show how the different dimensions of the social world each have their own characteristic structures. This becomes evident when we turn to the world of contemporaries with whom I am *not* in face-to-face contact. Schutz emphasizes that there is no sharp line dividing face-to-face situations from these other social interactions with contemporaries. Although one type of situation shades off into another, significant structural modifications are involved.

In the face-to-face situation the fellow-man and I were partners in a concrete We-relation. He was present in person, with a maximum of symptoms by which I could apprehend his conscious life. In the community of space and time we were attuned to one another; his Self reflected mine; his experiences and my experiences formed a common stream, *our* experience; we grew older together. As soon as my fellow-man leaves, however, my experience of him undergoes a transformation. I know that he is in some Here and Now of his own, and I know that his Now is contemporaneous with mine, but I do not participate in it, nor do I share his Here. I know that my fellow-man has grown older since he left me, and upon reflection, I know that strictly speaking, he has changed with each additional experience, with each new situation. But all this I fail to take into account in the routine of everyday life. . . . Until further notice I hold invariant that segment of my stock of knowledge which concerns you and which I have built up in face-to-face situations, that is, until I receive information to the contrary. But then this is information about a contemporary to whom I am oriented as a mere contemporary and not as a fellow-man. (II, 38–39)

The world of contemporaries itself has different strata. It involves persons whom I formerly encountered face to face; contemporaries whom I have never met but may soon meet; contemporaries of whose existence I am aware as reference points for typical social functions (e.g., the post office employees processing my mail); as well as a variety of collective social realities (e.g., governmental agencies) which exist and affect my life, but with whom I may have no direct contact.

"*Whereas I experience the individual Thou directly in the concrete We-relation, I apprehend the contemporary only mediately, by means of typifications*" (II, 42). More precisely, while typification affects my relation and interaction with my fellow man in face-to-face situations (for any such situation is conditioned by my knowledge at hand), the role that typification plays in the world of contemporaries is quite different.

A face-to-face interaction is constituted primarily by a "Thou-orienta-tion"; a social relation in the world of contemporaries, by a "They-orien-tation."

In contrast to the way I experience the conscious life of fellow-men in face-to-face situations, the experiences of contemporaries appear to me more or less anonymous processes. The object of the They-orientation is my knowledge of social reality in general, of the conscious life of other human beings in general, regardless of whether the latter is imputed to a single individual or not. The object of the They-orientation is *not* the existence of a concrete man, *not* the ongoing conscious life of a fellow-man which is directly experi-enced in the We-relation, *not* the subjective configuration of meaning which I apprehend if experiences of a fellow-man constitute themselves before my eyes. My knowledge of contemporaries stands by its very nature in an *ob-jective context of meaning.* . . . My knowledge of the world of contempo-raries is typical knowledge of typical processes. (II, 43–44)

It is important to discriminate these different dimensions of the social world, because the types of social relation and interaction that take place in each of these dimensions are themselves different. For example, if I board a train or mail a letter, I relate to and interact with contemporaries in a They-relation. For I orient my conduct on the expectation that the contemporaries involved in such situations—the railway employees and postal clerks—will have typical expectations, will orient themselves to me in typical ways, and perform typical functions.

Both dimensions of the social world exemplified by face-to-face situa-tions and the world of contemporaries share a time zone in which I actually and directly encounter others, or can potentially encounter others. Although Schutz is far sketchier in his discussion of other dimen-sions of the social world, it is clear that he thinks a fully developed phenomenology would also isolate the distinctive structures and relations characteristic of the "world of predecessors" and the "world of succes-sors."[40] In my actual everyday life, all these worlds shade into one an-other and are aspects of the *Lebenswelt*. Nevertheless, the phenome-nologist must be sensitive to the distinctive structures exhibited in these different dimensions of the social world.

When Schutz speaks of the different dimensions of the social world, he is using a matrix in which the primary variations are reflected in dif-ferent degrees of intimacy and anonymity, and in the different types of phenomenological time and space. But Schutz also perceived another type of matrix that was equally important for dividing up and under-standing the social world. This is a matrix in which we discriminate dif-ferent "*finite provinces of meaning* upon each of which we may bestow the accent of reality" (I, 230). Schutz develops a theory of "multiple realities" which is based upon William James's claim that a man lives within a variety of "subuniverses of reality."[41] The primary world in which we live is the intersubjective one of everyday life—the world of the natural attitude with its dominant pragmatic motives. As individuals living in such a world, we may in specific circumstances doubt the veracity of some aspect of it, but we do not doubt the existence of this world or of the persons with whom we interact. Individuals in their daily lives suspend doubt, not belief, in the *Lebenswelt*. This is what Schutz called the *epoché* of the natural attitude (I, 229).

But we also live our lives in other worlds or finite provinces of meaning. There is the world of dreams, of images and phantasms; the world of art and religious experience; the world of scientific contemplation; the play world of the child; the world of the insane; etc.

We speak of provinces of meaning and not of subuniverses because it is the meaning of our experiences and not the ontological structure of objects which constitutes reality. Hence we call a certain set of our experiences a finite province of meaning if all of them show a specific cognitive style and are—*with respect to this style*— not only consistent in themselves but also compatible with each other. (I, 230)

When I alter my attention from one finite province of meaning to another, I experience a "shock"—a modification in the tension of consciousness—which compels me to break through the limits of the specific province of meaning that has engaged my attention. Each of these different provinces of meaning has its own distinctive "cognitive style" and "accent of reality." Also, each exhibits its distinctive structures, spatial and temporal relations, systems of relevance, schemes of interpretation, etc. "The concept of finite provinces of meaning does not involve any static connotation as though we had to select one of these provinces as our home to live in, to start from or to return to. That is by no means the case. Within a single day, even within a single hour our consciousness may run through most different tensions and adopt most different attentional attitudes to life" (I, 233, n. 19). Schutz did not explore these different worlds or finite provinces of meaning as carefully as he analyzed the world of everyday life, which is "the archetype of our experience of reality" (I, 233), but some of his most fascinating and illuminating studies concern the structures and dynamics of these several worlds.[42]

One begins to grasp, tentative though it is, the magnitude of the comprehensive phenomenology of the social world that Schutz projects. The study of human beings and their social lives requires not only a constitutive phenomenology of the world of everyday life, with its several social dimensions, but also the classification, delimitation, and investigation of the other worlds within which we live. This requires bringing out the distinctive structures and dynamics of these several worlds, with their characteristic cognitive styles and accents on reality, as well as the various ways in which these different worlds are interrelated.

The Theorizing Self

Schutz's theory of multiple realities provides a new perspective for understanding social theory and the ideal type of the pure theorist. For the "world of scientific theory" is itself one of the multiple realities or finite provinces of meaning that he delineates. By returning to the theme of theory and the theorist's stance armed with this new perspective, I can complete my analysis of Schutz's phenomenology of the social world.

"Scientific theorizing," we are emphatically told, "does not serve any practical purpose" (I, 245). Schutz is not denying that theorizing can have practical consequences. He is fully aware that the desire to improve the world and to apply theory to technical applications are among men's strongest motives for engaging in scientific theorizing. "But neither these motives nor the use of its results for 'worldly' purposes is an element of the process of scientific theorizing itself. Scientific theorizing is one thing, dealing with science within the world of working is another" (I, 245–46). Over and over again Schutz emphasizes the need for the scientific theorist to assume the attitude of the disinterested observer (I, 246). The primary attitude, interest, and system of relevances for the scientific theorist are radically different from those of an individual—even the same individual—as he lives his daily life in pursuit of pragmatic interests.

If one objects that such an ideal is virtually impossible to sustain, this is not an objection at all. Schutz is perfectly aware that no one does or can live a complete life as a disinterested observer; he seeks to delineate the ideal type of the theorist which may be concretely realized only approximately and intermittently. "The theoretical thinker is interested in problems and solutions valid in their own right for everyone, at any place, and at any time, wherever and whenever certain conditions, from the assumption of which he starts, prevail. The 'leap' into the province of theoretical thought involves the resolution of the individual to suspend his subjective point of view" (I, 248). He must bracket the pragmatic and private concerns that dominate his everyday life.

Further, the system of relevances appropriate to the theorist is determined by the scientific problems at hand. While there is some discretion in what the scientist chooses to investigate, he enters "a precon-stituted world of scientific contemplation handed down to him by the historical tradition of his science" (I, 250). And in specifying the prob-lem at hand and what solutions are appropriate to it, the theorist is lim-ited by the norms, rules, and methodological procedures of the given sci-entific discipline. Although there is a distinctive social world in which the theorist functions—a community of scientists with its own rules and procedures for intersubjective communication—Schutz emphasizes that "the Theorizing self is solitary" (I, 253).

Everything I have said is relevant to any theorist or theoretical sci-entist, whether he studies natural, social, or cultural phenomena. Schutz never wavered in his staunch defense of the disinterestedness required for the pure theorist. The social theorist attempts to elaborate a model of the life-world, but this model is intended to be objective. It must conform to the canons of verifiability and testability by the scientific community.

This model, however, is not peopled with human beings in their full hu-manity, but with puppets, with *types;* they are constructed as though they could perform working actions and reactions. Of course, these working ac-tions and reactions are merely fictitious, since they do not originate in a liv-ing consciousness as manifestations of its spontaneity; they are only assigned to the puppets by the grace of the scientist. But if, according to certain defi-nite operational rules (the description of which is the business of a method-ology of the social sciences), these types are constructed in such a way that their fictitious working acts and performances remain not only consistent in themselves but compatible with all the pre-experiences of the world of daily life which the observer acquired within the natural attitude before he leaped into the theoretical province—then, and only then, does this model of the social world become a theoretical object, an object of an actual positing of being. It receives an accent of reality although not that of the natural atti-tude. (I, 255)

But now we need to probe deeper and pin down precisely what Schutz takes to be distinctive about the models and theories that we use in ac-counting for the social world. We need to make explicit a distinction that has been implicit in our discussion, and that is fundamental for the con-ceptual scheme that Schutz is developing. This is the distinction between *in-order-to motives* and *genuine because-motives*. Not only is this distinc-tion fundamental for Schutz, but, as I will show in my critique of him, it is fraught with ambiguities and unresolved difficulties.

Let us recall Schutz's statement that the basic epistemological problem of "every social science can . . . be summarized in the question: *How are sciences of subjective meaning-context possible?"* (*PSW*, 223). Like all sciences, the social sciences make objective meaning claims. Yet what is distinctive about the social sciences is that these claims concern the subjective meanings that are constitutive of actions of individuals in the social world. We cannot "understand a social thing without reducing it to the human activity which has created it and, beyond it, without referring this human activity to the motives out of which it springs" (II, 10). Again Schutz tells us, "We want to understand . . . social phenomena, and we cannot understand them apart from their placement within the scheme of human motives, human means and ends, human planning—in short—within categories of human action" (II, 85).

Human action itself is shaped by the projects envisioned by the actor. It is the project that is the primary and functional meaning of the action. A project is the completed act that the actor has fantasied in the future perfect tense. These distinctions enable us to characterize what Schutz terms the *in-order-to motive*.

> The motivational context is by definition the meaning-context within which a particular action stands in virtue of its status as the project of an act for a given actor. In other words, the act thus projected in the future perfect tense and in terms of which the action receives its orientation is the "in-order-to motive" (*Um-zu-Motiv*) for the actor. (*PSW*, p. 88)

Every human action necessarily involves an in-order-to motive. And Schutz makes the stronger claim that "it is obvious that an action has only one subjective meaning: that of the actor himself" (*PSW*, p. 32).

But this type of motive needs to be carefully distinguished from a different type which Schutz calls the *genuine because-motive*. In several different places Schutz gives essentially the same example to bring out the difference between them.

> Suppose I say that a murderer perpetrated his crime for money. This is an in-order-to statement. But suppose I say that the man became a murderer because of the influence of bad companions. This statement is of an order quite different from the first. The whole complicated structure of projection in the future perfect tense is inapplicable here. What our second statement does is to take a past event—namely, the murder—and connect this with an event still further back in the past, namely, the influence of bad companions. Now this is a *different* kind of meaning-context. This we are very likely to call an "explanation of the deed." But obviously what is being said in such an explanation is only that certain past experiences of the murderer have created a disposition on the part of the murderer to achieve his goals by violence rather than by honest labor. The difference, then, between the two kinds of motive as expressed in our two statements is that the in-order-to motive explains the

act in terms of the project, while the genuine because-motive explains the project in terms of the actor's past experiences. (*PSW,* p. 91)

These two types of motive can be distinguished by their temporality. An in-order-to motive explains an act in terms of a project. Even when I am speaking of past actions, this project has the character of futurity. If I have just returned from a visit to a friend and you ask me why I went out, I can now reply that "I went out in order to see a friend." The temporality expressed by the phrase "in order to see a friend" is future with reference to the act in question. On the other hand, the characteristic temporality of genuine because-motives is always that of the past.[43] In the search for such motives, one seeks to isolate those past experiences of an individual that will explain, through a causal relationship, the project that is the basis of the individual's in-order-to motive. Because they have been both neglected and misunderstood by social scientists and philosophers of social science, Schutz gives primary emphasis to the in-order-to motives; but he thinks that an adequate social science and theory must be concerned with both types of motives. "Social things are only understandable if they can be reduced to human activities; and human activities are only made understandable by showing their in-order-to or because-motives" (II, 13). Explanations involving reference to these two types of motive are compatible because *what* they explain and *how* they explain it are radically different. Further, the two types of explanation are interdependent because we must first grasp the in-order-to motive of an act in order to isolate the project which we attempt to explain in terms of genuine because-motives.

Every human action involves specific in-order-to and genuine because-motives, but the social theorist is concerned with *typical* ones. His models are "lifeless fictions," "constructs," "ideal types," "puppets," or "homunculi" created by him. If, then, these models are distinct from the actual ontological conditions of individual everyday human existence in the life-world, how do they enable us to understand and explain actual concrete social actions? And what are the methodological restrictions on the construction of such models?

We have already anticipated the way Schutz answers these questions with reference to what he calls the "postulates for scientific model constructs of the social world" (I, 42), but it will be helpful in this context to enumerate the three primary postulates involved. First, there is the "postulate of logical consistency." "The system of typical constructs designed by the scientist has to be established with the highest degree of clarity and distinctness of the conceptual framework implied and must be fully compatible with the principles of formal logic" (I, 43). This postulate is especially important in order to guarantee the "objective validity of the thought objects constructed by the social scientist" (I, 43).

Secondly, there is "the postulate of subjective interpretation." "In order to explain human actions the scientist has to ask what model of an individual mind can be constructed and what typical contents must be attributed to it in order to explain the observed facts as the result of the activity of such a mind in an understandable relation" (I, 43). It is this postulate that enables us to discern what is *distinctive* about the models or constructs that are appropriate for an adequate social theory. "The compliance with this postulate warrants the possibility of referring all kinds of human action or their result to the subjective meaning such action or result of an action had for the actor" (I, 43).

Finally, there is "the postulate of adequacy." This postulate is intended to answer the question: How do we ascertain that the models constructed are *adequate* for explaining human actions? "Each term in a scientific model of human action must be constructed in such a way that a human act performed within the life-world by an individual actor in the way indicated by the typical construct would be understandable for the actor *himself* as well as for his fellow-men in terms of common sense interpretations of everyday life. Compliance with this postulate warrants the consistency of the constructs of the social scientist with the constructs of common-sense experience of the social reality" (I, 44; italics added).[44]

Phenomenological Foundations: Cracks and Crevices

Having completed this outline of Schutz's understanding of a phenomenology of the social world and his conception of social theory, I can evaluate his contribution to the restructuring of social and political theory. In my discussion of analytic critiques of mainstream social science, two dominant themes emerged: first, that the social and political reality examined has distinctive characteristics that affect the ways in which we explain this reality; second, that an interpretation of this reality cannot be limited exclusively to discerning regularities among dependent and independent variables. Individuals in their social and political lives are self-interpreting beings. The ways in which they interpret their own actions and those of others are not externally related to, but constitutive of, those actions. To assume that social and political reality is simply a given which is the starting point for a correlational science of society and politics not only begs some of the most important relevant questions, but—as we have seen—encourages a variety of distortions and misconceptions.

I have also argued that we are not forced to choose between an either/or: *either* the social and political disciplines are similar in all respects to the natural sciences, *or* they are so logically distinct as to involve wholly different concepts, methods, and aims. On the contrary, I have tried to show that if we work through what is involved in a naturalistic self-understanding of the social sciences, we are ineluctably led to recognize how the world is a meaningful one for human beings, how such meanings arise, what sustains and challenges these meanings, and how they shape what we do. Further, a more robust understanding of social and political reality, and of the ways in which this reality is value-constituted, does not discredit or undermine the application of scientific techniques to the study of men in society. It helps us to comprehend the contributions and limitations of such an approach. What *is* challenged, of course, is the unwarranted presupposition that *only* by the study of regularities can we achieve legitimate empirical knowledge of social and political reality.

Many independent lines of inquiry about how human action is rule-governed, and how such action is embedded in value-constituted social practices and institutions, have led to a new orientation, emphasis, and set of problems. But we do not find in analytic philosophers a systematic attempt to develop an alternative conceptual approach that incorporates the genuine insights of their several analyses. In exploring the foundations of a phenomenology of the social world, Schutz sought to develop a conceptual scheme both rich and specific enough "to obtain organized knowledge of social reality." He was not content to leave such slippery concepts as "subjective meaning," "interpretation," and "intersubjectivity" at a vague intuitive level, but sought to pin down these concepts and integrate them into a scheme that seeks *objective* knowledge of social reality.

Schutz avoids the either/or that I presented in the confrontation between the synoptic visions of Sellars and Husserl. According to Sellars' understanding of man-in-the-world, social sciences are based on "correlational induction" of the manifest image; consequently, they are sciences of the manifest image which are to be ultimately incorporated into the scientific image of man as a complex physical system. While Husserl was not directly responding to Sellars, he attacked all forms of naturalism, objectivism, and scientific realism. The *telos* of Husserl's own reflections is the elaboration of a transcendental philosophy and phenomenology as the most basic "science," requiring a different conception of science from that of the objective sciences, and a wholly different approach to the study of individuals in their psychological and social lives.

But now we can see how Schutz rejects both these extremes. Using Sellars' terminology, Schutz shows how much richer the manifest image is than even Sellars suggests, and how it is possible to develop an objective science of this image which is not limited to procedures lumped together under the heading of "correlational induction." Such an interpretative science aims at elucidating the basic structures involved in the everyday world—structures rooted in the ways in which individuals subjectively interpret their experiences. And although Schutz owes an enormous debt to Husserl, he was rightfully critical of the claim that the "methods of the social sciences [including even a phenomenological constitutive psychology] are *toto coelo* different from those of the natural sciences" (I, 48).

In acknowledging the achievement of Schutz, one must recognize the tentativeness of much of his work. After his first book, Schutz published only essays and articles. As one reads through his collected papers and posthumously published manuscripts, one has a sense of always starting from scratch instead of building, exploring, and explicating on the basis of what has been previously established. Schutz was acutely aware of this deficiency, and toward the end of his life was working on a systematic presentation which he never completed.[45] Consequently, there is scarcely an aspect of Schutz's work that does not raise a variety of troubling questions which he left unanswered. There are serious cracks and crevices in his understanding of a phenomenology of the social world.

I will begin my critique of Schutz's work with a consideration of the highly important and ambiguous concept of *structure,* especially in regard to "structures of the life-world." For I believe that this indicates a fundamental difficulty not only in Schutz's work, but in phenomenology itself. Let us recall that after Husserl's early break with psychologism and historicism, there is a thematic continuity in his investigations. His search for beginnings, and for the essential structures of subjectivity, shows a primary drive toward the discovery of the most fundamental, universal, a priori structures of transcendental subjectivity. Even when Husserl turned his attention to the *Lebenswelt,* intersubjectivity, and history, his primary aim was to reveal ("unconceal") and elucidate basic transcendental structures of consciousness, and to achieve a knowledge of these with apodictic certainty.[46]

Throughout Schutz's intellectual career, he displayed an ambivalent attitude toward Husserl's project of a definitive transcendental philosophy and phenomenology. At times Schutz thought of his own work as a contribution to a constitutive phenomenology of the social world, and endorsed the orthodox Husserlian claim that this phenomenological discipline itself would be grounded in a more basic transcendental phenomenology.[47] But Schutz became increasingly skeptical about the claims made for such a transcendental phenomenology, especially in regard to elucidating the nature of intersubjectivity. In one of Schutz's last and most brilliant papers, he reviewed—and devastatingly criticized—Husserl's several attempts to clarify transcendental intersubjectivity. He concludes that "Husserl's attempt to account for the constitution of transcendental intersubjectivity in terms of the operations of a consciousness of a transcendental ego has not succeeded" (III, 82). The issues raised by this failure—and more generally by the internal difficulties of the very idea of a transcendental phenomenology—have direct consequences for Schutz's own work, and his understanding of the structures of the life-world.

What precisely are the nature and status of these structures? This question becomes acute when our chief concern is not the solitary ego but the social world. At times Schutz seems to be operating in an orthodox Husserlian context, searching for structures so basic as to be constitutive of any form of social life. Thus when Schutz deals with the structures of face-to-face situations, or the world of contemporaries, he is attempting to elucidate those structures manifested in any form of social life, whether the Greek polis or contemporary technological society. In both these historical contexts there are face-to-face interactions, and interactions with contemporaries whom we do not directly encounter. Presumably the basic structures of these two dimensions of the social world would be exhibited in widely disparate historical settings.

But suppose we are concerned with the distinctive historical structures of these two very different situations, and furthermore seek to understand not only the characteristics of face-to-face situations in the Greek polis, but also how such structures arise, are sustained, and pass away. It is perfectly clear that both Husserl and Schutz are aware of the differences in levels of structure. But throughout Schutz's work there is a fundamental ambiguity concerning the nature and status of "structures of the life-world." More serious, there is a failure to distinguish clearly those structures which are presumably fixed, permanent, and a priori from those which have specific historical roots and causes. In understanding social reality we want to understand not only the permanent a priori structures, if there are any, but also those changing features and structures that characterize different societies and periods. And we want to understand how such structures come into being, flourish, and decline. I reiterate that it would be unfair to say that Schutz was not aware of the distinction I am pressing; but he failed to develop those concepts, categories, and procedures which would clarify the difference in the levels and types of structures exhibited in social reality, and which would indicate the proper way of studying these different types of structures.

The problems that arise here continue to plague phenomenological sociology and ethnomethodology. There is frequently a lack of sharpness about the level and specificity of structures, and what influences their emergence, reproduction, and decline.[48] In this respect, for all the talk about the genesis of common-sense thinking—*whose* common-sense thinking?—and the constitution of meaning, there is in phenomenology a tendency corresponding to the tendency toward *reification* in many naturalistic approaches.[49]

A similar obscurity arises when we probe another concept at the heart of a phenomenological orientation: *constitution*. The centrality of this concept is evident from our explication of Schutz. In dealing with the problem of meaning—especially subjective meaning—Schutz emphasizes how meaning is constituted. Husserl himself returned over and over again to the task of elucidating constitution and discriminating the various types of it.[50] Schutz was extremely acute in isolating one of the central difficulties in the theory of constitution.

At the beginning of phenomenology, constitution meant clarification of the sense-structure of conscious life, inquiry into sediments in respect of their history, tracing back all *cogitata* to intentional operations of the on-going conscious life. . . . But unobtrusively, and almost unaware, it seems to me, the idea of constitution has changed from a clarification of sense-structure, from an explication of the sense of being, into the foundation of the structure of being: it has changed from explication into creation (*Kreation*). (III, 83)

But even this statement of a central ambiguity in the theory of constitution does not reveal the full dimensions of the problems harbored in it. Suppose we restrict ourselves to what Schutz takes to be the legitimate task for phenomenological constitutional analysis, i.e., *"the clarification of the sense-structure* of intersubjectivity and of the world accepted-by-me-as-objective" (III, 84). Still there are crucial ambiguities. Is our primary concern the a priori modes in which any transcendental ego constitutes a meaningful world? Are we dealing with the modes of constitution by which any wide-awake individual in the everyday world gives meaning to this world? Are we concerned with the ways whereby the group or class within which an individual functions influences the specific schemes of interpretation, forms of typification, and systems of relevance of his biographically determined situation?

No doubt the answer would be that an adequate phenomenology must deal with *all* these questions. Indeed, it might even be argued that both Husserl and Schutz emphasize that an adequate phenomenology must treat the *genesis* of meaningful structures. But the same ambiguities that arise in specifying what is meant by "constitution" arise in analyzing what is meant by "genesis." To lump all these different ways and levels of analysis under the heading of "constitution" obscures the crucial differences involved. One is tempted to say about the theory of constitution, as employed by Schutz, what he said about Weber's concept of "subjective meaning": as Schutz left this concept, "it was little more than a heading for a number of important problems which he did not examine in detail, even though they were hardly foreign to him" (*PSW*, p. xxxi).

The construction of the social world—with the emphasis on interpretative schemes, typifications based on the sedimentation of past experiences, and selective systems of relevance—requires us to ask questions which Schutz left unanswered. Suppose we turn our attention away from the presumably universal and a priori modes of constitution and typification, and focus on those which are affected by a determinate historical reality and which change in the course of historical development. We want to know how such distinctive models of interpretation and typification arise; why individuals typify the world in the ways in which they characteristically do; and what mechanisms operate in the selection among the possible schemes of interpretation open to us. Schutz's work points to the legitimacy and importance of these questions, but does not carry us very far in giving detailed answers to them. Even such expressions as "life-world," "common-sense thinking," and "the everyday world of man" can have an obscuring effect. They fail to indicate which aspects of the life-world are fixed and permanent, and which are variable and changing. The more one emphasizes the role of history and the sedimentation of past experiences in shaping how an individual constitutes his social world, and the more one is aware of the mediation of groups and classes in these processes of constitution, then the more one requires a detailed analysis of the processes and determinants involved in the construction of different forms of social and political reality.[51]

Many of the difficulties of Schutz's phenomenology of the social world come into sharp focus when we scrutinize the central distinction between in-order-to and genuine because-motives. Schutz's distinction parallels the distinction between "motives" and "causes" which has been so fundamental in post-Wittgensteinian analyses of the concept of action, but Schutz glosses over and at times seems oblivious of the many difficulties involved in elucidating this distinction.[52] His failure to confront the issues has consequences for his entire phenomenological scheme.

First, there is a crucial ambiguity in Schutz's understanding of genuine because-motives which raises the issue of whether and in what sense they can be legitimately called motives. At times Schutz uses this expression to refer to any past experience which exerts a causal influence on the selection of a specific project by an individual. In this general sense, genuine because-motives include past experiences of which an individual may be totally unaware. In the example that Schutz gives, a man may not realize that he became a murderer "because of the influence of bad companions." But if this is true, then it is difficult to see in what sense we can speak of this influence as a *motive*—even a genuine because-motive—for his present action. Is the fact that a person drank an excessive amount of alcohol before driving his car off a cliff a motive for this action? Is it or is it not a necessary condition of a motive that an individual be aware of it as his motive?

At times Schutz speaks of genuine because-motives in a much more restricted sense, referring to experiences of which an individual is fully aware. Consider another of his examples:

In the statement, "I open my umbrella because it is raining," there lies concealed a genuine because-motive. It can be described alternatively as follows: first I see that it is raining, then I remember that I could get wet in the rain and that that would be unpleasant. I am then ready to plan any appropriate preventive step, whether this be running for shelter or spreading my umbrella. This, then, explains the constitution of the project of opening my umbrella. It is motivated by the genuine because-motive. Once this is done, the in-order-to motive motivates the act which is itself being constituted on that occasion, using the project as its basis. In the in-order-to relation, the already existent project is the motivating factor; it motivates the action and is the reason why it is performed. But in the genuine because-relation, a lived experience temporally prior to the project is the motivating factor; it motivates the project which is being constituted at that time. This, then, is the essential difference between the two relations. (*PSW*, p. 92)

The process of thought represented by seeing that it is raining and reasoning that I ought to open my umbrella to avoid getting wet is a process fully within my consciousness. Precisely because of this, it makes sense to speak of the series of past lived experiences as a genuine because-motive.

This ambiguity is crucial because Schutz never fully clarifies the relation between genuine because-motives—especially those of which I am unaware—and in-order-to motives. This failure on his part has consequences even for understanding in-order-to motives. If the "act thus projected in the future perfect tense and in terms of which the action receives its orientation is the 'in-order-to motive' (*Um-zu-Motiv*) for the actor," then in what sense can an actor be mistaken or deceived about his in-order-to motives? Schutz also fails to distinguish between motives and intentions. I may have the explicit intention to kill X, but this does not reveal my motive—even my in-order-to motive. An individual need not be self-conscious about his projects. But if a project is a completed act which he imagines or fantasizes, then how can we avoid the consequence that an individual has privileged access to his own in-order-to motives?

If we move to the social level, it is difficult to see how Schutz can give an account of ideology or "false consciousness," if we assert that an individual or group of individuals are unaware of or mistake their *genuine* in-order-to motives. In common-sense thinking, no less than in social and political theory, we are frequently suspicious or skeptical of what individuals profess to be their in-order-to motives, not because we suspect them of overtly lying, but because we think they lack self-understanding. Often we question the self-professed claims about in-order-to motives of individuals because we discern causal influences or patterns of behavior which belie those claims. Although it is sometimes treacherous to do so, we frequently think that an outside observer—whether a fellow man, a social theorist, or a psychoanalyst—can better understand the genuine in-order-to motives of an individual than the individual himself. But if we accepted Schutz's characterization of an in-order-to motive as the act projected by an individual in the future perfect tense, how can we possibly distinguish between pseudo and genuine in-order-to motives?

Consider, for example, two individuals who perform the action of washing their hands, one of whom we have reason to believe is a healthy normal person and the other a compulsive neurotic. In the case of a healthy individual, we would normally accept as a statement of his motive that he did it in order to clean his hands. The completed act of having washed his hands is the project that he imagines in the future perfect tense. The neurotic presumably has the same type of project in mind, yet we are rightfully skeptical that cleaning his hands is his genuine in-order-to motive, even though this may well be the completed act that he projects in the future perfect tense. We are skeptical because, in observing his behavior, we realize that excessive washing of his hands is not

warranted by his situation. Our (or the analyst's) search for causal influences is a means for understanding the genuine in-order-to motive, and
not simply a means for discovering the because-motive.

These difficulties have the most serious consequences for interpreting
and applying what Schutz takes to be a primary postulate for scientific
models of the social world—the postulate of adequacy. Schutz tells us
that "each term in a scientific model of human action must be constructed in such a way that a human act performed within the life-world
by an individual actor in the way indicated by the typical construct would
be *understandable* for the actor himself as well as for his fellow-men in
terms of common-sense interpretation of everyday life" (I, 44; italics
added). But whether we think of psychoanalysis, or the Hegelian analysis
of "false consciousness," or Marxist analysis of ideology, we can say that
Schutz is ignoring or glossing over the complex mechanisms of resistance,
defense, or self-deception by which individuals fail to find "understandable" what may in fact be their genuine in-order-to motives. If we take
this postulate literally, it can lead to the construction of models that are
ideological rather than scientific, in that they reflect our biases and false
beliefs about ourselves and our in-order-to motives.

Further difficulties arise when we probe the meaning and relation of
genuine because-motives and in-order-to motives. Schutz hedges on the
crucial issue of how genuine because-motives *determine* a project. The
difficulty is illustrated in the following passage.

Over against the class of in-order-to motives we have to distinguish another
one which we suggest calling the "because" motive. The murderer has been
motivated to commit his acts because he grew up in an environment of such
and such a kind, because, as psycho-analysis shows, he had in his infancy such
and such experiences, etc. Thus, from the point of view of the actor, the
because-motive refers to his past experiences. These experiences have determined him to act as he did. What is motivated in an action in the way of "because" is the project of the action itself. In order to satisfy his needs for
money, the actor had the possibility of providing it in several other ways than
by killing a man, say by earning it in a remunerative occupation. His idea of
attaining this goal by killing a man was determined ("caused") by his personal situation or, more precisely, by his life history, as sedimented in his personal circumstances. (I, 70)

Schutz never provides a systematic analysis of what such causation means
and involves—how strong or weak it is. But the passage cited suggests
that we can find *specific* causes for the *specific* projects that we adopt; in
the example, we can say that "his idea of attaining this goal by killing a
man was determined ('caused') by his personal situation."

Let us assume, then, it is really possible to give a causal explanation of why an individual chooses a specific project—rather than merely one of why he has a general disposition to choose a specific project. Then, despite Schutz's claim that explanation with reference to in-order-to motives and genuine because-motives are two independent, different, but compatible modes of explanation, it begins to look as if explanations in terms of genuine in-order-to motives and genuine because-motives are mutually dependent and internally related. In order to isolate what one is trying to explain, one must identify the manifest in-order-to motive: one must know that an individual killed a man in order to satisfy his need for money, rather than some perverse sexual desire. But in what sense, if any, has one explained the act simply by naming the in-order-to motive? On the contrary, using Schutz's own example of the act of murder, it appears that identifying the relevant in-order-to motive does *not* explain the act; rather, it is only a necessary stage in giving a causal explanation of the act by isolating the determinants that led the murderer to have this specific project. Furthermore, the investigation of causal influences may result in a revision of what I take to be the *genuine* in-order-to motive.

The are also further difficulties that have consequences for the social sciences as interpretative disciplines. Schutz tends to think that, whatever importance we assign to causal factors or genuine because-motives, we can nevertheless isolate the problems of interpretation from those involved in causation. This tendency is supported by the very way in which Schutz characterizes in-order-to motives. For if such a motive is indeed the project imagined by an individual in the future perfect tense, then it is one thing to identify this motive—or even construct an ideal type of in-order-to motive—but quite another to inquire about causal determinants that explain "the project in terms of past experiences." But a problem that Schutz never squarely confronts—and a problem that critics of interpretative procedures constantly emphasize—is how we are to evaluate competing interpretations: how we are to determine which interpretation is the correct one, or at least better approximates the "facts."

To see the seriousness of this problem, let us grant Schutz's claim that the function of the social theorist is to develop models of social reality which involve constructs of *typical* human actions and interactions. According to the postulate of subjective interpretation, any such model of the social world must include constructs of the typical in-order-to motives of the individuals whose actions we are attempting to explain. But how do we know that the model we have constructed is adequate? How do we decide among different or competing models which purport to deal with the same social reality? What we take to be genuine in-order-to motives—and consequently properly scientific constructs of these motives—depends on the substantive theory of motivation that we accept. Taking account of what individuals claim to be their in-order-to motives (when this is possible), or what would be "understandable for the actor himself," may be a necessary condition for constructing a model of their genuine in-order-to motives, but it is certainly not a sufficient condition for doing so. A Freudian and a Marxist are likely to construct different models of the genuine in-order-to motives. These accounts or models may not only be different but incompatible, because each holds to a different theory about the genuine in-order-to motives of human action. According to Schutz, a characteristic of genuine in-order-to motives is that they have "causal efficacy": "Motivated by the way of in-order-to, therefore, is the 'voluntative fiat,' the decision: 'Let's go!' which transforms the inner fancying into a performance or an action gearing into the outer world" (I, 70). But Schutz never tells us how in fact or principle we can properly discriminate between in-order-to motives that do have this efficacy and those that do not, or how we can evaluate different claims about what are the genuine in-order-to motives that will explain the relevant actions.

These difficulties about the precise meaning of, and relationship between, genuine because-motives and genuine in-order-to motives cannot be corrected by adding a few more distinctions or refining the analysis that Schutz provided. They raise issues that go to the very heart of a phenomenology of the social world. They show that the major problem of the relation between causal analysis and interpretation of the everyday world is left unresolved by Schutz. They show that what we take to be genuine in-order-to motives are themselves dependent on both the meaning of such motives and the extent to which we can speak of them as caused. They show how inadequate Schutz's characterization of in-order-to motives is, insofar as he defines them as the projects or completed acts that an individual imagines or fantasizes. And they show how even a sympathetic appreciation of the need to account for in-order-to motives must confront the major and complex issues involved in discerning what are to be taken as genuine in-order-to motives. Finally, they show the extent to which a conception of social theory and social science as an interpretative discipline is dependent on—and not logically distinct from—causal analysis. While it is true that the study of regularities, or the causal relations between independent and dependent variables, is not sufficient to provide an interpretation of social reality, it is just as true and just as fundamental that we cannot make much headway in interpreting social reality unless we face the complex issues involved in causal analysis. *What we judge to be an adequate interpretation of social action is itself dependent on our understanding of the causal determinants of social action.*

The Theorist as Disinterested Observer: A Critique

I will conclude my critique of Schutz's phenomenology of the social world by discussing the ideal type of social theorist that he sketches for us. Schutz brings into sharp relief a conception of the social theorist that not only has its origins in Weber, but is shared by naturalists, descriptivists such as Winch, and orthodox phenomenologists. When the social theorist makes his leap in the finite province of meaning characteristic of pure theory, he adopts an attitude that is disinterested, objective, and aloof. He must discipline himself to bracket the cares and pragmatic interests that govern his everyday life. As delineated by Schutz, this ideal is a strenuous one that is frequently violated in practice, and that can only intermittently be approximated in the concrete life of an individual. Nevertheless, these contingencies do not affect its status as an ideal type. Schutz clearly believes that if we aspire to be genuine social theorists, we must strive toward this ideal. There is no need to review at this point the various reasons why this ideal has been endorsed by so many diverse thinkers and why it has proved so attractive. It is typically professed and argued for against a background of all the prejudices and biases that influence our understanding of social and political reality. But it should also be clear by now how double-edged such an ideal can be. The problems that it raises for a consistent phenomenology are acute.

Suppose we grant for the moment that phenomenological analysis—whether understood as transcendental phenomenology, or as the constitutive phenomenology of the natural attitude—can approximate what it takes to be its *telos*—an elucidation of the most fundamental structures by which we constitute a meaningful world. Presumably, if we can achieve or even approximate this *telos*—if we have some way of distinguishing what is genuinely a priori and universal from what only appears to be so—we might have a firm basis for making critical judgments about different forms of historical social and political reality. We should be in the ideal position of discriminating what in the human condition is genuinely universal and basic from what is not. If one of the characteristics of ideology or false consciousness is that it systematically *mis-takes* what is relative to a specific historical context for a permanent feature of the human condition, it might even be argued that a thoroughgoing phenomenological analysis is truly radical and critical. Indeed, phenomenology would enable us to see through the variety of ideological distortions that affect our understanding of social and political reality. This line of argument is endorsed by those who think that phenomenology holds great promise not only for the understanding of social and political reality, but for the critical evaluation of different historical forms of this reality.[53]

But what is lacking in phenomenology, with its hierarchy of *epochés* and bracketings, is anything that could serve as a basis for such critical evaluative judgments. What is worse, it turns this lack into a virtue—the presumed virtue of pure description. Consider again an example to which I have alluded: a phenomenological analysis of political life in the Greek polis, and in a contemporary technological society with its various devices for manipulating political opinion. Presumably there are basic structures common to both these forms of historical reality, and a transcendental phenomenology would elucidate them. Further, by using the techniques of phenomenology, we can also carefully describe the differences between these two forms of life. But what is lacking in phenomenology, with its drive toward pure description, is any ground for evaluating these very different forms of political life, for saying that one form better approximates what political life is or ought to be. The discrimination of what is genuinely universal and a priori from what is changing and variable is not *sufficient* to assess any one historical form of social and political reality as dehumanizing or alienating or repressive. These concepts seem to have no place in a purely conceived, disinterested, aloof phenomenological stance directed toward pure description.

I do not want to underestimate or denigrate what phenomenological analysis can achieve. There is much to be learned, for example, from a phenomenological analysis of the face-to-face interactions in concentration camps or mental institutions. But I do insist that a pure phenomenology shuns explicit critical evaluation of the different forms of social and political reality. Or more accurately, when phenomenologists do make such judgments—as they inevitably do—they are violating their most fundamental methodological tenets by illicitly introducing their own fundamental values and norms—values and norms which appear to be without any foundation in phenomenological analysis itself. While such an analysis might reveal how such norms are constituted, it lacks the intellectual resources for rational critical evaluation of these norms.

The same basic tension that lies at the heart of a naturalistic self-understanding of the social sciences, and is exhibited by those who tell us that the task of proper social theory is to understand the variety of forms of life, is also at the center of phenomenology. Despite the claims of phenomenologists to have discovered the most basic, radical, and critical discipline or method, this tension is found in an even more acute form in phenomenology. The ideal phenomenologist systematically removes himself from the pragmatic worldly interests of everyday social and political life. He must engage in the rigorous discipline of bracketing and performing the required *epochés*. He must turn his gaze to the processes of the constitution of meaning rooted in human subjectivity. As a pure theorist, he is not directly concerned with judging, evaluating, or condemning existing forms of social and political reality, or with changing the world. To the extent that he turns his gaze to such worldly activities—which of course are important to him—they too are phenomena to be described and elucidated from the perspective of pure theory. Whatever our practical goals and strivings as citizens, the aim of phenomenology is the theoretical one of advancing knowledge of structures and of processes of constitution. The tension that this understanding of *theoria* and the *bios theoretikos* creates—a tension poignantly illustrated by Husserl's conception of transcendental phenomenology and his profound and passionate concern with the fate of European humanity—is the beginning point and central problematic of those who have sought to develop a critical theory of society.[54]

Part IV

The Critical
Theory
of Society

Aт the conclusion of Part III I returned once again to a problem that has been with us since the beginning of this inquiry. For all the crucial differences among mainstream social scientists, and their analytic and phenomenological critics, there is a common motif that appears again and again concerning the role of theory and the theorist. Schutz has presented one of the sharpest formulations of the ideal theorist as disinterested observer: while the theorist may be passionately interested in the fate and quality of social and political life, he must bracket this practical interest in his pursuit of theory.

Although Schutz and Winch differ about the nature of social theory, they do not disagree about this substantive point. One of the main reasons why Winch thinks philosophy so relevant for the study of society is that it takes an uncommitted view toward different and competing ways of life. In this respect there is no essential disagreement among Schutz, Winch, and the mainstream social scientists who advocate objective, value-neutral research; their disagreements are about what really constitutes an adequate account of social and political phenomena. Thus thinkers who are at variance on almost every other issue take the defense of this ideal as virtually synonymous with a defense of free, self-corrective, open inquiry which is subject only to the critical norms of intersubjective discourse.

This very ideal of the theorist as disinterested observer is bound up with closely related categorial distinctions: the distinction between theory and practice, where "practice" is understood as the technical application of theoretical knowledge; the distinction between empirical and normative theory, where the former is directed toward the description and explanation of what *is,* while the latter deals with the clarification and justification of what *ought to be;* the distinction between descriptive and prescriptive discourse; and the distinction between fact and value.

Yet we have also found—especially among analytic philosophers—a persistent questioning of these very categorial dichotomies. Is practice properly conceived of as the technical application of theoretical knowledge—an application which can be used for the most diverse purposes, depending on one's goals and values? Can we really distinguish empirical from normative theory? When we deal with human action, can we always discriminate the descriptive and prescriptive components of discourse? Does the world neatly divide into facts and values? Must we follow Schutz when he suggests a type of existential schizophrenia in which the same individual who theorizes, and also engages in the practical world of everyday life, functions in two different worlds with different "accents of reality"?

In this part I will examine one of the most penetrating and sustained challenges to the ideal type of theorist outlined above. It is an orientation that has its roots in Hegel, and in Marx's use and understanding of *critique;* that has been given a classical formulation by the central figures of the Frankfurt School;[1] and that has been refined and developed by Jürgen Habermas. My primary interest in the critical theory of society is to show how it is related to the restructuring of social and political theory. What I take to be most central in this tradition is the way it attempts to at once recover and defend the critical moment or impulse required for any adequate social and political theorizing. As I read the contemporary scene, it is this critical impulse that is breaking out among thinkers trained in radically different traditions. There is a dialectical movement from the advocacy of empirical theory to the realization of the necessity for interpretation and understanding of social and political reality. And finally, there is growing recognition of the need for the type of critique that has a practical interest in the fate and quality of social and political life. The search for empirical correlations, the task of interpreting social and political reality, and the critique of this "reality," are not three distinct types of inquiry. They are three internal moments of theorizing about social and political life.

The procedure I will follow here is similar to the one used in Part III. To set the stage for an examination of the critical theory of society, I will first consider the conflict between the views of Edmund Husserl and Max Horkheimer, the director of the Frankfurt School. This will enable me to examine in detail the work of Jürgen Habermas, who has explored the epistemological foundations of critical theory.

Background: The Crisis in the Role of Science

To introduce the central problematic to which both Husserl and Horkheimer addressed themselves, we need to discern how the conception of theory and the ideal type of the theorist are at once continuous and discontinuous with the classical conception of *theoria* rooted in Greek philosophy. Even though modern and contemporary thinkers frequently use the same formulas as classical thinkers, their conception of theory and its relation to human action is radically different. This point has been nicely brought out by Jürgen Habermas:

> The *empirical-analytic* sciences develop their theories in a self-understanding that automatically generates continuity with the beginnings of philosophical thought. For both are committed to a theoretical attitude that frees those who take it from dogmatic association with the natural interests of life and their irritating influence; and both share the cosmological intention of describing the universe theoretically in its lawlike order, just as it is. In contrast, the *historical-hermeneutic* sciences, which are concerned with the sphere of transitory things and mere opinion, cannot be linked up so smoothly with this tradition—they have nothing to do with cosmology. But they, too, comprise a *scientistic consciousness,* based on the model of science. For even the symbolic meanings of tradition seem capable of being brought together in a cosmos of facts in ideal simultaneity. Much as the cultural sciences may comprehend their facts through understanding and little though they may be concerned with discovering general laws, they nevertheless share with the empirical-analytic sciences the methodological consciousness of describing a structured reality within the horizon of the theoretical attitude. Historicism has become the positivism of the cultural and social sciences. (*KI,* pp. 302–303)[2]

But the *bios theoretikos* in classical Greek thought was understood to be a form of life that has ultimate *practical* efficacy. It was conceived of as a discipline, a "way" that intrinsically cultivates and educates the soul by emancipating men from the enslavement by *doxa* or opinion; through it, gifted men could achieve autonomy and wisdom. The philosophical life is the very exemplar of the fullest type of *virtuous* life, where men can be most like the gods. But from a modern point of view, this classical understanding of the *bios theoretikos* reads like poetry and confuses fact and value, or theory and practice. Habermas continues:

> Thus, although the sciences share the concept of theory with the major tradition of philosophy, they destroy its classical claim. They borrow two elements from the philosophical heritage: the methodological meaning of the theoretical attitude and the basic ontological assumption of a structure of the world independent of the knower. On the other hand, however, they have abandoned the connection of *theoria* and *kosmos,* of *mimesis* and *bios theoretikos* that was assumed from Plato through Husserl. What was once supposed to comprise the practical efficacy of theory has now fallen prey to methodological prohibitions. The conception of theory as a process of cultivation of the person has become apocryphal. Today it appears to us that the mimetic conformity of the soul to the proportions of the universe, which seemed acces-

sible to contemplation, had only taken theoretical knowledge into the service of the internalization of norms and thus estranged its legitimate task. (*KI,* p. 304)[3]

The difficulty that Habermas is locating—at what at first might seem to be a very abstract level—has had enormous practical consequences that have reached crisis proportions. One of the deepest convictions throughout Western philosophic and scientific thought is the belief that genuine knowledge or *theoria* is the most efficacious means for enlightenment and liberation of both the individual and society. It was the hope of many pioneers in the social sciences that the time was now at hand when we would finally achieve the theoretical understanding necessary for the reform of human social existence. Yet increasingly we are faced with the paradox that this is not the consequence of inquiry in either the natural or the social sciences. We have seen that what is frequently offered as genuine knowledge of social and political reality turns out to be a subtle form of ideology. The hope that *theoria* could provide a sufficient rational basis for guiding our lives not only appears to be groundless, but is actively excluded by methodological prohibitions. Yet what is frequently proclaimed in the name of a new tough-minded rationality turns out, when measured by classical standards, to be hopelessly irrational. Even more troubling is the realization that science and technology have become powerful and invidious tools for manipulation, repression, and domination, rather than the way to enlightenment and freedom. The common reaction to this increasingly ominous state of affairs is either to fluctuate between forms of pessimistic despair that claim we are caught in a process which has its own logic, over which we can exert no control, or to attempt, through some form of romantic protest, to reject or escape from our scientific and technological civilization. It is a measure of our growing sense of impotence that even to label this situation a crisis has degenerated into a cliché.

Edmund Husserl and the Ideal of *Theoria*

T HIS crisis became acute in the nineteen thirties, when the disintegration of Western culture appeared to be no longer a mere logical possibility but an imminent and real one. This was the context within which Husserl wrote his *Crisis of the European Sciences and Transcendental Phenomenology*. Husserl claims that what has taken place in the modern world is a "positivistic restriction of the idea of science," and that this positivism "decapitates philosophy" (pp. 7, 9).[4] The leadership and guidance that philosophy as *theoria* was to provide "in the completely new shaping of European humanity" has collapsed.[5] What is at stake is not only the fate of philosophy and science, but Western Civilization itself. Husserl in the *Crisis* analyzes the stages of this collapse, and indicates the way to a recovery of this ideal of *theoria* conceived by classical Greek thought and reaffirmed at the beginning of the Renaissance. As Husserl tells this dramatic story of Western Civilization, Renaissance thinkers "after some hesitation" affirmed

nothing less than the "philosophical" form of existence: freely giving oneself, one's whole life, its rule through pure reason or through philosophy. Theoretical philosophy is primary. A superior survey of the world must be launched, unfettered by myth and the whole tradition: universal knowledge, absolutely free from prejudice, of the world and man, ultimately recognizing in the world the inherent reason and teleology and its highest principle, God. Philosophy as theory freed not only the theorist but any philosophically educated person. And theoretical autonomy is followed by practical autonomy. According to the guiding ideal of the Renaissance, ancient man forms himself with insight through free reason. . . . This means not only that man should be changed ethically [but that] the whole human surrounding world, the political and social existence of mankind, must be fashioned anew through free reason, through the insights of a universal philosophy. (p. 8)

The recovery and fulfillment of this guiding ideal are Husserl's primary objective in the *Crisis*. This cannot be accomplished by a nostalgic return to the ancients. It can be realized only by working through the stages of the falling away from this ideal; by criticizing the presuppositions involved at every point; and by "interrogating, concretely and analytically, actual subjectivity, i.e., subjectivity as having the actual phenomenal world in intuitive validity—which, properly understood, is nothing other than carrying out the phenomenological reduction and putting transcendental phenomenology into action" (p. 337). The only way out of the present crisis is by the difficult path of transcendental phenomenology and the type of "conversion" that it involves. Husserl culminated his career with a passionate plea for

a philosophy with the deepest and most universal self-understanding of the philosophic ego as the bearer of absolute reason coming to itself . . . that reason is precisely that which man *qua* man, in his innermost being, is aiming for, that which alone can satisfy him, make him "blessed"; that reason allows for no differentiation into "theoretical," "practical," "aesthetic," or whatever; that being human is teleological being and an ought-to-be, and that this teleology holds sway in each and every activity and project of an ego; that through self-understanding in all this it can know the apodictic *telos;* and that this knowing, the ultimate self-understanding, has no other form than self-understanding according to *a priori* principles as self-understanding in the form of philosophy. (pp. 340–41)

There is extraordinary eloquence and pathos in this apologia for the philosophic life of *theoria*. When we consider the darkness of the times —the nineteen thirties, when a life of reason was threatened externally and internally—one admires Husserl's courage in reaffirming what he took to be the deepest aspiration of European mankind. But while Husserl affirms the "absolute self-responsibility" of man based on genuine theoretical insight and self-understanding, he never succeeds in showing us concretely the intrinsic connection between the life of pure *theoria* and its practical efficacy in transforming mankind. Even more troubling, as we follow the thorny paths of his understanding of transcendental phenomenology and philosophy, are the deep internal cracks that break out, and that many of his followers have either ignored or attempted unsuccessfully to bridge. No more than those whom he radically opposes and so devastatingly criticizes, has Husserl himself made clear to us a life of reason where there is no differentiation into "theoretical" and "practical." Despite the nobility of his intentions, he leaves us with a deep abyss between the ideal of the *bios theoretikos* and the "transformation of the political and social existence of mankind."[6]

It is the gap between *theoria* and *praxis* that is the key point of criticism by the Frankfurt School. Despite Husserl's brilliant analysis of the crisis of the European sciences—an analysis largely shared by members of the Frankfurt School—and his critique of the positivistic restriction of the idea of reason and theory, Husserl himself was seen to be guilty of the same fault that he exposed in others. One is left with no basis for bridging the gap between *theoria* and *praxis,* for transforming social and political reality so that it would be in accord with Husserl's ideal of the life of reason. Despite his intentions and claims, his understanding of transcendental philosophy and phenomenology leaves us impotent in the face of the concrete historical determinations of social and political reality.[7]

The Critical Theory of Max Horkheimer

At the time that Husserl was struggling to understand the fundamental crisis of the times, we find a similar endeavor by members of the Frankfurt School. Despite their skepticism and suspicion regarding phenomenology, there are basic similarities in the analysis of the crisis. The Frankfurt thinkers, no less than Husserl, were critical of the positivistic and objectivistic tendencies that were increasingly affecting all intellectual disciplines. They too reacted against the "positivistic restriction of the idea of science," whereby all legitimate knowledge, all theory, was seen through the myopic vision of positivism. They too perceived that what was at issue was the nature of a rational life, and argued that the modern positivistic conception of reason was hopelessly irrational. But they found no solution in a life of pure *theoria,* and scorned the "delusion" of Husserl that phenomenology would "save" mankind. Rather, they called for a rethinking and further development of a critical theory of society that has its roots in Hegel and Marx. At just about the time that the first edition of Husserl's *Crisis* appeared, Max Horkheimer published an essay, "Traditional and Critical Theory," which virtually became a position paper for the Frankfurt thinkers.

By "traditional theory" Horkheimer means the conception of theory that has served as a regulative ideal for the natural sciences. The goal of such theory

is a universal systematic science, not limited to any particular subject matter but embracing all possible objects. The division of sciences is being broken down by deriving the principles for special areas from the same basic premises. The same conceptual apparatus which was elaborated for the analysis of inanimate nature is serving to classify animate nature as well, and anyone who has once mastered the use of it, that is, the rules of derivation, the symbols, the process of comparing derived propositions with observable fact, can use it at any time. (pp. 188–89)[8]

As Horkheimer develops this idea of traditional theory, he indicates—in a manner similar to Husserl—how it has its origins in the beginnings of modern philosophy, especially in the Cartesian conception of method.[9] He claims that, despite their internal differences, "there can be no doubt, in fact, that the various schools of sociology have an identical conception of theory" (p. 191). Horkheimer also thinks that phenomenologists share this commitment. He cites Husserl's statement that theory consists of "a systematically linked set of propositions taking the form of a systematically unified deduction" (p. 190).

Just as Husserl had stressed the close link between theory in the positive sciences and its technical application, so does Horkheimer:

The manipulation of physical nature and of specific economic and social mechanisms demand alike the amassing of a body of knowledge such as is supplied in an ordered set of hypotheses. The technological advances of the bourgeois period are inseparably linked to this function in the pursuit of science. On the one hand, it made facts fruitful for the kind of scientific knowledge that would have practical application in the circumstances, and, on the other, it made possible the application of knowledge already possessed. Beyond doubt, such work is a moment in the continuous transformation and development of the material foundations of that society. (p. 194)

Further, Horkheimer indicates how this traditional idea of theory supports a split in the individual who is the theorist.

The scholarly specialist "as" scientist regards social reality and its products as extrinsic to him, and "as" citizen exercises his interest in them through political articles, membership in political parties or social service organizations, and participation in elections. But he does not unify these two activities, and his other activities as well, except, at best, by psychological interpretation. (pp. 209–210)

It is the explicit recognition of the connection of knowledge and interest that distinguishes critical from traditional theory, and that justifies calling such theory critical. It might seem that the expression *"critical theory"* is redundant, insofar as *theoria* was to be the means for distinguishing reality from appearance, knowledge from mere belief and opinion. But one of the persistent claims by the Frankfurt School is that this critical or negative function of theory has been suppressed or abandoned. When traditional theory is applied to existing social and political reality, it no longer provides a rational basis for criticizing this "given" reality.[10]

By criticism, we mean that intellectual, and eventually practical effort which is not satisfied to accept the prevailing ideas, actions, and social conditions unthinkingly and from mere habit; effort which aims to coordinate the individual sides of social life with each other and with the general ideas and aims of the epoch, to deduce them genetically, to distinguish the appearance from the essence, to examine the foundations of things, in short, really to know them. (p. 270)

Critical theory has a fundamental *practical interest* that guides it—a practical interest in radically "improving human existence," of fostering the type of self-consciousness and understanding of existing social and political conditions so that "mankind will for the first time be a conscious subject and actively determine its own way of life."

There is a human activity which has society itself for its object. The aim of this activity is not simply to eliminate one or another abuse, for it regards such abuses as necessarily connected with the way in which the social structure is organized. Although it itself emerges from the social structure, its purpose is not, either in its conscious intention or in its objective significance, the better functioning of any element in the structure. On the contrary, it is suspicious of the very categories of better, useful, appropriate, productive, and valuable, as these are understood in the present order, and refuses to take them as nonscientific presuppositions about which one can do nothing. (pp. 206–207)

Horkheimer also emphasizes that the critical theorist is not content to take a merely negative stance toward existing social conditions. The "theoretician and his specific object are seen as forming a dynamic unity with the oppressed class, so that his presentation of societal contradictions is not merely an expression of the concrete historical situation but also a force within it to stimulate change" (p. 215).

Let us examine this conception of critical theory against the background of Marx's early reflections on the nature and function of critique. Marx declared "that we do not anticipate the world dogmatically, but rather wish to find the new world through criticism of the old," and "even though the construction of the future and its completion for all times is not our task, what we have to accomplish at this time is all the more clear: *relentless criticism of all existing conditions,* relentless in the sense that the criticism is not afraid of its findings and just as little afraid of the conflict with the powers that be."[11] The purpose of such a radical critique is to further human emancipation.[12] But why should one think that such a critique can have practical efficacy, that it can become a "material force"? The classic Marxist answer is that such a critique becomes efficacious and leads to revolutionary praxis to the extent that it correctly analyzes and speaks to the human condition of the oppressed class (more accurately, the exploited class)—the proletariat, who alone can become the agent for the radical transformation of society. Although Horkheimer is less emphatic and concrete in his expectations than Marx, he echoes Marx when he says that critical theory "becomes a genuine force, consisting in the self-awareness of the subjects of a great historical revolution" (p. 231), and when he tells us that the critical theorist's thinking "should in fact be a critical, promotive factor in the development of the masses" (p. 214).

Consequently, critical theory is not externally related to the subjects that concern it. It does not consist solely of hypotheses and descriptions of existing social reality which are to be verified or falsified by existing facts. It is not a theory which pretends to be disinterested and thereby disguises or suppresses the interests that guide it. It is not a theory that pretends to be neutral and divorced from action—a theory which the social engineer or the private citizen may or may not seek to implement. Critical theory aspires to bring the subjects themselves to full self-consciousness of the contradictions implicit in their material existence, to penetrate the ideological mystifications and forms of false consciousness that distort the meaning of existing social conditions. Critical theorists see the distinction between theory and action which is accepted by advocates of traditional theory, as itself an ideological reflection of a society in which "theory" only serves to foster the status quo. By way of contrast, critical theory seeks a genuine unity of theory and revolutionary praxis where the theoretical understanding of the contradictions inherent in existing society, when appropriated by those who are exploited, becomes constitutive of their very activity to transform society.

We know that Marx became increasingly impatient with vague talk about the promise of critique, and turned his attention more and more to the specific analysis of capitalism.[13] Marx scorned the conviction of young Hegelians that somehow the intellectual criticism of society would automatically lead to revolutionary changes of material conditions. But through his successive transformations and self-criticisms, Marx never significantly wavered in his belief that the proletariat would be the agent of revolutionary change, and that this would be both the vindication and the validation of critique. Critique for Marx became the detailed critique of political economy.

But here we find one of the key weaknesses in Horkheimer's conception of critical theory. The world of the nineteen thirties was radically different from the period when Marx was writing. Yet we do not find in Horkheimer any systematic attempt to refine and develop an historically relevant critique of political economy. Instead, he simply refers to Marx. "The Marxist categories of class, exploitation, surplus value, profit, pauperization, and breakdown are elements in a conceptual whole, and the meaning of this whole is to be sought not in the preservation of contemporary society but in the transformation into the right kind of society" (p. 218). Again: "The concepts Marx uses such as commodity, value, and money, can function as genera when, for example, concrete social relations are judged to be relations of exchange and when there is a question of the commodity character of goods" (p. 225). But these passing references to Marx lack what Hegel calls "the seriousness of the concept" (*der Ernst des Begriffs*). Horkheimer fails to consider the many problems that arise in the differing interpretations, precise meanings, and applications of these Marxist concepts. He also fails to meet the serious challenges of those who claim that such categories are no longer relevant for understanding advanced capitalist societies.

Furthermore, in the thirties Horkheimer and other Frankfurt thinkers were becoming increasingly ambivalent about whether one could still expect a genuine proletarian revolution. But the consequences of this growing skepticism were not directly faced.[14] Central to Marx's understanding of critique is the belief that there is an exploited class which, when it comes to a full understanding and self-consciousness of its true historical situation, will be the agent of revolutionary praxis. For critical theorists it became a central issue—some might say, their Achilles heel —to determine who is or will become this revolutionary class; who are the subjects to whom critical theory is addressed. Indeed, what is the function of critical theory, if no such class seems to exist? It is not surprising that Horkheimer and other central Frankfurt thinkers became less and less interested in a systematic development of an historically relevant critique of political economy, and more concerned with the critique of ideology in its variety of expressions.

We might put the issue another way. In his *Grundrisse,* Marx with remarkable perspicacity entertained the possibility of significant structural changes in the development of capitalism.

But to the degree that large industry [*die grosse Industrie*] develops, the creation of real wealth comes to depend less on labour time and on the amount of labour employed than on the power of the agencies set in motion during labour time, whose powerful effectiveness is itself in turn out of all proportion to the direct labour time spent on their production, but depends rather on the general state of *science* and on the progress of *technology,* or the application of this science to production.[15]

If we take this suggestion seriously—and grasp the extent to which Marx's prediction has been realized in contemporary technological societies—then, at the very least, the original Marxist critique of political economy needs radical revision. For this change affects all those concepts which Horkheimer claims form a "conceptual whole," especially the absolutely central one of surplus value. But we do not find in Horkheimer any attempt to begin the type of detailed revision that such a changed historical situation requires.

There is another central difficulty in Horkheimer's conception of critical theory. Horkheimer realizes that from the perspective of traditional theory, critical theory appears to be "subjective and speculative, one-sided and useless" (p. 218). The way in which Horkheimer sets up the contrast between traditional and critical theory may remind us of the passage from Hegel cited in the Introduction (p. xix); we seem to be faced with opposing claims where "one barren assurance . . . is of just as much value as another." Despite the acute analyses, the rich polemic, and the passionate commitment, we lack a sustained argument that moves from traditional to critical theory. Such an argument requires showing how the conflicts and contradictions inherent in traditional theory force us to move beyond it. Otherwise we face an impasse where one is in effect being told, "Here I stand and there you stand."

Despite many hints and suggestions, and a great deal of polemic, I do not think that any of the classic figures associated with the Frankfurt School—including Horkheimer, Adorno, and Marcuse—has advanced such a sustained argument: one that explores the epistemological foundations and inadequacies of traditional theory and justifies the move to critical theory. This is precisely the project that has been attempted by Jürgen Habermas. He examines Marx's critique of political economy with the aim of distinguishing what is still legitimate and what must be rejected.[16] He subjects critical theory itself to analysis by re-examining its epistemological foundations. Moreover he has sought to meet directly some of the deepest challenges of the analytic philosophy of science, as well as phenomenology and hermeneutics.

Yet the full dimensions of Habermas' project are even more ambitious. He develops an historical interpretation of the relation of theory and praxis from Aristotle until the present, which locates the main moments and changes in the understanding of the relation of theory and praxis. We find "an historically oriented attempt to reconstruct the prehistory of modern positivism with the systematic intention of analyzing the connections between knowledge and human interests" (*KI*, p. vii), which involves critical interpretations of Kant, Fichte, Hegel, Marx, Nietzsche, Dilthey, Comte, Peirce, Mach, and Freud. We also find an assessment of the methodological biases of mainstream social science.[17] Habermas has been developing a comprehensive theory of communicative competence and a consensus theory of truth that grows out of his earlier investigations and ranges over a variety of technical problems in the philosophy of language and theoretical linguistics.[18] He draws upon all this research to sketch a theory of crises in advanced capitalism.[19] But for all the ambitiousness of Habermas' investigations, there is also a certain intellectual modesty that pervades his work, and an awareness of its programmatic nature. Considering what Habermas has taken on in an age that both yearns for and is deeply suspicious of a "synoptic vision," it is no wonder that he has been attacked from a variety of points of view. It is an indication of the centrality and importance of the issues that Habermas examines that he has been judged worthy of such critical attention.[20]

Jürgen Habermas' Comprehensive Critical Theory of Society

I will not examine all aspects of Habermas' investigations, but concentrate on his understanding and justification of a critical theory of society. Habermas has been developing a complex dialectical synthesis which encompasses what he takes to be legitimate in both naturalistic and phenomenological approaches. At the same time he seeks to go beyond both of these by showing that social and political theory *must* be critical. Whereas the dominant biases make a sharp distinction between descriptive theory and prescriptive normative theory, and a categorial distinction between theory understood as "disinterested observation," and action, Habermas challenges the epistemological foundations of these distinctions.

The Confusion of the Practical and the Technical

Let me begin with what Habermas takes to be the most fundamental problem that the social and political theorist faces today. Focusing on Aristotle and Hobbes, Habermas contrasts the classical and the modern conceptions of politics. The "old doctrine of politics" has become alien to us in three respects. First, "politics was understood to be the doctrine of the good and just life; it was the continuation of ethics. Aristotle saw no opposition between the constitution formulated in the *nomoi* and the ethos of civil life; conversely, the ethical character of action was not separable from custom and law. Only the *politeia* makes the citizen capable of the good life; and he is altogether a *zoon politikon,* in the sense that he is dependent on the city, the *polis,* for the realization of human nature" (*TP,* p. 42).

Second, "the old doctrine of politics referred exclusively to *praxis* in the narrow sense of the Greeks. This had nothing to do with *techne,* the skillful production of artifacts and expert mastery of objectified tasks. In the final instance, politics was always directed toward the formation and cultivation of character; it proceeded pedagogically and not technically" (*TP,* p. 42).[21]

Third, "Aristotle emphasizes that politics, and practical philosophy in general, cannot be compared in its claim to knowledge with rigorous science or with apodictic *episteme*. For its subject matter, the Just and the Excellent in its context of a variable and contingent *praxis,* lacks ontological constancy as well as logical necessity. The capacity of practical philosophy is *phronesis,* a prudent understanding of the situation, and on this the tradition of classical politics has continued to base itself, by way of the *prudentia* of Cicero, down to Burke's 'prudence' " (*TP,* p. 42).

In sharp contrast to these characteristics of the classical understanding of politics, we can isolate the three following principles emerging from the work of Thomas Hobbes.

First, the claim of scientifically grounded social philosophy aims at establishing once and for all the conditions for the correct order of the state and society as such. Its assertions are to be valid independently of place, time, and circumstances, and to permit an enduring foundation for communal life, regardless of the historical situation. Second, the translation of knowledge into practice, the application, is a technical problem. With a knowledge of the general conditions for a correct order of the state and of society, a practical prudent action of human beings toward each other is no longer required, but what is required instead is the correctly calculated generation of rules, relationships, and institutions. Third, human behavior is therefore to be now considered only as the material for science. The engineers of the correct order can disregard the categories of ethical social intercourse and confine themselves to the construction of conditions under which human beings, just like objects within nature, will necessarily behave in a calculable manner. This separation of politics from morality replaces instruction in leading a good and just life with making possible a life of well-being within a correctly instituted order. (*TP,* p. 43)

Habermas sets up this contrast in order to explore several interrelated themes. He isolates the major historical "moments" in the transition and transformation of the classical understanding of politics to the modern one. He also examines the legacy of Hobbes's conception of social philosophy as it has worked itself out in the contemporary world, showing the theoretical and practical paradoxes to which it leads.

This contrast and tension help to locate what Habermas considers the primary problem of the political or social theorist today.

How, within a political situation, can we obtain clarification of what is practically necessary and at the same time objectively possible? This question can be translated back into our historical context: how can the promise of practical politics—namely, of providing practical orientation about what is right and just in a given situation—be redeemed without relinquishing, on the one hand, the rigor of scientific knowledge, which modern social philosophy demands in contrast to the practical philosophy of classicism? And on the other, how can the promise of social philosophy to furnish an analysis of the interrelationships of social life, be redeemed without relinquishing the practical orientation of classical politics? (*TP*, p. 44)

To appreciate the full dimensions of these questions, we must examine the legacy of the modern conception of social knowledge. In industrially advanced societies there is an

escalating scale of continually expanded technical control over nature and a continually refined administration of human beings and their relations to each other by means of social organization. In this system, science, technology, industry, and administration interlock in a circular process. In this process the relationship of theory to praxis can now only assert itself as the purposive-rational application of techniques assured by empirical science. The social potential of science is reduced to the powers of technical control—its potential for enlightened action is no longer considered. The empirical, analytical sciences produce technical recommendations, but they furnish no answer to practical questions. (*TP*, p. 254)

The intelligibility of this claim depends on understanding the contrast between the *practical* and the *technical*. When we examine the categorial scheme that Habermas has been developing, we will see how fundamental for him this distinction is. But our very difficulty in grasping the difference between the two—for we now commonly think of the practical as being a matter of technical application or know-how—helps underscore Habermas' point. We not only confuse the practical with the technical, but in both thought and action tend to reduce distinctively practical issues to the matrix of technical application. The following passage indicates what Habermas takes to be the categorial distinction between the practical and the technical. It also indicates the consequences of confusing practical and technical issues.

The real difficulty in the relation of theory and praxis does not arise from this new function of science as technological force, but rather from the fact that we are no longer able to distinguish between practical and technical power. Yet even a civilization that has been rendered scientific is not granted dispensation from practical questions: therefore a peculiar danger arises when the process of scientification transgresses the limit of technical questions, without, however, departing from the level of reflection of a rationality confined to the technological horizon. For then no attempt at all is made to attain a rational consensus on the part of citizens concerned with the practical control of their destiny. Its place is taken by the attempt to attain technical control over history by perfecting the administration of society, an attempt that is just as impractical as it is unhistorical. (*TP*, p. 255)

In a number of studies Habermas has examined the prevailing tendency to reduce all problems of "action" to problems of technical control and manipulation—a tendency that results in "depoliticization of the mass of the population and the decline of the political realm as a political institution" (*TRS*, p. 75).[22] When practical discourse is eliminated or suppressed, the public realm loses—in the classical sense of politics—its political function. The problem has become urgent in our time not only because science and technology are the most important productive forces in advanced industrial societies, but because a technological consciousness increasingly affects all domains of human life, and serves as a background ideology that has a legitimating power.[23] Much of Habermas' work exposes and criticizes this ideological consciousness which seeks to suppress the distinction between the practical and the technical, and to treat all problems of action as technical.

The Criticism of Marx

Even if we accept Habermas' diagnosis of what is happening in the contemporary world—where "the more the growth and change of society are determined by the most extreme rationality of processes of research . . . the less rooted is this civilization, now rendered scientific, in the knowledge and conscience of its citizens" (*TP*, p. 256)—the central question arises: do we have any resources or weapons to combat this tendency? Habermas warns against those prophets of despair who think that science and technology have their own internal logic over which there is no possibility of human direction. But he is equally critical of those who think that when the revolution comes, the very nature of science and technology itself will be transformed.[24]

Habermas does think that there is a rational discipline that can serve as a basis for this desperately needed criticism—criticism that has a practical intent. He thinks that the classic Frankfurt thinkers were right in their attempt to recover the concept of critique implicit in Marx. But Habermas does not appropriate Marx uncritically. On the contrary, his explicit and implicit criticisms of Marx are penetrating. They are dialectical in the sense that Habermas seeks to extract from Marx what he takes to be legitimate, important, and relevant to the critique of advanced industrial societies, and to reject and expose what is no longer valid. His critical examination of Marx proceeds on two levels. First, taking seriously Marx's critique of political economy as developed in *Capital*, Habermas argues for the need to revise the theory of surplus value, the theory of the falling rate of profit, the theory of crises, the original form of Marx's understanding of class conflict, and the theory of imperialism. Further, since capitalism has developed and changed, we need to realize the ever greater extent to which economic motives for accumulation are embedded into political motives.[25] In these various criticisms of Marx, Habermas' main intent is to show how the altered structure and dynamics of advanced industrial societies—both capitalist and communist—require a rethinking of those major Marxist concepts that Horkheimer claimed formed part of a conceptual whole.

But there is another level of criticism directed against Marx. Habermas claims that Marx never explicitly reflected on the nature of critique itself, and that he failed to distinguish the ways in which critique differs both from pure philosophy and from positive science. "Marx never explicitly posed for himself the epistemological question concerning the conditions of the possibility of a philosophy of history with political intent" (*TP*, p. 242). Or again: "Marx never explicitly discussed the specific meaning of a science of man elaborated as a critique of ideology and distinct from the instrumentalist meaning of natural science. Although he himself established the science of man in the form of a critique and not as natural science, he continually tended to classify it with the natural sciences" (*KI*, p. 45). This failure or ambiguity has had the most serious practical consequences.

Contrary, then, to those humanistic interpreters who see Engels as the great corrupter of Marx by elaborating a positivistic and scientistic understanding of Marxism, Habermas argues that we find such positivistic tendencies in Marx himself. When these positivistic tendencies are exaggerated and exploited, Marxism becomes a positive science.[26] According to "true believers," Marxism is *the* positive science—true, correct, and complete—and as such, distinguished from false "bourgeois science." But once this positivistic reading of Marx becomes rigidified—and it has taken on some very subtle forms[27]—then Marxism becomes vulnerable to certain criticisms: first, that on scientific grounds alone it is too vague to meet the criteria of a good scientific theory; further, that what is clear and specific in Marxism has been falsified by historical events. What is lost, submerged, or repressed in this dispute about Marxism as the "true" science—a dispute which since the time of Marx has broken out over and over again in a variety of forms—is precisely the critical intent or sting of Marxism: "the experience of an emancipation by means of critical insight into relationships of power" (*TP*, p. 253).

The Dissolution of Epistemology

Habermas' dialectical criticism of Marx and "orthodox" Marxism enables us to specify the context for the ambitious inquiry that he has undertaken in *Knowledge and Human Interests*.

I am undertaking an historically oriented attempt to reconstruct the pre-history of modern positivism with the systematic intention of analyzing the connection between knowledge and human interests. In following the process of the dissolution of epistemology, which has left the philosophy of science in its place, one makes one's way over abandoned stages of reflection. Re-treading this path from the perspective that looks back toward the point of departure may help to recover the forgotten experience of reflection. That we disavow reflection is positivism. (*KI*, p. vii)

By the "dissolution of epistemology" Habermas means the abandonment of the critical reflection practiced by Kant when philosophy still had a sovereign role in relation to science, and was the basis for understanding and assessing the various forms of knowledge. The "critique of knowl-edge was still conceived in reference to a system of cognitive faculties that included practical reason and reflective judgment as naturally as critique itself" (*KI*, p. 3). The narrative that Habermas relates is one where the critique of knowledge, in this robust Kantian sense, has shrunk to a methodological concern with the nature of the positive sciences. "For the philosophy of science that has emerged since the mid-nineteenth century as the heir of the theory of knowledge is methodology pursued with a scientistic self-understanding of the sciences. 'Scientism' means science's belief in itself: that is, the conviction that we can no longer un-derstand science as *one* form of possible knowledge, but rather must identify knowledge with science" (*KI,* p. 4).

Habermas conducts his inquiry in a way that illustrates what he means by critique. He seeks to recover the "abandoned stages of reflection"—all that has been repressed and forgotten. However—to follow out the Freudian analogy that Habermas self-consciously adopts—what has been repressed is not something that is exclusively a part of the past. On the contrary, it exerts its influence on the present and breaks out in distorted forms. It is not simply that the "stages of reflection" have been aban-doned. After all, this is what positivists such as Comte believed would and should occur with the triumph of the positive sciences, and the identification of knowledge with what is discovered by the empirical sci-ences. Nor is Habermas suggesting that if only intellectuals had been more self-conscious about the consequences of their views at crucial stages in this dissolution, then that dissolution might never have oc-curred. Such an intellectualistic understanding of what has happened in the last two hundred years underestimates and distorts the both subtle and complex ways in which the development of "science, technology, and administration is a circular process," and the interaction and mutual reinforcement between the material conditions of advanced industrial so-cieties and a positivistic self-understanding of knowledge and science.

Habermas' "historically oriented" study means to show us that if we work through the intellectual expression of this dissolution—if we subject the legitimation of a positivistic self-understanding of knowledge and science to critical examination—then we can further liberate ourselves from ideological mystifications. While Habermas is absolutely clear that such a critical project is not sufficient to bring about the transformation of institutions and practices required for concrete emancipation— he is well aware of Marx's warning against mere intellectual criticism— he insists that such a critical reflection is absolutely necessary for any form of praxis that aims at furthering human emancipation.

We can also draw an analogy between Habermas' project in *Knowledge and Human Interests* and Hegel's *Phenomenology*. There is, of course, a significant nonanalogy in the scope of these two works and what each author claims to have shown. Habermas sharply criticizes Hegel for succumbing to an "Identity-philosophy" in which subject and object, thought and being, are "unified," and where *Geist* supposedly actualizes and completes itself in the form of Absolute Knowledge.[28] But despite these nonanalogies, Habermas' "stages of the dissolution" are analogous to the successive "forms of consciousness" that Hegel portrays. Just as Hegel shows the disparity between the meaning or intention of each stage and its actual consequences, or the disparity between the self-understanding that each form of consciousness has of itself and the concrete reality that underlies it, so too Habermas traces the implicit conflicts and contradictions that break out in his "prehistory of modern positivism." Further, according to Hegel it is by following and comprehending this "highway of despair"—a process whereby reason reflects upon the different forms it has taken in the course of its development— that we can achieve a full understanding of the contribution and limitation of each form of consciousness. It is by this movement of reflection that reason comes to a complete self-understanding. While Habermas makes no such ambitious claims, and indeed explicitly rejects them, he thinks that Hegel had a penetrating grasp of the movement of self-reflection. It is this movement that Habermas wants to recover. Habermas' ultimate aim is to show how the dynamics of self-reflection are relevant for a critical understanding of contemporary social and political reality.

The Three Cognitive Interests

From what I have said—and Habermas himself insists that this is his aim—his historically oriented work has a "systematic intention." Although this systematic intention can be discerned throughout his writings, the outlines emerged with clarity only in the nineteen sixties and were set forth in his inaugural lecture at the University of Frankfurt in 1965. The most central concept in Habermas' systematic understanding of knowledge is that of interest. While "interest" is a literal translation of the German *Interesse,* its use invites misunderstanding because, in contemporary English, "interests" are attributed to private individuals or politically motivated groups. In political science it is common to think of politics itself as the ways in which such competing interests are expressed, mediated, and played off against one another. Habermas' *Interesse,* however, refers primarily to "cognitive interests" or "knowledge-constitutive interests," which he claims have a "quasi-transcendental status." (We shall see later that the epistemological status of these interests is one of the most problematic features of his work.) Habermas searches for a way to characterize such interests that mediates between the claim that they are like any other contingent empirical fact about individuals, and the claim that they are rooted in a transcendental subjectivity isolated from historical development.

"Cognitive Interest" is therefore a peculiar category, which conforms as little to the distinction between the empirical and the transcendental or factual and symbolic determinations as to that between motivation and cognition. For knowledge is neither a mere instrument of an organism's adaptation to a changing environment nor the act of a pure rational being removed from the context of life in contemplation. (*KI*, p. 197)

Such interests or orientations are *knowledge-constitutive* because they shape and determine what counts as the objects and types of knowledge: they determine the categories relevant to what we take to be knowledge, as well as the procedures for discovering and warranting knowledge claims. And such interests are *basic* because they are "rooted in specific fundamental conditions of possible reproduction and self-constitution of the human species" (*KI*, p. 196).

To grasp what this means, we need to realize that Habermas' concern is not merely epistemological, in the sense in which epistemology can be separated from an examination of human nature. Thinking through the issues of the status and types of human knowledge requires thinking through the issue of what man *is* and *can be*. Habermas is developing a philosophical anthropology that singles out the distinctive characteristics of human social life that are the grounds of these basic knowledge-constitutive interests. He isolates three primary cognitive interests: the technical, practical, and emancipatory. Corresponding to these three nonreducible cognitive interests are three types of sciences or disciplines. "The approach of the empirical-analytic sciences incorporates a *technical* cognitive interest; that of the historical-hermeneutic sciences incorporates a *practical* one; and the approach of critically oriented sciences incorporates the *emancipatory* cognitive interest" (*KI,* p. 308). Each of these cognitive interests is grounded in one dimension of human social existence: work, interaction, or power. Work corresponds to the technical interest which guides the empirical-analytic sciences; interaction, to the practical interest which guides the historical-hermeneutic disciplines; power, to the emancipatory interest which guides the critical disciplines —the critical social sciences.

Habermas argues that we must not only carefully distinguish these three cognitive interests and the three aspects of social life in which they are rooted, but also understand the specific ways in which they are interrelated. In a subtle interpretation of Hegel's Jena writings, Habermas argues that we find in them a preliminary statement of these three dimensions of social existence and the distinctive dialectic relevant to each.[29] According to Habermas, however, Hegel, under the drive of the "Identity-philosophy," in his *Phenomenology* merged them into a single all-embracing dialectic of *Geist* realizing itself in history. This monistic drive in Hegel shows up in Marx, too. For although Marx at times displayed acute insight into the differences between the dialectic of work or labor and communicative interaction, he tends to assimilate or reduce the levels of communicative interaction and power to the dialectic of work or labor.[30] By "work" or what Habermas, following Weber, calls "purposive-rational" (*Zweckrational*) action, Habermas means

instrumental action or rational choice or their conjunction. Instrumental action is governed by *technical rules* based on empirical knowledge. In every case they imply conditional predictions about observable events, physical or social. These predictions can prove correct or incorrect. The conduct of rational choice is governed by *strategies* based on analytic knowledge. They imply deduction from preference rules (value systems) and decision procedures; these propositions are correctly or incorrectly deduced. Purposive-rational action realizes defined goals under given conditions. But while instrumental action organizes means that are appropriate or inappropriate according to criteria of an effective control of reality, strategic action depends on the correct evaluation of possible alternative choices, which result from calculation supplemented by values and maxims. (*TRS,* pp. 91–92)

Work, as a primary level of action, refers to the ways in which individuals control and manipulate their environment in order to survive and preserve themselves. Habermas thinks that Marx's analysis of the dialectic of labor is based on the concept of work, for Marx stresses that "labor is above all a process between man and nature, a process in which man through his actions mediates, regulates, and controls his material exchange with nature" (*KI,* p. 27). Furthermore Marx emphasizes—and Habermas agrees—that labor is a dynamic social process by which men shape and constitute themselves in historically determinate ways. The disciplines that correspond to this type of purposive-rational action or control are the empirical-analytic sciences, which embody, and are oriented by, a technical interest. This does *not* mean that scientists engaged in these disciplines are primarily interested in the technical application of their theories, or that theories in these disciplines are to be given an instrumental interpretation in the sense that they are merely instruments for systematically relating observation statements.[31] A practitioner in these disciplines can and indeed ought to take a "disinterested" attitude, in the sense that he should exclude subjective biases and beliefs from the validity of his knowledge claims. It is not in these ways that such disciplines are oriented by a technical cognitive interest. Rather, what Habermas stresses is that the very *form* of this type of knowledge necessitates the isolation (constitution) of objects and events into dependent and independent variables, and the investigation of regularities among them. This type of knowledge is based on a model of negative feedback in which there can be confirmation and falsification of hypotheses.[32] The search for hypothetical-deductive theories, which permit the deduction of empirical generalizations from lawlike hypotheses, and the requirement of controlled observation and experimentation, indicate "that theories of the empirical sciences disclose reality subject to the constitutive interest in the possible securing and expansion, through information, of feedback-monitored action. This is the cognitive interest in technical control over objectified processes" (*KI,* p. 309).

It is essential to realize that Habermas is not criticizing or denigrating this type of knowledge. On the contrary, insofar as he claims that it is grounded in the dimension of human life that involves human survival, he is stressing its importance and its basic quality for any social life. Habermas' primary object of attack is the ideological claim that this is the *only* type of legitimate knowledge, or the standard by which all knowledge is to be measured.

I am concerned with knowledge-guiding interests which in each case form the basis for a whole system of inquiries. In contrast to positivistic self-understanding, I should like to point out the connection of empirical-analytic science with technical interests in acquiring knowledge. But this has nothing to do with 'denunciation'. . . . On the contrary, I regard as abortive, even reactionary, the attempts which characterized the old methodological dispute, namely, attempts to set up barriers from the outset in order to remove certain sectors altogether from the clutches of a certain type of research.[33]

Habermas is following out one strain of the transcendental turn in philosophy taken by Kant. Although Habermas is sharply critical of the notion of a transcendental ego which is somehow "outside" of history, he agrees with Kant that while there are no internal limits on what we can learn from the empirical-analytic sciences, there are categorial limits on these disciplines. They are by no means the measure of all legitimate knowledge, nor are they to be identified with what all genuine knowledge will become when it is fully "legitimated." He also agrees with the phenomenological analysis—especially Husserl's—of the positive sciences as internally unlimited and categorially bounded.

According to Habermas, the level of human action characterized as work or purposive-rational action, and the technical interest that guides the disciplines concerned with it, must be sharply and carefully distinguished from the action that he calls "interaction" or "communicative action," and the practical interest that orients the related disciplines.

By "interaction" . . . I understand *communicative action,* symbolic interaction. It is governed by binding *consensual* norms, which define reciprocal expectations about behavior and which must be understood and recognized by at least two acting subjects. Social norms are enforced through sanctions. Their meaning is objectified in ordinary language communication. While the validity of technical rules and strategies depends on that of empirically true or analytically correct propositions, the validity of social norms is grounded only in the intersubjectivity of the mutual understanding of intentions and secured by the general recognition of obligations. (*TRS*, p. 92)

For Habermas, interaction is a nonreducible type of action requiring a distinctive set of categories for the description, explanation, and understanding of it. Individuals shape and determine themselves not only through their work, but also through communicative action and language. If we are to understand the ways in which the human species has formed itself in the course of its historical development, it is just as important and fundamental to understand the historical forms of communicative action as those of purposive-rational action. And of course we must also understand the complex ways in which these two levels of action are interrelated. Habermas draws upon a wide variety of resources to clarify what he means by interaction and to justify his claim that it is a nonreducible level of action, including the phenomenological and hermeneutic traditions, the conception of the social sciences as interpretative disciplines, and the types of analyses that Wittgenstein provides of language games and forms of life in the *Philosophical Investigations*. What he takes to be vital and correct in these seemingly disparate approaches is the primary emphasis on a level of communicative action and intersubjectivity that is basic for understanding social and political life.

Habermas' most powerful line of argument for establishing the autonomy and nonreducibility of communicative action is to show that the attempt to give a rational account of the empirical-analytic sciences which is limited to those concepts shaped by the technical interest is self-defeating. In this respect, too, his argument and approach have a Hegelian quality. In the *Phenomenology,* when Hegel examines the successive forms or shapes (*Gestalten*) of consciousness, the contradictions within a given stage emerge most acutely when we realize the inability of a specific form of consciousness to provide a rational account of itself. Each of these forms of consciousness is understood as implicitly making the claim to give a true, complete, total account of knowledge and the object of knowledge. But there is an internal crisis in this "highway of despair" when we comprehend how a particular form of consciousness fails to account for itself—when we grasp that the very intelligibility of its claim to true and complete knowledge presupposes concepts and categories which from its own point of view are "unreal."

In just this manner, Habermas argues, the self-understanding of the empirical-analytic sciences breaks down. Suppose we take seriously the claim that these sciences can in principle provide us with a true and complete account of knowledge and reality. If such a claim is warranted, then we ought to be able to explain the very possibility of the empirical-analytic knowledge achieved by the scientific community. But what we discover is that the intelligibility of such a community, with its distinctive forms of intersubjectivity and communication, presupposes a level of action—symbolic interaction—and a set of categories needed to account for that action, which are richer and more inclusive than those explicitly countenanced by the technical cognitive interests.[34] The consequence of such an argument is not to denigrate the empirical-analytic sciences or to lessen the value of what we can learn from them, but rather to make us self-conscious that the very intelligibility of these disciplines requires a more comprehensive concept of rationality.

The disciplines that are concerned with symbolic interaction exhibited in a scientific community of investigators, and more generally with communicative action in *all* aspects of human life, are the historical-hermeneutic disciplines.

The *historical-hermeneutic sciences* gain knowledge in a different methodological framework. Here the meaning of validity of propositions is not constituted in the frame of reference of technical control. . . . For theories are not constructed deductively and experience is not organized with regard to the success of operations. Access to the facts is provided by the understanding of meaning, not observation. The verification of lawlike hypotheses in empirical-analytic sciences has its counterpart here in the interpretation of texts. Thus the rules of hermeneutics determine the possible meaning of the validity of statements of the cultural sciences. (*KI*, p. 309)

These disciplines are guided and shaped by a knowledge-constitutive *practical* interest—an interest that has as its aim *not* technical control and manipulation, but the clarifying of the conditions for communication and intersubjectivity.

Habermas is sharply critical of the monopolistic tendencies of the positivistic self-understanding of the empirical-analytic sciences, but he is just as critical of the claim that the historical-hermeneutic disciplines provide the most fundamental knowledge of man and the world. This is the point of his remark that "historicism has become the positivism of the cultural and social sciences." Each of these "self-understandings" mistakes the part for the whole. And they do so because they fail to realize that there is a nonreducible plurality of fundamental cognitive interests.

Thus far I have stressed Habermas' claim that the media of social life, the knowledge-constitutive interests, and the types of inquiry guided by these interests, are autonomous and not reducible to each other. But there is a danger of which Habermas is acutely aware: that we will mistake the nonreducibility of these two levels of action—work and interaction—and the disciplines corresponding to them, for a mutual indifference and isolation. The most perspicuous way to state Habermas' point is that only when we comprehend the distinctive characteristics of these nonreducible media and cognitive interests can we seriously investigate the interrelationships and dynamics between them.[35] While critical of positivists and vulgar Marxists who understand social life exclusively in terms of concepts shaped by a technical interest, he is equally critical of the idealistic tendency to bracket symbolic interaction and isolate it from work and labor. The specific historical forms of work and labor exert a powerful *causal* influence on the nature and quality of symbolic interaction. The free and open communication that is the aim of the practical interest requires the existence of determinate social institutions and practices. On both these points he is in essential agreement with Marx. Consequently, while Habermas is deeply suspicious of the tendency to think that there are historical material conditions that automatically bring about the "realm of freedom," he is sufficiently Marxist to maintain that free symbolic interaction or unconstrained communication cannot concretely exist unless nonalienating and nonexploitative material conditions exist.

Habermas' dialectical synthesis also becomes evident when viewed against the background of competing claims about the nature of the social sciences by naturalists and phenomenologists. In the course of this inquiry we have seen that thinking through a naturalistic self-understanding of these disciplines leads to an examination of the problems of interpreting social and political reality. But it is just as true, and no less fundamental, that in the interpretation of social and political reality we must have recourse to the causal analysis which is so central for naturalists. Otherwise we would be unable to isolate and criticize those rationalizations which are advanced as scientific or self-evident truths, but turn out to be ideological mystifications.[36]

Habermas' synthesis comes into sharp focus when we examine the third type of knowledge-constitutive interest: the emancipatory interest. It is at once derivative, and the most basic cognitive interest. If we reflect upon the forms of knowledge and rationality guided by the technical and practical interests, we become increasingly aware of the internal demand of reason for free, open communication, and for the material conditions permitting such communication. A consistent, adequate understanding of the empirical-analytic sciences demands the existence—as Peirce and so many who have followed him have argued—of an open, self-critical community of inquirers. And the practical interest that governs the historical-hermeneutic disciplines seeks to promote such open, nondistortive communication. Implicit in the knowledge guided by the technical and practical interests is the demand for the intellectual and material conditions for emancipation, i.e., the ideal state of affairs in which nonalienating work and free interaction can be manifested.

Here too one cannot underestimate Habermas' debt to Hegel and the tradition of German idealism, for the very way in which he formulates what he means by the emancipatory interest. Central to this tradition—from Kant through Fichte to Hegel—has been the theme that when reason or knowledge is properly understood, we realize that there is in it a primary interest or demand to become fully actualized. "Reason . . . means the will to reason. In self-reflection knowledge for the sake of knowledge attains congruence with the interest in autonomy and responsibility. The emancipatory cognitive interest aims at the pursuit of reflection as such" (*KI,* p. 314). But Habermas agrees with Marx's critique of German idealism, and therefore believes that an emancipatory interest cannot be realized by a solitary ego or Absolute Spirit, but only in and through the concrete social and political lives of men.

It is this emancipatory cognitive interest that provides the epistemological basis for Habermas' understanding of critique, and the goal of the critical social sciences.

The systematic *sciences of social action,* that is economics, sociology and political science, have the goal, as do the empirical-analytic sciences, of producing nomological knowledge. A critical social science, however, will not remain satisfied with this. It is concerned with going beyond this goal to determine when theoretical statements grasp invariant regularities of social action as such and when they express ideologically frozen relations of dependence that can in principle be transformed. To the extent that this is the case, the *critique of ideology,* as well, moreover, as *psychoanalysis,* take into account that information about lawlike connections sets off a process of reflection in the consciousness of those whom the laws are about. Thus the level of [nonreflective] consciousness, which is one of the initial conditions of such laws, can be transformed. Of course, to this end, a critically mediated knowledge of laws cannot through reflection alone render a law itself inoperative, but can render it inapplicable.
    The methodological framework that determines the meaning of the validity of critical propositions of this category is established by the concept of *self-reflection.* The latter releases the subject from dependence on hypostatized powers. Self-reflection is determined by an emancipatory cognitive interest. (*KI,* p. 310)

Many points in this dense passage call for comment. Habermas refers to the critique of ideology and psychoanalysis because he believes that in different ways these two disciplines, as practiced by Marx and Freud, provide the epistemological model for what he means by critique. Both are anticipated by the dynamics of self-reflection in German idealism, especially as exemplified in Hegel's *Phenomenology.* We can also grasp what Habermas is up to by appealing to a much older model in philosophy, the Socratic model of self-knowledge whereby, through a process of dialogue, the participants achieve self-knowledge and self-reflection which are therapeutic and effect a cognitive, affective, and practical transformation involving a movement toward autonomy (*Mündigkeit*) and responsibility.

Habermas, however, argues that this Socratic model must be modified in two significant respects if it is to serve as an adequate model for a critical theory of society. First, it is a fiction that Socratic dialogue is possible everywhere and at any time. Throughout history violence has deformed repeated attempts at dialogue, and recurrently closed off the path to unconstrained communication. Genuine dialogue and unconstrained communication depend on the existence of those social and political institutions that allow for and foster such dialogue. Further, we must understand how the self-formative processes of men, expressed through historical forms of work and interaction, have resulted in systematically distorted communication.

Second, the very concept of dialogue involves and presupposes an intersubjective context. This is, of course, implicit in the Socratic ideal of dialogue. Hegel and Marx not only revived—in opposition to the subjectivist turn that has infected so much modern philosophy—the classical appreciation of the intrinsic political nature of men, but also explored the historically changing forms of intersubjectivity. Just as any viable understanding of critical social theory demands an epistemological clarification and justification of its foundations, Habermas argues that today an adequate epistemology must itself be a social theory. But we still need to pin down what Habermas understands by critique, and how it is guided by an emancipatory interest. We can do this by turning to those features of the psychoanalytic model of therapeutic interpretation that he emphasizes.

Psychoanalysis and the Critique of Ideology

Psychoanalysis is a discipline that incorporates methodological self-reflection. It requires a "depth hermeneutics" in which psychoanalytic interpretation is directed to the various ways in which the patient-subject fundamentally and systematically misunderstands himself, and fails to grasp the significance of the symptoms from which he suffers.

The technique of dream interpretation goes beyond the art of hermeneutics insofar as it must grasp not only the meaning of a possibly distorted text, but the *meaning of the text distortion itself,* that is the transformation of a latent dream thought into the manifest dream. In other words, it must reconstruct what Freud called the "dreamwork." (*KI,* pp. 220–21)

Such interpretation is not disinterested. The analyst is concerned with and guided by his interest in helping the patient to overcome his suffering and the debilitating symptoms that he exhibits. The analyst can only achieve this by helping to bring to consciousness the individual's distinctive self-formative processes. And "*the act of understanding* to which it leads is *self-reflection*" (*KI,* p. 228).

Following Freud, Habermas emphasizes that this is not merely a matter of imparting information to the patient or applying a theory in a technical or strategic manner (though a skilled therapist will at times manipulate his patient). What is required is an *achievement* by the patient—and by the therapist, too—that is aimed at dissolving resistances. Freud warns that

the pathological factor is not his [the patient's] ignorance in itself, but the root of the ignorance in his inner *resistances*. It was they that first called this ignorance into being, and they still maintain it now. The task of the treatment lies in combating these resistances. Informing the patient of what he does not know because he has repressed it is only one of the necessary preliminaries to the treatment. If knowledge about the unconscious were as important for the patient as people inexperienced in psychoanalysis imagine, listening to lectures or reading books would be enough to cure him. (*KI*, p. 229)

Thus while a therapeutic treatment requires analytic reconstruction, it must aim at the patient's own recollection and appropriation. This highlights one of the most important features of the psychoanalytic model: a technical manipulation of the patient-subject by the analyst is *not* sufficient; the treatment must set off a process of depth self-reflection in the patient-subject himself. "Analytic knowledge is also moral insight" (*KI*, p. 236). Such analytic knowledge on the part of the patient is self-reflection insofar as it exhibits certain features.

First, it includes two movements equally: the cognitive, and the affective and motivational. It is critique in the sense that the analytic power to dissolve dogmatic attitudes inheres in analytic insight. Critique terminates in a transformation of the affective-motivational basis, just as it begins with the need for practical transformation. Critique would not have the power to break up false consciousness if it were not impelled by a *passion for critique*. (*KI*, p. 234)

The analyst (critical theorist) is searching for the causes of the distorted self-formative processes of the patient-subject—causes hidden from the patient's consciousness. This discovery can be achieved only through a process of reconstruction and interpretation in which the analyst comes to understand how the patient's present behavior is related to the unconscious processes affecting it. But the success of therapy ultimately depends not on the analyst's understanding of the patient, but on the extent to which the patient by his own self-reflection can appropriate this analytic understanding and dissolve his own resistances. It is this depth knowledge that effects a transformation in the patient—a transformation which, while certainly not utopian, liberates him from the distorting causal efficacy of processes not initially accessible to his consciousness. Further, the experience of self-reflection by the patient is the criterion for the correctness of the depth interpretation of his condition.

For if the patient rejects a construction, the interpretation from which it has been derived cannot yet be considered refuted at all. For psychoanalytic assumptions refer to conditions in which the very experience in which they must corroborate themselves is suspended: the experience of reflection is the only criterion for the corroboration or failure of hypotheses. If it does not come about, there is still an alternative: either the interpretation is false (that

is, the theory or its application to a given case) or, to the contrary, the resistances, which have been correctly diagnosed, are too strong. The criterion
in virtue of which false constructions fail does not coincide with either controlled observation or communicative experience. The interpretation of a case
is corroborated only by the successful continuation of a self-formative process, that is by the completion of self-reflection, and not in any unmistakable
way by what the patient says, or how he *behaves*. (*KI*, p. 266)

This last point is especially important for understanding both psychoanalytic therapy and critical theory, and also helps sharpen an issue that
arose in my examination of Winch and Schutz. Both Winch and Schutz
argue that the concepts and models that the theorist employs must be
based on the ways in which individuals interpret their own actions and
the actions of others. But both are finally unclear about this relation—
about what effective limits common-sense thinking places on the constructions of the theorist. Both even acknowledge that psychoanalysis is
a discipline where the interpretations developed by the analyst involve
concepts which may be unintelligible to the subjects themselves. We have
seen too why this problem is central for understanding the status of social
and political theory: stressing that individuals ascribe meaning to their
actions and situations, and that this self-interpretation is constitutive of
social and political reality, is dialectically important for opposing those
who think that concepts such as "interpretation" and "subjective meaning" have no role to play in social and political theory. But the problems
that arise in distinguishing correct from incorrect, or better from worse,
interpretations must be faced and not obscured. Individuals may have
not only occasional false beliefs about what they are doing, but systematically distorted misconceptions of themselves, the meaning of their actions, and their historical situations. The recognition of the appropriate-
ness of an interpretation by the subjects involved is not sufficient to
justify the correctness of the interpretation. Winch and Schutz are sensitive to the distortions that can result in social theory when the theorist
imposes his own standards and biases on the social actors he is studying.
But they seem insensitive to the distortions that can and do result when
theories reflect the biases of those investigated.

Habermas wants to preserve the "truth" implicit in the demand that
ultimately the subjects themselves must be able to appropriate the interpretations of their actions developed by the theorist. At the same time
he wants to avoid the consequence of endorsing a conception of theory
which is only an ideological reflection of prejudices and false beliefs. His
critique of ideology is directed at isolating and exposing this consequence. The theorist may propose a correct interpretation of an individual

or group, but one which is strongly resisted and rejected by the subjects. (According to Marx, this happens both when the proletariat has not yet achieved a true consciousness of its historical condition, and when the capitalist denies that his actions are shaped by bourgeois ideology.) But the subjects may also corroborate a false or distorted interpretation of their actions, precisely because they understand their own actions in systematically distorted ways. Consequently there are two extremes to avoid: assuming that corroboration by the subjects either constitutes verification of the interpretation or is irrelevant to it. This is why Habermas stresses that "the interpretation of a case is corroborated only by the successful *continuation of a self-formative* process, that is by the completion of self-reflection, and not in any unmistakable way by what the patient says, or how he *behaves*" (*KI,* p. 266).

It is essential to discriminate—as Habermas does not always carefully do—those features of the psychoanalytic model that he appropriates and thinks relevant for an understanding of critique from those which he rejects. Habermas uses the psychoanalytic model to illustrate a form of knowledge that exhibits the essential features of critique—a form of knowledge guided by an emancipatory interest that requires a depth interpretation achievable only through an analysis of self-formative processes. But this does not mean that Habermas endorses psychoanalytic theory's claim to provide the basic or the most perspicuous categories for the interpretation of human behavior. Freud himself thought of the therapeutic situation as a primary and one-to-one relationship between two unequals. He not only was skeptical of extending this relationship to a group, but doubted the ability of the individual to engage in self-analysis. Further, there is a way of construing the analytic situation in which its success is due primarily to the type of technical manipulation and authoritative power relationship that Habermas deplores. As Freud says in a passage cited by Habermas:

Cruel though it may sound, we must see to it that the patient's suffering, to a degree that is in some way or other effective, does not come to an end prematurely. If, owing to the symptoms having been taken apart and having lost their value, his suffering becomes mitigated, we must reinstate it elsewhere in the form of some appreciable privation; otherwise, we run the danger of never achieving any improvements except quite insignificant and transitory ones. (*KI,* p. 234)

Habermas is aware that his analogy between psychoanalysis and critical social theory is—like all analogies—selective, and has defended himself against the charge that his own understanding of psychoanalysis is both idealized and mistaken.[37] The use he makes of the psychoanalytic model is shaped by, and shapes, his understanding of Hegel and Marx.

If we think of Hegel's analysis of the self-formation and self-reflection of human beings not from the point of view of the philosophic "we" who contemplates and comprehends this process, but from the perspective of the subjects who undergo it, then each of the forms of consciousness can be understood as a life-experience in which the subjects cling to what they take to be their reality. It is only in the dialectical working out of these situations that the participants confront the existential conflicts and contradictions implicit in their situation, and realize the disparity between their initial "certitude" and the "truth." In the course of this experience —which involves a cognitive, affective, and practical transformation as moments of a single process—there is a movement toward emancipation and autonomy. The most famous example is the dialectic of master and slave. The slave initially clings to his bondage and grasps his reality as the master's slave, only to discover through the experience of "service and obedience"—the condition for "absolute fear"—that he has a mind of his own (*der eigene Sinn*), and that his reality is not exhausted in being the master's slave. The dialectical movement here—which according to Hegel results initially in the most abstract sort of freedom for the slave—is characteristic of each of the successive forms of consciousness.[38] In each stage there is a critical moment of insight that dissolves the determinate form of false consciousness which has imprisoned the subject. Habermas sharply criticizes Hegel for ordering the successive forms of consciousness into a single story of the realization of *Geist,* but this does not diminish his conviction that Hegel understood and captured the experience of self-reflection.

Habermas agrees with Marx, however, that the all-embracing dialectic of *Geist* is a mystification; that Hegel failed to understand the concrete historical ways in which men form themselves through labor; and that the experience of self-reflection is systematically distorted by these historical material conditions of production. While Habermas accuses Marx of succumbing to an inverted form of Hegel's reductionism where the self-formation of the human species is interpreted exclusively through the dialectic of labor, Habermas does claim that Marx showed us the nature of critique. In the drive toward a specific detailed analysis of the structures and dynamics of capitalism, Marx's critique is guided by an emancipatory interest. The primary intention is not to lay bare the iron laws of political economy from a disinterested perspective; indeed, insofar as Marx speaks in this manner, Habermas argues that he is betraying his own critical intent. Rather, Marx's aim is to provide a detailed interpretation of capitalism which will give the proletariat a true understanding of its historical situation and lead to revolutionary praxis. Habermas sees in *Capital* no sharp break with Marx's earliest speculations, but the fulfillment of a *promise* of critique formulated in the early writings.[39] Habermas' criticisms of Marx are many: that the most basic categories of a critique of political economy need to be drastically revised; that Marx at times succumbed to and endorsed a positivistic self-understanding of critique; that he failed to examine the epistemological foundations of critique itself; that he is guilty of a reductionism that has the most serious intellectual and practical consequences. Nevertheless Habermas argues that what now must be recovered and developed is both the theory and practice of critique.

Habermas' endeavor to recover and further develop a critical theory of society modeled on Marx's critique of ideology and on Freud's psychoanalysis, raises many complex issues that need to be probed. There are, of course, issues of interpretation. To what extent is Habermas' interpretation of Freud and Marx correct? Will the analogies that Habermas draws between critique as practiced by Marx and Freud, and a critical theory of society itself, stand up to rational scrutiny? But for the purposes of this inquiry, the most important and difficult problems concern Habermas' systematic attempt to articulate and justify critique as a distinctive form of knowledge with its own epistemological integrity. This has been one of the main objects of attack by his critics.

In his investigations since the publication of *Knowledge and Human Interests,* the detailed clarification and justification of critique has been a dominant concern. Although Habermas' social theory of knowledge, which includes technical, practical, and emancipatory interests, is extremely ambitious in its aims, his recent attempt to develop a comprehensive theory of communicative competence, and to defend a consensus theory of truth, aspires to even more. Habermas has set for himself the goal of developing nothing less than a comprehensive theory of rationality encompassing both theoretical and practical reason. He is building upon some of the most sophisticated and technical recent work in philosophy of language and theoretical linguistics. This project is still very much in process; Habermas himself insists that what he has achieved thus far is not really a detailed theory, but a theory sketch and a program of what needs to be done—one which to date is more suggestive than substantive and convincing.[40]

Communicative Competence and Rationality

There are some who have been disappointed by this linguistic turn in Habermas' investigations. They think he has become so "sophisticated" and "subtle" that he has given up the attempt to unite theory and praxis.[41] There is certainly some truth in this charge. We need not be vulgar Marxists to appreciate that in the final analysis, when Marx himself referred to the unity of theory and praxis, he meant revolutionary praxis; he was not only the author of *Capital,* but a political organizer. Despite the criticisms and modifications of Marx by critical theorists, the promise of critical theory as originally formulated was that it had a practical intent, that it could and would lead to political revolutionary action. The enthusiastic revival of interest in critical theory by many young radicals in the nineteen fifties and early sixties stemmed from this hope. Their rapid disenchantment in the late sixties reflected bitter disappointment: the realization that critical theory had failed to provide any *strategic* orientation in what was to be done.

Furthermore, the very self-understanding of the nature of a theory with practical intent by critical theorists requires the existence of a group or class of individuals to whom it is primarily addressed, and who will be the agents of revolution. But as critical theory became more sophisticated, this central practical demand played less and less of a role. No critical theorist, including Habermas, has been absolutely clear on this point in the way that Marx was. To whom is critical theory addressed— fellow intellectuals? Who are the agents of revolution—students who read these esoteric books? If critical theorists blur these hard issues, then what is the difference between a critical theory of society and a liberal bourgeois ideology? Despite the lip service paid to Marx, are not critical theorists betraying what even *they* take to be the vital core of Marxism— the development of a theory with genuine practical intent? What difference is there between the rarefied conception of critical theory, and the errors of the young Hegelians that Marx so ruthlessly attacked and exposed?

These questions cannot be brushed aside, though it is inaccurate to say that Habermas has not seriously struggled with them. I will return to them when I consider Habermas' most recent reflections on the relation of theory and praxis. It is important, however, to see why Habermas has taken a "linguistic turn," what this means for him, and how the problems that he is now examining grow out of, and were implicit in, his earliest investigations. These central problems can be directly related to what I have tried to show in the course of this inquiry.

Habermas' sketch of a comprehensive theory of communicative competence must be understood in the context of a search for a comprehensive theory of rationality—a topic that is increasingly central for different lines of philosophic, social, and political inquiry. Despite the many diverse attacks on a positivistic self-understanding of knowledge and science, it would be irresponsible to ignore the challenge that positivism presents—a challenge which may be formulated as follows: Whatever disagreements there may be about the characteristics of the natural sciences, mathematics, and logic, there can be no doubt that these disciplines are the exemplars of warranted knowledge. One of the depth motivations for restricting the domain of legitimate knowledge to these disciplines or those which can be modeled upon them, was the revulsion against the belief that there are other forms of knowledge and other means of gaining knowledge. Positivists claimed that when we examine these other pretenders to knowledge, we discover that they lack what is characteristic of scientific knowledge: rational procedures for testing, validating, and rejecting hypotheses.

Tough-minded positivists have never been satisfied with general pronouncements and manifestos; clear, rigorous formulation and explication are required. Few movements in the history of philosophy have set such explicit standards for legitimate cognitive claims—standards by which the positivists' theses themselves were to be judged. This demand has been one of the great virtues of positivism. It says to its adversaries: if you assert that there are other forms of knowledge and other means for testing knowledge claims, you must clearly and rigorously state what these are and provide convincing justifications of their legitimacy.

It is, however, precisely this central virtue of positivism that led to its downfall. There is not a single major thesis advanced by either nineteenth-century positivists or the Vienna Circle that has not been devastatingly criticized when measured by the positivists' own standards for philosophic argumentation. The original formulations of the analytic-synthetic dichotomy and the verifiability criterion of meaning have been abandoned. It has been effectively shown that the positivists' understanding of the natural sciences and the formal disciplines is grossly oversimplified. Whatever one's final judgment about the current disputes in the postempiricist philosophy and history of science—disputes among Kuhnians, Popperians, and mavericks like Paul Feyerabend, Imre Lakatos, and Stephen Toulmin, as well as moderates such as Dudley Shapere, Peter Achinstein, Mary Hesse, and Ernan McMullin—there is rational agreement about the inadequacy of the original positivist understanding of science, knowledge, and meaning. But if positivism is fundamentally mistaken, then what is a proper account of science and knowledge? There are fierce disagreements among those who stress different features of scientific inquiry.

Earlier I suggested that the best way to appreciate Kuhn's contribution to this discussion is by realizing the significance of the new questions that he raises and the lines of investigation that he has opened up—not by damning him for the solutions or nonsolutions he proposes. Many of these important questions cluster about the nature of rationality. The most perspicuous way of stating Kuhn's central insight concerning "paradigm-switches," or the decision among competing theoretical orientations, is that while this involves rational processes—and is not a matter of whim, arbitrary fiat, or irrational decision—our standard theories of rationality are not rich enough to illuminate these processes adequately. Even though Kuhn stresses the importance of "persuasive techniques" and "conversion," it is perfectly clear that he wants to distinguish between rational means of persuasion and nonrational or irrational means.

When Kuhn's investigations are seen from this point of view, we can also view them as part of a larger movement and change of orientation in recent philosophy. The problems that now come into focus are not localized ones restricted to the status and choice of paradigms or theories in the natural sciences. The same or analogous problems arise in clarifying what we mean in general by alternative conceptual schemes or frameworks, and what processes are involved when one conceptual scheme replaces or displaces another. In many areas of recent discussion—including the mind-body problem, scientific materialism and realism, the theory of action, and the theory of meaning and reference—philosophers are now confronting similar basic problems: problems in the theory of rationality.[42]

Habermas' theory of communicative competence, which he calls a "universal pragmatics," has the aim of systematically investigating "the general structures which appear in every possible speech situation, which are themselves produced through the performance of specific types of linguistic expressions, and which serve to situate pragmatically the expressions generated by the linguistically competent speaker." In keeping with the spirit in which I have examined Habermas' work thus far, I want to focus on a single theme that underlies this theory, because it bears directly on the epistemological understanding and justification of a critical theory of society. This theme can be clarified by stating a central objection to Habermas' social theory of knowledge.

There appears to be a lack of symmetry in Habermas' analysis of those disciplines guided by a technical and a practical interest, as opposed to those guided by an emancipatory interest. In the first two, Habermas is primarily interested in the *formal* conditions of the types of knowledge involved. To claim, for example, that the empirical-analytic sciences are guided by a technical interest which requires that the objects studied be constituted in certain ways in order to formulate hypothetical-deductive systems, does not prejudice the issue of which theoretical schemes will be corroborated or falsified in the course of scientific inquiry. Again, to note the ways in which the historical-hermeneutic disciplines differ from the empirical-analytic sciences in the "objects" that they study, the methods employed in studying them, and the criteria used in evaluating competing interpretations, does not prejudice—or illuminate—the issue of how we are to judge among competing interpretations.

But an emancipatory interest, and the disciplines supposedly guided by it, appear to be something quite different. Such a cognitive interest is not merely *formal,* it is *substantive* and *normative.* It dictates what ought to be the aim both of our study of society and of society itself—human emancipation. Habermas seems to be doing precisely what he accuses others of—smuggling in his own normative biases under the guise of an objective analysis of reason as self-reflection. Whatever our sympathy with such an understanding of the role of critique, we must recognize it for what it is: a substantive normative theory which cannot be justified by an appeal to the formal conditions of reason and knowledge.

This objection is a variation on the claim that there is a categorial and unbridgeable dichotomy between fact and value, the *is* and the *ought,* the descriptive and prescriptive modes of discourse. To those who accept some form of these dichotomies, it has always seemed, despite their claims to "overcome" them, that Hegelians and Marxists are guilty of conceptual confusion. This objection has frequently been advanced against Marx himself. It is claimed that what informs Marx's work is a normative blueprint of what society ought to be like, and that this normative bias is the basis of his critique of political economy. In another context I have argued that to view Marx in this way—whether to criticize or to defend him—is a fundamental mistake.[43]

What Habermas seeks to establish in his theory of communicative competence—at a much more abstract and self-consciously epistemological level—parallels what Marx sought to accomplish in his own critique of political economy. Marx argues that, implicit in the concrete historical forms of alienation and exploitation that now exist, are the real dynamic potentialities for radically transforming this existing historical situation. Marx's orientation, like Hegel's, bears a stronger affinity to classical thought—especially Aristotle—than it does to such moderns as Hume. It is precisely by studying what *is*—what now exists in a determinate historical form—that we can discover the real historical potentialities of human beings. We can do this because we do not assume that what now exists is opaque and must be taken as a brute given; rather it is an historical expression of what is essential. Hegel would say that what is essential shows or manifests itself (*erscheinen*) through appearance; Marx, that what now exists is itself the result of an historically alienated form of human production which can be radically transformed. If we speak the language of norms—a language of which both Hegel and Marx were deeply suspicious because it suggests that norms are "cut off" from what is—then we would say that norms are *not* externally related to what human beings actually do, but are *presupposed* and *anticipated* in the determinate alienated forms of action by which men now shape themselves.

In a parallel manner Habermas argues that human discourse or speech —even in its systematically distorted forms—both *presupposes* and *anticipates* an ideal speech situation in which both the theoretical and practical conditions exist for unrestrained communication and dialogue. To explain what this means, I need to clarify a distinction that plays an increasingly important role in Habermas' most recent work: the distinction between *action* and *discourse*.

Communicative *action*—which may involve speech as well as nonverbal communication—requires a background consensus that is accepted or taken for granted, while *discourse* arises when this background consensus is disturbed or called into question.

Discourses help test the truth claims of opinions (and norms) which the speakers no longer take for granted. In discourse, the 'force' of the argument is the only permissible compulsion, whereas co-operative search for truth is the only permissible motive. Because of their communicative structure, discourses do not compel their participants to act. Nor do they accommodate processes whereby information can be acquired. They are purged of action and experience. The relation between discourses and information is one where the latter is fed into the former. The output of discourses . . . consists in recognition or rejection of problematic truth claims. Discourses produce nothing but arguments.[44]

Habermas is well aware that this characterization of discourse is a theoretical construct; in actual life the distinction between communicative action and communicative discourse is fluid, not fixed. He uses this construct to make much more explicit than in his earlier work the distinctions among experience, action, and argumentation. Habermas claims that there are generic features characteristic of all discourse—dialogue-constitutive universals—as well as features which enable us to discriminate different types and levels of discourse. Thus there are distinctive types of discourse corresponding to the different types of knowledge guided by the primary cognitive interests.

Building on Wittgenstein's understanding of language games, and Austin's and Searle's analysis of speech acts—as well as Chomsky's analysis of linguistic competence—Habermas notes that all linguistic communication presupposes a background consensus. This consensus can be analyzed as involving four different nonreducible validity claims (*Geltungsansprüche*), of which the claim to truth stressed in the preceding quotation is only one. These claims include the *comprehensibility* of the utterance; the *truth* of its propositional content (when assertions are made); the *legitimacy* or rightness of its performative content; and the *veracity* of the speaker. In normal contexts of communicative action, these four claims are not questioned; but when a language game is disturbed or the background consensus breaks down, then the appropriate form and level of discourse is required in order to assess the implicit claim to validity. Any of the four claims may be questioned.[45]

Such questioning calls for a discourse in which the relevant claim to validity is examined and tested. The aim of such discourse is to distinguish an *accepted* consensus—one which is now challenged—from a *rational* consensus. The claims to validity implicit in the initial speech situation must then be judged with regard to the argumentation of the appropriate discourse. It is argumentation itself that is the basis for determining whether a consensus is rational or not. This is not to deny that in any given instance we may be mistaken: we may judge a consensus to be rational where further reflection and argumentation indicate that it is not.

What are the *criteria* for determining whether the consensus reached is a rational one? What are the criteria of argumentation itself? Habermas claims that there are no fixed decision procedures or explicit criteria which will definitively set off a rational consensus from one which is not; we can only have recourse to argumentation itself. But it may be objected that this merely pushes the question back one step further. Argumentation presupposes a consensus: how else can we rationally agree about what are sound and unsound, or better and worse, arguments? We seem to be on the verge of a vicious infinite regress or a vicious circle. Habermas not only is aware of this possibility, but develops his argument to bring out its full force.

Is there a solution? Habermas thinks so: what is required is an understanding of the sense in which an ideal speech act is both presupposed and anticipated in every speech act.

No matter how the intersubjectivity of mutual understanding may be deformed, the *design* of an ideal speech situation is necessarily implied in the structure of potential speech, since all speech, even intentional deception, is oriented toward the idea of truth. This idea can be analyzed with regard to a consensus achieved in unrestrained and universal discourse. In so far as we master the means for the construction of the ideal speech situation, we can conceive the ideas of truth, freedom, and justice, which interpenetrate each other—although of course only as ideas. On the strength of communicative competence alone, however, and independent of the empirical structures of the social system to which we belong, we are quite unable to realize the ideal speech situation, we can only anticipate it.[46]

Habermas' theory of communicative competence can be understood as an attempt to elucidate and justify the above statements. His aim is to provide an analysis of speech acts which will show how implicit in speech is the normative foundation of what ideal speech requires. To claim that "the *design* of an ideal speech situation is necessarily implied in the structure of potential speech," is to claim that every speech act implicitly makes a claim to validity—a claim which can be rationally assessed in ideal speech. In normal communicative interaction we do not question these claims to validity, but any one of them can be questioned, in which case the correctness of the claim must be established. This in turn requires discourse which itself presupposes and anticipates ideal discourse or ideal speech.

But what is "ideal speech"? Ideal speech is that form of discourse in which there is no other compulsion but the compulsion of argumentation itself; where there is a genuine symmetry among the participants involved, allowing a universal interchangeability of dialogue roles; where no form of domination exists. The power of ideal speech is the power of argumentation itself. What Habermas calls ideal speech comes remarkably close to Peirce's understanding of the ideal community of inquirers —a parallel that Habermas readily acknowledges. Like Peirce, Habermas thinks that such an ideal is presupposed and anticipated in *all* inquiry—even deformed inquiry—and that it serves as the critical standard for any given inquiry.

But we should also note the practical turn in Habermas' grand argument. This is indicated in the preceding citation by Habermas' linkage of truth, freedom, and justice. If we pursue what is required to even approximate such ideal speech and ideal dialogue, we realize that it demands an "ideal form of life"—one where objective social institutions and practices exist permitting free, symmetrical, responsible, unconstrained discourse. The ideal speech situation requires the existence of an ideal community, and it is through speech and discourse that such a form of life is manifested.[47] This is why Habermas insists that "on the strength of communicative competence alone . . . and *independent of the empirical structures of the social system to which we belong,* we are quite unable to realize the ideal speech situation, we can only anticipate it" (italics added).

Although Habermas has reservations about speaking of such an ideal as regulative—because it can become *constitutive* of human interactions —his thinking about its status closely parallels Kant in stressing that it is presupposed and anticipated in speech, and can exert a regulative power over men. The chain of reasoning that leads Habermas to this conclusion has been succinctly summarized by T. A. McCarthy:

> The analysis of speech shows it is oriented toward the idea of truth [more generally, toward the idea of validity—R.J.B.]. The analysis of 'truth' leads to the notion of a discursively achieved consensus. The analysis of 'consensus' shows this concept to involve a normative dimension. The analysis of the notion of a grounded consensus ties it to a speech situation which is free from all external and internal constraints, that is, in which the resulting consensus is due simply to the force of the better argument. Finally, the analysis of the ideal speech situation shows it to involve assumptions about the context of interaction in which speech is located. The end result of this chain of argument is that the very structure of speech involves the anticipation of a form of life in which autonomy and responsibility are possible. 'The critical theory of society takes this as its point of departure.' Its normative foundation is therefore not arbitrary, but inherent in the very structure of social action which it analyzes.[48]

Each stage of this grand argument requires far more careful and detailed explication, clarification, and justification, if it is to be rationally persuasive.[49] But the issues that Habermas locates are the ones that must be confronted in order to make progress in both the theory of rationality and the justification of the very idea of a critical theory of society. We can see now how Habermas would answer the objection that he is smuggling in his own substantive normative biases. He would certainly not deny that a critical theory guided by an emancipatory interest is substantive and normative; but such a normative foundation is *not* arbitrary and unjustified. The normative foundation of a critical theory is implicit in the very structure of social action that it analyzes.[50]

Theory and Praxis

Habermas' understanding of the relation of theory and praxis—especially in light of his distinction between action and discourse—is considerably more complicated than it may have originally appeared. I can complete my explication and interpretation of Habermas by returning to this theme. This will also provide a basis for evaluating the charge that Habermas has abandoned a serious attempt to unify theory and praxis.

In his new introduction to the fourth edition of *Theory and Practice,* Habermas tells us:

> The mediation of theory and praxis can only be clarified if to begin with we distinguish three functions, which are measured in terms of different criteria: the formation and extension of critical theorems, which can stand up to scientific discourse; the organization of processes of enlightenment, in which such theorems are applied and can be tested in a unique manner by the initiation of processes of reflection carried on within certain groups toward which these processes have been directed; and the selection of appropriate strategies, the solution of tactical questions, and the conduct of political struggle. On the first level, the aim is true statements, on the second, authentic insights, and on the third, prudent decisions. (*TP*, p. 32)

Habermas now seeks to distinguish carefully what seemed to be blended together in his earlier work. With the introduction of the concept of discourse in which "problematic claims to validity of opinions and norms" are analyzed, tested, and evaluated through the appropriate form of argumentation, we render "inoperative all motives except solely that of a cooperative readiness to arrive at an understanding." "Discourse therefore requires the virtualization of constraints on action" (*TP*, p. 18). In this respect Habermas emphasizes that dimension of the tradition of *theoria* which requires, in the search for truth, a bracketing of the constraints of action; the primary norm is to pursue and follow the best argument.

What is distinctive about Habermas' understanding of theoretical discourse is that it can no longer be conceived of with reference to a solitary ego or consciousness; it is essentially an intersubjective linguistic process requiring a community of inquirers. Like Peirce, he also wants to insist that it is an eminently fallible and self-corrective process which can never achieve absolute finality. The very nature of argumentation presupposes the possibility of further argumentation. The aim of such theoretical discourse is "true statements," and the criteria for testing and evaluating such truth claims are those intersubjective norms accepted by a free, unconstrained community of inquirers.

Earlier I made a distinction between the form of knowledge exemplified by Freud's psychoanalysis and Marx's critique of ideology, and the substantive claims made by these disciplines. Now we can see why this distinction is so important. Both psychoanalysis and the critique of ideology are based upon "critical theorems" concerning, respectively, the human psyche and the nature of political economy. These critical theorems themselves are subject to further argumentation in theoretical discourse. Indeed, Habermas' criticism of both Marx's critique of ideology and Freud's understanding of the human psyche can be understood as furthering the theoretical discourse required for testing, evaluating, modifying, and even rejecting what can no longer be rationally warranted.

If this were all that Habermas had to say about the nature of theory and theoretical discourse, there might be little difference between his claims and those of naturalists, conceptual analysts, and phenomenologists. At their best, all three approaches have emphasized that when it comes to assessing claims to knowledge about social and political reality, there must be a bracketing of the constraints of action; only argumentation itself can clarify, explicate, and justify knowledge claims. And Habermas agrees: it would be the grossest distortion of his thinking to say that he was denying or compromising this ideal of rational inquiry. On the contrary, he has shown how much of the social and political inquiry professing commitment to such an ideal falls short of it. The sharpest way, then, of stating Habermas' point is that a conception of social and political theory that *limits* itself to the ideal conditions for theoretical discourse leaves us with a myopic vision of the relation of theory and praxis.

The second function involved in the mediation of theory and praxis is "the organization of processes of enlightenment, in which such [critical] theorems are applied and can be tested in a unique manner by the initiation of the processes of reflection carried on within certain groups toward which these processes have been directed." This second function itself has a theoretical and a practical dimension. The theoretical dimension directs us to the need to provide an epistemological clarification and justification of this form of knowledge, i.e., critique. The results of theoretical discourse, then, are not neutral in regard to action. Nor is there a categorial and unbridgeable gap between explanation, understanding and interpretation on the one hand, and praxis and action on the other. It is precisely the application of warranted critical theorems in the process of enlightenment that mediates theory and praxis.

To the extent that such enlightenment is successful, processes of self-reflection and self-understanding are initiated among those to whom it is directed, thereby dissolving reified power relations and resistances.[51] The failure of such enlightenment may be due to many factors, and may even necessitate a re-examination of those very critical theorems that have been presumed to be warranted. Consequently there is a reciprocal and dynamic relation between theoretical discourse that aims at establishing critical theorems, and the application and testing of these theorems in the context of enlightenment. Critique is a form of "therapeutic knowledge"— not in the debased sense so characteristic of contemporary fashions, but in the classical sense of *paideia* (education) directed to the cultivation, formation, and "turning" of the human psyche.

Habermas has focused on the theoretical clarification and justification of critique. The reasons for this should now be clear: much of modern thought has implicitly or explicitly attacked the very legitimacy of this form of knowledge. But Habermas has not been very illuminating about the practical dimensions of how one is to go about—in concrete political contexts—organizing the "processes of enlightenment."

In his most recent work Habermas emphasizes the third function of the mediation of theory and praxis: "the selection of appropriate strategies, the solution of tactical questions, and the conduct of political struggle." It is in regard to this third function that he most directly answers the charge that he has abandoned the project of seeking a unity of theory and praxis. Like Hegel and Marx—and unlike some of their followers—Habermas does *not* think that the approximation of a transformed consciousness in a concrete historical situation automatically leads to effective political action. His claim is even stronger: theory can never be used directly to justify political action. When this demand is placed upon theory—when it is assumed that theoretical statements can provide an absolute authority in deciding what is to be done—both theory and praxis are mutilated. "Stalinist *praxis* has furnished the fatal proof that a party organization which proceeds instrumentally and a Marxism which has degenerated into a science of apologetics complement each other only too well" (*TP,* p. 36).

Theory cannot have the same function for the organization of action, of the political struggle, as it has for the organization of enlightenment. The practical consequences of self-reflection are changes in attitude which result from insight into causalities in the past, and indeed result of themselves. In contrast, strategic action oriented toward the future, which is prepared for in the internal discussion of groups, who (as the avant-garde) presuppose for themselves already successfully completed processes of enlightenment, cannot be justified in the same manner by reflective knowledge. (*TP,* p. 39)

The importance of the distinctions among the contexts of unconstrained theoretical discourse, enlightenment, and strategic political action, cannot be underestimated. In one sense Habermas is much closer to Hegel—and Freud—than to Marx. We might interpret his thought as a retreat from Marx to Hegel, because it now becomes clear that the immediate aim of critique is insight into causalities *in the past.* It is therefore retrospective insofar as its aim is to initiate self-reflection by which we become aware of, and liberated from, the historical compulsions of the past. But such a "liberation" does not solve the problem of what is to be done. As Hegel himself so brilliantly realized—a point frequently suppressed or glossed over by his interpreters—the freedom that results when the bondsman realizes that he has a mind of his own is only the most abstract and empty type of freedom. It is not yet concrete freedom, and can arise in a world in which nothing has substantially changed.

But it would be false to claim that Habermas is simply retreating from Marx to Hegel, for he is highlighting a central problem that must be faced by anyone who takes Marx seriously. The intent of critical theorems is to provide us with an accurate depth understanding of our historical situation. Such theory can only become efficacious—a material force—to the extent that it correctly interprets this situation and initiates self-reflection. While theory understood in this manner is intimately related to the formation of a political consensus among those engaged in strategic action, it does not and cannot play the role of legitimizing and justifying what is to be done.

The organization of action must be distinguished from this process of enlightenment. While the theory legitimizes the work of enlightenment, as well as providing its own refutation when communication fails, and can, in any case, be corrected, it can by no means legitimize *a fortiori* the risky decisions of strategic action. Decisions for the political struggle cannot at the outset be justified theoretically and then be carried out organizationally. The sole possible justification at this level is consensus aimed at in practical discourse, among the participants, who, in the consciousness of their common interests and their knowledge of circumstances, of the predictable consequences and secondary consequences, are the only ones who can know what risks they are willing to undergo, and with what expectations. There can be no theory which at the outset can assure a world-historical mission in return for the potential sacrifices. (*TP,* p. 33)

By some, this insistence on the gap between theoretical justification and political or strategic action will be interpreted as a grand "cop-out." Those who think that the unity of theory and praxis means—or ought to mean—that theory will tell us precisely how "to change the world," will find this conclusion inevitable. They fail to realize—whether they are "vulgar Marxists" or "bourgeois" engineers—that they are trying to reduce all political action to technical control and manipulation. What they want is a theory or science so secure and so well grounded that it provides, once and for all, authoritative decision procedures for what is to be done. Ironically, those "Marxists" who claim that it is possible to achieve such a science—or that we already have it—are the true progeny of that great bourgeois thinker, Hobbes. They do not dispute the ideal implicit in Hobbes's project: that it is possible to achieve a scientific understanding of human beings and society which will provide a definitive basis for reconstructing or revolutionizing society. They claim that Marxism, when "properly" understood, has fulfilled or is fulfilling this promise; it is the "true" science which stands opposed to all forms of ideology. They fail to grasp that this makes science itself into ideology.

Habermas' radical opposition to all such "true believers"—whether of the right or the left—brings us full circle to the central questions that he posed at the beginning. The three functions of the mediation of theory and praxis show how Habermas answers these questions. "The rigor of scientific knowledge, which modern social philosophy demands," is relevant to the level of theoretical discourse. In theoretical discourse we seek an interpretation of social and political reality based on an understanding of structural regularities and causal determinants that have shaped this reality. We seek nomological knowledge, but our aim is "to determine when theoretical statements grasp invariant regularities of social action as such and when they express ideologically frozen relations of dependence that can in principle be transformed" (*KI,* p. 310). Such theoretical interpretations are subject only to the compulsion of the better argument. Theoretical discourse is fallible and self-corrective; it is always open to further testing and criticism, for no interpretation has absolute certainty or authority. Theoretical discourse itself presupposes and anticipates an ideal discourse carried on by an ideal community of inquirers.

Theoretical discourse is intimately and dynamically related to the processes of enlightenment characteristic of systematic critique. It provides the basis for a depth interpretation by which we can attain an insight "into the causalities in the past" and initiate self-reflection. This results in a cognitive, affective, and practical transformation in the subjects addressed. To the extent that such critique is effective in initiating genuine self-reflection, it provides a partial confirmation of the correctness of the critical theorems established in theoretical discourse. To the extent that it fails, it may require re-examination and further argumentation about the validity of our critical interpretations. Here too Habermas is calling attention to a fundamental ambiguity intrinsic to the human condition. We are never in a position to know with absolute certainty that critical enlightenment has been effective—that it has liberated us from the ideologically frozen constraints of the past, and initiated genuine self-reflection. The complexity, strength, and deviousness of the forms of resistance; the inadequacy of mere "intellectual understanding" to effect a radical transformation; the fact that any claim to enlightened understanding may itself be a deeper and subtler form of self-deception—these obstacles can never be completely discounted in our evaluation of the success or failure of critique.

When we turn to those concrete situations which require practical discourse directed toward political action, we see most clearly how Habermas seeks to redeem the promise of the classical—specifically, the Aristotelian—understanding of praxis. Such practical discourse is grounded in theoretical discourse and the processes of enlightenment. But while theory and enlightenment inform practical discourse, no theory can legitimize the "risky decisions of strategic action," or guarantee a world-historical role to political actors. "The sole possible justification at this level is consensus aimed at in practical discourse, among the participants" (*TP*, p. 33).

This is the level of praxis requiring practical judgment and phronesis. Practical discourse directed toward political action cannot be reduced to technical control or the technical application of theoretical knowledge, for this distorts human social life and the medium of communicative action. All the lines of Habermas' investigations converge in emphasizing that the most urgent practical problem of our time is to oppose all those intellectual and material tendencies that undermine or suppress practical discourse, and to work toward the achievement of those objective institutions in which such practical discourse can be concretely realized. By his own admission, Habermas has not gone far in showing us how this is to be achieved in advanced technological societies. But few contemporary thinkers have been as perceptive and systematic in uncovering and relentlessly criticizing the powerful tendencies that conspire to undermine such praxis, and in focusing our attention on the vital need to redeem the promise of the classical politics without relinquishing the rigor of scientific knowledge.

The Unresolved Difficulties in Habermas

Habermas' attempt to develop a comprehensive critical theory of society is extraordinarily ambitious, immensely suggestive, and extremely frustrating. One cannot help admiring his encyclopedic knowledge, his broad historical perspective, and his mastery of current research in philosophy as well as the social and political disciplines. He has the rare ability to understand a wide variety of conflicting positions from the inside. Even when one sharply disagrees with his interpretations, they are always incisive and provocative. He has a keen sense of the central problems that must be confronted in furthering the development of social and political theory. He combines analytic skill with a drive toward synthesis and totality in seeking a critical understanding of human social life.

But Habermas' weaknesses are the other side of these virtues. There is an unsatisfactory abstractness and programmatic quality in his investigations. Part of this difficulty is due to the complexity of the issues, and his constant attempt to break new ground. Frequently, however, no sooner have we grasped what Habermas is up to in one domain of inquiry, than he passes on to another. He moves all too rapidly from a reconstruction of epistemology focusing on the primacy of cognitive interests, to a comprehensive theory of communicative competence and a universal pragmatics, then to a theory of social evolution and the crisis potential of advanced capitalism. There is, of course, a rationale for such a procedure: in the best tradition of dialectical thinking, Habermas shows us that in order to clarify and resolve issues in one area of inquiry, one is required to make progress with interrelated issues. But Habermas' overview is at times so breathtaking that crucial ambiguities are left unresolved, and persuasive concrete specification omitted.

Consider, for example, the heart of his theory of social knowledge: the primary knowledge-constitutive interests. Habermas does not pin down the precise epistemological status of these interests, or even the status of the claim that these three primary interests exist. Clearly he wants to avoid two extremes: that they are merely contingent empirical interests, or that they are rooted in a transcendental ego outside of and beyond human history. He endeavors to show that these interests are rooted in the very conditions of human social life, and speaks of them as "quasi-transcendental." But this designation is not very helpful in clarifying their positive status. Many critics have raised a variety of objections to this reconstruction of epistemology, and Habermas has sought to meet these objections. But his responses raise many more issues than they resolve. Habermas, who has engaged in a constant process of self-criticism, is far more trenchant in posing relevant questions than in providing clear, unambiguous answers.

Habermas' qualified concept of the transcendental or the "quasi-transcendental" departs so radically from the tradition of transcendental philosophy from Kant to Husserl, that the use of such terms obscures more than it illuminates. My quarrel with Habermas involves far more than the use of philosophical nomenclature. Habermas wants to preserve the central claim of transcendental philosophy that there are *categorially* distinct object domains, types of experience, and corresponding forms of inquiry. But he has not succeeded in establishing this central thesis.

The difficulties and unresolved ambiguities that I am locating are not limited to rarefied epistemological concerns, but have the utmost consequence for all of Habermas' thought. His typical strategy in criticizing previous thinkers is to show that they confuse categorially distinct levels of action. Thus, according to Habermas, Marx was guilty of stretching the concept of praxis to encompass both instrumental action and symbolic interaction. Hegel was guilty of a monistic drive that blurred the distinctions among the different levels of action, and of claiming that they could be comprehended in a single all-encompassing dialectic of *Geist*. Presumably, Peirce succumbs to the temptation of "reducing" all action to instrumental action.[52] But the validity of these criticisms is itself dependent on the acceptance of Habermas' categorial distinctions. The tables can be turned on Habermas by arguing that he seeks to introduce hard and fast distinctions where there is really only continuity. We can see this clearly when he uses the distinctive cognitive interests and their corresponding object domains to demarcate categorially distinct types of inquiry. Despite his protestations, it begins to look as if Habermas is guilty of the type of hypostatization that he so brilliantly exposes in others.

Habermas' thesis is that there are categorially distinct but interrelated forms of knowledge and inquiry. Both these emphases must be noted, for he wants not only to preserve the unity of rational discourse, but to show how it differentiates itself in its various modes. But has Habermas really justified the important claim that there are categorially different forms of knowledge and inquiry? I do not think so, for two primary reasons—the first centers on his metatheoretical understanding of the various disciplines, and the second on the actual practice and controversies within these disciplines.

One need not deny that a technical cognitive interest has played a major role in shaping the history and form of the empirical-analytic sciences, and that we are living in a time when there is a relentless drive to make all knowledge claims satisfy the demands of a technical interest. Habermas is extremely incisive in following out the distortive theoretical and practical consequences involved in such a project. But this is far different from saying that the empirical-analytic sciences are guided by a technical interest that determines the form of knowledge that such inquiries yield. At several points in this study, I have indicated that the post-empiricist philosophy and history of science is deeply questioning the categorial distinctions that separate even the hard natural sciences from what Habermas calls the historical-hermeneutical disciplines. One of the lessons to be learned from such inquiries is that the very characteristics thought distinctive of disputes in the historical-hermeneutical disciplines have their analogues in research controversies in the natural sciences. Reference to a technical interest is not sufficient to characterize the empirical-analytic sciences, for at their very foundation they require interpretative principles and a rational resolution of the conflict of interpretations.

Similarly, when Habermas claims that the historical-hermeneutical disciplines operate within a distinctive "methodological framework," his thesis is suspect. In the context of Continental—especially German—thought, with its vital tradition of the theory and practice of hermeneutics, there is a certain plausibility in claiming that such a discipline operates in a distinctive methodological framework. But Habermas never fully specifies what this framework is, nor does he meet the challenge of those who claim that there is a continuity—not necessarily a reduction—in all forms of rational inquiry.

It is here that we can see how a second set of considerations converge with metatheoretical ones to call into question Habermas' categorial distinctions. What has been most prominent in the historical-hermeneutical disciplines in the last decade or so is the attempt to apply techniques used successfully in the empirical-analytic disciplines to the study of texts and history. No doubt there have been exaggerated claims: scientism has been rampant in the proclamations of those who advocate the "new" history or the "new" archaeology. Habermas would not deny that the empirical-analytic sciences should be pressed to their limits, and that one can never predict the potential significance of such disciplines for critically understanding human life. But the primary issue in many of these internal disputes is whether in fact there are any sharp categorial distinctions to be made. I fail to see how these issues can be resolved by any type of "quasi-transcendental" or transcendental analysis. There is no clear boundary between "information"—Habermas' label for the cognitive output of the empirical-analytic sciences—and practical knowledge.

A similar point is even more dramatically illustrated in recent disputes about psychoanalysis and psychotherapy. We have seen how much of Habermas' case for a distinctive form of self-reflective knowledge, guided by the emancipatory interest, is warranted by his appeal to psychoanalysis and the critique of ideology. But what Habermas actually does is offer us an interpretation of psychoanalysis that highlights these emancipatory and self-reflective themes. This very interpretation of the psychoanalytic situation has been under severe attack. According to behavioral psychotherapists, whatever success even classical psychoanalysis has had in curing patients is *not* due to anything like the processes of self-reflection and analytic insight that Habermas stresses. Rather they claim that what actually takes place is a complex pattern of negative and positive reinforcement. Further, they assert, once we better understand the type of conditioning that takes place between patient and analyst, we can perfect the techniques and efficacy of such conditioning. It is not my intention to endorse this interpretation, but to emphasize that tangled disputes about the dynamics and structure of the therapeutic situation cannot be resolved by categorial analysis.

There is, then, a deep unresolved conflict in Habermas between the transcendental pole of his thinking which emphasizes a priori categorial distinctions, and more pragmatic tendencies that emphasize the continuity and overlapping similarities and differences in all forms of rational inquiry. Habermas has been extremely perceptive and forceful in exposing various forms of reductionism, whether they take a physicalist or historicist form. But the alternative he proposes is suspect. It is a fiction—and not a useful methodological one—to suggest that there are categorially different types of inquiry and knowledge. But it is not a fiction—rather, it is the locus of the most important controversies about the nature and limits of human knowledge, as it pertains to social and political inquiry—to see how the battle of competing technical, practical, and emancipatory cognitive interests continues to rage.

In presenting the outlines of Habermas' comprehensive theory of communicative competence, I have tried to show that his theory sketch is not an incidental afterthought or a turning away from the central problems that have preoccupied him. On the contrary, it is here that Habermas attempts to clarify and justify the foundations of a critical theory of society. The ambitiousness of his program cannot be underestimated: according to Habermas, such a theory seeks to clarify the formal characteristics of *all* speech acts. I have indicated that Habermas' researches published to date at best lay out the idea of such a theory—what a universal pragmatics might look like—and provide a few key suggestions for developing it. But here I want to focus on one central difficulty—a difficulty which in one form or another has plagued critical theorists from the earliest days.

Suppose for the moment that Habermas can clarify and justify the complex stages of his grand argument, viz., that all potential or actual speech presupposes and anticipates ideal speech, which in turn requires the material conditions—the ideal form of community life—in which such speech can be concretely realized. If this line of argumentation can be justified, then one clear consequence is that this chain of entailments is true under *any* empirical conditions. It is just as true for the individual who consciously seeks to deceive, as for groups guilty of self-deception or systematically distorted communication. But then it must be asked whether such a theory sheds any light on what leads human beings to overcome forms of distortive communication and work toward the conditions required for ideal speech. What seems to be lacking here is any illumination on the problem of human agency and motivation. In a new form we have the old problem that has faced every critical theorist: under what conditions will agents who have a clear understanding of their historical situation be motivated to overcome distorted communication and strive toward an ideal form of community life? What are the concrete dynamics of this process? Who are or will become its agents?

Habermas might reply that to require a comprehensive theory of communicative competence to answer such questions is to place an illegitimate demand upon it. The aim of such a theory is to provide a rational reconstruction of the formal conditions required for communicative competence. Only after we have a clear understanding of what is required for communicative competence can we examine the historical forms of social evolution and the real potentialities for future development. But I do not think that such a reply is entirely satisfactory.

According to Habermas, there are categorially different types and levels of action involved in social formation, and different types of crises that can break out in the development of society. Furthermore, there are a variety of ways in which these crises may be met or overcome. But there is no *necessity* that the resolution of a crisis will take the form of a movement toward an ideal form of community life. To be sure, according to Habermas this is always a real possibility; he has incisively attacked those who, citing the complexity of modern technological societies, believe the opposite. But even if we are convinced by Habermas' eloquent defense of such an ideal and its relevance to our historical situation, we want to know whether the present form of society indicates that such an ideal can be approximated. Do we have reason to think that individuals will strive to overcome distorted forms of communication? Do we have reason to believe that the ideal which Habermas claims is presupposed and anticipated in any form of communication will be realized, rather than the more ominous possibilities that confront us? And we want to gain some illumination—not a blueprint—of what forms of political activity can further the realization or approximation of this ideal.

Earlier I suggested that there is a strain in Habermas' thought that can be interpreted as a movement from Marx to Hegel. But it now begins to look as if there is a return to Kant. It looks as if—at this crucial juncture —Habermas is reformulating Kant's categorical imperative. One *ought* to act in such a manner as to further the realization of the ideal which is the ground of rational life; one *ought* to act so that his actions further the realization of the ideal form of community life (the kingdom of ends?). But if this is the direction of Habermas' thought, then he must confront the serious challenge that Hegel and Marx presented to a Kantian orientation, when they exposed how such a "noble" ideal can become impotent in the course of concrete history.

Once again we return to the central problem of the relation of theory and praxis. If one is to fulfill the promise of developing a critical theory that has practical intent, then it is not sufficient to recover the idea of self-reflection guided by an emancipatory interest. It is not sufficient to develop a critique of ideology and contemporary society which exposes the powerful tendencies to suppress practical discourse and force all rationality into the form of instrumental reason. It is not sufficient even to show that a critical theory can serve to further enlightenment and affect a transformation in political agents.

All the preceding is necessary. But, as Habermas so acutely shows, the very idea of practical discourse—of individuals engaged in argumentation directed toward rational will formation—can easily degenerate into a "mere" ideal, unless and until the material conditions required for such discourse are concretely realized and objectively instituted. Habermas, who has taught us this lesson so well, does not offer any real understanding of how this is to be accomplished. It is of little help to label such concrete problems "strategic," for this is only a name for our ignorance.[53] I do not raise these criticisms of Habermas by way of suggesting that others have succeeded where he has not. Rather, in the final analysis we must honestly confront the gap that has always existed—and still exists—between the idea of such a critical theory of society and its concrete practical realization.

The Restructuring of Social and Political Theory

AT the beginning of this study I claimed that there is a coherence, power, and direction in what initially appear to be diverse and unrelated critiques of mainstream social science and the naturalistic interpretation of social and political inquiry. I have now worked through a great variety of material, attempting to assess its strengths and weaknesses and to sort out what is right and wrong. But my primary objective has been to show how we can critically interpret what has been happening as contributing to a restructuring of social and political theory. In this concluding section I want to review some of the major stages or moments in this restructuring.

Let us return to the generalized picture of social and political inquiry that has been widely held by mainstream social scientists. Without reducing their self-understanding to caricature, or suggesting that mainstream social science is more monolithic and homogeneous than it really is, we have discovered common framework assumptions, attitudes, and expectations. There is a shared sense of what is and what ought to be the character of such a discipline, and of what constitutes scientific knowledge and explanation. Such a self-understanding reflects a total orientation that has substantive consequences for comprehending the nature of empirical knowledge; the relations of theory and practice, fact and value; the dichotomy between empirical and normative theory; and the education and role of the theorist. The optimism and self-confidence about what can and will be achieved in the social sciences is far more muted and qualified than a few decades ago. But it would be naive to underestimate the extent to which the framework assumptions and categorial distinctions of a mainstream orientation are still widely held.

One cannot give an adequate account of the pervasiveness and dominance of such an orientation simply by appealing to its intellectual origins or to the weight of the epistemological and methodological reasons advocated in support of it. Without succumbing to a simplistic reflex theory of the relation of ideas to the underlying social and political reality, we must nevertheless recognize the extent to which what we think, believe, and even feel, is shaped by our social and political lives. As the social and political worlds themselves function more like a grand complex interlocking system, as technology and bureaucracy spread, as technical, instrumental, or systems "rationality" affect and infect all dimensions of human life, there is a continual reinforcement of such a mainstream orientation. In this respect a mainstream perspective reflects what our social and political lives are in the process of becoming. This is one of the primary reasons why—despite all the criticisms—such an orientation is so resistant to fundamental change. Just as a mainstream orientation is rooted in modern society and politics, so too are the protest and challenge to it. Subsequent history has not refuted but confirmed Marx's penetrating insight that the very structure and dynamics of modern society generate basic conflicts and contradictions. What has become far more ambiguous today is our understanding of this crisis potential, and the ways in which crises can be diffused, suppressed, or managed.

We are confronted with a plethora of characterizations of the crisis of our times and the appropriate response to it. As I indicated earlier, even our talk about "crises" tends to degenerate into clichés. The most typical response to this situation has been despair, which takes a variety of forms. There is the temptation to cultural pessimism, to the belief that the forces at work in contemporary technological societies are so powerful and lawlike that it is naive or utopian to even attempt collective rational self-determination of the quality of human life. There is the despair of romantic protest; of the "great refusal"; of the retreat to pure theory; of the nostalgia for a golden era that never existed; of the frenzied seeking for ever new forms of individual salvation through physical or "spiritual" narcotics. There is the despair of that form of activism that spurns the very attempt to gain a rational understanding of what we are doing and why, and there is its reaction—the despair of apathy.

In this inquiry I have followed the course of another response to our contemporary situation: the response of those who are unwilling to submit to despair, although they are profoundly dissatisfied with existing forms of social and political reality, as well as with the typical ways we think about this reality and attempt to understand and explain it. What is required is a fundamental re-examination of the very categories by which we understand human action, and seek to relate theory to practice. The root issues concern the most basic questions about what human beings are, what they are in the process of becoming, and what they may yet become.

Initially, the most striking characteristic of the narrative that I have been relating is the negative moment in the critique of mainstream social science. At the core of a naturalistic understanding of social and political inquiry is the demand for empirical explanatory theories of human behavior. When this idea of empirical theory is fully articulated, it requires that we discover basic invariants, structures, or laws that can serve as a foundation for theoretical explanations—explanations which will take a deductive form, and from which we can derive counterfactual claims about the relations of independent and dependent variables. It has been projected that the social sciences, as they mature, will discover well-tested bodies of empirical theory which will eventually coalesce in ever more adequate and comprehensive theories. Yet if we judge the results to date of the endeavor to discover such theories, there is no hard evidence that this expectation is being fulfilled. There is lots of talk about such theories, elaborate classificatory schemes, post hoc interpretations, and programs of research, but scarcely anything that resembles nontrivial theories of even the "middle range."

The rationalizations for this disparity between expectation and fulfillment, which play on metaphors of the "youth," "immaturity," "preparadigmatic" and "paradigmatic" stages of scientific inquiry, have become thin and unconvincing. These rationalizations move in a closed circle. They presuppose what ought to be at issue: whether we have good reason to think that social and political inquiry should follow the development of the natural sciences.

We have seen how the case for a naturalistic understanding of the social sciences is based upon dubious interpretations of the natural sciences. These fluctuate between forms of naive empiricism that emphasize the collecting and processing of data—that is, building from the ground up—and more sophisticated forms of empiricism that emphasize the construction of hypothetical-deductive explanatory systems. Yet these conceptions of what is presumably most vital and central in the natural sciences have been challenged and modified as a result of postempiricist analyses in the philosophy and history of science.

When we examine those empirical theories that have been advanced, we discover again and again that they are not value-neutral, but reflect deep ideological biases and secrete controversial value positions. It is a fiction to think that we can neatly distinguish the descriptive from the evaluative components of these theories, for tacit evaluations are built into their very framework. Further, a close analysis of the basic categorial distinctions between empirical and normative theory, fact and value, descriptive and evaluative discourse, private subjective attitudes and public observable behavior, reveals how they break down and misrepresent the ways in which we describe, explain, and understand human action.

We have detected a fundamental ambivalence toward the status of normative theory. The official view holds that of course there is a proper place for normative theory, once we carefully distinguish it from the aims, methods, and claims of empirical theory. But this official tolerance is combined with a tendency to call into question the rationality—indeed, the very possibility—of a normative theory that evaluates the quality of social and political life.

This ambivalence is also reflected in the typical attitudes toward the relation between empirical knowledge and its practical application. We are constantly told that the more adequately we understand how the variables in social and political life interact, the better able we will be to apply this knowledge, make informed policy decisions, and solve practical problems. But we are also told that any such application must always involve reference to aims, goals, and purposes which cannot themselves be justified by scientific inquiry. While we are reassured of how relevant empirical inquiry is to making enlightened decisions, we are treated to pious generalities or outright skepticism when it comes to how we are to determine the ends, goals, and purposes to be achieved. A professed modesty regarding the nature and limits of empirical research is frequently combined with a dangerous arrogance about how such "expert" knowledge can already determine policy decisions, and serve as a basis for piecemeal or wholesale engineering.

For all these reasons, I think that Habermas is right when he argues that we are confronted with a relentless drive to transform all "real" issues concerning social and political life into technical questions where we are exclusively interested in the relations of means and ends, or the relationships among variables which lend themselves to technical control. This tendency itself must be seen in a larger social and political context where there is an "escalating scale of continually expanded technical control over nature and a continually refined administration of human beings and their relations to each other by means of social organization."[54] Increasingly, the only image of human beings that makes sense to many mainstream social scientists is one where individuals are exclusively motivated to maximize their private wants, desires, and interests, whatever these happen to be.

Although the points of attack have been most prominent in the critiques of mainstream social science, there has also emerged an alternative understanding of the nature of human action and of social and political reality. With this shift—this change of emphasis—new types of problems come into the foreground, and a new understanding arises of the tasks of social and political theory. I have argued that in the work of Anglo-Saxon thinkers from Berlin, through Winch and Louch, to Wolin, MacIntyre, Taylor, Pitkin, Ryan, and many others, common themes recur that have been pursued in a variety of ways. There has been not only a persistent questioning of the categorial distinctions so deeply embedded in a mainstream orientation, but a cumulative argument for a shift in perspective and categorial framework.

Against the view that we can divide all relevant social and political phenomena on the one hand into what is publicly observable like any other physical phenomena, and on the other hand into what is private and subjective, they have argued that this misrepresents what human action is. Human action cannot be properly identified, described, or understood unless we take account of the intentional descriptions, the meanings that such actions have for the agents involved, the ways in which they interpret their own actions and the actions of others. These intentional descriptions, meanings, and interpretations are not merely subjective states of mind which can be correlated with external behavior; they are constitutive of the activities and practices of our social and political lives. If we are to understand what human beings are, then we must uncover those models, interpretative schemes, and tacit understandings that penetrate human thought and action. Any conception of what is "strictly speaking" empirical or observable that excludes this dimension of human life, or simply relegates it to a realm of subjective opinion, is emasculated and epistemologically unwarranted.

The insistence on understanding human action with reference to the meaning that action has for agents is *not* a license for unbridled subjectivism, although this is frequently alleged by those who would classify all phenomena as either objective and physical or subjective and mental. One of the most dominant themes in analytic philosophy has been that language and human action are rooted in intersubjective contexts of communication, in intersubjective practices and forms of life.

This shift of emphasis affects the ways in which we understand the fact-value dichotomy. One need not deny that there are specific contexts in which it is important to distinguish biased value judgments from factual claims. But the obsession with this type of situation, and the misguided attempt to overgeneralize from it, has blinded many to the extent to which interpretations that are constitutive of social and political practices involve categories of assessment and evaluation. There has been a persistent tendency in mainstream social science to neglect, suppress, or underestimate this essential feature of social and political practices. What is taken for granted as the starting point for empirical research, as the realm of "brute fact" that presumably grounds such research, is itself the product of complex processes of interpretation which have historical origins.

The turning of attention to the analysis of practices, forms of life, and intersubjective meanings, and to understanding how social and political life consists of *moral* paradigms, enables us to see what underlies and is presupposed by the study of regularities and correlations. The debates about whether or not there is a logical incompatibility between the concepts required for describing and understanding social and political life, and those required for the study of nonhuman natural phenomena, have become increasingly sterile.

Social and political practices exhibit regularities and correlations, and it is necessary to understand these in order to understand social and political life. Furthermore we must ask how such practices arise, are sustained, and change. But how are we to understand the significance of the regularities and correlations discovered? Do they reveal invariant regularities of social action? Do they express ideologically frozen relations of dependence? Even the de facto applicability of the models and theories we construct to explain the workings of society and politics presupposes that the agents accept de jure standards of what is proper and reasonable behavior. These standards may appear so obvious and basic that we fail to realize that they are always open to rational criticism.

Any attempt to understand social and political life that ignores the study of regularities and correlations is itself threatened by ideological distortion. An adequate theoretical understanding of social and political life must seek to discover and uncover the ways in which agents understand themselves and interpret what they are doing. This task itself requires the investigation of the regularities and correlations exhibited in human practices. Furthermore, it is never sufficient to construct a model or ideal type of human action which simply reflects the common-sense constructs of everyday life. We must also ask whether there are systematic distortions or ideological mystifications in the agents' understanding of what they are doing. We must investigate the causes of these distortions and mystifications. We could not even begin to make a distinction between what human beings think they are doing and what they are actually doing, unless we appeal to independent evidence that reveals this disparity. The very evidence that we draw upon involves the appeal to regularities and correlations. This distinction, however, is not to be construed as a distinction between subjective mental beliefs of agents and their actual physical behavior. Rather it is a distinction between the self-understanding of the agents—a self-understanding preformed by intersubjective interpretative schemes—and those practices and activities that are taken for granted, that seem so basic that we frequently forget they involve tacit interpretations and evaluations.

I have also tried to show how the themes and preoccupations dominant in Anglo-Saxon critiques of mainstream social science are shared, reinforced, and further articulated in phenomenological investigations. Here too there is an attack on the basic epistemological dualisms that have penetrated so much of modern thought and shaped the categorial framework of mainstream social science. Here too there has been a shift of perspective so as to focus on the understanding of human action with reference to the meaning that such action has for the agents. As Schutz forcefully argues, meaning is not simply attached to or correlated with physical behavior; it is constitutive of human action. Just as analytic philosophy teaches that, to understand human action, one must understand how language and action are grounded in intersubjective practices and forms of life, so the phenomenological investigations of Schutz reveal a corresponding emphasis.

The main value of phenomenology, as it pertains to the understanding of social and political life, does *not* lie in its elaborate intellectual scaffolding: the hierarchy of different types of *epoché,* or the different levels of phenomenological analysis culminating in a transcendental phenomenology that aspires to lay bare the fundamental a priori structures of transcendental subjectivity and intersubjectivity. Rather, its main contribution to the restructuring of social and political theory is the way it forces us to examine critically the taken-for-grantedness of the social and political worlds. It turns our gaze to the constitution of social and political meanings, and thereby initiates new types of empirical and theoretical questions. It presents a challenge to develop empirical techniques by which we can uncover the common-sense constructs, interpretative schemes, modes of typification, and systems of relevance exhibited in everyday life. It reveals the necessity of grounding our models and theories of the social and political worlds in these first-order common-sense constructs.

But there are serious deficiencies and tensions within the phenomenological program. There is a fundamental ambiguity about the very meaning of the structures of the *Lebenswelt,* and a lack of clarity about how we are to distinguish those structures which are fundamental and a priori from those that are the product of historical forms of political and social life. There is a lack of clarity about the precise nature of the causal factors that influence the character of common-sense constructs and interpretative schemes. There is a failure to indicate how we are to evaluate and adjudicate among competing second-order interpretations of social and political phnomena, and how we are to avoid constructing models and theories that simply reflect the ideological biases of the agents we are studying.

Many of these difficulties can be traced back to the misguided attempt to isolate the interpretation of social and political reality from the study of regularities, correlations, and historical causes. Schutz is mistaken when he suggests that the analyses of genuine because-motives and in-order-to motives are two independent although complementary forms of inquiry. They are dialectically interrelated. We cannot explain human action unless we have a preliminary grasp of the in-order-to motives of human agents. But if we are to distinguish genuine from pseudo in-order-to motives, we must understand the causal influences operative in the formation of such motives. In this respect there is a tendency in phenomenology—as in the conceptual analysis advocated by Winch—to isolate and separate what is inseparable and dialectically interrelated.

It therefore becomes evident that an adequate theoretical understanding of society and politics must be critical. This critical dimension becomes most explicit among the advocates of a critical theory of society. I have raised doubts about Habermas' claim that there are categorially different forms of knowledge and inquiry; however, I do think he reveals powerfully the dialectic that moves from the systematic study of regularities and correlations to the necessity of seeking interpretations of the historical forms of social and political reality—interpretations that disclose the hidden causalities operative in the processes of social formation to the critical self-reflection and self-understanding of human agents. We find in his work one of the most systematic attempts to explore the meaning of critique, to clarify what it presupposes, and to probe its epistemological foundations. But the point to be emphasized is that Habermas has articulated a dialectical movement of thought that has much broader consequences—a dialectical movement likewise exhibited in the work of many who have begun from different starting points and worked in different intellectual traditions.

The most important feature in the restructuring of social and political theory has been the reassertion of the necessity and legitimacy of the critical function of theory. In this respect the restructuring of social and political theory reflects and contributes to a larger intellectual movement of our times. We are coming to realize that human rationality cannot be limited to technical and instrumental reason; that human beings can engage in rational argumentation in which there is a commitment to the critical evaluation of the quality of human life; that we can cultivate theoretical discourse in which there is a rational discussion of the conflict of critical interpretations, and practical discourse in which human beings try not simply to manipulate and control one another, but to understand one another genuinely and work together toward practical—not technical—ends.

The realization that an adequate theoretical understanding of society and politics must be critical has become explicit in the widely different critiques of mainstream social science that I have explored. It is already suggested by Isaiah Berlin when he claims that "the first step to understanding of men is the bringing to consciousness of the model or models that dominate and penetrate their thought and action," and that "the second task is to analyse the model itself, and this commits the analyst to accepting or modifying or rejecting it, and in the last case, to providing a more adequate one in its stead."[55] This critical theme reappears like a leitmotif throughout the work of the Anglo-Saxon critics of mainstream social science. It is affirmed by Sheldon Wolin when he writes:

Systems theories, communication theories, structural-functional theories are unpolitical theories shaped by the desire to explain certain forms of nonpolitical phenomena. They offer no significant choice or critical analysis of the quality, direction, or fate of public life. Where they are not alien intrusions, they share the same uncritical—and therefore untheoretical—assumptions of the prevailing ideology as that which justified the present "authoritative allocation of values" in our society.[56]

We can read the work of Winch, Louch, MacIntyre, Taylor, Ryan and Pitkin as stages in an argument showing that political and social theory is to be construed as genuine moral theory—"moral theory" in a sense that is much closer to the understanding of the human sciences as "moral sciences," in the eighteenth-century sense of this expression. They have shown that we cannot neatly separate the empirical study of human nature from the critical evaluation of the "quality, direction, and fate of public life." When Hanna Pitkin, for example, turns to the question of the "significance that Wittgenstein might have for political theory itself—for its actual substance, as distinct from the study of its history," she indicates that Wittgenstein has "something new and important to add to our objective self-knowledge"; that "like Nietzsche and Marx, Wittgenstein teaches that our thought is a reflection of our activity"; that like Freud he is concerned to liberate us from illusion, from mental pictures which "hold us captive."

Self-knowledge, perspective on ourselves, acceptance of the truth of human limitations, is alienating, one might suggest, only so long as it is confined to the intellectual realm, is kept out of contact with—our real, inner selves and our real, outer lives. Like Freudian doctrine, it can be distorted into a new, supersophisticated weapon of propaganda and manipulation, but like Freudian doctrine it can be a humanizing and liberating force where it takes the form of genuine insight rather than merely superficial, intellectual mastery.[57]

It is striking how the thought expressed here, and indeed the very language, complement and reinforce the themes that are central to Habermas' understanding of the nature and function of critique.

At first sight, it might seem somewhat strange that the type of insight Pitkin claims Wittgenstein and linguistic philosophy can help us to achieve in political theory is precisely what others have claimed to find in Husserl and phenomenology. Just as in linguistic philosophy an initial stage of uncommitted descriptivism has yielded to a growing self-conscious affirmation of the critical function of theory, so in phenomenology the same dialectical movement has occurred. Here too there is a growing realization of the internal necessity for theory to become critical. Consider how the words of Richard Zaner, a student of Schutz, support those of Pitkin.

If social scientific knowledge is at the same time knowledge of the self, of the social scientist himself, and conversely—and this circumstance necessitates making thematic the taken-for-granted typifications (beliefs, values, concepts, etc.) of beings whose typifications they are (the postulate of subjective interpretation of meaning)—then it is clearly evident that this task opens out onto an even more fundamental set of problems. The fact of "taken for grantedness" itself, the fact that typifications even arise in human consciousness, the fact that human beings themselves understand, live in, and act on the social world as the common matrix of their lives in terms of these typifications—all these point to a dimension of issues which undergird those of the social sciences and are systematically presupposed by them. These issues, I have argued, form the prime subject of phenomenological criticism. A truly radical discipline of criticism, then, is one that has the task of explication, and it relates to social science as the soil relates to the tree which is nourished by it, on and through which it can thrive.[58]

In citing these passages from such diverse thinkers, I do not want to suggest that they are all really saying the same thing; they are not. There is still a great deal of uncertainty about the precise meaning of critique, and a great deal of work to be done to articulate what it involves. But I do assert that underlying the manifest differences of philosophical styles and concern, a similar dialectical pattern is exhibited.

There is a common illusion that the history of thought proceeds in terms of clearly demarcated intellectual positions—positions that can be characterized in terms of either/or. In the contemporary understanding of social and political inquiry, this has played a significant role. Either social and political theory *must* be explanatory and empirical, it is thought, or it is not genuine theory at all. Either the theoretical understanding of the social and political worlds *must* be interpretative, or it is totallly inadequate. Either theory *must* be critical about the quality of social and political life, or it is not theory. But as Hegel has taught us, the history of culture develops by the assertion and pursuit of what appear to be irreconcilable conflicts and oppositions. We can discern in these "moments" a pattern that reveals how we grasp both their "truth" and their "falsity." As we work through these moments, we learn how what is true in each of them can be integrated into a more comprehensive understanding that enables us to reject what is false, partial, one-sided, and abstract. Hegel's insight still helps us understand what is going on, including specifically what is going on in the restructuring of social and political theory. In the final analysis we are not confronted with exclusive choices: *either* empirical theory *or* interpretative theory *or* critical theory. Rather, there is an internal dialectic in the restructuring of social and political theory: when we work through any one of these moments, we discover how the others are implicated. An adequate social and political theory must be *empirical, interpretative,* and *critical.*

One must be careful to neither exaggerate nor denigrate this new shared awareness of the nature, aims, and tasks of social and political theory. There is always the danger of thinking that intellectual criticism is itself sufficient to bring about fundamental change. We must learn again and again that it is not. One must not underestimate the fallibility of the critical enterprise and the power of resistances. But one must also beware of thinking that history is always working behind the backs of human beings, that critique can never be efficacious, never become a "material force." We can recognize that there will be no significant movement toward emancipation unless there is a transformation of social and political practices and institutions. But we must also recognize that human beings are capable of bringing to consciousness the interpretations, evaluations, and standards that they tacitly accept, and can subject them to rational criticism. We are still vastly ignorant of the material conditions necessary for critique to play a role in the transformation of existing forms of social and political reality.

But we do know—or ought to know—that if we fail to attempt the project of critique—if we do not seek a depth understanding of existing forms of social and political reality; if we are unwilling to engage in the type of argumentation required for evaluating the conflict of interpretations; if we do not strive to realize the conditions required for practical discourse—then we will surely become less than fully human.

Notes*

Introduction

1. See *Praxis and Action,* Part IV, for the reason I am skeptical about such a priori or transcendental arguments.
2. *The Phenomenology of Mind,* pp. 134–35.
3. See Hannah Arendt, *The Human Condition;* and Jürgen Habermas, *Theory and Practice.*
4. Jürgen Habermas, *Theory and Practice,* p. 44.

PART I
Empirical Theory

1. *Philosophy, Politics and Society* (First Series), ed. Peter Laslett, p. vii.
2. David Easton, *The Political System,* p. 4.
3. Alan Ryan, " 'Normal' Science or Political Ideology?", *Philosophy, Politics and Society* (Fourth Series), p. 86.
4. Clark L. Hull, *Principles of Behavior,* p. 400.
5. *Social Theory and Social Structure* has appeared in three editions and numerous printings. It was first published in 1949, revised in 1957, and revised again and enlarged in 1968. Many of the passages cited in my text are taken from the Introduction to the first edition, in which Merton proposed the need for "theories of the middle range." This Introduction was reprinted in the 1957 edition. In the 1968 enlarged edition, however, Merton expanded and revised his original introduction into two full-length chapters. In these new chapters Merton defends his conception of theories of the middle range against many of the criticisms that had been made of it during the intervening twenty years, and also gives a fuller characterization of the scientific status of sociology that takes account of recent work in the history and philosophy of science. Unless otherwise noted, all page references to Merton are to the first edition of *Social Theory and Social Structure.*
6. In the 1968 edition of *Social Theory and Social Structure,* Merton extends his list of natural scientists for whom there is no equivalent yet in the social sciences. "Perhaps sociology is not yet ready for its Einstein because it has not

* Bibliographical details for works cited are given in the Bibliography.

237

yet found its Kepler—to say nothing of its Newton, Laplace, Gibbs, Maxwell or Planck" (p. 47).

7. C. Wright Mills, *The Sociological Imagination,* especially Chapters 2 and 3.

8. Karl Popper emphasizes this point in *The Poverty of Historicism:* "The more fruitful debates on method are always inspired by certain practical problems which face the research worker; and nearly all debates on method which are not so inspired are characterized by that atmosphere of futile subtlety which has brought methodology into disrepute with the practical researcher" (p. 57).

9. A difficulty that one frequently discovers in the literature of the social sciences is the disparity between general statements about the nature of theories, scientific explanation, laws, etc., and the examples cited to illustrate these points. Merton is no less guilty of this than many of his less sophisticated colleagues. Since in this context I am interested in eliciting Merton's understanding of the nature and function of theory in the social sciences, I am passing over the many questions that can be raised about the adequacy of Merton's "reformulation" of Durkheim. Recent scholarship calls into question the historical and empirical accuracy of Merton's logical reconstruction. See Steven Lukes, *Emile Durkheim: His Life and Work,* Chapter 9; Dominick La Capra, *Emile Durkheim: Sociologist and Philosopher,* Chapter 4; Jack Douglas, "The Sociological Analysis of Social Meanings of Suicide," *Archives européennes de sociologie,* 7 (1966); and Hannan C. Selvin, "Durkheim's *Suicide* and Problems of Empirical Research," *American Journal of Sociology,* 62 (1958).

10. Robert K. Merton, *Social Theory and Social Structure* (1968 enlarged edition), p. 52.

11. Neil J. Smelser, *Essays in Sociological Explanation.* Unless otherwise noted, all page references to Smelser are to this volume.

12. Neil J. Smelser, "Some Replies and Some Reflections," *Sociological Inquiry,* 39 (Spring 1969), p. 217.

13. George C. Homans, "Bringing Men Back In," *American Sociological Review,* 29 (December 1964). Unless otherwise noted, all page references to Homans are to this article.

14. See also George C. Homans, *The Nature of Social Science.*

15. Two significant comprehensive attempts to clarify and answer these and related questions are: Ernest Nagel, *The Structure of Science,* and Carl G. Hempel, *Aspects of Scientific Explanation.*

16. Ernest Nagel, "A Formalization of Functionalism," *Logic Without Metaphysics,* p. 248.

17. Richard S. Rudner, *Philosophy of Social Science,* pp. 108–09.

18. Alan Ryan, *The Philosophy of Social Sciences,* pp. 190–91.

19. Neil J. Smelser, "Some Personal Thoughts on the Pursuit of Sociological Problems," *Sociological Inquiry,* 39 (Spring 1969) p. 160.

20. *Ibid.,* p. 162.

21. *Ibid.,* p. 163.

22. *Ibid.,* p. 164.

23. *Ibid.*

24. *Ibid.,* p. 166. For further criticisms of Smelser's work, see my comments and Smelser's reply in the "Review Symposium" of *Essays in Sociological Explanation, Sociological Inquiry,* 39 (Spring 1969).

25. Homans does *not* succeed where Smelser, Parsons, and Merton have failed. For a critique of Homans, see Peter P. Ekeh, *Social Exchange Theory.*

26. Richard S. Rudner, *Philosophy of Social Science,* p. 101.

27. Ernest Nagel, *The Structure of Science.* Unless otherwise noted, all page references to Nagel are to this volume.

28. David Easton, *The Political System,* p. 221.

29. For an examination of the differences between Weber's views and the interpretation of these by mainstream social scientists, see Alvin W. Gouldner, "Anti-minotaur: The Myth of Value-Free Sociology," *For Sociology;* and Denis Wrong's Introduction in *Max Weber,* ed. Dennis Wrong (Makers of Modern Social Science). One of the best discussions of the complexities of Weber's reflections on value issues is W. G. Runciman, *A Critique of Max Weber's Philosophy of Social Science.* A sharp critique of Weber is to be found in the writings of Leo Strauss. See his discussion of Weber, "Natural Right and the Distinction Between Fact and Values," *Natural Right and History,* where Strauss writes: "I contend that Weber's thesis necessarily leads to nihilism, or to the view that every preference, however evil, base, or insane, has to be judged before the tribunal of reason to be as legitimate as any other preference" (p. 42).

30. Max Weber, "Science as a Vocation," *From Max Weber: Essays in Sociology,* ed. H. H. Gerth and C. Wright Mills, p. 143.

31. Max Weber, "The Meaning of Ethical Neutrality," *The Methodology of the Social Sciences,* trans. and ed. Edward Shils and Henry A. Finch, p. 20.

32. *Ibid.*

33. *Ibid.,* p. 21.

34. Max Weber, "Science as a Vocation," p. 151.

35. Karl R. Popper, *The Poverty of Historicism.* Unless otherwise noted, all page references to Popper are to this volume.

36. Philip M. Hauser, "The Chaotic Society: Product of the Social Morphological Revolution," *American Sociological Review,* 34 (February 1969). Unless otherwise noted, all page references to Hauser are to this article.

37. Jürgen Habermas, *Knowledge and Human Interests,* p. 304. See my discussion of this point in Part IV, pp. 175 ff.

PART II
Language, Analysis, and Theory

1. Isaiah Berlin, "Does Political Theory Still Exist?" *Philosophy, Politics and Society* (Second Series), ed. Peter Laslett and W. G. Runciman, p. 19.
2. Introduction, *Philosophy, Politics and Society* (Second Series), p. vii.
3. *Ibid.*
4. See *Praxis and Action,* Part IV, "The Concept of Action: Analytic Philosophy." See also Hanna F. Pitkin's perceptive discussion of the concept of action in *Wittgenstein and Justice.*
5. Isaiah Berlin, "Does Political Theory Still Exist?" Unless otherwise noted, all page references to Berlin are to this essay.
6. Peter Winch, *The Idea of a Social Science,* pp. 72, 119, 94; italics added. Unless otherwise noted, all page references to Winch are to this monograph.
7. For critical discussion of Winch's work, see the exchange between A. R. Louch and Peter Winch: A. R. Louch, "The Very Idea of a Social Science," *Inquiry,* 6 (1963); Peter Winch, "Mr. Louch's Idea of a Social Science," *Inquiry,* 7 (1964); A. R. Louch, "On Misunderstanding Mr. Winch," *Inquiry,* 8 (1965). See also Louch's discussion of Winch in *Explanation and Human Action,* and the exchange between I. C. Jarvie and Peter Winch, "Understanding and Explanation in Sociology and Social Anthropology," *Explanation in the Behavioural Sciences,* ed. Robert Borger and Frank Cioffi. A number of the essays in the anthology *Rationality,* ed. Bryan R. Wilson, critically examine Winch's claims; see especially Alasdair MacIntyre, "Is Understanding Religion Compatible with Believing?" and "The Idea of a Social Science." Other critical discussions of Winch are to be found in Jürgen Habermas, *Zur Logik de Sozialwissenschaften;* Albrecht Wellmer, *Critical Theory of Society;* Hanna F. Pitkin, *Wittgenstein and Justice;* George Henrik von Wright, *Explanation and Understanding;* and Martin Hollis, "Witchcraft and Winchcraft," *Philosophy of the Social Sciences,* 2 (1972).
8. Winch's interpretation of Wittgenstein's remarks about "forms of life" are extremely dubious and controversial. Winch speaks of " 'science,' 'art,' etc." as forms of life, and this way of speaking has become fashionable among many philosophers who claim to be influenced by Wittgenstein. But Wittgenstein himself never made any such claims. It would be closer to his intentions to say, for example, that in science too there are varied forms of life, rather than to speak of science in general as a form of life. This is important because much of the polemical force of Winch's contrast between the study of social phenomena and science presupposes an understanding of science as a single, monolithic form of life. This not only departs from Wittgenstein, but violates the type of discriminating analysis and clarification that he demanded. For a

subtle discussion of the complexities of the notion of a "form of life," see Hanna F. Pitkin, *Wittgenstein and Justice*, pp. 132 ff.

9.   At times Winch fails to distinguish between the task of a philosopher and the task of the student of society—a lack of clarity that has caused much misunderstanding. Winch sometimes writes as if we have two options in the study of society—philosophy or science. Since he argues that the notion of a human society involves "a scheme of concepts that are logically incompatible with the kinds of explanation offered in the natural sciences," and that many of the more important theoretical issues concerning the social sciences belong to philosophy rather than science, he may *seem* to say that the proper study of society belongs to philosophy. This is how A. R. Louch reads Winch (see "The Very Idea of a Social Science," *Inquiry*, 6 [1963]). But such an interpretation is mistaken, even though Winch is partly responsible for it.

Winch does hold that the investigation of the "concept of the social" belongs to philosophy, and that in elucidating the notion of a form of life, philosophy elucidates what is distinctive about social phenomena. But this does not mean that the philosopher usurps the role of the student of society; rather, he helps to clarify the proper function of the student of society. Once we understand what is involved in the notion of a form of life, then we can turn our attention to the study of the *specific* forms of life in our own and alien societies. The student of society describes and interprets these varied forms of life, which can only be done by investigating their structures. "Just as the requirements of mathematics place limits on the acceptable forms of natural scientific theory, so do the requirements of philosophy place limits on the *acceptable forms of social scientific theory.*" ("Mr. Louch's Idea of a Social Science," *Inquiry*, 7 [1964], p. 205, italics added.)

But this clarification introduces another ambiguity. Winch speaks here of "the acceptable forms of social scientific theory," yet his original monograph suggests that he is calling into question the very idea of a *scentific* study of society, and the very possibility of a social scientific theory.

10.   Winch's claims about different "standards of rationality" have given rise to extensive philosophic controversy. Many of the articles dealing with this controversy have been collected in the volume *Rationality,* ed. Bryan H. Wilson.

11.   Alasdair MacIntyre, "The Idea of a Social Science," *Against the Self-Images of the Age,* p. 223.

12.   *Ibid.,* p. 221.

13.   See F. Waismann, "Language Strata," *How I See Philosophy*.

14.   For a discussion of the complexities involved in applying the concept of causality to the study of human behavior, see Donald Davidson, "Action, Reasons, and Causes," *Journal of Philosophy,* 60 (1963); Charles Taylor, *The Explanation of Behaviour;* Hanna F. Pitkin, *Wittgenstein and Justice;* and George Henrik von Wright, *Explanation and Understanding*.

15.   Hanna F. Pitkin, *Wittgenstein and Justice*, pp. 267–68.

16. R. Harré and P. F. Secord attempt to show, in *The Explanation of Social Behaviour,* how an understanding of a human being as a rule-following agent can serve as the basis for a *scientific* study of social behavior. In their preface they write: "The idea that a human being *must* be regarded in his social behaviour as a rule-following agent has been the basis of much contemporary criticism of social science, and has indeed been used by such writers as P. Winch . . . to attack the very conception of a scientific study of human social behaviour. We believe that this conclusion is mistaken, and that it derives from a misleading conception of the nature of science, developed in the schools of positivist philosophy" (p. v).

17. Peter Winch, "Understanding a Primitive Society," *Ethics and Action,* p. 42.

18. For Louch's criticism of Winch see the references in note 7.

19. "Mr. Louch's Idea of a Social Science," *Inquiry,* 7 (1964), p. 205.

20. A. R. Louch, *Explanation and Human Action.* Unless otherwise noted, all page references to Louch are to this book.

21. One should not underestimate the conceptual difficulties in the description of human performances. Witness the recent disputes about what is "deviant" behavior and what counts as "suicide." See Jack D. Douglas, *The Social Meanings of Suicide;* and, *Deviance & Respectability: The Social Construction of Moral Meanings,* ed. Jack D. Douglas.

22. On the appeal to "brute facts" or "brute data" in the social sciences, see Charles Taylor, "Interpretation and the Sciences of Man," *Review of Metaphysics,* 25 (1971), pp. 8 ff.

23. "Second Thoughts on Paradigms," *The Structure of Scientific Theories,* ed. Frederick Suppe, p. 459.

24. Alan Ryan, " 'Normal' Science or Political Ideology?", *Philosophy, Politics and Society* (Fourth Series), ed. Peter Laslett, W. G. Runciman, and Quentin Skinner, p. 89.

25. Thomas S. Kuhn, *The Structure of Scientific Revolutions,* 2nd ed. Unless otherwise noted, all page references to Kuhn are to this edition.

26. The critical literature on Kuhn is now already voluminous, but see the following where a number of the criticisms mentioned have been advanced: *Criticism and the Growth of Knowledge,* ed. Imre Lakatos and Alan Musgrave; Israel Scheffler, *Science and Subjectivity;* Carl R. Kordig, *The Justification of Scientific Change;* Dudley Shapere, "The Structure of Scientific Revolutions," *Philosophical Review,* 73 (1964), and "Meaning and Scientific Change," *Mind and Cosmos,* ed. R. Colodny; Stephen Toulmin, *Human Understanding;* Gerd Buchdahl, "A Revolution in Historiography of Science," *History of Science,* 4 (1965).

27. Margaret Mastermann, "The Nature of a Paradigm," *Criticism and the Growth of Knowledge,* ed. Imre Lakatos and Alan Musgrave.

28. "Reflections on My Critics," *Criticism and the Growth of Knowledge,* p. 234.

29.   In a footnote to his paper, "Second Thoughts on Paradigms," Kuhn writes: "Whatever paradigms may be, they are possessed by any scientific community, including the schools of the so-called 'pre-paradigm period.' My failure to see that point clearly has helped make a paradigm seem a quasi-mystical entity or property which, like charisma, transforms those infected by it. There is transformation, but it is not induced by the acquisition of a paradigm" (p. 461).

30.   Kuhn refers to such empirical techniques without elaborating what they are (see *The Structure of Scientific Revolutions*, p. 176). But if one examines the research that Kuhn mentions as examples of how we can empirically investigate the characteristics of scientific communities, these techniques do *not* distinguish between scientific communities and other closely knit intellectual communities.

31.   Even the isolation of the sense of a paradigm as an exemplar does not really help to distinguish science from other types of intellectual inquiry. Consider, for example, the role of exemplars in analytic philosophy—a field that Kuhn does not think of as scientific inquiry. Russell's analysis of definite descriptions, Ryle's analysis of mental concepts, and Wittgenstein's discussion of private languages have each served as powerful exemplars that guided philosophers in developing puzzle-solutions based upon the original exemplars. And like the exemplars that Kuhn discusses, they served as concrete models for analysis, rather than as full-blown theories or sets of rules for the solution of problems. Of course these exemplars were not universally accepted, but Kuhn himself has emphasized that even in science the acceptance of exemplars is by small groups of individuals. Furthermore, as a field like philosophy (or any humanistic discipline) becomes increasingly specialized, we find "invisible colleges," technical journals, exchange of prepublished papers, and explicit references to key papers and authorities. None of this belittles the importance of exemplars in science. I want to insist, however, that the role exemplars play in *any* closely knit intellectual endeavor is just as important.

32.   On occasion Kuhn slides from talk about the choice of "paradigms" to the choice of "theories." But Kuhn does not identify theories with paradigms. A theory *may* serve as paradigm, but so may other elements. His new terminology of "exemplars" is intended to communicate more clearly that a paradigm need not be a theory. Kuhn has further misgivings about the term "theory" because, in much of the literature of philosophy of science, theories are understood as well-formulated hypothetical-deductive systems. Kuhn insists that—contrary to the claims of logical empiricists—such hypothetical-deductive systems are far less significant in actual scientific inquiry than philosophers of science realize.

33.   In a similar vein, Kuhn says ("Reflections on My Critics," *Criticism and the Growth of Knowledge*): "What I am denying then is neither the existence of good reasons nor that these reasons are of the sort usually described. I am,

however, insisting that such reasons constitute values to be used in making choices rather than rules of choice. Scientists who share them may nevertheless make different choices in the same concrete situation. Two factors are deeply involved. First, in many concrete situations, different values, though all constitutive of good reasons, dictate different conclusions, different choices. In such cases of value-conflict (e.g., one theory is simpler but the other is more accurate) the relative weight placed on different values by different individuals can play a decisive role in individual choice. More important, though scientists share these values and must continue to do so if science is to survive, they do not all apply them in the same way. Simplicity, scope, fruitfulness, and even accuracy can be judged quite differently (which is not to say they may be judged arbitrarily) by different people. Again they may differ in their conclusions without violating any accepted rule" (p. 262).

34.   For an explanation of what Kuhn means by "translation," see *The Structure of Scientific Revolutions*, pp. 202 ff., and "Reflections on My Critics," *Criticism and the Growth of Knowledge*, pp. 268 ff.

35.   "Reflections on My Critics," *Criticism and the Growth of Knowledge*, p. 262.

36.   For a challenging overview of the issues involved in speaking of alternative conceptual frameworks and "choosing" among them, see Richard Rorty, "The World Well Lost," *Journal of Philosophy*, 69 (1972).

37.   "Reflections of My Critics," *Criticism and the Growth of Knowledge*, pp. 244–45.

38.   In order not to extend my discussion to unmanageable proportions, I have focused on the use and abuse of Kuhn among some political scientists and theorists. But the discussion of Kuhn has played a fundamental role in almost every one of the social sciences including sociology, anthropology, psychology, and economics. For a sampling of this literature see Robert W. Friedrichs, *A Sociology of Sociology;* the "Special Issue of Radical Paradigms in Economics," *Review of Radical Political Economics,* 3 (1971); *Historical Conception of Psychology,* ed. Mary Henle, Julian Jaynes, and John J. Sullivan; and *Reinventing Anthropology,* ed. Dell Hymes.

39.   David B. Truman, "Disillusion and Regeneration: The Quest for a Discipline," *American Political Science Review,* 59 (1965). Unless otherwise noted, all page references to Truman are to this article.

40.   Gabriel A. Almond, "Political Theory and Political Science," *American Political Science Review,* 60 (1966). Unless otherwise noted, all page references in the text are to this article.

41.   J. Peter Euben, "Political Science and Political Silence," *Power and Community: Dissenting Essays in Political Science,* ed. Philip H. Green and Sanford Levinson, p. 8.

42.   Not only is this claim false, but Almond fails to realize that his brief historical sketch exhibits the very features of the histories of disciplines that Kuhn severely criticizes. Almond's sketch is written from the perspective of our present "scientific" breakthroughs, where we evaluate earlier contribu-

tions with reference to current "scientific" standards. Although the terminology is Kuhn's, the substantive content of Almond's conception of the history of political theory is closer in spirit to Comte. For a critique of the way in which many social scientists approach the history of their own discipline, see Robert K. Merton, *The Sociology of Science.*

43. For a critique of Almond's work, and more generally of the underlying epistemological and methodological assumptions of his approach, see Alasdair MacIntyre, "Is a Science of Comparative Politics Possible?" *Against the Self-Images of the Age;* Charles Taylor, "Neutrality in Political Science," *Philosophy, Politics and Society* (Third Series), ed. Peter Laslett and W. G. Runciman; Charles Taylor, "Interpretation and the Sciences of Man," *Review of Metaphysics,* 25 (1971); Alan Ryan, " 'Normal Science' or Political Ideology?", *Philosophy, Politics and Society* (Fourth Series), ed. Peter Laslett, W. G. Runciman, and Quentin Skinner; and Alan Ryan, *The Philosophy of the Social Sciences,* pp. 154 ff.

44. On the meaning and self-understanding of the behavioral revolution in political science, see David B. Truman, "The Implications of Political Behavior Research," *Items,* 5 (1951), Social Science Research Council; and Robert A. Dahl, "The Behavioral Approach in Political Science: Epitaph for a Monument to a Successful Protest," *American Political Science Review,* 55 (1961).

45. This passage is cited in Sheldon Wolin, "Paradigms and Political Theories," *Politics and Experience,* ed. Preston King and B. C. Parekh. Unless otherwise noted, all page references to Wolin are to this article.

46. In drawing the analogy between Kuhn's "image of science" and the history of political theory, Wolin overlooks two important warnings that Kuhn frequently reiterates. The first is a warning against the trivialization of Kuhn's thesis. Kuhn frequently tells us that, in studying the history of most disciplines, we can isolate periods of tradition punctuated by periods of rapid change that then give rise to new traditions. But this general point, he stresses, fails to bring out anything distinctive about the development of science. For example, in commenting on the comparison of art and science, Kuhn writes: "In both the historian can discover periods during which practices conform to a tradition. . . . In both he is able to isolate periods of relatively rapid change. . . . That much, however, can probably be said about the development of any human enterprise." (Thomas Kuhn, "Comment" in a symposium on "The New Reality in Art and Science," *Comparative Studies in Society and History,* 11 [1969], p. 409.)

The second warning concerns the mistake of thinking that paradigms can be identified with major theories, for this neglects the reasons why Kuhn has adopted the language of paradigms. In the "Comment" cited above, Kuhn writes that he "never intended to limit the notions of paradigm and revolution 'to major theories,' " that the special importance of those concepts is that "they permit a fuller understanding of the oddly non-cumulative character of events like the discovery of oxygen, of X-rays, or of the planet Uranus" (p. 412).

For further comments on the differences between paradigms and theories, see his postscript to *The Structure of Scientific Revolutions,* pp. 182 ff.

47. Kuhn is quite emphatic on this point. "In no area is the contrast between art and science clearer. Science textbooks are studded with the names and sometimes the portraits of old heroes, but only historians read old scientific works. In science new breakthroughs do initiate the removal of suddenly outdated books and journals from their active position in a science library to the desuetude of a general depository. . . . Unlike art, science destroys its past" (see the "Comment" listed in note 46, p. 407).

48. That this is a parody of what Wolin wants to claim is clear from remarks in another essay. He writes that the behavioral revolution "has succeeded in transforming political science," but the transformation effected is one of *methodology,* not theory. "Whatever else it may be, a revolution without an initiating theory cannot qualify as a revolution by Kuhn's criterion." (Sheldon Wolin, "Political Theory as a Vocation," *Machiavelli and the Nature of Political Thought,* ed. Martin Fleisher, p. 26.)

But here, too, Wolin's infatuation with Kuhn obscures what he wants to say. Wolin is simply mistaken in saying that, according to Kuhn, a scientific revolution requires an initiating *theory* (see note 46). Further, while I think Wolin is right in insisting that political theories ought to offer "significant choice or critical analysis of the quality, direction, or fate of public life," there is no basis in Kuhn's analysis of science for making such a distinction between "genuine" political theories and "pseudo-political" theories, or for insisting that political theories must be critical in the sense that Wolin intends.

49. It would be tedious to show the many different ways the term "paradigm" has been used, even by those who think they are using it as Kuhn did. J. G. A. Pocock is still another political scientist (a political historian) for whom the notion of a paradigm is central. But the meaning he attaches to it and the use he makes of it are quite different from those of Almond, Truman, Wolin, and Kuhn. See J. G. A. Pocock, *Politics, Language and Time.*

50. Peter Winch, *The Idea of a Social Science,* p. 87.

51. A. R. Louch, *Explanation and Human Action,* p. 77.

52. Alan Ryan, " 'Normal Science' or Political Ideology?", *Philosophy, Politics and Society* (Fourth Series) p. 93.

53. The way the dominant paradigm of political society influences what is considered useful inquiry, and limits the language and concepts employed to investigate problems, is illustrated by John H. Scharr, "Legitimacy in the Modern State," *Power and Community: Dissenting Essays in Political Science,* ed. Philip Green and Sanford Levinson; Charles Taylor, "Interpretation and the Sciences of Man," *Review of Metaphysics,* 25 (1971); Alasdair MacIntyre, "Is a Science of Comparative Politics Possible?", *Against the Self-Images of the Age;* and Quentin Skinner, "The Empirical Theorists of Democracy and Their Critics: A Plague on Both Their Houses," *Political Theory,* 1 (1973).

54. It is difficult to pin down Wolin's attitude toward behaviorism. In "Paradigms and Political Theories" he contrasts "behavioral theory" with "traditional theory" (p. 152), but in "Political Theory as a Vocation" he denies that behaviorism is a *political* theory (pp. 26, 30). He draws the analogy between behaviorism and normal science, yet claims that the dominant paradigm of political scientists is an "ideological paradigm." Wolin's ambivalence is also indicated by what he takes to be the important subversive role of behavioral findings. "One of the most interesting and disturbing features of behavioural findings is their subversiveness. Many of the common notions about the quality of the democratic electorate have been shaken. The same might be said about prevailing beliefs about the democratic character of politics, decision-making in American communities, and the representativeness of elected officials." ("Paradigms and Political Theories," p. 152.)

55. See Alan Ryan's discussion of this point when he argues that the de facto applicability of the classical economic model of brokerage requires that "the actors should accept *de jure* standards of what is rational and acceptable behaviour" (" 'Normal Science' or Political Ideology?", pp. 96–97). Ryan not only develops a theme suggested by Berlin in his earlier essay, when he argued that the models and paradigms that human beings accept shape their beliefs and behavior, but also supports Louch's contention that classical economics is a moral theory. See also Charles Taylor's analysis of the depth and significance of a negotiating or brokerage model for the interpretation of political and social reality in "Interpretation and the Sciences of Man."

Louch's, Ryan's, and Taylor's analyses are also supported and explored by radical economists who have been challenging mainstream economic theories and research. These economists have also been influenced by Kuhn, and use the concept of a paradigm in ambiguous and conflicting ways. But what stands out in their work, too, are the nonanalogies between Kuhn's understanding of the natural sciences and the social sciences, especially the way in which economic reality can itself be understood as a moral paradigm. See the *Review of Radical Political Economics* 3 (1971). See also Edward J. Nell, "The Revival of Political Economy," *Social Research,* 39 (1972).

56. During the early years of the behavioral revolution, Hannah Arendt acutely noted this tendency in behaviorism: "The unfortunate truth about behaviorism and the validity of its laws is that the more people there are, the more likely they are to behave and less likely to tolerate nonbehavior. Statistically, this will be shown in the leveling out of fluctuation. In reality, deeds will have less and less chance to stem the tide of behavior, and events will more and more lose their significance; that is, their capacity to illuminate historical time. Statistical uniformity is by no means a harmless scientific ideal; it is the no longer secret political ideal of a society which, entirely submerged in the routine of everyday living, is at peace with the scientific outlook inherent in its very existence" (*The Human Condition,* p. 40).

57. For an historical examination of the concept of ideology, see George

Lichtheim, "The Concept of Ideology," *The Concept of Ideology and Other Essays*. See also Alasdair MacIntyre's discussion of ideology in *Against the Self-Images of the Age;* and John Plamenatz, *Ideology*.

58. Charles Taylor, "Neutrality in Political Science," *Philosophy, Politics and Society* (Third Series), ed. Peter Laslett and W. G. Runciman, p. 42.

59. *Ibid.*

60. *Ibid.*, pp. 56–57.

61. Alasdair MacIntyre, "Is a Science of Comparative Politics Possible?", *Against the Self-Images of the Age*, p. 278. See Hanna F. Pitkin's perceptive discussion of the dispute between Socrates and Thrasymachus, and its relation to modern disputes in political science. Hanna F. Pitkin, *Wittgenstein and Justice*, Chapter 8. For further confirmation of the ideological bias of contemporary definitions of legitimacy, see John H. Schaar, "Legitimacy in the Modern State," *Power and Community: Dissenting Essays in Political Science*, ed. Philip Green and Sanford Levinson.

62. Quentin Skinner, "The Empirical Theorists of Democracy and Their Critics: A Plague on Both Their Houses," *Political Theory*, 1 (August 1973), pp. 303–04.

63. See Wilfrid Sellars, "Empiricism and the Philosophy of Mind," *Science, Perception, and Reality*. See also my discussion of the "myth of the given" in Part IV of *Praxis and Action*.

64. For a detailed and subtle examination of how the ideal of objectivity is confused with objectivism in the policy sciences, see Laurence H. Tribe, "Policy Science: Analysis of Ideology," *Philosophy & Public Affairs*, 2 (1972).

65. Charles Taylor, "Interpretation and the Sciences of Man," *Review of Metaphysics*, 25 (1971), p. 27.

66. *Ibid.*, p. 24.

PART III
The Phenomenological Alternative

1. See J. J. C. Smart, *Philosophy and Scientific Realism;* David M. Armstrong, *A Materialist Theory of Mind;* and the readings in *Materialism and the Mind-Body Problem*, ed. David M. Rosenthal.

2. See my discussion in *Praxis and Action*, Part IV.

3. P. F. Strawson, *Individuals, An Essay in Descriptive Metaphysics*, p. 10.

4. Wilfrid Sellars, "Philosophy and the Scientific Image of Man," *Science, Perception and Reality*.

5. *Ibid.*, pp. 7–8.

6. Maurice Merleau-Ponty, *Phenomenology of Perception*, pp. viii–ix.

7. Wilfrid Sellars, "Philosophy and the Scientific Image of Man," *Science, Perception and Reality*, p. 25. Unless otherwise noted, all page references to Sellars are to this article. For a general overview of Sellars' philosophy, see

my article "Sellars' Vision of Man-in-the-World," *Review of Metaphysics*, 20 (1966).

8. For the details of Sellars' argument, see his exchange with R. M. Chisholm, "Intentionality and the Mental," *Minnesota Studies in the Philosophy of Science*, Vol. II.

9. See Wilfrid Sellars, "Phenomenalism," *Science, Perception and Reality; Science and Metaphysics*, Chapter 1; and "Science, Sense Impressions, and Sensa: A Reply to Cornman," *Review of Metaphysics*, 24 (1971).

10. For details of Sellars' concept of a person, see: *Science and Metaphysics*, Chapters 6 and 7; "Metaphysics and the Concept of a Person," *The Logical Way of Doing Things*, ed. Karel Lambert; and ". . . this I or he or it (the thing) which thinks . . . ," *Proceedings and Addresses of the American Philosophical Association*, 44 (1970–71).

11. Wilfrid Sellars, "Empiricism and the Philosophy of Mind," *Science, Perception and Reality*, p. 173.

12. For an explanation of what Sellars means by "behaviorism" and "behavioristics," see "Philosophy and the Scientific Image of Man," pp. 22 ff.

13. My discussion of Husserl is based primarily on *The Crisis of European Sciences and Transcendental Phenomenology*. Unless otherwise noted, all page references to Husserl are to this volume.

Among those influenced by Husserl, as well as Husserl scholars, an intellectual battle has raged concerning the status of this work in Husserl's corpus. At one extreme there are those who claim that the *Crisis* represents a break with Husserl's earlier work; at the other extreme, those who argue that it represents a continuous development. Although the manifest issue is the correct interpretation of the "historical" Husserl, the latent issue frequently concerns what are the most important or promising directions for phenomenological analysis. See Aron Gurwitch, "The Last Work of Edmund Husserl," *Studies in Phenomenology and Psychology;* Maurice Merleau-Ponty, "The Philosopher and His Shadow," *Signs;* Paul Ricoeur, *Husserl: An Analysis of His Phenomenology;* Maurice Natanson, *Edmund Husserl: Philosopher of Infinite Tasks;* Enzo Paci, *The Function of the Sciences of Man;* William Leiss, "Husserl's *Crisis*," and Paul Piccone, "Reading the *Crisis*," *Telos*, no. 8 (1971). For a general review of some of the controversies concerning the *Crisis*, see David Carr's introduction to the English translation of the *Crisis*.

14. For a careful analysis of the development of Husserl's concept of constitution, see Robert Sokolowski, *The Formation of Husserl's Concept of Constitution*.

15. Sellars has not directly taken up this hypothetical challenge posed by Husserl. But how he might meet such a criticism is indicated by the way he treats Kant's claims about the transcendental ego. See Wilfrid Sellars, ". . . this I or he or it (the thing) which thinks . . ."

16. Husserl is perfectly aware of how absurd the transcendental turn appears

to the "natural" man's understanding, and to "common sense." "The complete inversion of the natural stance of life, thus into an 'unnatural' one, places the greatest conceivable demands upon philosophical resolve and consistency. Natural human understanding and the objectivism rooted in it will view every transcendental philosophy as a flighty eccentricity, its wisdom as useless foolishness; or it will interpret it as a psychology which seeks to convince itself that it is not psychology. No one who is truly receptive to philosophy is ever frightened off by difficulties" (p. 200).

17.   Since the Second World War one of the most intense and complex debates concerning the sciences of human life has taken place between phenomenologists and structuralists. Much of this debate has focused on the significance and consequences of Levi-Strauss's structural anthropology. Although the issues are tangled, one frequently senses that the disputants are arguing at cross purposes. Sometimes it appears as if the primary issue concerns those who claim that there are depth structures by which we can account for the manifest complexity of human experience versus those who presumably deny this central claim. But this way of presenting the issue is misleading. Perhaps no philosopher since Kant has given such prominence to "primary structures" in elucidating human life as Husserl has. The key issues concern what are the meaning, nature, and status of these structures; how are they related or not related to the "ego"; what are our means of knowing them; and in what ways they explain or account for the variety of human social life. For a critical review of the debate between structuralists and phenomenologists, see Bob Scholte, "The Structural Anthropology of Claude Levi-Strauss," *Handbook of Social and Cultural Anthropology,* ed. John J. Honegmann.

18.   For an examination of the background of phenomenology's contribution to the study of psychology and psychiatry, see Herbert Spiegelberg, *The Phenomenological Movement,* and his more recent study, *Phenomenology in Psychology and Psychiatry.*

19.   The "Americanization" of Schutz is not only reflected in the content of his thought, but also in his philosophical style. His first book (the only full-length book that Schutz published), *Der sinnhafte Aufbau der sozialen Welt* (1932), addresses itself almost exclusively to the controversy concerning the foundations of the social sciences that had taken shape during the prior fifty years in Germany. It is far more detailed, dense, and technical than many of Schutz's later writings. The works that Schutz published in English consist entirely of articles and papers written for a variety of occasions. An English translation of his book was published in 1967 with the title *The Phenomenology of the Social World.* His papers have now been collected in three volumes. In 1970 Richard M. Zaner published and edited an annotated manuscript of Schutz, *Reflections on the Problem of Relevance.* In 1973 Thomas Luckmann published Volume I of *The Structures of the Life-World,* which is based upon the unfinished *magnum opus* on which Schutz was working at the time of his death in 1959. For a bibliography of Schutz's writings,

and writings on Schutz through 1970, see *Phenomenology and Social Reality: Essays in Memory of Alfred Schutz,* ed. Maurice Natanson.

20. One of the first papers that Schutz published in English was "William James's Concept of the Stream of Thought Phenomenologically Interpreted." Published originally in 1941, it is now reprinted in Volume III of his *Collected Papers.* The paper is a landmark in the exploration of phenomenological themes of William James's work. Until its publication, there was scarcely an American scholar who appreciated the affinity between James and the phenomenological movement. It is only now—over thirty years after the appearance of Schutz's article—that the full dimensions of phenomenological motifs in James have been seriously explored. Schutz's discussions of James, Dewey, and Mead are always fresh and perceptive. For references, see the indexes to the three volumes of his *Collected Papers.*

21. See "Concept and Theory Formation in the Social Sciences," *Collected Papers,* III. This paper was written specifically as comment on a symposium held in December 1952 at the Eastern Division of the American Philosophical Association, in which Ernest Nagel and Carl G. Hempel delivered the main papers. Nagel's and Hempel's original papers are printed in *Science, Language and Human Rights,* American Philosophical Association, Eastern Division, Vol. I.

22. See the Bibliography for the relevant works of these authors.

23. For an indication of Schutz's growing influence on the social sciences, see Maurice Natanson, *Phenomenology and the Social Sciences* (two volumes); and George Psathas, *Phenomenological Sociology.* Recently there is evidence that phenomenology is even taking root in England—at least among young sociologists. See Paul Filmer, Michael Philipson, David Silverman, David Walsh, *New Directions in Sociological Theory.* This volume also includes a good bibliography of the literature related to phenomenology and the social sciences. Recently Maurice Roche has explored some of the relations between conceptual analysis and phenomenology as they relate to the social sciences. See Maurice Roche, *Phenomenology, Language and the Social Sciences.*

24. The relation between Schutz and Husserl is a complex one. When Schutz published *Der sinnhafte Aufbau der sozialen Welt,* he freely acknowledged his intellectual debt to Husserl, although he had not yet met Husserl. He sent a copy to Husserl, and Husserl was sufficiently impressed to ask Schutz to become his assistant. Schutz declined, but it was the beginning of a friendship between them. What is especially interesting in regard to Schutz's intellectual development is that when Schutz wrote his book, Husserl had scarcely published anything that dealt directly with the relation of phenomenology to the social sciences. It was Schutz's perspicacity to detect how phenomenological themes might be applied to the study of the foundations of the social sciences. But Schutz was never a slavish disciple of Husserl. Indeed, what caused Schutz the greatest difficulty was Husserl's treatment of intersubjectivity—the

theme that is Schutz's most central concern. Schutz became increasingly skeptical about Husserl's understanding of, and claims about, transcendental phenomenology. Schutz's papers on Husserl are in Volume III of his *Collected Papers*. See especially "The Problem of Transcendental Intersubjectivity in Husserl."

25.   Unless otherwise noted, all references to Schutz are to *The Phenomenology of the Social World* and his *Collected Papers* (three volumes). *The Phenomenology of the Social World* is abbreviated *PSW*. References to his *Collected Papers* are indicated by the volume number, followed by the page number: I, 1.

26.   Talcott Parsons' Introduction to Max Weber, *The Theory of Social and Economic Organization*, p. 9.

Parsons played a major role in making Weber's work available to an English-reading public, and in stressing the importance of Weber for the social sciences, especially sociology. But Parsons' own biases have influenced his presentation of Weber and have affected the way in which a generation of mainstream social scientists have read and interpreted Weber. "What Weber did was to take an enormous step in the direction of bridging the gap between the two types of science, and to make possible the treatment of social material in a systematic scientific manner rather than as an art. But he failed to complete the process, and the nature of the half-way point at which he stopped helps to account for many of the difficulties of his position" (Parsons' Introduction, p. 11). Parsons leaves no doubt that *he* has taken the next step which he thinks that Weber should have taken. What Parsons labels Weber's unsatisfactory "half-way" point can be turned against Parsons himself and many other mainstream social scientists. Weber saw clearly what many mainstream social scientists have failed to see or saw dimly: that an adequate social theory must not only examine causal relationships in the human and cultural field, but also be sensitive to the distinctive concepts and procedures required for the *interpretation* of social reality. We are only beginning to realize how Weber was much more profound and perceptive about these issues than those who "progressed" beyond him.

27.   Ernest Nagel, *The Structure of Science*, p. 484. See also Karl R. Popper, *The Poverty of Historicism*, p. 139, and "On the Theory of the Objective Mind," *Objective Knowledge*.

28.   Schutz stresses the importance of "the social scientist as disinterested observer" on many occasions. See I, 36; I, 63; II, 69.

29.   See Schutz's "Appended Note," *PSW*, pp. 43–44.

30.   The precise nature and meaning of intersubjectivity became one of the most important and enigmatic issues for Husserl. The thrust of Husserl's earlier work, with its focus on the solitary ego, seemed to provide no place for genuine intersubjectivity. Yet Husserl claimed that intersubjectivity lies at the very heart of subjectivity. Husserl's most important attempt to clarify the meaning of intersubjectivity is found in the fifth meditation of his *Cartesian Meditations*. For a perceptive discussion of what precisely Husserl means by

intersubjectivity, and what he establishes in his fifth meditation, see David Carr, "The 'Fifth Meditation' and Husserl's Cartesianism," *Philosophy and Phenomenological Research,* 34 (1973). See Alfred Schutz, "The Problem of Transcendental Intersubjectivity in Husserl," *Collected Papers,* III. See also Richard M. Zaner, "Theory of Intersubjectivity: Alfred Schutz," *Social Research,* 28 (1961).

31.   This discrimination of three types or phases of a phenomenological inquiry is intended as a heuristic device. I do not suggest that they can be neatly distinguished, or even that Schutz explicitly made this distinction. In my analysis of Schutz I have focused on the first two phases of his investigations. For the application of his categorial scheme, see Part II, "Applied Theory," of his *Collected Papers,* Vol. II.

32.   Although I am not primarily concerned with Schutz's intellectual development in this inquiry, it should be pointed out that an important reversal takes place. *The Phenomenology of the Social World* follows the more orthodox Husserlian "egology," beginning with the primacy of the solitary ego and systematically introducing distinctions in order to "construct" the social world. But increasingly, Schutz became aware of the difficulties of moving in this direction. In his later writings it becomes more and more evident that he takes "intersubjectivity" and the "social" as a starting point. This shift of emphasis indicates what has become one of the most problematic features in the attempt to apply phenomenology to the elucidation of the social world. The tension between the pull to Cartesianism or egology, and the pull to the primacy of intersubjectivity, is also central to Merleau-Ponty's and Paul Ricoeur's interpretations of Husserl and phenomenology.

33.   In a later formulation Schutz writes: "Meaning . . . is not a quality inherent in certain experiences emerging within our stream of consciousness but the result of an interpretation of a past experience looked at from the present *Now* with a reflective attitude. As long as I live *in* my acts, directed toward the objects of these acts, the acts do not have meaning. They become meaningful if I grasp them as well-circumscribed experiences of the past and, therefore, in retrospection. Only experiences which can be recollected beyond their actuality and which can be questioned about their constitution are, therefore, subjectively meaningful" (I, 210).

34.   In *The Phenomenology of the Social World, Verhalten* has been translated as "behavior." But in Schutz's later English writings, he uses the expression "conduct" to refer to the meaning-endowing experiences which he originally called *Verhalten.* "We avoid the term 'behavior' because it includes in present use also subjectively non-meaingful manifestations of spontaneity such as reflexes" (I, 211). The shift here is not merely linguistic, because Schutz wants to distinguish his analysis sharply from a concept of behavior that includes or is restricted to physical processes that lack any meaning component. According to Schutz human behavior or conduct—as distinct from physical motion—is essentially and intrinsically meaningful.

35.   I have presented the bare outlines of Schutz's characterization of "ex-

perience," "behavior" (conduct), and "action." These distinctions serve as a basis for further important refinements. For example, Schutz distinguishes between covert and overt conduct and action. Overt actions "gear into the outer world by bodily movements" (I, 211–12). Schutz calls this type of action "working." "Working, then, is action in the outer world, based upon a project and characterized by the intention to bring about the projected state of affairs by bodily movements" (*Ibid.*). Once Schutz discriminates the various types of actions, he introduces finer distinctions among "sensible," "reasonable," and "rational" actions. For details, see *PSW*, pp. 57 ff.; *Collected Papers*, I, 209 ff; and "The Problem of Rationality in the Social World," *Collected Papers*, II.

36. Schutz emphasizes and explores the role of choice of interpretative schemes. "For the choice is by no means prescribed from the start as either obvious or exclusive; as a matter of fact, no lived experience can be exhausted by a single interpretive scheme" (*PSW*, p. 85). Schutz's most systematic investigation of the nature of choice is to be found in "Choosing among Projects of Action," *Collected Papers*, I.

37. For a discussion of the significance of this motif in John Dewey, see *Praxis and Action*, Part III.

38. Schutz increasingly emphasized the theory of relevances, claiming that it was of the utmost importance for understanding the social sciences. In his posthumously published papers, he distinguished three interrelated types of relevance: motivational, thematic, and interpretational. For details see *Reflections on the Problem of Relevance*, ed. Richard M. Zaner; and Alfred Schutz and Thomas Luckmann, *The Structures of the Life-World*.

39. Schutz's remarks about the "social distribution of common sense knowledge" are barely developed and appear almost incidentally. But since Schutz's death there is a whole body of literature, and indeed a new field of empirical inquiry, that bears directly on the issue of the social distribution of common-sense knowledge. This is one of the central problems of sociolinguistics. See for example Joshua Fishman, ed., *Readings in the Sociology of Language*, and *Advances in the Sociology of Language;* Dell Hymes, ed., *Language in Culture and Society;* William Labov, *Sociolinguistic Patterns;* John Gumperz and Dell Hymes, eds., *Directions in Sociolinguistics;* and Pier Paolo Giglioli, ed., *Language and the Social Context*.

40. See *PSW*, p. 223; II, 56 ff.; III, 117 ff.

41. See "On Multiple Realities," *Collected Papers*, I; and "Symbol, Reality and Society," Part VI, *Collected Papers*, I.

42. See especially the papers in Part II, "Applied Theory" of the *Collected Papers*, II.

43. Schutz speaks of "genuine" because-motives in order to distinguish them from "pseudo" because-motives or because-statements. "Now, ordinary language fudges this distinction and allows the translation of every 'in-order-to' statement into a 'because' statement. 'Because I wanted to talk to A, I went

out' or 'I'm going out because I want to talk to A.' Let us call any because-statement which is logically equivalent to an in-order-to statement a 'pseudo because-statement.' " (*PSW*, p. 89).

44.   In "The Problem of Rationality in the Social World," Schutz gives a slightly different and more detailed statement of his postulates. In this other context Schutz indicates how the several requirements he lists may be condensed "into another postulate for the building up of the ideal types, that of rationality. It may be formulated as follows: The ideal type of social action must be constructed in such a way that the actor in the living world would perform the typified act if he had a clear and distinct scientific knowledge of all the elements relevant to his choice and the constant tendency to choose the most appropriate means for the realization of the most appropriate end" (II, 86).

45.   See Thomas Luckmann's preface to *The Structures of the Life-World* for a description of the problems that he faced in editing Schutz's unfinished manuscript.

46.   It is sometimes argued that in the *Crisis* Husserl gave up or compromised his search for such structures. But he writes there: "The life-world does have, in all its relative features, a *general structure*. This general structure, to which everything that exists relatively is bound, is not itself relative. We can attend to it in its generality and, with sufficient care, fix it once and for all in a way equally accessible to all" (*Crisis*, p. 139).

47.   See the Appended Note in *PSW*, pp. 43–44.

48.   These difficulties are illustrated in the papers collected in Maurice Natanson, *Phenomenology and the Social Sciences;* and George Psathas, *Phenomenological Sociology*. There seems to be no consensus about what are the permanent, fixed, a priori structures of the social world, nor any clear statement of the criteria for distinguishing such structures from those that change historically.

49.   Thomas Luckmann and Peter L. Berger—both of them highly influenced by Schutz—have made a beginning toward distinguishing between different forms of externalization, objectification, and reification. But at best they have made some important preliminary distinctions, rather than developing an adequate conceptual scheme. Both also exhibit the deep tension between structures and processes of constitution fundamental for any human consciousness, and those that have specific historical roots and causes. See Peter L. Berger and Thomas Luckmann, *The Social Construction of Reality;* and Peter L. Berger and S. Pullberg, "Reification and the Sociological Critique of Consciousness," *New Left Review*, no. 35 (1966).

50.   See Robert Sokolowski, *The Formation of Husserl's Concept of Constitution.*

51.   The claim that I am making about Schutz can also be made about Husserl: that he indicates the centrality of questions concerning the social and political *change* of historical structures without investigating what is involved

in these changes. A number of thinkers who have felt the urgency of these issues have attempted a fusion of Husserl and Marx. The most ambitious of these fusions is Enzo Paci, *The Function of the Sciences and the Meaning of Man.* See the journal *Telos,* where a number of articles for and against this fusion have appeared—especially those of Paul Piccone and Pier Aldo Rovatti. For a review of the uneasy alliance of phenomenology and Marxism, see Fred R. Dallmayr, "Phenomenology and Marxism: A Salute to Enzo Paci," *Phenomenological Sociology,* ed. George Psathas.

52.   For a discussion of the issues involved in distinguishing motives and causes, see my discussion in *Praxis and Action,* Part IV. See also Hanna F. Pitkin, *Wittgenstein and Justice.*

53.   See for example Richard M. Zaner, "Solitude and Sociality: The Critical Foundations of the Social Sciences," *Phenomenological Sociology,* ed. George Psathas; and John O'Neill, "Can Phenomenology be Critical?", *Sociology as a Skin Trade.*

54.   For an eloquent apologia of Husserl's stance, see Robert Sokolowski, "Husserl's Protreptic," *Life-World and Consciousness: Essays for Aron Gurwitsch,* ed. Lester E. Embree. Sokolowski tells us that "finally, all this means that phenomenology alone is *autonomous and absolutely self-responsible,* the law unto itself. It aims at a life of intellectual autonomy, responsibility, and underived evidences. In doing this it is being faithful to the traditional sense of philosophy" (p. 77). But Sokolowski, no more than Husserl, spells out what this means concretely—how phenomenology provides substantive guidance in developing a moral and political community.

PART IV
The Critical Theory of Society

1.   The expression the "Frankfurt School" became popular after the Second World War to refer to the group of intellectuals associated with the *Institut für Sozialforschung* founded in Frankfurt in 1923. Forced to leave Germany in the early nineteen thirties, the Institute kept its intellectual identity under the strong directorship of Max Horkheimer. During the thirties, when the Institute had moved to Morningside Heights in New York, much creative and original work was published in its journal, *Zeitschrift für Sozialforschung.* After the Second World War the writings of the Frankfurt School had an extensive impact. First rediscovered by young student radicals in Germany, they soon exerted an international influence. In the late nineteen forties the Institute was officially invited to return to its original home, Frankfurt. After some hesitation Horkheimer, who was still director, accepted the invitation and was appointed Professor at the University of Frankfurt. Horkheimer and Theodor Adorno were the most prominent members of the Institute who returned. During the fifties and early sixties, they were enthusiastically welcomed and avidly read by many young German intellectuals. But as German

radical students became more militant in the late sixties, the Frankfurt thinkers became one of the main targets of attack.

There are now several informative accounts in English of the history and development of the Frankfurt School. The most comprehensive is Martin Jay, *The Dialectical Imagination: A History of the Frankfurt School and the Institute of Social Research, 1923–1950.* See my review of Jay's book, "The Frankfurt School," *Midstream,* September 1973. Jay's book contains an excellent bibliography of primary and secondary sources relating to the Frankfurt School. George Lichtheim was one of the most informed and sympathetic writers about the School; see his collection of essays, *From Marx to Hegel.* See also Albrecht Wellmer, *The Critical Theory of Society;* Trent Schroyer, *The Critique of Domination;* David Frisby, "The Frankfurt School: A Critical Theory of Society," *Approaches to Sociology,* ed. J. Rex. The significance of the Frankfurt School is also examined by William Leiss, *The Domination of Nature;* Norman Birnbaum, *Toward a Critical Sociology;* Göran Therborn, "Frankfurt Marxism: A Critique," and "Habermas: A New Eclectic," *New Left Review,* no. 63 (1970) and no. 67 (1971).

2.   This passage is cited from Habermas' inaugural lecture at the University of Frankfurt in 1965: "Knowledge and Human Interests." Habermas begins his analysis with a contrast of Horkheimer and Husserl. An English translation of this lecture is included as an appendix of *Knowledge and Human Interests.*

I have used the following abbreviations to refer to the English translations of Habermas' works: *Knowledge and Human Interests, KI; Legitimation Crisis, LC; Theory and Practice, TP; Toward a Rational Society, TRS.* The English translations of Habermas' works involve some editorial reordering of the German originals. See the Bibliography for Habermas' works and the English translations available.

3.   Compare this description of the classical meaning of the *bios theoretikos* with that of Sheldon Wolin in "Political Theory as a Vocation," *Machiavelli and the Nature of Political Thought,* ed. Martin Fleisher. Although Wolin's orientation is very different from that of the Frankfurt thinkers, he shares with them a critique of the degeneration of theory in political science.

4.   Unless otherwise noted, all page references to Husserl are to the English translation of the *Crisis.*

5.   Although Husserl speaks of "European humanity," he uses this expression as a rough equivalent to "Western Civilization."

6.   One of the most sympathetic and helpful discussions of these problems, especially as they relate to the "problem of history," is David Carr, *Phenomenology and the Problem of History.* Carr's careful textural study of Husserl's developing views on the nature and significance of history for phenomenology shows how deep and unresolved are the tensions between the idea of pure *theoria,* and the concrete problems of political and social existence of mankind.

7.   On many occasions, members of the Institute sharply criticized phenom-

enology as developed by both Husserl and Heidegger. But the relationships between the Frankfurt thinkers and phenomenology are more complex than this persistent critique might indicate. Before he joined the Institute, Herbert Marcuse had been profoundly influenced by Heidegger, and some have argued that this influence has persisted. Nevertheless, in the nineteen thirties Marcuse sharply attacked Husserl's concept of essence (see "The Concept of Essence," *Negations*). Theodor Adorno also persistently criticized Husserl. His most systematic criticism appears in *Zur Metakritik der Erkenntnistheorie*. Horkheimer explicitly criticized Husserl and phenomenology, but in a footnote to his essay, "The Latest Attack on Metaphysics," in *Critical Theory*, observed that Husserl's *Crisis* "with its extremely abstract discussion of problems has more to contribute to contemporary historical tasks than does pragmatism for all its vaunted relevance or the writing and thinking, supposedly addressed to the 'man in the street,' of many young intellectuals who are in fact ashamed of their role" (pp. 146–47).

8.   Unless otherwise noted, all page references to Horkheimer are to "Traditional and Critical Theory," *Critical Theory*.

9.   Compare Sheldon Wolin's analysis of "methodism" and its influence on contemporary political science in "Political Theory as a Vocation," *Machiavelli and the Nature of Political Thought*.

10.   This has also been a persistent theme in Marcuse's work. See *Negations, Reason and Revolution*, and *One Dimensional Man*. For a discussion of some of the difficulties of Marcuse's conception of critical theory, see my article "Herbert Marcuse: An Immanent Critique," *Social Theory and Practice*, 1 (1971).

11.   *Writings of the Young Marx on Philosophy and Society*, ed. Loyd D. Easton and Kurt H. Guddat, p. 212.

12.   See especially, "On the Jewish Question," *Writings of the Young Marx on Philosophy and Society*.

13.   Marx's dissatisfaction with the vague promise of critique is discussed in my book *Praxis and Action*, Part I.

14.   Jay carefully traces this ambivalence, and the ways in which the Frankfurt thinkers moved away from Marx, in *The Dialectical Imagination*. See also my discussion of this point in "Herbert Marcuse: An Immanent Critique," *Social Theory and Practice*, 1 (1971).

15.   Karl Marx, *Grundrisse*, ed. and trans. Martin Nicolaus, p. 704 (italics added).

16.   For Habermas' critical discussion of Marx see *Theory and Practice*, and *Knowledge and Human Interests;* see also Albrecht Wellmer, *The Critical Theory of Society*. Habermas' most recent attempt to sketch a theory of crises in late or advanced capitalism is in *Legitimation Crisis*.

17.   See *Zur Logik der Sozialwissenschaften;* and Jürgen Habermas and Niklas Luhmann, *Theorie der Gesellschaft oder Sozialtechnologie—Was leistet die Systemforschung?*

18.   See "On Systematically Distorted Communication," *Inquiry*, 13 (1970);

"Towards a Theory of Communicative Competence," *Inquiry,* 13 (1970);
"Der Universalitaetsanspruch der Hermeneutik," *Hermeneutik und Ideologiekritik;* "Vorbereitende Bermerkungen zu einer Theorie der kommunikativen
Kompetenz," *Theorie der Gesellschaft oder Sozialtechnologie—Was leistet
die Systemforschung?;* "Wahrheitstheorien," *Festschrift für W. Schulz.*

19. See *Legitimation Crisis.*

20. The critical literature on various aspects of Habermas' investigations is
already quite extensive. See Fred R. Dallmayr, "Critical Theory Criticized:
Habermas's *Knowledge and Human Interests* and its Aftermath," *Philosophy
of the Social Sciences,* 2 (1972). Dallmayr discusses a number of Habermas'
critics. See also the other articles by Nikolaus Lobkowicz, Christian Lehnhart,
Melvyn Alan Hill, and Christopher Nichols in this issue of *Philosophy and
the Social Sciences.* Habermas answers his critics in his new introduction to
the fourth edition of *Theory and Practice,* and in "A Postcript to *Knowledge
and Human Interests,*" *Philosophy of the Social Sciences,* 3 (1973). See also
Continuum, 8 (1970), an issue dedicated to a discussion of the Frankfurt
School.

21. In *Theory and Practice* Habermas acknowledges his intellectual debt to
Hannah Arendt for emphasizing the importance of the distinction between
techne and *praxis* in Aristotle. But the similarity between Habermas and
Arendt is much deeper than this. Both agree in their reading of the historical
development of the fusion and confusion of the classical meaning of politics
with the modern conception of social life. Both see this as involving a major
historical transformation in which politics has been "reduced" to one form of
social life, and political science "reduced" to one of the social sciences. Both
argue that the systematic undermining of the classical sense of politics has had
the most serious theoretical and practical consequences in the modern world.
When we examine Habermas' categorial scheme, we will also see how his
basic distinction between interaction (communicative action) and work
closely parallels Arendt's distinction between action and work. Yet I do not
mean to suggest their understanding of politics, or of political theory and its
relation to action, is the same. On the contrary, their sharp differences—
especially in regard to the relation of theory and praxis—are as important as
their similarities.

22. See especially the essays in *Toward a Rational Society,* and *Legitimation
Crisis.*

23. See the concluding chapter, "On Theory and Praxis in Our Scientific
Civilization," in *Theory and Practice;* and "Technology and Science as
'Ideology,' " *Toward a Rational Society.*

24. For Habermas' critique of these "extremes," see "Technology and Science as 'Ideology.' "

25. For the details of these criticisms, see the discussion of Marx in *Theory
and Practice,* in *Knowledge and Human Interests,* and in "Towards a Reconstruction of Historical Materialism," *Theory and Society,* 2 (1975).

26. Albrecht Wellmer, who was a student of Habermas, has explored the

latent positivistic and scientistic tendencies in Marx. See his *Critical Theory of Society*.

27.   I include here the work of Louis Althusser. It may be thought that this is an error because Althusser explicitly attacks positivism and a positivistic reading of Marx. But underlying Althusser's intellectual dexterity is a rigid distinction between ideology and Marxist science. This new "science," which supposedly represents a radical epistemological break or rupture with the past, has finally fulfilled the promise of a definitive, true, well-grounded science of human beings. While Althusser never tires of telling us how different this new science is from anything that preceded it, he is remarkably unilluminating about what it is and what are its essential characteristics. In this respect we find a parallel with the less sophisticated scientistic interpretations of Marx that make essentially the same type of claim. For critiques of Althusser's conception of the new Marxist philosophy and science, see Norman Geras, "Louis Althusser—An Assessment," *New Left Review*, no. 71 (1972); André Glucksmann, "The Althusserian Theatre," *New Left Review*, no. 72 (1972); Leszek Kolakowski, "Althusser's Marx," *The Socialist Register*, 1971.

28.   For Habermas' criticisms of Hegel, see *Theory and Practice* and *Knowledge and Human Interests*.

29.   See "Labor and Interaction: Remarks on Hegel's Jena *Philosophy of Mind*," *Theory and Practice*.

30.   Habermas' criticism of Marx presupposes the validity of the categorial distinction between work and interaction. Habermas is accusing Marx of merging what ought to be sharply distinguished. But one can turn Marx against Habermas, for Marx shows the dangers that can result from making such a dichotomy. This is precisely the danger of an "idealism" that wants to separate the processes of "symbolic interaction" from the dialectics of labor. As Habermas himself notes, Marx did not think that a transformation of the material conditions of human life automatically brings about free symbolic discourse and rational determination of social life. Rather than charging Marx with some sort of category mistake, a more penetrating interpretation would indicate that Marx is calling into question the very categorial distinction that Habermas takes to be fundamental.

31.   Habermas, following many other Frankfurt thinkers, characterizes the type of action relevant to the empirical-analytic sciences as "instrumental." But what he means by "instrumental" is quite different from the meaning of this term as used by analytic philosophers of science. Among the latter, "instrumentalism" is commonly used to identify a specific interpretation of the role of theories in the sciences, and is frequently contrasted with "scientific realism." Theories are "instruments" by which we can systematically relate observation statements. According to the pragmatic interpretation that Habermas gives to the empirical-analytic sciences, they are instrumental because the information they yield is "technically utilizable." See "Rationalism Divided in Two: A Reply to Albert," *Positivism and Sociology*, ed. Anthony

Giddens, p. 206, for a clarification of what Habermas means by "instrumental."

32. Mary Hesse shows how Habermas' conception of the empirical-analytic sciences can be compared with the model of a learning-machine in which there is negative feedback. See Mary Hesse, "In Defence of Objectivity." See also George Henrik von Wright's analysis of causation and action in *Explanation and Understanding*. Von Wright's analysis of the role of causation in the natural sciences provides independent support for Habermas' interpretation of the empirical-analytic sciences guided by a technical interest. For a comprehensive survey and comparison of analytic and continental interpretations of the nature of science, see Gerhard Radnitzky, *Contemporary Schools of Metascience*.

33. Jürgen Habermas, "Rationalism Divided in Two: A Reply to Albert," *Positivism and Sociology*, p. 218.

34. See Habermas' discussion of Peirce in *Knowledge and Human Interests*, Chapters 5 and 6. Karl-Otto Apel, who has edited the German edition of Peirce's writings, has developed a similar argument. See Karl-Otto Apel, *Analytic Philosophy of Language and the Geisteswissenschaften*, and "Szientifik, Hermeneutik, Ideologie-Kritik: Entwurf einer Wissenschaftslehre in erkenntnis-anthropologischer Sicht," *Man and the World*, 1 (1968). The similarities and differences between Habermas and Apel are discussed by Fred R. Dallmayr, "Reason and Emancipation: Notes on Habermas," *Man and the World*, 5 (1972); and Gerhard Radnitzky, *Contemporary Schools of Metascience*, Vol. II.

35. For an illustration of how Habermas shows the complex historical interrelationships between these two levels of action, see "Towards a Reconstruction of Historical Materialism," *Theory and Society*, 2 (1975), and *Legitimation Crisis*.

36. See my earlier discussion of ideology and the critique of ideology in Part II, pp. 107–10.

37. For criticisms of Habermas' interpretation of Freud and his analogy between psychoanalysis and critical theory, see Christopher Nichols, "Science or Reflection: Habermas on Freud," *Philosophy of the Social Sciences*, 2 (1972); H. J. Geigel, "Reflexion und Emanzipation," and H. G. Gadamer, "Rhetorik, Hermeneutik und Ideologiekritik," in *Hermeneutik und Ideologiekritik*. For Habermas' replies to these critics, see the new introduction to *Theory and Practice*, and "A Postscript to *Knowledge and Human Interests*."

38. See Alexander Kojève's interpretation of the master-slave dialectic in *Introduction to the Reading of Hegel*.

39. This indicates the sharpest disagreement between Habermas' and Althusser's interpretation of Marx. Althusser claims to have discovered a radical epistemological break in Marx's development—a break between the early humanistic Marx and the genuinely scientific Marx. This disagreement involves more than the attempt to "rediscover" the historical Marx. According

to Habermas, Marx's relevance for us is his practice of *critique;* for Althusser, Marx is the originator of a new definitive *science.*

40.   See T. A. McCarthy's lucid systematic exposition and critical discussion of Habermas' comprehensive theory of communicative competence, "A Theory of Communicative Competence," *Philosophy of the Social Sciences,* 3 (1973). See also Albrecht Wellmer, "Communication and Emancipation: Reflections on the 'Linguistic Turn' in Critical Theory," *Philosophy and Social Theory, Stony Brook Studies in Philosophy,* 1 (1974).

41.   See Oskar Negt, "Revolution und Geschichte: Eine Kontroverse mit Jürgen Habermas," *Politik als Protest.*

42.   The recent interest in, and controversies about, John Rawls's *A Theory of Justice* are directly related to the theory of rationality. Rawls characterizes the main idea of this theory of justice as centering about "the principles that free and rational persons concerned to further their own interests would accept in an initial position of equality as defining the fundamental terms of their association" (p. 11). Rawls too is attacking prevailing dogmas about the nature of human rationality. Although I do not want to underestimate the fundamental differences between Rawls and Habermas, they share a common basic theme; there are mutual entailments among the concepts of rationality, freedom, and equality.

43.   See *Praxis and Action,* Part I.

44.   Jürgen Habermas, "A Postscript to *Knowledge and Human Interests,*" *Philosophy of the Social Sciences,* 3 (1973), p. 168.

45.   On the four claims to validity, see the new introduction to *Theory and Practice,* p. 18; and "Vorbereitende Bermerkungen zu einer Theorie der kommunikativen Kompetenz," *Theorie der Gesellschaft oder Sozialtechnologie—Was Leistet die Systemforschung?*

46.   Jürgen Habermas, "Towards a Theory of Communicative Competence," *Inquiry,* 13 (1970), p. 372.

47.   For a clarification of the meaning and conditions of "ideal speech," see Jürgen Habermas, "Wahrheitstheorien."

48.   T. A. McCarthy, "A Theory of Communicative Competence," *Philosophy of the Social Sciences,* pp. 153–54.

Although based on contemporary philosophy of language and theoretical linguistics, Habermas' argument exhibits some striking parallels with the one that Socrates develops in the *Phaedrus.* Socrates too is concerned with the conditions for speech, and argues that the analysis of speech is oriented to the idea of truth—even when speech is intended to deceive. Further, the analysis of truth leads to the analysis of the conditions for ideal speech—the type of discourse characteristic of true philosophic friends. There is even a parallel with the four validity claims that Habermas specifies; when Socrates analyzes the requirements for speech, he emphasizes the importance of each of these features. Socrates' argument is intended to show that all speech—even the deceptive speech of Lysias—presupposes and anticipates ideal speech. And

just as Habermas' line of argument leads him to recognize the reciprocal relation between ideal speech, which is essentially dialogic, and an ideal form of
life, so the primary practical problem for Socrates becomes one of constructing or reconstructing a polis in which such ideal speech can be realized.

49.   See T. A. McCarthy's critical remarks in "A Theory of Communicative Competence," pp. 148 ff.

50.   See Habermas' new introduction to *Theory and Practice*, where he confronts the charge that "the normative basis for a critical sociology is smuggled
in surreptitiously" (*TP*, p. 15).

51.   In his writings after *Knowledge and Human Interests*, Habermas introduces a more refined distinction "between reconstruction and 'self-reflexion'
in a critical sense." In "A Postscript to *Knowledge and Human Interests*" he
writes: "It occurred to me only after completing the book that the traditional
use of the term 'reflexion,' which goes back to German Idealism, covers (and
confuses) two things: on the one hand, it denotes the reflexion upon the conditions of potential abilities of a knowing, speaking and acting subject as such;
on the other hand, it denotes the reflexion upon unconsciously produced constraints to which a determinate subject (or a determinate group of subjects,
or a determinate species subject) succumbs in its process of self-formation"
(p. 182). See Section 6 of this postscript for the significance of this distinction
between "reconstruction" and "self-reflexion."

52.   See my new introduction to the German edition of *Praxis and Action*
for a critical evaluation of Habermas' interpretation of Peirce.

53.   See also Dick Howard's criticism of Habermas, "A Politics in Search of
the Political," *Theory and Society*, 2 (1974); and the interview with Habermas by Boris Frankel, "Habermas Talking: An Interview," *Theory and Society*, 2 (1974).

54.   Jürgen Habermas, *Theory and Practice*, p. 254.

55.   Isaiah Berlin, "Does Political Theory Still Exist?", *Philosophy, Politics
and Society* (Second Series), ed. Peter Laslett and W. G. Runciman, p. 19.

56.   Sheldon Wolin, "Political Theory as a Vocation," *Machiavelli and the
Nature of Political Thought*, p. 26.

57.   Hanna F. Pitkin, *Wittgenstein and Justice*, p. 316.

58.   Richard M. Zaner, "Solitude and Sociality: The Critical Foundations
of the Social Sciences," *Phenomenological Sociology: Issues and Applications*,
ed. George Psathas, p. 42. See also John O'Neill, "Can Phenomenology be
Critical?", *Sociology as a Skin Trade;* and Paul Piccone, "Phenomenological
Marxism," *Telos*, no. 9 (1971).

Bibliography

Adorno, Theodor W., ed. *Der Positivismusstreit in der deutschen Soziologie.* Damstadt und Neuwied: Hermann Luchterhand Verlag, 1972.

Almond, Gabriel A. "Political Theory and Political Science." *American Political Science Review,* 60 (1966), 869–79.

Althusser, Louis. *For Marx.* New York: Vintage Books, 1970.

Apel, Karl-Otto. *Analytic Philosophy of Language and the Geisteswissenschaften.* Dordrecht, Holland: D. Reidel Publishing Co., 1967.

———. "Szientifik, Hermeneutik, Ideologie-Kritik: Entwurf einer Wissenschaftslehre in erkenntnis-anthropologishcher Sicht." *Man and the World,* 1 (1968), 37–63.

Arendt, Hannah. *The Human Condition.* New York: Doubleday Anchor Books, 1959.

Armstrong, David M. *A Materialist Theory of Mind.* New York: Humanities Press, 1968.

Berger, Peter L., and Luckmann, Thomas. *The Social Construction of Reality.* New York: Anchor Books, 1967.

Berger, Peter L., and Pullberg, S. "Reification and the Sociological Critique of Consciousness." *New Left Review,* no. 35 (1966), 56–77.

Berlin, Isaiah. "Does Political Theory Still Exist?" In *Philosophy, Politics and Society,* Second Series. Oxford: Basil Blackwell, 1962.

Bernstein, Richard J. "Einleitung." In *Praxis und Handeln.* Frankfurt am Main: Suhrkamp Verlag, 1975.

———. "The Frankfurt School." *Midstream,* September 1973, 55–66.

———. "Herbert Marcuse: An Immanent Critique." *Social Theory and Practice,* 1 (1971), 97–111.

———. " 'A Philosopher's Perspective' on Neil Smelser's *Essays in Sociological Explanation." Sociological Inquiry,* 39 (1969), 207–13.

———. *Praxis and Action.* Philadelphia: University of Pennsylvania Press, 1971.

———. "Sellars' Vision of Man-in-the-World." *Review of Metaphysics,* 20 (1966), 113–43, 290–316.

Birnbaum, Norman. *Toward a Critical Sociology.* New York: Oxford University Press, 1971.

Borger, Robert, and Cioffi, Frank, eds. *Explanation in the Behavioural Sciences.* Cambridge: Cambridge University Press, 1970.

Buchdahl, Gerd. "A Revolution in Historiography of Science." *History of Science,* 4 (1965), 55–69.

Carr, David. "The 'Fifth Meditation' and Husserl's Cartesianism." *Philosophy and Phenomenological Research,* 34 (1973), 14–35.

———. *Phenomenology and the Problem of History.* Evanston, Ill.: Northwestern University Press, 1974.

Cicourel, Aaron V. *Cognitive Sociology.* Harmondsworth, Middlesex, England: Penguin Books, 1973.

———. *Method and Measurement in Sociology.* New York: The Free Press, 1964.

Dahl, Robert A. "The Behavioral Approach in Political Science: Epitaph for a Monument to a Successful Protest." *American Political Science Review,* 55 (1961), 763–72.

Dallmayr, Fred R. "Critical Theory Criticized: Habermas's *Knowledge and Human Interests* and its Aftermath." *Philosophy of the Social Sciences,* 2 (1972), 211–29.

———. "Phenomenology and Marxism: A Salute to Enzo Paci." In *Phenomenological Sociology,* edited by George Psathas. New York: John Wiley & Sons, 1973.

———. "Reason and Emancipation: Notes on Habermas." *Man and the World,* 5 (1972), 79–109.

Davidson, Donald. "Actions, Reasons, and Causes." *Journal of Philosophy,* 60 (1963), 685–700.

Douglas, Jack D., ed. *Deviance and Respectability: The Social Construction of Moral Meanings.* New York: Basic Books, 1970.

———. *The Social Meanings of Suicide.* Princeton: Princeton University Press, 1967.

———. "The Sociological Analysis of Social Meanings of Suicide." *Archives européennes de sociologie,* 7 (1966), 249–76.

Easton, David. *The Political System: An Inquiry into the State of Political Science.* New York: Alfred A. Knopf, 1967.

Ekeh, Peter. *Social Exchange Theory: The Two Traditions.* Cambridge: Harvard University Press, 1974.

Euben, J. Peter. "Political Science and Political Silence." In *Power and Community: Dissenting Essays in Political Science,* edited by Philip Green and Sanford Levinson. New York: Vintage Books, 1970.

Feyerabend, Paul K. "Against Method: Outline of an Anarchistic Theory of Knowledge." In *Minnesota Studies in the Philosophy of Science,* Vol. 4, edited by Michael Radner and Stephen Winokur. Minneapolis: University of Minnesota Press, 1970.

Filmer, Paul; Phillipson, Michael; Silverman, David; and Walsh, David. *New Directions in Sociological Theory.* London: Collier-Macmillan, 1972.

Fishman, Joshua A., ed. *Advances in the Sociology of Language.* The Hague: Mouton, 1971.

————, ed. *Readings in the Sociology of Language.* The Hague: Mouton, 1968.

Frankel, Boris. "Habermas Talking: An Interview." *Theory and Society,* 1 (1974), 37–58.

Friedrichs, Robert W. *A Sociology of Sociology.* New York: The Free Press, 1970.

Frisby, David. "The Frankfurt School: A Critical Theory of Society." In *Approaches to Sociology: An Introduction to the Major Trends in British Sociology,* edited by J. Rex. London: Routledge & Kegan Paul, 1974.

Garfinkel, Harold. *Studies in Ethnomethodology.* Englewood Cliffs, N.J.: Prentice-Hall, 1967.

Gadamer, H. G. "Rhetorik, Hermeneutik und Ideologiekritik," *Hermeneutik und Idealogiekritik.* Frankfurt am Main: Suhrkamp Verlag, 1971.

Geigel, H. J. "Reflexion und Emanzipation," *Hermeneutik und Ideologiekritik.* Frankfurt am Main: Suhrkamp Verlag, 1971.

Geras, Norman. "Althusser's Marxism: An Assessment." *New Left Review,* no. 71 (1972), 57–86.

Giglioli, Pier Paolo, ed. *Language and Social Context.* Baltimore: Penguin Books, 1972.

Glucksmann, André. "The Althusserian Theatre." *New Left Review,* no. 72 (1972), 68–92.

Gouldner, Alvin W. *For Sociology: Renewal and Critique in Sociology Today.* New York: Basic Books, 1973.

Gumperz, John, and Hymes, Dell, eds. *Directions in Sociolinguistics.* New York: Holt, Rinehart and Winston, 1972.

Gurwitsch, Aron. *Studies in Phenomenology and Psychology.* Evanston, Ill.: Northwestern University Press, 1966.

Habermas, Jürgen. *Erkenntnis und Interesse.* Frankfurt am Main: Suhrkamp Verlag, 1968.

————. *Knowledge and Human Interests.* Translated by Jeremy J. Shapiro. Boston: Beacon Press, 1971.

————. *Legitimation Crisis.* Translated by Thomas McCarthy. Boston: Beacon Press, 1975.

————. *Legitimationsprobleme im Spatkäpitalismus.* Frankfurt am Main: Suhrkamp Verlag, 1973.

————. "On Systematically Distorted Communication." *Inquiry,* 13 (1970), 205–18.

————. "A Postscript to *Knowledge and Human Interests.*" *Philosophy of the Social Sciences,* 3 (1973), 157–85.

————. "Rationalism Divided in Two: A Reply to Albert." In *Positivism and Sociology,* edited by Anthony Giddens. London: Heinemann Educational Books, 1974.

————. *Technik und Wissenschaft als 'Ideologie.'* Frankfurt am Main: Suhrkamp Verlag, 1968.

————. *Theorie und Praxis.* Frankfurt am Main: Suhrkamp Verlag, 1971.

————. *Theory and Practice*. Translated by John Viertel. Boston: Beacon Press, 1973.

————. *Toward a Rational Society*. Translated by Jeremy J. Shapiro. Boston: Beacon Press, 1970.

————. "Towards a Reconstruction of Historical Materialism." *Theory and Society*, 2 (1975), 287–300.

————. "Towards a Theory of Communicative Competence." *Inquiry*, 13 (1970), 360–75.

————. "Der Universalitätsanspruch der Hermeneutik." In *Hermeneutik und Ideologiekritik*. Frankfurt am Main: Suhrkamp Verlag, 1971.

————. "Wahrheitstheorien." In *Wirklichkeit und Reflexion: Walter Schulz z. 60. Geburtstag*. Edited by H. Fahrenbach. Pfullingen: Neske, 1973.

————. *Zur Logik der Sozialwissenschaften*. Frankfurt am Main: Suhrkamp Verlag, 1970.

Habermas, Jürgen, and Luhmann, Niklas. *Theorie der Gesellschaft oder Sozialtechnologie—Was leistet die Systemforschung?* Frankfurt am Main: Suhrkamp Verlag, 1971.

Harré, R., and Secord, P. F. *The Explanation of Social Behaviour*. Oxford: Basil Blackwell, 1972.

Hauser, Philip M. "The Chaotic Society: Product of the Social Morphological Revolution." *American Sociological Review*, 34 (1969), 1–18.

Hegel, G. W. F. *The Phenomenology of Mind*. Translated by J. B. Baillie. New York: Macmillan, 1949.

Hempel, Carl G. *Aspects of Scientific Explanation*. New York: The Free Press, 1965.

————. "Problems of Concept and Theory Formation in the Social Sciences." In *Science, Language, and Human Rights*. Philadelphia: University of Pennsylvania Press, 1952. (Papers for the symposia held at the annual meeting of the Eastern Division of the American Philosophical Association.)

Henle, M.; Jaynes, J.; and Sullivan, J. J., eds. *Historical Conceptions of Psychology*. New York: Springer Publishing Co., 1973.

Hesse, Mary. "In Defence of Objectivity." In *Proceedings of the British Academy*, Vol. 58. London: Oxford University Press, 1972.

Hollis, Martin. "Witchcraft and Winchcraft." *Philosophy of the Social Sciences*, 2 (1972), 89–103.

Homans, George C. "Bringing Men Back In." *American Sociological Review*, 29 (1964), 809–18.

————. *The Nature of Social Science*. New York: Harcourt Brace Jovanovich, 1967.

Horkheimer, Max. *Critical Theory*. New York: The Seabury Press, 1972.

————. *Kritische Theorie*. Edited by Alfred Schmidt. 2 vols. Frankfurt am Main: S. Fischer, 1968.

Howard, Dick. "A Politics in Search of the Political." *Theory and Society*, 1 (1974), 271–306.

Hull, Clark L. *Principles of Behavior*. New York: Appleton-Century-Crofts, 1943.

Husserl, Edmund. *Cartesian Meditations: An Introduction to Phenomenology*. Translated by Dorion Cairns. The Hague: Martinus Nijhoff, 1960.

————. *The Crisis of European Sciences and Transcendental Phenomenology*. Translated with an introduction by David Carr. Evanston, Ill.: Northwestern University Press, 1970.

Hymes, Dell, ed. *Language in Culture and Society*. New York: Harper & Row, 1964.

————, ed. *Reinventing Anthropology*. New York: Pantheon Books, 1972.

Jarvie, I. C. "Understanding and Explanation in Sociology and Social Anthropology." In *Explanation in the Behavioural Sciences*, edited by Robert Borger and Frank Cioffi. Cambridge: Cambridge University Press, 1970.

Jay, Martin. *The Dialectical Imagination*. Boston: Little, Brown and Company, 1973.

Kolakowski, Leszek. "Althusser's Marx." *The Socialist Register* (1971), 111–28.

Kordig, Carl R. *The Justification of Scientific Change*. New York: Humanities Press, 1971.

Kuhn, Thomas S. " 'Comment' on the Relations of Art and Science." *Comparative Studies in Society and History,* 11 (1969), 403–12.

————. "Reflections on My Critics." In *Criticism and the Growth of Knowledge,* edited by Imre Lakatos and Alan Musgrave. Cambridge: Cambridge University Press, 1970.

————. "Second Thoughts on Paradigms." In *The Structure of Scientific Theories,* edited by Frederick Suppe. Urbana: University of Illinois Press, 1974.

————. *The Structure of Scientific Revolutions*. 2nd ed. enl. Chicago: University of Chicago Press, 1970.

Labov, William. *Sociolinguistic Patterns*. Philadelphia: University of Pennsylvania Press, 1972.

LaCapra, Dominick. *Emile Durkheim: Sociologist and Philosopher*. Ithaca, N.Y.: Cornell University Press, 1972.

Lakatos, Imre, and Musgrave, Alan, eds. *Criticism and the Growth of Knowledge*. Cambridge: Cambridge University Press, 1970.

Laslett, Peter, ed. *Philosophy, Politics and Society*. First Series. New York: Macmillan, 1956.

————, and Runciman, W. G., eds. *Philosophy, Politics and Society*. Second Series. Oxford: Basil Blackwell, 1962.

Leiss, William. *The Domination of Nature*. New York: George Braziller, 1972.

————. "Husserl's Crisis." *Telos,* no. 8 (1971), 109–20.

Lichtheim, George. *The Concept of Ideology and Other Essays*. New York: Vintage Books, 1967.

————. *From Marx to Hegel.* New York: Herder and Herder, 1971.

Louch, A. R. *Explanation and Human Action.* Berkeley: University of California Press, 1969.

————. "On Misunderstanding Mr. Winch." *Inquiry,* 7 (1965), 212–16.

————. "The Very Idea of a Social Science." *Inquiry,* 6 (1963), 273–86.

Lukes, Steven. *Emile Durkheim: His Life and Work.* London: Allen Lane, The Penguin Press, 1973.

McCarthy, T. A. "A Theory of Communicative Competence." *Philosophy of the Social Sciences,* 3 (1973), 135–56.

MacIntyre, Alasdair. *Against the Self-Images of the Age.* New York: Schocken Books, 1971.

Marcuse, Herbert. *Negations.* Boston: Beacon Press, 1968.

————. *One Dimensional Man.* Boston: Beacon Press, 1964.

————. *Reason and Revolution.* New York: Oxford University Press, 1941.

Marx, Karl. *Grundrisse.* Translated with a foreword by Martin Nicolaus. New York: Vintage Books, 1973.

————. *Writings of the Young Marx on Philosophy and Society.* Edited and translated by Loyd D. Easton and Kurt H. Guddat. New York: Anchor Books, 1967.

Mastermann, Margaret. "The Nature of a Paradigm." In *Criticism and the Growth of Knowledge.* Edited by Imre Lakatos and Alan Musgrave. Cambridge: Cambridge University Press, 1970.

Merleau-Ponty, Maurice. *Phenomenology of Perception.* Translated by Colin Smith. New York: Humanities Press, 1962.

————. *Signs.* Translated by Richard C. McCleary. Evanston, Ill.: Northwestern University Press, 1964.

Merton, Robert K. *Social Theory and Social Structure.* Glencoe, Ill.: The Free Press, 1949. (Rev. and enl. ed., The Free Press, 1957; enl. ed., The Free Press, 1968.)

————. *The Sociology of Science.* Chicago: University of Chicago Press, 1973.

Mills, C. Wright. *The Sociological Imagination.* New York: Oxford University Press, 1959.

Nagel, Ernest. "A Formalization of Functionalism." In *Logic without Metaphysics.* Glencoe, Ill.: The Free Press, 1956.

————. "Problems of Concept and Theory Formation in the Social Sciences." In *Science, Language, and Human Rights.* Philadelphia: University of Pennsylvania Press, 1952. (Papers for the symposia held at the annual meeting of the Eastern Division of the American Philosophical Association.)

————. *The Structure of Science.* New York: Harcourt Brace Jovanovich, 1961.

Natanson, Maurice. *Edmund Husserl: Philosopher of Infinite Tasks.* Evanston, Ill.: Northwestern University Press, 1973.

————, ed. *Phenomenology and Social Reality: Essays in Memory of Alfred Schutz.* The Hague: Martinus Nijhoff, 1970.

————, ed. *Phenomenology and the Social Sciences.* 2 vols. Evanston, Ill.: Northwestern University Press, 1973.

Negt, Oskar. "Revolution und Geschichte: Eine Kontroverse mit Jürgen Habermas." In *Politik als Protest.* Frankfurt am Main: Suhrkamp Verlag, 1971.

Nell, Edward J. "The Revival of Political Economy." *Social Research,* 39 (1972), 32–52.

Nichols, Christopher. "Science or Reflection: Habermas on Freud." *Philosophy of the Social Sciences,* 2 (1972), 261–69.

O'Neill, John. *Sociology as a Skin Trade.* New York: Harper Torchbooks, 1972.

Paci, Enzo. *The Function of the Sciences and the Meaning of Man.* Translated with an introduction by Paul Piccone and James E. Hansen. Evanston, Ill.: Northwestern University Press, 1972.

Parsons, Talcott, and Smelser, Neil J. *Economy and Society.* New York: The Free Press, 1956.

Peabody, Gerald E. "Scientific Paradigms and Economics: An Introduction." *Review of Radical Political Economics,* 3 (1971), 1–16.

Piccone, Paul. "Phenomenological Marxism." *Telos,* no. 9 (1971), 3–31.

————. "Reading the Crisis." *Telos,* no. 8 (1971), 121–29.

Pitkin, Hanna F. *Wittgenstein and Justice.* Berkeley: University of California Press, 1972.

Plamenatz, John. *Ideology.* New York: Praeger, 1970.

Pocock, J. G. A. *Politics, Language and Time.* New York: Atheneum, 1971.

Popper, Karl R. "Normal Science and Its Dangers." In *Criticism and the Growth of Knowledge,* edited by Imre Lakatos and Alan Musgrave. Cambridge: Cambridge University Press, 1970.

————. *Objective Knowledge: An Evolutionary Approach.* Oxford: Oxford University Press, 1972.

————. *The Open Society and Its Enemies.* 5th ed. London: Routledge & Kegan Paul, 1966.

————. *The Poverty of Historicism.* Rev. ed. London: Routledge & Kegan Paul, 1972.

Psathas, George. *Phenomenological Sociology.* New York: John Wiley & Sons, 1973.

Radnitzky, Gerhard. *Contemporary Schools of Metascience.* New York: Humanities Press, 1970.

Rawls, John. *A Theory of Justice.* Cambridge: Harvard University Press, 1971.

Review of Radical Political Economics: Special Issue on Radical Paradigms in Economics, 3 (1971).

Ricoeur, Paul. *Husserl: An Analysis of His Phenomenology.* Translated by

Edward G. Ballard and Lester E. Embree. Evanston, Ill.: Northwestern University Press, 1967.

Roche, Maurice. *Phenomenology, Language and the Social Sciences.* London: Routledge & Kegan Paul, 1973.

Rorty, Richard M. "The World Well Lost." *Journal of Philosophy,* 69 (1972), 649–65.

Rosenthal, David M., ed. *Materialism and the Mind-Body Problem.* Englewood Cliffs, N.J.: Prentice-Hall, 1971.

Rudner, Richard S. *Philosophy of Social Science.* Englewood Cliffs, N.J.: Prentice-Hall, 1966.

Runciman, W. G. *A Critique of Max Weber's Philosophy of Social Science.* Cambridge: Cambridge University Press, 1972.

Ryan, Alan. " 'Normal' Science or Political Ideology?" In *Philosophy, Politics and Society,* Fourth Series, edited by Peter Laslett, W. G. Runciman, and Quentin Skinner. Oxford: Basil Blackwell, 1972.

———. *The Philosophy of the Social Sciences.* London: Macmillan, 1970.

Scharr, John H. "Legitimacy in the Modern State." In *Power and Community: Dissenting Essays in Political Science.* New York: Vintage Books, 1970.

Scheffler, Israel. *Science and Subjectivity.* Indianapolis: Bobbs-Merrill Co., 1967.

Scholte, Robert. "The Structural Anthropology of Claude Levi-Strauss." In *Handbook of Social and Cultural Anthropology.* Edited by John J. Honigman. Chicago: Rand McNally, 1973.

Schroyer, Trent. *The Critique of Domination.* New York: George Braziller, 1973.

Schutz, Alfred. *Collected Papers.* Vol. I. Edited and with an introduction by Maurice Natanson. The Hague: Martinus Nijhoff, 1962.

———. *Collected Papers.* Vol. II. Edited by Avrid Brodersen. The Hague: Martinus Nijhoff, 1964.

———. *Collected Papers.* Vol. III. Edited by I. Schutz. The Hague: Martinus Nijhoff, 1966.

———. *The Phenomenology of the Social World.* Translated by George Walsh and Frederick Lehnert. Evanston, Ill.: Northwestern University Press, 1967.

———. *Reflections on the Problems of Relevance.* New Haven: Yale University Press, 1970.

Schutz, Alfred, and Luckmann, Thomas. *The Structures of the Life-World.* Evanston, Ill.: Northwestern University Press, 1973.

Sellars, Wilfrid. "Metaphysics and the Concept of a Person." In *The Logical Way of Doing Things,* edited by Karel Lambert. New Haven: Yale University Press, 1969.

———. *Science and Metaphysics.* New York: Humanities Press, 1969.

———. *Science, Perception and Reality.* New York: Humanities Press, 1963.

————. "Science, Sense Impressions, and Sensa: A Reply to Cornman." *Review of Metaphysics,* 24 (1971), 391–447.

————. ". . . this I or he or it (the thing) which thinks. . . ." *Proceedings and Addresses of the American Philosophical Association,* 44 (1970–71), 5–31.

Sellars, Wilfrid, and Chisholm, Roderick M. "Intentionality and the Mental." In *Minnesota Studies in the Philosophy of Science,* Vol. II, edited by Herbert Feigl, Michael Scriven, and Grover Maxwell. Minneapolis: University of Minnesota Press, 1958.

Selvin, Hanan C. "Durkheim's Suicide and Problems of Empirical Research." *American Journal of Sociology,* 62 (1958), 609–19.

Shapere, Dudley. "Meaning and Scientific Change." In *Mind and Cosmos,* edited by Robert G. Colodny. Pittsburgh: University of Pittsburgh Press, 1966.

————. "The Structure of Scientific Revolutions." *Philosophical Review,* 73 (1964), 383–94.

Skinner, Quentin. "The Empirical Theorists of Democracy and Their Critics: A Plague on Both Their Houses." *Political Theory,* 1 (1973), 287–306.

Smart, J. C. C. *Philosophy and Scientific Realism.* New York: Humanities Press, 1963.

Smelser, Neil J. *Essays in Sociological Explanation.* Englewood Cliffs, N.J.: Prentice-Hall, 1968.

————. *Social Change in the Industrial Revolution.* London: Routledge & Kegan Paul, 1959.

————. "Some Personal Thoughts on the Pursuit of Sociological Problems." *Sociological Inquiry,* 39 (1969), 155–68.

————. "Some Replies and Some Reflections." *Sociological Inquiry,* 39 (1969), 213–17.

————. *Theories of Collective Behavior.* New York: The Free Press, 1963.

Sokolowski, Robert. *The Formation of Husserl's Concept of Constitution.* The Hague: Martinus Nijhoff, 1970.

————. "Husserl's Protreptic." In *Life-World and Consciousness,* edited by Lester E. Embree. Evanston, Ill.: Northwestern University Press, 1972.

Spiegelberg, Herbert. *The Phenomenological Movement.* The Hague: Martinus Nijhoff, 1965.

————. *Phenomenology in Psychology and Psychiatry.* Evanston, Ill.: Northwestern University Press, 1972.

Strauss, Leo. *Natural Right and History.* Chicago: University of Chicago Press, 1953.

Strawson, P. F. *Individuals: An Essay in Descriptive Metaphysics.* London: Methuen & Co., 1959.

Sweezy, Paul M. "Toward a Critique of Economics." *Review of Radical Political Economics,* 3 (1971), 59–66.

Taylor, Charles. *The Explanation of Behaviour.* New York: Humanities Press, 1964.

———. "Interpretation and the Sciences of Man." *Review of Metaphysics,* 25 (1971), 3–51.

———. "Neutrality in Political Science." In *Philosophy, Politics and Society,* Third Series, edited by Peter Laslett and W. G. Runciman. Oxford: Basil Blackwell, 1969.

Therborn, Göran. "Frankfurt Marxism: A Critique." *New Left Review,* no. 63 (1970), 65–96.

———. "Habermas: A New Eclectic." *New Left Review,* no. 67 (1971), 69–83.

Toulmin, Stephen. *Human Understanding.* Vol. I. Princeton, N.J.: Princeton University Press, 1972.

Tribe, Laurence H. "Policy Science: Analysis or Ideology?" *Philosophy and Public Affairs,* 2 (1972), 66–113.

Truman, David B. "Disillusion and Regeneration: The Quest for a Discipline." *American Political Science Review,* 59 (1966), 865–73.

———. "The Implications of Political Behavior Research." *Items* (Social Science Research Council), 5 (1951), 37–39.

von Wright, George Henrik. *Explanation and Understanding.* Ithaca, N.Y.: Cornell University Press, 1971.

Waismann, F. "Language Strata." In *How I See Philosophy.* New York: St. Martin's Press, 1968.

Weber, Max. *Max Weber.* Edited by Denis Wrong. Makers of Modern Social Science. Englewood Cliffs, N.J.: Prentice-Hall, 1970.

———. *The Methodology of the Social Sciences.* Translated and edited by Edward A. Shils and Henry A. Finch. New York: The Free Press, 1949.

———. "Science as a Vocation." In *From Max Weber: Essays in Sociology,* translated and edited by H. H. Gerth and C. Wright Mills. New York: Oxford University Press, 1946.

———. *The Theory of Social and Economic Organization.* Edited by Talcott Parsons. New York: The Free Press, 1947.

Wellmer, Albrecht. "Communication and Emancipation: Reflections on the 'Linguistic Turn' in Critical Theory." In *Stony Brook Studies in Philosophy.* Edited by P. Bryns, C. Evans, and D. Howard, 1 (1974).

———. *Critical Theory of Society.* New York: Herder and Herder, 1971.

Wilson, Bryan R., ed. *Rationality.* Oxford: Basil Blackwell, 1970.

Winch, Peter. *Ethics and Action.* London: Routledge & Kegan Paul, 1972.

———. *The Idea of a Social Science and Its Relation to Philosophy.* London: Routledge & Kegan Paul, 1958.

———. "Mr. Louch's Idea of a Social Science." *Inquiry,* 7 (1964), 202–08.

Wittgenstein, Ludwig. *Philosophical Investigations.* New York: Macmillan, 1953.

Wolin, Sheldon S. "Paradigms and Political Theories." In *Politics and Experi-*

ence, edited by Preston King and B. C. Parekh. Cambridge: Cambridge University Press, 1968.

————. "Political Theory as a Vocation." In *Machiavelli and the Nature of Political Thought,* edited by Martin Fleisher. New York: Atheneum, 1972.

Zaner, Richard M. "Solitude and Sociality: The Critical Foundations of the Social Sciences." In *Phenomenological Sociology: Issues and Applications,* edited by George Psathas. New York: John Wiley & Sons, 1973.

————. "Theory of Intersubjectivity: Alfred Schutz." *Social Research,* 28 (1961), 71–93.

Index of Names

Adorno, Theodor W., xvii, 184

Almond, Gabriel, 32, 109; and his application of Kuhn's ideas, 97–99, 102, 105, 244 n. 42

Althusser, Louis, 260 n. 27, 261 n. 39

Arendt, Hannah, xxi, 259 n. 21; on behaviorism, 247 n. 56

Aristotle, 5, 100, 185–186

Austin, J. L., xvi, 74, 118, 211

Bacon, Francis, 10

Berger, Peter, 255 n. 49

Bergson, Henri, xvii, 142

Berlin, Isaiah, 67, 83, 109, 113; and his critique of empirical theory, 59–63; on political theory, 57, 58, 106, 110, 111, 233; on the task of the theorist, 84

Burke, Edmund, 186

Carr, David, 257 n.6

Chomsky, Noam, 211

Cicero, 186

Comte, Auguste, 5, 190

Dahl, Robert, 110

Davidson, Donald, 93

Durkheim, Emile: on suicide, 11–13

Easton, David, 3, 32; on facts and values, 45–46

Einstein, Albert, 100

Eulau, Hans, 32, 99

Feyerabend, Paul K., 93

Freud, Sigmund, 72, 205; on dream interpretation, 200–201; Habermas' criticism of, 214–215; and the therapeutic situation, 203

Galileo, 100; discovery-concealment of, 127, 128

Garfinkel, Harold, 18, 136

Goffman, Erving, 18

Habermas, Jürgen, xvii, xxi, xxii, 53; communicative competence and rationality, 205–213, 229; and the confusion of the practical and the technical, 185–188; and his critical theory of society, 174–176, 184–225; criticism of Marx, 188–189, 260 n. 30; on the dissolution of epistemology, 190–191, 263 n.51; on psychoanalysis and the critique of ideology, 200–205; on theory and praxis, 213–219, 259 n. 21, 260 n. 31; the three cognitive interests of, 191–200; unresolved difficulties in, 219–225

Harré, R., 242 n. 16

Hauser, Philip M.: on social engineering, 50–53

Hegel, G. W. F., xvii, xix, xx, 4, 57–59, 107, 174, 179, 182, 184; and the forms of consciousness, 196, 204, 210; on the history of cul-

Index of Subjects

"Abstracted empiricism," 8, 10
Action, xi, 44, 51, 58; communicative, 210, 211, 195, 196; "dysfunctional," 40; Habermas' view of, 224, 260 n. 31; human, 62, 154–157, 229–232; language of, 63–74; as a moral concept, 74–84; "purposive-rational," 193, 195; Schutz's view of, 143–145, 254 n. 35; theory of, 113; Weber's definition of, 144–145
Analysis, 5; categorial, 223; causal, 166, 198; conceptual, 64, 69; functional, 16, 27; paradigm of theoretic, 12, 13; phenomenological, 160, 167, 168
Analytic-synthetic dichotomy, 207
Anomaly, 86–87, 96, 98, 102, 105
Argument, xiii–xiv; "impossibility," 41, 42, 64, 70, 78, 112, 134; about justice, 110; "transcendental," 64
Argumentation, 211, 214, 215

Behavior: "meaningful," 65; rule-governed and rule-following, 65–67; as used by Schutz, 143–145, 253 n. 34; voting, 66, 68, 69
Behaviorism, 102, 247 n. 56; as a form of reductive materialism, 37; as a methodological orientation, 37; Wolin's attitude toward, 247 n. 54
Bias, 44, 58, 59, 111, 114, 138, 185, 194, 202; a priori, 73; conceptual, 77, 80; epistemological, 75, 77;

ideological, 62, 96, 107, 109, 110; methodological, 184; normative, 209, 213; of a scientific mentality, 79; value, 107, 109
Biographically determined situation, 146
Bios Theoretikos, 53, 102, 169, 178; in classical Greek thought, 175
Bourgeois ideology, xiii, 206

Capitalism, 184, 188, 189, 204, 220; Marx's analysis of, 182–183
Cartesian dualism, 138
Categorical imperative, 47, 224
Categories, 138, 139, 192; of assessment and appraisal, 76, 77, 78, 80, 82, 83; causal, 69; for interaction, 195–196; moral, 76–78, 80; objectivistic, 134; theoretical, 137
Causal efficacy, 166
Causal influence, 162–165
Causation, 69, 261 n. 32
Cognitive Interests, 192–200, 208, 209, 220–222
Conceptual scheme, 25, 69
Consciousness, 141, 151; "false," 71, 108, 163, 164, 182; forms of, 191, 196, 204; stream of, 142, 143, 144, 145, 148; "true," 109, 203
Consensus, 210, 211
Constitution, 160–161
Constructs, 165, 210; common-sense, 139–140, 147

Technical, the, 187–188
Telos: of phenomenology, 167; of politics, xxii
Theoretical system, 9
Theoria, 53, 169, 175, 180, 214; Edmund Husserl and the ideal of, 176–178
Theories of the middle range, 8, 16, 43, 227, 237 n. 5
Theorist, 54, 100, 175; attitude of the, 44, 173; contemporary systematic, 15; critical, 181; as disinterested observer, xix, 53, 152, 153, 167–169, 173, 174; Habermas' view on the, 186–188, 202–203; the scientific, 152; the social, 9, 165; task of the, 84, 111
Theorizing self, 152, 153
Theory, 137, 243 n. 32; choice, 91–93; of communicative competence, 184, 206, 208–212, 220, 223, 224; continuity, 5; critical, xxii, 180–184, 219, 223, 233–236; economic, 81, 82; explanatory, 24–32; and fact, 20, 21; function of, 10, 13; general system of, 17; history of, 14–15; Homan's view of, 22–24; hypothetical-deductive, 194; of justice, 262 n. 42; moral, 234, 247 n. 55; of multiple realities, 151, 152; political, 57, 58, 60, 61, 62, 63; and praxis, 184, 187, 206, 213–219, 225; of relevances, 254 n. 38; restructuring of, 235–36; social, xxi, 82; structural-functionalist, 29; systematic, 11–16, 23; traditional, 179, 180, 182–184; understanding truth and falsity in, xix, xx. *See also* Empirical theory; Normative theory
Therapeutic situation, 203

They-orientation, 150
Thoughts, 123; central core of, 119, 120; dialectical movement of, 233
Thou-orientation, 150
Tradition: American intellectual, 135; Anglo-Saxon, xx, xxii, 114; Continental, xxi; of *Geisteswissenchaften,* 137; German, 198, 222; modern scientific, 118; of *Theoria,* 74
Transcendental: concept of the, 220, 249 n. 16; "turn," 131, 134
True believers, 189, 218
Typifications, 147, 148, 149, 161, 235

Universal pragmatics, 208

Validity claims (*Geltungsansprüche*), 109, 211–213, 214, 262 n. 48
Value, 45, 46, 49, 53; axioms, 47, 48; conflict, 243 n. 33; judgments, 39–40; Louch's view of, 76; neutral, 104; positions, 47–48; shared, 92, 93
Verstehen, 37, 63; analysis of, 136–141; Weber's notion of, 71
Vienna Circle, 5, 207

Wahrheit (Truth), xx
"We" relation, 148, 149, 150
Wertfrei, 46, 61, 136, 137
Wissenschaft, xix
Work ("purposive rational action"), 193, 194, 195, 197
World: of contemporaries, 149–150, 159; of everyday life, 128, 134, 145, 146–152; of scientific theory, 152. *See also Lebenswelt*